THE
LAWMEN

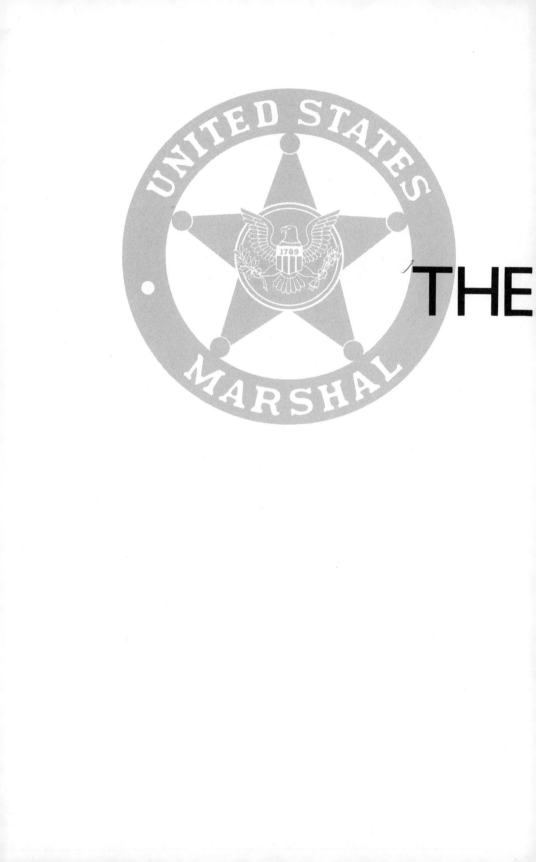

THE

LAWMEN

UNITED STATES MARSHALS

AND THEIR DEPUTIES, 1789–1989

FREDERICK S. CALHOUN

SMITHSONIAN INSTITUTION PRESS

WASHINGTON AND LONDON

Editor: Rosemary Sheffield
Production Editor: Rebecca Browning
Designer: Linda McKnight

Library of Congress Cataloging-in-Publication Data

Calhoun, Frederick S.
    The lawmen: United States marshals and their deputies,
  1789–1989 / Frederick S. Calhoun.
        p.   cm.
    Includes bibliographical references.
    ISBN 0-87474-396-6
    1. United States marshals–History.   2. United States–
  Constitutional history.   I. Title.
  KF8794.C35   1989
  363.2'82'097309–dc20   89-21806

British Library Cataloging-in-Publication Data available

On the cover: Painting by Edward C. Ward, *Enter the Law,*
1925, from the collection of the Thomas Gilcrease Institute of
American History and Art, Tulsa, Oklahoma

For permission to reproduce individual illustrations appearing
in this book, please correspond directly with the owners of the
works, as listed in the captions. The Smithsonian Institution
Press does not retain reproduction rights for these illustrations
individually or maintain a file of addresses for photo sources.

Manufactured in the United States of America
97 96 95 94 93 92 91 90   5 4 3 2 1

∞ The paper used in this publication meets the minimum
requirements of the American National Standard for
Permanence of Paper for Printed Library Materials
Z39.48-1984.

To Stanley E. Morris, who gave the marshals back their history, and to the men and women — brave marshals all — who made that history so compelling

CONTENTS

PREFACE AND ACKNOWLEDGMENTS

The history of the United States marshals and their deputies is a story of constitutional implementation. Since 1789 the marshals have been the civilian enforcement power of the federal government and its courts. Their history as federal lawmen illustrates how the Constitution has worked – or failed to work – over the past two centuries.

Because the marshals uphold the Constitution, their duties have involved them in most of the significant events in American history. They confronted Whiskey Rebels, arrested seditionists, traced counterfeiters, challenged filibusters, and chased fugitive slaves. After the Civil War, marshals protected the newly freed slaves and established federal law in the territories. During their second century, marshals subdued labor strikes, enforced Prohibition, desegregated schools and colleges, and contained an Indian uprising. Present-day marshals pursue federal fugitives, protect the federal judiciary and its participants, keep custody of federal prisoners until they are tried, and execute the orders of the federal courts.

The subject of this book, then, is the Constitution. The context is federal law enforcement; the example is the work of the U.S. marshals and their deputies.

This is an official history of the U.S. marshals and their deputies. As the first historian for the U.S. Marshals Service, I have received tremendous support from the organization and from the individuals who compose it. I have also enjoyed considerable latitude in my interpretations and conclusions. Fortunately, I have also had wise counsel from many sources. What is good in the book reflects that counsel; that which is still bad shows simply my native southern stubbornness.

In any undertaking such as this, a good archivist is essential. I was fortunate to work with Cynthia G. Fox, who is quite simply the best archivist at the National Archives. She guided me through the maze of judicial records, suggested other sources, conducted research, commented on drafts of the manuscript, and became my friend. She first suggested using the implementation of the Constitution as a theme, then waited patiently for me to discover it on my own. The book could hardly have been started, much less completed, without her.

Other archivists also helped. Clarence Lyon, Ron Swerczek, Mary Rhonan, and John Roberts of the National Archives were invaluable. Bill Grover read the manuscript and made numerous suggestions to improve it. I particularly want to thank the staffs of the following institutions: the Library of Congress and its Manuscript Division, the Huntington Library, the Kansas State Historical Society, the Oklahoma Historical Society, the Western History Collections of the University of Oklahoma, the Minnesota Historical Society, the Massilon Historical Society, the Arizona Historical Society, the Buffalo and Erie County Historical Society, and my friend Bob Plowman and his colleagues at the Mid Atlantic Regional Archives in Philadelphia.

Several college students researched particular aspects of the marshals' history, then shared the fruits of their labors with me. They were Kathy Smith of Minnesota, Sandra Hannah of Virginia, and Greg Girardin of Maine. Mark Rivera worked for me for a year before deciding that psychology was more attractive than history—or perhaps I drove him to it.

I imposed on several friends to read drafts of the book. Their comments were insightful and useful. For their help, I thank Reis Kash, Robert Christman, Roy and Peggy Williams, Steve Boyle, Bill Dempsey, and Jeff Miller. Jerry Auerbach and Jerry Elston provided me able legal advice and wise counsel. Jack McCrory first hired me, then served as a sounding board for many of my ideas. John and June Gilchriese opened their home and their hearts to me. I am deeply indebted to each of them.

A number of marshals allowed me to interview them at length about their roles in the recent past. I want to thank Al Butler, Frank Vandegrift, Herschel Garner, Robert Haislip, James Redpath, Bill Stubblefield, Don Forsht, Jesse Grieder, Cecil Miller, Bill Shoemaker, Bill Opel, Bob Christman, Reis Kash, Charles E. Burrows, and Bill Hall.

Many helped with friendship and kindness. Throughout the Marshals Service I have made many friends and have received tremendous support and encouragement. Listing everyone who has helped would rival the length of this already long volume. I am indebted to all, but in particular I thank Bob Leschorn, Dick Bippus, Roger Arechiga, Chuck Kupfer, Louis McKinney, Dave Neff, Tony Odom, and David Stanton. Each of them exemplified what is best about being a deputy U.S. marshal. My good friend Romolo Imundi exemplified what is best about being a U.S. marshal.

John Hubbell and the board of editors of Kent State University Press first indicated to me that I had a book worthy of publication. I am indebted to them for their confidence.

Mary Lou Brown, Vyleen Hofer, Cynthia Mason, and Jeannie Trevino helped with the word processing of the manuscript.

Ana-Marie Sullivan helped with the research, commented on the various drafts of the manuscript, selected the illustrations, and endured daily contact with me. She is one of those rare individuals who combines intelligence with common sense; her contributions to the work are distinguishable by both.

John Twomey, Howard Safir, and Gary Mead suffered my interference with their efforts to manage the U.S. Marshals Service. Each has helped me understand the current activities of the marshals; each has illustrated to me the type of people the office has always attracted. I have benefited immeasurably by my association with them. For the past four years Mr. Twomey has consistently proved to be the best of all possible supervisors. He allows me enough rope to hang myself, then cuts the noose before too much damage is done.

I also want to express my thanks to K. Michael Moore, who was sworn in as the first presidentially appointed director of the U.S. Marshals Service on December 6, 1989, just as this book went to press. He faces the formidable task of taking the marshals into their third century. To the extent that history ever enlightens the future, then I hope this volume will help him. I also wish him the best.

Ken and Holly Hargreaves once again patiently put up with my obsession for my work. By allowing me to talk incessantly about it, they helped me clarify my ideas even as they challenged my assertions. I am richer for their friendship.

I am also enriched by a gentle wife and two remarkable children. My wife, Leslie, shares with me the important things in life – Austin and Emily.

In the epilogue to this book, I describe the recent history of the U.S. marshals. It is an awkward attempt, partly because I was an eyewitness to most of it and partly because I am writing about a man whom I admire and like. I claim no historical objectivity for that section. I do claim that it is an honest evaluation of an honorable man who, through a stunning and intelligent force of will, transformed an organization. My successors will better assess his many contributions. I merely wished to pay my respects. The dedication expresses my admiration.

INTRODUCTION

United States Marshal Robert Forsyth may have expected trouble. He took two of his deputies with him to Mrs. Dixon's house in Augusta, Georgia, on January 11, 1794, because the Allen brothers, Beverly and William, had reportedly been seen there. The forty-year-old Forsyth, a veteran of the American Revolution, knew how to take care of himself, but in the four years he had served the new federal government as the first marshal in the District of Georgia, he had experienced little, if any, difficulty or resistance. Most of his work had consisted of routine administrative duties, and his search for the Allen brothers was no different. He merely wanted to serve them with some court papers in a civil suit. Nonetheless, Forsyth took the precaution of bringing two of his deputies with him.

When the three officers entered Mrs. Dixon's house, they found the Allens talking with friends. Wishing to spare the brothers embarrassment, Forsyth asked to speak to them privately outside. Instead of following the marshal, however, the brothers ran up to the second floor and darted into the nearest room, bolting the door behind them. Beverly Allen loaded, primed, and cocked his pistol.

Hearing Forsyth and his deputies approach, Beverly aimed his pistol toward the door and squeezed the trigger. The ball splintered through the wooden door and struck Forsyth fair in the head. He was dead before his body hit the floor, the first of four hundred or more marshals to be killed performing their duties. Although the two deputies promptly arrested the Allens, the brothers later escaped from the local sheriff and were never brought to trial.[1]

Almost two hundred years later, on February 13, 1983, Marshal Kenneth Muir and his deputies set up a roadblock on the outskirts of Medina, North Dakota. They had an arrest warrant for Gordon Kahl, a federal fugitive wanted for refusal to pay his taxes. As the leader of the violence-prone Posse Comitatus group, Kahl had, in effect, declared a private war on the United States government. Coming down the highway, Kahl and his carload of supporters stopped before Muir's roadblock. Almost immediately, they opened fire on the lawmen with automatic weapons. The gun battle raged only a few minutes before Kahl made his escape, leaving Marshal Muir and Deputy Robert Cheshire dead. Four months later, Kahl was killed in a shoot-out with marshals, FBI agents, and local police in Arkansas.[2]

These two episodes illustrate the violent side to the history of U.S. marshals and their deputies. For more than a century after the establishment of the federal government in 1789, U.S. marshals provided the only nationwide civilian police power available to the president, Congress, and the courts. Even after the creation of more than fifty specialized federal law enforcement agencies during the twentieth century, the marshals retained the broadest jurisdiction and authority. For two hundred years U.S. marshals and their deputies have been the instruments of civil authority for all three branches of government. This role has involved the marshals in most of the major historical episodes in America's past. The history of the marshals is, quite simply, the story of how the American people govern themselves.

The offices of U.S. marshal and deputy marshal were created by the first Congress in the Judiciary Act of 1789, the same legislation that established the federal judicial system. The marshals were given extensive authority to support the federal courts within their judicial districts and to carry out all lawful orders issued by judges, Congress, or the president. As a balance to this broad grant of authority, Congress limited the tenure of marshals to four-year, renewable terms, serving at the pleasure of the president. Until the mid-twentieth century the marshals hired their own deputies, often firing those who had worked for the previous marshal. Thus, the limitation on the marshal's term of office frequently extended to the deputies as well.

The primary function of the marshals was to support the federal courts. They served the subpoenas, summonses, writs, warrants, and other process issued by the courts; made all the arrests; and handled all the prisoners. They also disbursed the money, paying the fees and expenses of the court clerks, U.S. attorneys, jurors, and witnesses. They rented the courtrooms and jail space and hired the bailiffs, criers, and janitors. The marshals also took care of the details by making sure the water pitchers were filled, the prisoners were present, the jurors were available, and the witnesses were on time.

But those were only some of the marshals' duties. When George Washington set up his first administration, and the first Congress began passing laws, both branches of government quickly discovered an inconvenient gap in the constitutional design. It had no provision for a regional administrative structure stretching throughout the country. Both Congress and the executive were housed at the national capital. No agency represented the federal government's interests at the local level. The need for a regional organization quickly became apparent. Congress and the president solved part of the problem by creating specialized agencies, such as customs and revenue collectors, to levy the tariffs and taxes. Yet numerous other jobs needed to be done. The only officers available to do them were the U.S. marshals and their deputies.

Thus, the marshals also provided local representation for the federal government within their districts. They took the national census every ten years through 1870. They distributed presidential proclamations, collected a variety of statistical information on commerce and manufacturing, supplied the names of government employees for the national register, and performed other routine tasks needed for the central government to function effectively. Over the past two hundred years Congress and the president also called on the marshals to carry out unusual missions, such as registering enemy aliens in wartime, capturing fugitive slaves, sealing the American border against armed expeditions aimed at foreign countries, and swapping spies with the Soviet Union.

These diversified duties precluded the marshals from developing any particular specialty. They were not only law enforcers but also administrators. They needed to be adept in accounting procedures and pursuing outlaws, in quelling riots and arranging court sessions. The legacy of their history was the avoidance of specialization. Even today, in this age of experts, U.S. marshals and their deputies are the general practitioners within the law enforcement community. Although the FBI, Customs, the Border Patrol, and other federal agencies are restricted by legislation to specific, well-defined duties and jurisdictions, the marshals are not. Consequently, they are called upon to uphold the government's interests and policies in a wide variety of circumstances.

For the American people the marshals personified the authority of the federal government within their communities. The frequent outbursts of opposition to federal power that characterize much of American history were often first directed at individual marshals or deputies. The Whiskey Rebels of 1794, for example, violently opposed a national tax on whiskey. They expressed that opposition by taking Marshal David Lenox prisoner. Similar reactions obtained toward such noxious federal measures as the 1850 Fugitive Slave Law, the post-Civil War Reconstruction acts, and the desegregation of the South in the 1960s.

Nor was opposition to the federal government restricted to individual citizens or groups of citizens. State and local governments also took umbrage at federal measures. Their anger too was often directed at individual marshals who suffered interference, arrest, and imprisonment as a result. In March 1809 the Pennsylvania state legislature passed a resolution calling on all citizens to resist Marshal John Smith's court-ordered efforts to collect money from the state in the complicated *Olmstead* case. When Smith went to the house of a defendant with a writ of attachment in hand, eight state militiamen greeted him with bayonets. "In the name and by the authority of the United States, I command you to lay down your arms and permit me to proceed," Marshal Smith declared. "In the name and by the authority of the commonwealth of Pennsylvania, I command you to resist him," ordered General Bright, the commander of the squad. Turning to Marshal Smith, Bright warned that any further effort to enter the property would be "at the peril of your life."

After taking down the names of the militiamen, the marshal returned to the courthouse, where he promptly called on the secretary of state for permission to raise a posse of two thousand men. The next day, Smith returned alone to the defendant's house, which was still guarded by General Bright and his men. Circling around back, he scaled the fence and served his process on the defendant through the back door. Later, General Bright and his men were indicted and found guilty of resisting a federal court order. Bright was sentenced to three months in prison, his men to one month. All were later pardoned by President James Madison.[3]

Other instances of interference by local governments abound. After the Civil War, dozens of deputies were incarcerated in the South for enforcing federal laws. Deputy W. B. Blackburn was indicted by the Circuit Court of Tuscaloosa County, Alabama, in 1884 for carrying a concealed weapon. The evidence against him consisted of eyewitness accounts by two moonshiners he had arrested. Other deputies were arrested for murder or attempted murder, depending on the results of their gunfights with moonshiners and other criminals.[4]

Yet, in performing their duties in the face of opposition from the local populace and governments, the marshals constituted an important barrier between civilian government and military rule. They were the civilian enforcers of the law. Whenever the marshals were overcome by opposition, the president had little choice but to call out the military. Marshal David Lenox's brief captivity by the Whiskey Rebels persuaded President Washington to muster thirteen thousand state militiamen to put down the rebellion. The marshals in the Southern states after the Civil War enforced the new civil rights acts, but they frequently called on the army for assistance. And on the night of September 30, 1962, President John F. Kennedy reluctantly sent military forces to the University of Mississippi in Oxford, after a major riot erupted when marshals attempted to enforce James Meredith's court-ordered enrollment.

At the Pentagon in October 1967, anti–Vietnam War demonstrators confronted a thin, single-file line of marshals blocking them from the Defense Department. Behind the marshals, and clearly supplying the government's muscle, were large numbers of regular army troops. Standing between the rioters and the army, the marshals symbolized the government's civilian power, which, when overcome, allowed the army to intervene. At the same time, the marshals were on hand to make arrests, a civilian power not usually bestowed on the military. In a government based on civilian supremacy, the military was restricted to emergency support.

Early on, the federal government adopted measures to make its authority more palatable to the American people. Those who enforced federal laws at the local level generally came from that locality. They understood the people, for they were dealing with their friends and neighbors. This was particularly important in the nineteenth century, when lack of communications made the national government distant and seemingly foreign, but everyone knew or had heard of the marshal because he had been active in community affairs and politics for years.

For most of their history, U.S. marshals enjoyed a surprising degree of independence in performing their duties. No central administration existed to supervise their work until the late 1950s. Even then the Executive Office for U.S. Marshals had no real power over the districts until it was transformed into the U.S. Marshals Service in 1969 and given control of the district budgets and the hiring of deputies. Before that, each marshal was practically autonomous, receiving only general guidance from the executive branch.

As a result, the marshals, working with the federal judges and U.S. attorneys in their districts, enjoyed a wide latitude in determining how they would enforce the law. For most of them the solution was to go as easily as possible. Few of them wanted to offend their friends and neighbors, particularly because they knew all too well that the job of marshal was temporary. Unless they were prepared to leave their homes after their commissions expired, the marshals struggled to balance the enforcement of federal laws against the feelings of the local populace.

In July 1832 the District Court of Kentucky ordered Marshal John M. McCalla to seize more than ten thousand acres of land from about thirty people who had lost their court case to keep it. The marshal estimated that the defendants could organize "a formidable combination of tenants, retainers, and friends, who can muster from one to three hundred men, armed and resolved to resist to extremity." Although McCalla was "ready and willing" to raise a posse and evict the tenants, still he hesitated. "This is a case," he wrote to Attorney General Roger B. Taney, "in which my feelings, I confess, are with the defendants." The Supreme Court, rendering its decision in another case, had affirmed the arguments upon which the defendants had relied, but too late for them to appeal. "The most of them are ignorant of law and indeed of almost every thing else except . . . that justice if not law is on their side," the marshal observed. Yet, whatever his personal feelings, Marshal McCalla knew his duty.[5]

The marshals' dedication to duty was not boundless; they did not carry out orders blindly. In the months immediately before the opening of the Civil War, marshals throughout the South resigned. Although a unique situation, their resignations illustrated the effect of selecting marshals from within the districts they served. Pushed to the limit, these marshals chose loyalty to their communities over obedience to the federal government.

Most of the time a comfortable balance between law enforcement and community sensitivities was easy to achieve. Few people disputed the marshals' right to arrest mail robbers, counterfeiters, or others who broke federal laws. Nor were there many objections to the marshals' serving process. People generally accepted the principle that the purpose of the courts and trials was to settle disputes, not create them.

Yet, in attempting to obviate the American people's distaste for strong government, succeeding presidents and senates ultimately committed a disservice to the development of the office of U.S. marshal as a professional organization. The system of appointments, for which the only criteria were presidential nomination and Senate confirmation, retarded the professional growth of marshals. Most marshals did not last in office long enough to develop the skills and experience that mark a professional. Nor were they necessarily selected on the basis of their law enforcement credentials. Nor were they provided any training until fairly recent times. These factors also slowed the professional development of the deputies.

Quite simply, the office of marshal was a patronage job, subject to all the abuses of such a system. From 1789 to 1896 each marshal hired practically as many deputies as he wanted. They were paid on a fee system, collecting set amounts for performing particular tasks, such as serving summonses, writs, or warrants. In 1896 Congress established a salary for both the marshals and their deputies, and the attorney general imposed limits on the number of deputies each marshal could hire, but the marshal continued to do his own hiring. In 1937 the Department of Justice invoked a new regulation requiring the marshals to submit résumés and security checks on their deputies, but this was essentially a veto power over the marshals' hiring practices, not an active measure to select deputies for each district.

Finally, in 1972 the Marshals Service, a recently created headquarters agency superimposed on the individual districts, took control of all hiring and training of deputies nationwide. The selection of U.S. marshals remained in the hands of the president.

Professionalism is a twentieth-century phenomenon in the United States, particularly in law enforcement. Before World War I, federal law – the only law the marshals enforced – was limited and comparatively simple. The complex rules and regulations of today did not exist then. Few marshals and deputies had difficulty in quickly learning their duties and carrying them out with proficiency. Indeed, those officers with managerial and accounting experience may have been better suited to the position, because the biggest problem besetting the marshals of the 1800s was not to catch lawbreakers but to account for the monies used to run the courts. A small army of accountants at the Treasury and Justice departments audited them at every turn, disallowing their expenditures on the slightest excuse. Pursuing mail robbers and other outlaws must have seemed a welcome relief to the headache of keeping track of the courts' funds.

This, then, is the two-hundred-year story of how men and women enforced the law and served the courts, of how they fought and died in support of the ideal of self-government. But more than that, it is the story of the clumsy, inefficient, and peculiar method by which we Americans choose to govern ourselves. The thousands of men and women who served as marshals or deputies were, first and foremost, Americans. They took upon themselves the difficult and dangerous task of enforcing the laws. When they failed, it was an American failure more than a personal one, and when they succeeded, it was an American success. In a government of laws, not men, they were the lawmen.

I
PART ★

CONSTITUTION AND COURTS
1789–1861

1

AGENTS OF FEDERALISM

1789–1794

Nathaniel Ramsay stood his ground. Across the fields surrounding the Monmouth, New Jersey, courthouse, British troops were attacking. The American forces were hastily retreating. Arriving on the field, General George Washington was outraged to learn that General Charles Lee had ordered his men to run before battle had been properly joined. As a stopgap, Washington ordered Lieutenant Colonel Ramsay and his regiment to stall the British advance long enough for the Americans to regroup. It was June 28, 1778, the second year of American independence.

Fighting hand to hand, Ramsay's regiment took on the British troops. Ramsay fought with sword and pistol against mounted British dragoons. Although he was wounded several times and his men were dying around him, he refused to retreat. One redcoat aimed his pistol point-blank in Ramsay's face, but at the last second his aim was jarred. The exploding powder from the shot burned deeply along one side of Ramsay's face, scarring him for life. Eventually overwhelmed by wounds and British troops, Ramsay was taken prisoner.

But he had given Washington time to organize a counterattack. That night, the British deserted the field. The victory lifted the morale of the American forces. It was the first significant engagement after the debilitating winter at Valley Forge. Washington's success proved the new country's mettle.

Eleven years later, on September 26, 1789, President George Washington nominated Nathaniel Ramsay to be the first U.S. marshal for the two-day-old federal district court in Maryland. Ramsay's appointment, although clearly a reward for his bravery at the Battle of Monmouth Courthouse, also illustrated Washington's desire to appoint marshals who were loyal to the new government and well known and well liked in their communities.

Paroled by the British in 1780, Ramsay had retired from the army. He returned to Maryland, where he had lived and practiced law since his graduation from the College of New Jersey in 1767. His legal practice thrived, and he invested his profits in real estate, becoming a wealthy landowner. From 1785 to 1787, Ramsay represented Maryland in the Second Continental Congress. He was a staunch Federalist and a strong supporter of the new federal government and its untried Constitution. When Washington appointed him U.S. marshal, Ramsay was forty-eight years old.[1]

In selecting the first marshals, the president sought men not of national stature but, like Ramsay, of local reputation. The marshals would enforce the laws and orders of the federal government and its courts and administer its interests and affairs. The marshals' success depended on their acceptance by the local communities. For many Americans, their marshal was the federal government. Upon the U.S. marshals fell the burden of federalism.

THE JUDICIARY ACT OF 1789

United States marshals trace their origins to the sea. The Judiciary Act of 1789, which created the federal judicial system, including the office of marshal and deputy marshal, was modeled on the colonial vice-admiralty courts established by England in 1697 over its American colonies. These courts heard cases involving the laws of the sea, the British trade and revenue acts, and the disputes among men of the sea. Essentially, the jurisdiction of the courts encompassed three general areas. First, and most voluminous, were the cases involving ordinary maritime disputes, such as controversies over seamen's wages, salvage rights, contracts, and similar causes. The second category, which obtained only in wartime, concerned issues resulting from the capture of enemy ships. The third category arose from the laws of trade and the imposition of customs duties. These cases became increasingly important and controversial. As Parliament tightened England's commercial stranglehold on the unruly colonists, a move for independence began that culminated in the American Revolution.[2]

During the Revolution, the Second Continental Congress encouraged the creation of admiralty courts among its member states. In essence Congress relied on each of its member states to perfect its own admiralty courts to hear the wartime-prize cases brought within the jurisdiction of that state. As a consequence the courts had no national uniformity, although in general the former colonies modeled their courts on the British version of an earlier day. These courts applied international law and a series of defining resolutions passed by Congress in judging the cases. However, Congress eventually asked the states to prohibit jury trials within the admiralty courts because the jurors tended to sympathize with the parties to the suit who were from their state. Most of the state legislatures complied with the request. Congress reserved the right to hear cases on appeal from the state admiralty courts, provided that the state legislatures approved of allowing the decisions of their courts to be heard by Congress.[3]

When the first United States Congress designed the federal court system for the new nation, it borrowed the organization and structure of the colonial and wartime admiralty courts, broadening their jurisdiction and adding a clearer definition of the appeals procedures. Unlike the courts within each state and local area, the vice-admiralty courts extended throughout the colonies. They applied a comprehensive system of laws that transcended the particular whims and desires of local voters, judges, and sheriffs. They were, in effect, national courts, which made them extremely useful as models for a federal court structure.

Included in the borrowing was an office that went by the title of United States marshal. It too owed its origins to the colonial admiralty system. The marshals of the British and American vice-admiralty courts served the writs, subpoenas, and other court process, took possession of condemned ships and goods, made arrests, kept custody of the court's prisoners, hung convicted pirates and murderers, and carried out all the orders of the courts. When the first U.S. Congress defined the federal court system, it retained the office through which the courts exercised their power.[4]

Senate Bill 1 of the First Session of the First Congress became, after lengthy and heated debate, the Judiciary Act of September 24, 1789. The act provided a charter for the federal judicial system by specifying the jurisdiction and powers of the district and circuit courts, and the qualifications and authority of federal judges, district attorneys, court clerks, U.S. marshals, and deputy marshals. Invited by Article III, Section 1, of the newly ratified Constitution to "ordain and establish" a court structure for the new national government, the first Senate moved quickly to the task. But its labors were immediately embroiled in a bitter contest between the Federalists, who wanted a strong federal government, and the Anti-Federalists, who jealously guarded the rights of the states.

The result was a typically American compromise. The Federalists stymied an Anti-Federalist motion to limit the district courts' jurisdiction to admiralty and maritime cases only. The Anti-Federalists succeeded in limiting the appellate review of federal courts to issues of law, excluding questions of fact. The final form of the act satisfied neither side, for most of the participants recognized it as a clumsy, inefficient system. As soon as the act passed, the Congress directed the attorney general to report on ways to improve it. Yet the judicial system's very clumsiness and inefficiency served it well in successfully achieving its contradictory purposes of exerting federal authority and protecting the rights of the states and the freedoms of individual citizens.

To a remarkable extent the sections of the judiciary bill pertaining to marshals escaped the attacks and amendments of the bill's opponents. The need for some kind of enforcement authority was widely recognized and generally accepted, even by the Anti-Federalists. It would have made no sense to pass laws without provision for their enforcement. The Judiciary Act assigned this task to the marshals. The language of the assignment was so broadly written that few could find reason to challenge it. The act instructed the marshal of each district "to execute throughout the District, all lawful precepts directed to him, and issued under the authority of the United States." To assist him in his duties, each marshal was allowed to appoint deputies and "to command all necessary assistance in the execution of his Duty."[5]

The marshals were also placed in a subordinate role within the legal system then being devised. They were empowered only to enforce court decisions, federal laws, and orders of the president. By concentrating their efforts on restricting the power and authority of the courts, judges, and federal laws, the Anti-Federalists were at the same time also limiting the powers of the marshals.

In addition, the marshals were the only officials created by the act with a strict limit placed on their term. Unlike the attorneys, the marshals served four-year terms, "removable from office at pleasure." Although their terms could be renewed, they could also be fired at any time, and their renewal in office was dependent on the concurrence of the Senate. U.S. attorneys were not put under a similar restriction until thirty years later. The act also required each marshal to post a $20,000 bond to protect the United States from any attempt by errant marshals to cheat on their fees or abscond with the large amounts of government funds they handled. Until the marshals were put on a salary in 1896, the federal government had frequent opportunities to collect on those bonds.

PRESIDENTIAL PRECEPTS

The Judiciary Act of 1789 imposed upon the U.S. marshals the duty of executing all lawful precepts—written orders—issued under the authority of the United States. As designed by the Constitution, each branch of the federal government represented lawful authority in the United States, each could issue precepts, each could command the marshals to do its beckoning. This meant that the marshals not only served the process of the federal courts, its warrants, summonses, subpoenas, and so forth but also responded to orders from the president and Congress.

The presidents found in the marshals a convenient regional structure to carry out administrative functions. Appointed by the president, the marshals served at his will and answered to him. The courts in effect were the marshals' clients, for whom they performed a number of services, but it was the president for whom they worked.

President Washington placed the supervision of the U.S. marshals and attorneys under the purview of the secretary of state. It was a logical decision, given the way in which the federal government was originally organized. The attorney general's role within the administration was severely limited, barely more than a part-time position. The occupant was merely the government's attorney, paid on retainer and expected to have other clients. His principal responsibilities were to provide legal opinions to the president and heads of departments and to represent the government before the Supreme Court. Between 1789 and the 1850s the attorney general had little say in the administration of the federal government and, thus, no control over the marshals and attorneys.

That job fell to the secretary of state, whose domestic functions were far more extensive in the 1790s than they are today. "Generally," one historian has written, "all functions not related to finances or military and naval affairs were placed under the Secretary of State." The secretary "handled correspondence with state governors, administered territorial governments, and directed federal marshals and districts attorneys." Fortunately for the secretary, his clerk, and his messenger, the foreign affairs of the United States were conducted at a fairly minimal level. The domestic duties that devolved on the office did not prove onerous. Jefferson, for example, had plenty of time for frequent vacations at Monticello.[6]

In supervising the work of the marshals, Jefferson and his successors provided general policy instructions and occasionally gave specific directions for the capture of criminals. In February 1797, Secretary of State Timothy Pickering, for example, asked Marshal David Meade Randolph of Virginia to hurry to Norfolk and arrest five men who were hiding aboard the French frigate *Medusa*. The men were wanted for the murder of Captain Andrew Peyton, the late master of the brig *James* out of Philadelphia. However, Randolph arrived in Norfolk too late; the men had escaped.[7]

The various secretaries of state relied on the district marshals for more than the capture of fugitives and outlaws. One of the secretary's duties was the promulgation of laws and proclamations, but the Department of State had no nationwide structure to distribute material at the local level. Consequently, the marshals handled such tasks.

Throughout the 1790s and into the nineteenth century, U.S. marshals conducted a considerable amount of the federal government's business at the local level. In 1795 Secretary of State Edmund Randolph, a former attorney general, asked each marshal to distribute a proclamation of thanksgiving issued by the president. Similarly, Randolph's successor, Timothy Pickering, relied on the marshals to summon their congressmen and senators back to Philadelphia for a special session of Congress. Pickering also called on the marshals to distribute a circular letter to the clerks of the courts of record in their districts and to arrange for the publication in local newspapers of changes in the laws regulating the opening date of the courts. The marshal whose district encompassed the nation's capital was given the additional job of maintaining the lists of foreign residents and their servants who enjoyed diplomatic immunity; because those individuals could not be summoned into court, the marshal who performed the summoning needed to know who they were.[8]

Such duties led the marshals of this and later periods to consider themselves more than law enforcement officials. Marshal James Prince of Massachusetts, for example, described himself in 1812 as the "Executive Civil Officer of the Nation within this District." Prince's predecessors and successors would have readily agreed with the title.[9]

CONGRESSIONAL PRECEPTS

During the 1790s, Congress passed a number of laws that required the marshals to perform various duties that lay well outside the judicial sphere. The most important of these in terms of the amount of work involved was the national census. The Constitution specified a census every ten years, but it made no mention of who should conduct it. On March 1, 1790, Congress passed "An Act providing for the enumeration of the Inhabitants of the United States," making the marshals responsible for coordinating the count. Once again, the marshals were the logical choice because of their positions across the country.

Each marshal divided his district into specific sections and hired assistant marshals to take the count within each division. The title of assistant marshal was used to distinguish the enumerators from deputy marshals. The assistant marshals traveled from house to house, town to town, counting all the inhabitants of each household except Indians who paid no taxes. In their returns the assistants distinguished between free persons and slaves, males and females, whites and blacks, those under sixteen and those sixteen or older. Some marshals added information on the occupation of the head of the household, but that was not requested by Congress.

For this tedious work each assistant received a small fee based on a sliding scale according to the population density of his section. The rate was $1 for every 150 people in rural areas and $1 for every 300 people in cities or towns with more than 5,000 people. If the population was especially dispersed, as it was in Maine, for example, the assistant was allowed up to $1 for every 50 people, provided the marshal and the local district judge agreed to such an exorbitant rate. The assistants earned an additional $2 for every handwritten copy of the returns. No fewer than two copies were required by the act, one to be sent to the capital and one to be lodged with the clerk of the district court for local inspection. Each assistant had to provide his own pen and paper.

The marshal supervised his assistants to make sure they made their returns promptly and in good order. Once the individual returns came to him, he compiled them into a single volume listing the inhabitants of his district. One copy of the complete returns was filed with the clerk. The second copy was sent to the president, who then transmitted the entire national census to the Congress. The marshals received from $100 to $500, depending on the size of the population of their district. William Peck of Rhode Island, for instance, received $100, and Edward Carrington of Virginia got $500.[10]

President Washington delegated the responsibility for coordinating the census to Secretary of State Thomas Jefferson. Because Jefferson had not yet returned to France, where he had been the American minister, Washington's personal secretary, Tobias Lear, issued the instructions in Jefferson's name in a circular letter to all marshals on March 5, 1790. The law originally allowed nine months for the count, but the deadline was later extended because of difficulties encountered by the marshals and their assistants. On October 27, 1791, Washington sent the final tally to Congress. The census totaled 3,929,214 free people in the United States.[11]

The results surprised many people. They expected the population to be considerably larger. One compiler of census information noted that "the census was supposed by many to be inaccurate, and the assumed error was imputed, I know not on what evidence, to the popular notion that the people were counted for the purpose of being taxed, and that not a few had, on this account, understated to the deputy marshals the number of persons in their families." Jefferson, whenever he distributed copies of the published results to American ministers and consuls abroad, warned that the numbers were far too low. He even added his own estimates in red ink. Later censuses, however, proved that the marshals' tallies, not Jefferson's, were closer to the true numbers.[12]

Based on the marshals' returns, Congress apportioned the representation in the House of Representatives. Government officials also found the census a useful source of information. In 1793 Postmaster General Timothy Pickering asked for a copy of the returns to use in determining where to build new postal roads. Later censuses required the marshals to collect additional information, such as the number and type of factories in their districts, the number of males of military age, and other statistics that Congress and the president found helpful in governing the country.[13]

The census was a burdensome duty for the marshals. When Congress ordered them to take the third head count in 1810, it reminded them that their assistants were to make "an actual inquiry at every dwelling house, or of the head of every family within each district, and not otherwise." This requirement was tremendously difficult to accomplish, considering the primitive transportation of the day.

Often the marshals had trouble keeping their assistants at the task. Marshal Andrew Moore of Virginia, for example, eventually gave up on his assistant in Norfolk County. Secretary of State James Monroe promptly sent back the incomplete returns submitted by Moore with instructions to hire as many assistants as necessary but to get the count for Norfolk. "It is hoped," Monroe cautioned, "that you will not fail to accomplish this important objective, as a failure might be of essential injury to the state, and would on other considerations, afford real cause of regret." This stricture applied to all the counts taken by the marshals.[14]

The marshals continued to coordinate the census every ten years through 1870. In 1880 the count was taken by the newly created Bureau of the Census, which relieved the marshals of the task.

Other laws passed by Congress imposed additional administrative duties on the marshals. In 1798 Congress gave the marshals the responsibility for registering all enemy aliens in wartime. In cooperation with the district U.S. attorney the marshals also gained increased law enforcement responsibilities, such as dealing with foreign vessels in American ports, handling and housing prisoners, and selling condemned ships and goods. These additional duties complemented the orders of the president to establish the marshals as a regional organization for the federal government.

JUDICIAL PRECEPTS

Despite the increasing number of jobs assigned the marshals by the president and Congress, their most important duty remained to support the federal courts. The marshals acted as the administrative and disbursing officers of the courts, making the arrangements to hold court and paying the bills and fees. The marshals also served as the liaison between the executive and judicial branches of government. They were responsible for accounting for the courts' expenditures to the first auditor of the Treasury, who monitored each marshal's accounts and paid out the money. During the 1790s, banks were few and unreliable, and money was difficult to transport. At first the Treasury Department established an account for each marshal at the nation's capital. It required each marshal to report in detail how the money was spent. These reports were closely audited. Each marshal was also expected to grant power of attorney to someone in the capital for receiving the marshal's money. The marshal could then issue checks and letters of credit against the funds held by his attorney. Direct withdrawal from the Treasury accounts by a marshal's creditors was not allowed.[15]

But this system proved too cumbersome, imposing as it did a long wait between the time the marshals expended money for the courts and the recipients received the cash. In early 1793 the Treasury Department began depositing the money due the marshals in the Bank of the United States. Because the bank had branches throughout the country, the marshals were able to receive their reimbursements and fees sooner. On July 2, 1793, Secretary of the Treasury Alexander Hamilton decentralized the system to make it more convenient. He instructed the collectors of customs in port cities and the supervisors of revenue in the interior to pay set amounts to each marshal to cover court expenses for six-month periods. The marshals continued to report their spending to the Treasury Department, but they at least had cash on hand to pay witnesses, jurors, jailers, and others.[16]

Yet this early decentralization proved equally unwieldy because the secretary of the Treasury reserved the power to determine how much money each marshal needed for the next court term. The marshals found themselves increasingly shortchanged.

Washington's second secretary of the Treasury, Oliver Wolcott, Jr., completed the decentralization begun by Hamilton. On January 23, 1797, Wolcott informed the marshals, collectors, and supervisors that thenceforth each marshal would submit to his local collector or supervisor six-month estimates of how much money the courts in his district would need. The collectors or supervisors would transfer those funds to the marshals. At the end of the six months the marshals would submit detailed accounts of how the money was spent to the Treasury Department, which would audit the accounts. If the first auditor determined that the marshal had misspent funds or made a mistake in his accounts, the collectors or supervisors were instructed to withhold that amount from the next disbursement. The individual marshals' estimates were added together and submitted to Congress for budget appropriations.[17]

The marshals of the 1790s functioned as the business managers of their districts. Each marshal arranged for a place to hold court and to house its prisoners. Marshal Robert Forsyth of Georgia, for example, spent $2 in July 1791 to clean his courtroom, and David Randolph in Virginia bought curtains and fuel for one of his courts in July 1792. Because court was held at various places throughout a district during the course of a year, considerable travel and administrative work were required. The marshals paid the fees, travel, and other expenses of the U.S. attorneys, court clerks, jurors, and witnesses. The marshals also attended court to ensure that the proceedings functioned smoothly, the bills were paid, and the necessary participants were present.[18]

The marshals hired the criers to open court and the bailiffs to officiate, each of whom received 50 cents a day. Deputy marshals were prohibited from acting as bailiffs. They appeared in court only to escort prisoners, to testify, or to preserve order during potentially disruptive trials. The bailiffs fell into a separate category of employment. They were paid out of a separate appropriation of Congress, and their authority was limited to the courtroom and its immediate environs.[19]

Because marshals handled the funds of the courts, the Judiciary Act of 1789 required each nominee to post a $20,000 bond before taking the oath of office. Normally, the candidate asked local businessmen and friends to pledge portions of the total. These bondsmen were financially liable for any mistakes or malfeasance of the marshal, which put considerable strain on many friendships. The marshal's bond also covered the actions of his deputies. Judges could dismiss the deputies for cause, but this authority was intended as a protection to the government against any collusion between the marshal and his deputies to defraud the Treasury or otherwise misbehave.

Each marshal earned $5 for each day he attended court. The courts during the early 1790s met infrequently, so the amount accrued was small. Marshal John Skinner of North Carolina received $10 for the two days that court met during the October 1790 term. He was paid another $10 for the November term but only $5 for the single day that court was in session in January 1791. Skinner's colleague in New Jersey, Thomas Lowry, fared little better. He attended one-day sessions of court during the November 1789 and February, April, May, August, October, and November 1790 terms. The April 1791 term, perhaps because court had not met for four months, was busy for an unheard-of twelve days, but the May term returned to normal with a two-day session.[20]

In 1793 the marshals were given a regular advance of $200 a year, paid in two equal installments, to cover "incidental expenses," primarily those jobs not covered by fees. Eventually this $200 evolved into a salary. The marshals also earned fees from personally serving the process of the courts and skimming a percentage off the fees earned by their deputies. The deputies were entitled to no more than three-fourths of the fees they earned serving process, making arrests, and performing other duties. The other fourth (or more) went to the marshals and court expenses. Each marshal could make private arrangements with his deputies to receive higher percentages of the deputy's fees.[21]

To forestall anyone from falsifying his accounts or embezzling the government's money, the Treasury Department required each marshal to swear to his accounts in open court and to obtain the signed approval of the district judge. When the accounts arrived at the capital, they were closely scrutinized by Treasury auditors. If the auditors suspected a marshal of cheating on his accounts, the Treasury Department instructed the local U.S. attorney to investigate and, if warranted, to prosecute the wayward marshal for embezzlement or perjury.

The lack of business in the courts, combined with the pittance the marshals and their deputies received as fees, made the job of marshal a poor way to earn a living. Indeed, few people expected the courts to be active. "How beneficial this office may be," George Washington observed in 1791, "I know not. At the present, the mere emoluments of it can not be, I should suppose, an object; but as a step, it may be desired by such as have nothing better in prospect." Alexander Hamilton called the office of marshal "a troublesome and unprofitable place," an opinion shared by many marshals.[22]

Many individuals saw the office as an honorary position. When the job opening was first announced in North Carolina in 1790, Hugh

Williamson suggested to President Washington that he appoint John Skinner. "The Office of Marshal would probably be the more acceptable to Mr. Skinner," Williamson advised, "from the Idea that it is considered as being honourable rather than profitable. He is very independent in his circumstances." After serving five years as marshal of New York, Aquilla Giles described the position to President Adams as "an office of considerable responsibility, but of little emolument." He kept the job, he explained, in the hope that a better-paying position within the government would become available.[23]

Deputy marshals also suffered financial hardships because of the lack of business in the courts. Deputy John C. Barrett, for example, described to Marshal Joseph Scott of Virginia the work of the court in Norfolk during the summer of 1801. "I am disposed to think that the business in this court will turn out very inferior to my expectations," he observed, "for, since I first left this place until now, there has eminated from the office no business of any kind." Barrett repeated the complaint in November 1802: "Business in our line in this place, is unusually dull."[24]

It took many years for the business of the courts to increase. In January 1802, Judge Henry Innes of Kentucky reported to Secretary of State James Madison that only 870 cases were heard in his court from March 1790 to March 1801. The majority of them were tried from 1798 to 1801. Kentucky can hardly be considered unique among the other districts, whose business was probably just as slow.[25]

Some efforts were made to ease the financial hardships of the marshals and deputies. As early as 1790, Congress asked Attorney General Edmund Randolph to examine the functioning of the judiciary and suggest reforms to the Judiciary Act. Randolph urged, among other measures, that court clerks and marshals be allowed higher earnings. "Their posts now produce mere trifles," he informed Congress, which ignored the suggestion.[26]

2

REBELLION, SEDITION, AND WAR
1789–1815

Boston harbor bustled with activity in August 1793, and like other American ports, it involved the local United States marshals in a number of admiralty cases concerning the laws of the sea. The French war against Great Britain, Spain, and Holland further increased this work because U.S. courts adjudicated various prize cases resulting from naval battles. On August 21, Marshal John Brooks asked his deputy, Samuel Bradford, to serve a writ of replevin issued by a prize court to seize the British schooner *Greyhound,* which had been taken by a French frigate still anchored in the harbor.

As soon as Bradford stepped aboard the *Greyhound,* a dozen armed French marines from the frigate blocked his path to the helm. Replevin in hand, Bradford insisted that the marines get out of his way. The commander refused. Bradford took the only option open that preserved the dignity of the court: He stayed aboard the schooner.

Marshal Brooks tried to end the impasse through negotiations with the French consul in Boston, but the French would not recognize the court order. However, Bradford's presence aboard the *Greyhound* blocked any plans to put the schooner to sea. Even the French realized that to refuse a court order was one thing but to harm or kidnap an officer of the court was quite another.

The deputy had gambled that time was his best ally. The French frigate needed to return to war patrol in the Atlantic. On August 24 the marines withdrew from the *Greyhound,* and the frigate set sail. Bradford promptly hired a pilot to steer the *Greyhound* to the Boston wharves.[1]

When Bradford reviewed his part in the *Greyhound* affair, he proudly concluded that he had "legally executed his precept." It was an apt summary typical of the myopic vision imposed upon the marshals by their duty and their oath. The French resistance to the deputy was symptomatic of the strained neutrality of the United States during the war and its inability to offer a more forceful response to the provocations and disrespect shown by all the belligerents. But great issues of state were of less concern to Deputy Bradford—or any marshal—than that he had an order to execute and he was bound to do it.[2]

The marshals were not policymakers. They executed policy, taking their instructions from the president, the Congress, or the courts. Frequently, their orders issued from great constitutional challenges that translated into risk and trouble for the marshals. Their roles in these moments of crisis illustrate how events transpired, not why they did.

REBELLION

Of all the problems confronting George Washington when he took the presidential oath of office for the first time on April 30, 1789, that of raising money was by far the most serious. Not only did the new government have to support its ongoing operations, but it also had assumed responsibility to pay off the huge Revolutionary War debt inherited from the defunct Articles of Confederation government, a staggering total of almost $75 million. The only fundraising methods available to Washington were the tariff on imports and whatever tax proposals he could persuade Congress to approve. A personal income tax was more than a century away from acceptance. Indeed, barely two decades had passed since American colonists, led now by many of the same men who had led them then, took up arms in rebellion against Great Britain over issues related in part to taxes. Washington and the other members of the federal government could only hope that representation would make taxation more palatable to the American people.

Washington selected Alexander Hamilton to handle the problem of raising money. Brilliant, ambitious, and dedicated to making the new government a success, the new secretary of the Treasury quickly instituted a number of programs, including new bond issues to replace revolutionary war bonds, a plan for a national bank, and tariff schedules. Although these measures incurred opposition, particularly among followers of Thomas Jefferson, it was not until Hamilton proposed a tax on whiskey that instant, widespread, and popular resistance arose. Jefferson's dislike of the national bank and other Hamiltonian measures resulted in the development of a two-party system in the United States. The tax on whiskey culminated in an armed rebellion against the government.

Americans of the 1790s loved their whiskey and drank huge quantities of it, but the love of spirits alone did not lead to the rebellion. Whiskey was an economic staple for wheat and grain farmers because it was fairly easy to make and transport. A farmer needed only grain, firewood, metal containers, and copper tubing to produce whiskey, and a wagon to carry it to market.

In such backwoods locations as western Pennsylvania, at that time the very edge of the frontier, whiskey was the principal cash crop. Even so, by the time the farmers paid the costs of transporting it over the mountains to market, their margin of profit was slim. When Hamilton's whiskey tax became law on March 3, 1791, most of those farmers assumed that it would eat up their small profit. In addition, the law provided for an array of tax collectors with brands and paint to mark the stills and make life miserable for the distillers.

Hamilton argued that opponents of the tax failed to understand that its cost could be passed on to the consumer. However true his point may have been, the essential problem was that the tax required the producer to make a cash advance long before he sold the whiskey. For farmers and others on the frontier who had no cash to spare, the excise was especially burdensome. Consequently, opposition was particularly intense in the poorest sections of the country, such as the settlements clustered around the small village called Pittsburgh along the Monongahela and Allegheny rivers.

Opposition to the whiskey tax soon took the form of physical attacks on collectors, inspectors, and supervisors. On September 6, 1791, Robert Johnson, the collector for Washington and Allegheny counties in Pennsylvania, was attacked by a band of sixteen men wearing women's dresses as disguises. They cut off his hair, tarred and feathered him, and took his horse, leaving him, Hamilton wrote Washington, "in that mortifying and painful situation." Johnson, however, recognized some of his attackers and swore out warrants against them in federal court. Marshal Clement Biddle dispatched his deputy, Joseph Fox, to arrest the culprits.

Fox left the district office in Philadelphia for the long trek across the state apparently without fully understanding the extent of the opposition to the tax and its enforcers. When he arrived in Allegheny County in October, the intensity of the feeling struck him immediately. He feared for his life. Keeping both his identity and his mission a secret, Fox struck upon what Hamilton later called an "injudicious and fruitless expedient" to serve the warrants. Rather than serve them himself, Fox hired John Connor, an old cattle drover, to make the noxious deliveries. His strategy was of doubtful legality and undoubted cowardice, which he compounded by not telling Connor that he was delivering arrest warrants.

For helping Fox, Connor was whipped, tarred and feathered, relieved of his horse and money, bound with rope, and left in the woods for five hours before someone discovered him. Deputy Fox immediately fled the county, returning to Philadelphia with his warrants unserved. They remained unserved for two years. Perhaps Connor would have taken consolation in knowing that unserved warrants earned deputies no fees.[3]

Meanwhile, violent opposition to the tax continued unabated. The Whiskey Rebels, as they came to be called, continued to tar and feather various collectors, witnesses, and supporters and payers of the tax. On May 31, 1794, the federal district court in Pennsylvania issued process against seventy-five distillers in western Pennsylvania. Despite a new law allowing conveniently located state courts to hear whiskey tax cases, these processes were made returnable to the district court. The respondents would have to cross the state to appear in court. Marshal David Lenox, rejecting his predecessor's decision to use deputies in such cases, "came to the determination of doing the duty in person."[4]

The processes Lenox took to western Pennsylvania were not arrest warrants but simple summonses designating a particular day (August 12) for the defendants to appear in court to show cause why an arrest warrant for failure to pay the tax should not be issued. If the defendant failed to show adequate cause, an arrest warrant would be issued and service on the defendant again obtained by the marshal. The distinction was an important one to both Lenox and the federal court, if not to the seventy-five distillers, for Lenox believed it proved the court's desire to go as mildly as possible in enforcing the excise law. To the men summonsed, it meant the probability of two trips to Philadelphia.[5]

The marshal left Philadelphia on June 22, 1794, and traveled through Cumberland, Bedford, and Fayette counties, serving summonses. He encountered little difficulty or resistance. Indeed, Lenox later pointed out that in Fayette County "I met many instances of personal respect and attention from some of the persons on whom I had served process." His luck, however, did not hold.

On July 14, Lenox entered Allegheny County, and there the tenor of his reception changed dramatically. Upon arriving, Lenox called on General John Neville, the inspector of the revenue for the tax survey encompassing western Pennsylvania. Neville offered to accompany the marshal, sparing him the necessity of hiring a local guide, and they set out on horseback the next morning. "In the course of a few hours," Lenox later reported to Hamilton, "I served process on four persons all of whom shewed much contempt for the Laws of the United States." At their fifth stop, that contempt turned violent.

Shortly before noon on July 15, Lenox and Neville arrived at William Miller's farm to serve Miller a summons commanding him "to set aside all manner of business and excuses" and appear before the district judge in Philadelphia on August 12. According to Lenox, Miller "in much agitation refused to receive a Copy of the process against him." As Lenox and Miller argued, Neville glanced across the field and saw thirty to forty men running toward them. The inspector called to the marshal to hurry, and he and Lenox set off. Proceeding at a normal pace, they "were fired upon at the distance of forty or fifty yards." Lenox stopped his horse and "upbraided them with their conduct." The mob responded with shouts and curses, but no more shooting. Lenox and Neville went on their way without additional molestation.[6]

Shortly before dawn the next morning, another group of forty armed men approached Neville at his home on Bower Hill. Hearing them, Neville called out for an explanation. The leader, John Holcroft, who thought he was talking to Lenox, responded that they were friends from Philadelphia coming to act as the marshal's guard. Neville's demand that the men stand off was accompanied by a shot from his rifle that mortally wounded Oliver Miller, William's father. For almost half an hour a gun battle raged between the rebels and Neville, his wife, a visiting woman, and some of his eighteen slaves. No one on Neville's side was injured; the rebels suffered four more casualties before retreating.

Meanwhile, in Pittsburgh, Marshal Lenox was packing his bags. Hearing of the fight at Bower Hill, he postponed his departure "to remain in th[is] Country to see the issue." Throughout the remainder of the day, he helped Neville's son Presley enlist the support of the local militia to protect Bower Hill that night. The next morning, after no attack was made, the commander of the militiamen sent all but a dozen of them home.[7]

After lengthy debate the rebels decided to return to Bower Hill and compel General Neville to resign as inspector of the revenue. About five hundred armed men gathered at Couch's Fort under the leadership of James McFarlane. Marshal Lenox and Presley Neville spent the afternoon of July 17 in Pittsburgh, trying unsuccessfully to persuade the general of the militia and the county judge to return the militiamen to Bower Hill. At 3 p.m. Lenox, Presley Neville, and three volunteers left for Bower Hill to join in its defense.[8]

Unbeknownst to Lenox and his party, the rebels had already surrounded the house, though not before General Neville managed to hide in the nearby thickets. Lenox and his four companions rode straight into the ring of waiting rebels. The small party "proceeded to within half a Mile of General Neville's House where we were all made Prisoners of the insurgents," Lenox later reported. "Soon after the firing commenced and continued with some intermission for about an hour when we perceived the buildings on fire." The dozen defenders surrendered, after which they were allowed to leave unharmed. Neville's home burned to the ground, and the rebels looted his remaining possessions, including the contents of his wine cellar.[9]

After the battle, the five hundred rebels regrouped to celebrate their victory with Neville's liquor. A brief council was called, which decided to take Lenox and Presley Neville to Couch's Fort to determine their fate. The three men who had accompanied them from Pittsburgh were either released or allowed to escape. Surrounded by the rebels, many of whom were by this time drunk with success and Neville's whiskey, Lenox and Neville marched "in the most painful and humiliating situation" to Couch's Fort.[10]

Fortunately for Lenox, a few of the rebels protected him from the others. "On my arriving at the place of Rendezvous and being announced," the marshal later remembered, "four or five of a large party there fired towards me without injuring me, tho' by the light of the moon my person was plainly exposed to them at [but] few yards distance." His protectors cursed the men and ordered them to cease fire. As a committee began deliberating what to do with the marshal, Lenox reported, "two fellows advanced from among the Crowd towards me with their Knives drawn." In a loud voice Lenox told the rebels that he hoped he "was not to be assassinated in that way." The two men slashed his coat before being driven away. To prevent additional attacks, Lenox was moved into a house within the fort, where he rejoined Presley Neville.[11]

The rebel leaders agreed to release Lenox and Neville, provided that the marshal promise to deliver no more summonses west of the Allegheny Mountains. Lenox, who had already served all but one of the processes, readily agreed. Neville offered to guarantee the promise. The two men then requested an escort out of the rebel camp.

Lenox, Neville, and their three rebel escorts had gone less than half a mile from camp when they chanced upon a small group of rebels who were "much intoxicated." When the drunkards found out one of the men was Lenox, they shouldered their rifles. An escort, Benjamin Parkinson, threw himself between Lenox and the drunken rebels, saving the marshal's life. The disappointed rebels ordered Lenox and Neville to return with them to Couch's Fort. On the way, Lenox, who wanted nothing more to do with the Whiskey – and whiskeyed – Rebels, decided to escape. He and Parkinson were a short distance ahead of the others when Lenox spurred his horse and rode into the woods. After galloping a short distance, he reined in his horse to listen for any pursuit but heard none. He then carefully made his way back to Pittsburgh, arriving at 3 a.m. on July 18. Presley Neville also managed to escape and return to Pittsburgh.[12]

While the marshal recuperated from his ordeal and tried to figure out what to do, another group of rebels came into town to demand that he surrender all the summonses he had served. Although they made thinly veiled threats, Lenox refused to hand over his precepts. He explained that the summonses were not arrest warrants but orders to appear in court on a certain day. The rebel committee consulted Hugh Brackinridge, a locally prominent lawyer, who concurred in the marshal's description that the papers were "an initiatory process; and that judgement could not be taken; that there must be another writ, and service of it, in order to found a judgement." Satisfied with that answer, the group left town.[13]

Meanwhile, the peaceful citizens of Pittsburgh grew increasingly worried about the bands of armed rebels roaming the mountains surrounding the town. Their fears were heightened by the presence of both the marshal and the inspector of the revenue at local boardinghouses. The idea circulated that Lenox and General Neville should be turned over to the rebels in order to spare Pittsburgh from attack. "In such a situation," Lenox decided, "it behoved us to keep a good look out and to think of our personal safety." Both men agreed that it was time to leave Pittsburgh and go to Philadelphia, the national capital.

Perhaps fearing recapture, Lenox turned over all the served precepts to a Major Craig for safekeeping. Because the roads were infested with rebels, Lenox and Neville rode a barge down the Ohio River into western Virginia before crossing overland to Philadelphia, which they reached on August 8. "That I met *some* difficulties and encountered *some* opposition is very true," Lenox concluded in his report to Secretary of the Treasury Hamilton, but, he pointed out, "it was my duty to execute the processes."[14]

While Lenox and Neville were making their circuitous way to Philadelphia, President Washington decided to act. Warned of the troubles endured by both men, he called a meeting of his cabinet sometime before August 2. A 1792 law empowered the president to call out the state militias to suppress insurrections if an associate justice of the Supreme Court or a local district court judge notified him that the opposition to the laws was beyond the powers of the marshal to suppress. At the cabinet meeting, Washington asked Attorney General William Bradford to explain the situation to Justice James Wilson and get the required notification from him.[15]

Justice Wilson came through with the notification on August 4. "From the evidence which has been laid before me," he wrote Washington, though he neglected to mention that the administration itself had supplied the evidence, "I hereby notify you that, in the Counties of Washington and Allegheny in Pennsylvania, laws of the United States are opposed, and the Execution thereof obstructed by combinations too powerful to be suppressed by the ordinary course of judicial proceedings or by the Powers vested in the Marshal of that District." Upon receiving the notification, Secretary of State Randolph, at Washington's request, began drafting a proclamation for the president's signature. In tough language it called on the rebels to lay down their arms and return to their homes. At the same time, Secretary of War Henry Knox initiated the complex arrangements for the state militias to march on western Pennsylvania.[16]

The wait for Wilson's letter, combined with an irritating reluctance by Pennsylvania state officials to take action, dampened Washington's outrage over the attacks on the marshal and the inspector. Knowing the militia would take weeks to organize its march, the president sent a commission, headed by Attorney General Bradford, to the troubled area to negotiate peace. On August 7, 1794, Bradford's commission left for western Pennsylvania, Washington issued his proclamation calling for an end to the insurrection, and Knox ordered the governors of Pennsylvania, New Jersey, Maryland, and Virginia to muster a total of thirteen thousand militiamen prepared to march.

The Bradford commission had until the end of September to effect a peaceful solution. Although the commission persuaded hundreds of rebels to sign an oath of allegiance to the government, enough rebels remained unrepentant that on September 24 the president issued a proclamation ordering the militia to suppress the rebellion. Washington placed the combined militia under the command of the governor of Virginia, the famous American Revolution general Lighthorse Harry Lee. Hamilton, at his own request, also accompanied the expedition, serving as its second in command. Washington also marched with the militia as far as Bedford, Pennsylvania, the only time in American history that a president has taken the field at the head of his army. Somewhere in the midst of the thousands of soldiers rode three civilians: Marshal David Lenox, U.S. Attorney William Rawle, and Judge Richard Peters. Supported by the militia, they were, respectively, to arrest, prosecute, and try the rebel leaders for treason.[17]

After numerous delays caused by poor organization and bad weather, the army straggled into Pittsburgh early in November. By November 9 the marshal, the attorney, and the judge believed they had enough evidence against eighteen rebel leaders to warrant their arrest. On the night of November 13, known forever after in the local folklore as the Dismal Night, most of the suspects were arrested. The ensuing trials dragged on for a year before all but two of the defendants were acquitted. The two guilty men were sentenced to hang, but President Washington eventually pardoned them.[18]

Two years after that rebellious summer, former marshal Lenox applied to Washington to pardon Benjamin Parkinson for any crimes he might have committed during the insurrection. Lenox explained that Parkinson, one dark night, threw himself between the marshal and a group of drunken rebels. Washington granted the request.[19]

The end of the insurrection in western Pennsylvania did not quiet the opposition to the excise tax, but all organized resistance to the government ceased. In 1809 Congress repealed the whiskey tax and abolished the offices of surveyor, inspector, and collector. Because some back taxes were still due from distillers, Congress transferred the duty of collecting them to the U.S. marshals.[20]

The outcome of the Whiskey Rebellion substantiated the federal government's power. Four years later, in March 1799, an auctioneer named John Fries incited a small rebellion in eastern Pennsylvania against a 1798 federal tax on houses. Marshal William Nichols arrested several men who had interfered with tax assessors. Fries hastily organized an armed band to rescue the prisoners. President John Adams, like his predecessor, could not allow the challenge to federal authority to go unanswered, and the militia marched again on Pennsylvania. Both the Whiskey and the Fries rebellions illustrated that the marshals, as the civilian enforcers of the law, faced first the opposition to it.[21]

SEDITION

Rebellions composed only a part of the tumult the new federal government faced as it tried to establish its authority. By the end of Washington's first term, the feud between Jefferson and Hamilton was open and increasingly divisive. Each man had his own vision of what the government should be; each cultivated a substantial following within the government and among the people. For a time President Washington tried to mediate between the two men, but eventually he sided with Hamilton. On December 31, 1793, Jefferson resigned as secretary of state. He retired to Monticello, where he openly led the opposition to the administration's fiscal program and foreign policy. His followers called themselves Democratic-Republicans, or simply Republicans. Hamilton's supporters called themselves Federalists.

The French Revolution exacerbated the split between the two embryonic parties. The Republicans sympathized with the French and excused their bloody excesses as the price of liberty; the Federalists interpreted the revolution as illustrative of the tyranny of the mob, proof of the need for strong government to control the masses. When the Republicans began establishing "Democratic clubs" throughout the United States, Hamilton and his supporters saw them as harbingers of revolution. The concept of loyal opposition held little credence during the 1790s.

In part the problem arose because the nation's founders neither expected nor knew how to handle the development of political parties. The Constitution had no provision for opposing parties, because no one foresaw sustained, organized opposition to the government. Although objections to specific policies had been predicted, criticism of government actions, particularly coming from organized groups of private citizens, seemed almost treasonous.

For several years such battles raged primarily in the newspapers. Each party had its own organs to tout its philosophical and practical beliefs, as well as to libel the beliefs of its rivals. By mid-decade, Congress too was split along party lines, with the Federalists in the ascendancy. The election of 1796 pointed out the failings of the original constitutional procedures for presidential elections: The person with the most votes became president, and the runner-up became vice president. As a consequence Federalist John Adams assumed the presidency on March 5, 1797, with seventy-one electoral votes, and Republican Thomas Jefferson became his vice president with sixty-eight votes. That the two were not speaking to each other, that they each adamantly disagreed with the other, and that they worked to defeat the other's policies were constitutional inconveniences that went unrectified until the adoption of the Twelfth Amendment in 1804.

Shortly after Adams took the oath, relations with France deteriorated to the brink of war. French interference with American trading ships convinced the Federalists that war was the only answer. The famous XYZ affair, in which representatives of the French demanded a $240,000 bribe before they would even begin negotiations with Americans, further exasperated the Federalists. Adams, however, shied from war. He preferred instead to strengthen America's military posture by appointing George Washington head of the newly organized armies and asking Congress to establish a Department of the Navy. While he prepared the country, an undeclared naval war broke out with France.

The international tensions had domestic repercussions. Many Republicans were profoundly sympathetic with the French people. They remembered the assistance the lonely colonies had received from France during the gloomiest days of the American Revolution. The successful overthrow of Louis XVI and Marie Antoinette brought France into the democratic fold. Its subsequent declaration of war on regal Britain confirmed France as the champion of democracy. Consequently, the Republicans severely criticized the Federalists' warlike attitude toward America's former ally and fellow democracy.

The Federalists interpreted the criticism as treasonous. As part of the war preparations against France, Congress passed three measures in the summer of 1798 that were aimed directly at their domestic opponents. The alien acts of June and July allowed the president to deport any alien whom he considered dangerous to the public safety and, in wartime, to imprison aliens who were loyal to the enemy. The third act, however, was by far the most dangerous to American citizens. The Sedition Act of July 14, 1798, provided for the fine and imprisonment of unlawful combinations against the government or of anyone who published any "false, scandalous, and malicious writing" about the government, Congress, or the president. The only redeeming feature of the act was the provision for its expiration in 1801.

Secretary of State Timothy Pickering took the guiding hand in enforcing the Sedition Act. Each day he scoured Republican newspapers looking for seditious comment, hoping to arrest anyone who dared complain about government policies. Pickering also urged U.S. attorneys to review the Republican papers in their districts for objectionable materials. District Attorney (as the U.S. attorneys were called in those days) Richard Harrison of New York, for example, assured Pickering on August 17, 1799, that he had arranged for the daily delivery of the *Argus,* a widely read Republican paper. Harrison promised "to pursue your Directions to prosecute the publisher for every Libel appearing therein against the Government or its officers." In the fall of 1799 he indicted the *Argus's* publisher, Mrs. Ann Greenleaf. Although Greenleaf's trial was postponed until the spring of 1800, her printer, David Frothingham, was tried and convicted under New York state law for libeling Alexander Hamilton, a private citizen at the time. The circumstances forced Greenleaf to sell the *Argus* in March 1800, one month before her trial was to begin. Having thus silenced her, Pickering agreed with Harrison's suggestion to drop the charges.[22]

During the two and a half years the act was enforced, the government arrested twenty-five people for violating it; ten were convicted and sent to prison. All of them were Republican editors or printers, except Luther Baldwin and two of his drinking buddies. On July 27, 1798, Baldwin and his friends stepped outside their favorite tavern in Newark, New Jersey, to watch President Adams and a parade in his honor pass down Broad Street. As the president and his entourage reached the city limits, Newark saluted Adams with a sixteen-gun cannonade. "There goes the President and they are firing at his ass," said one of the men, to whom Baldwin drunkenly replied that he "did not care if they fired thro' his ass." For that seditious slander of the president, Baldwin was fined $150 and jailed until he paid it. His friends were also fined and jailed as a lesson to all Republicans to avoid spirits and spirited comments about the president.[23]

Baldwin's arrest emphasized the tragedy underlying the Sedition Act, the greatest threat to freedom of speech and the press ever approved by a peacetime Congress. Of the ten men who went to prison for expressing their views on Federalist policies and officials, none symbolized the danger of the Sedition Act better than Matthew Lyon, a Republican congressman from Vermont and the first person arrested for violating the act. Nor did any other case show more clearly the role of the U.S. marshals in enforcing the pernicious law.

Lyon came to America from his native Ireland as an indentured servant. Hard work allowed him to purchase his freedom and earned him considerable wealth. He fought alongside Ethan Allen during the revolution. After the war, he founded the town of Fairhaven, Vermont, and married the governor's daughter. Although a wealthy man, he never forgot the poverty of his youth. That experience brought him into the Republican party and gave him a profound sympathy for the common people. He was elected to Congress in 1796, one of only a few Republican members from New England.[24]

Once in Congress, Lyon showed himself to be a fierce defender of Republican virtues and an abrasive enemy of Federalist policies and pomp. He made many enemies with his quick tongue and temper, but one particular incident united the Federalists against him. On January 30, 1798, Roger Griswold, a leading Federalist congressman from Connecticut, belittled Lyon's Revolutionary War service in a speech before the House. Lyon promptly spat in Griswold's face. That ungentlemanly response almost got him expelled from the House and earned him the nickname "the Spitting Lyon."[25]

Lyon's sedition, not his spittle, caused him the most trouble. During the 1798 election campaign his vitriolic attacks on the president and the Federalists assumed greater importance because the Federalist majority in Congress was slim; they needed desperately to win as many seats as possible. To help his own campaign, Lyon founded a new newspaper on October 1, 1798: *The Scourge of Aristocracy and Repository of Important Political Truths*. Four days after the first issue appeared, the federal grand jury indicted him for sedition. That evening a deputy marshal arrested him.[26]

The circuit court trial opened on October 8 in Rutland, Vermont. Lyon acted as his own attorney. Justice William Paterson and district judge Samuel Hitchcock presided at the trial, which was prosecuted vigorously by Charles Marsh. The fairness of the trial was questionable. After Marsh rested the government's case, Justice Paterson immediately began instructing the jury until Lyon asked if he could present his defense. The judge "politely sat down" and allowed the defendant to put forth his case. For two and a half hours, Lyon attacked the Sedition Act as unconstitutional, explained his innocence, and asserted that the alleged seditious comments he had made were not seditious, because they were true. At one point he asked Justice Paterson "whether he had not frequently dined with the President, and observed his ridiculous pomp and parade." After an hour's deliberations, the jury returned a verdict of guilty. The next day, Justice Paterson announced his intention of making an example of Lyon. He sentenced him to four months in jail, fined him $1,000, and ordered him to pay the $60.96 court costs.[27]

Marshal Jabez G. Fitch took custody of the convicted congressman. Fitch was the second marshal for the district of Vermont, his predecessor, Lewis R. Morris, having been elected to Congress as a staunch Federalist. Fitch had been a lieutenant in the Continental Regiment during the American Revolution and was taken prisoner by the British in August 1776. He received his first appointment as marshal from George Washington on June 9, 1794. President Adams renewed the appointment four years later. Fitch's reappointment confirmed his good standing as a Federalist. He could be depended on to do his duty and keep the faith.[28]

Fitch had no sympathy for seditionists, especially if they were Republican congressmen. He refused Lyon's request to stop briefly at the congressman's home to pick up his papers. Instead of lodging Lyon in the local Rutland jail, Fitch took his prisoner on a forty-four-mile trek to Vergennes. When they reached the city, Fitch marched the entire length of the town, purposefully passing the place where the state legislature was in session.

Lyon's cell measured twelve by sixteen feet. It had no fireplace or stove or any way to close the small barred window at the top of the wall. Although the window offered the only source of light, it also provided gusts of cold October wind.

Lyon continued his reelection campaign from this chilly headquarters. At first Marshal Fitch refused to supply him with pen and ink unless he submitted his letters for censorship. After four days, however, the marshal relented, and Lyon was allowed to correspond freely with his fellow Republicans. The election returns gave Lyon a plurality, but he fell one vote short of the majority he needed under Vermont law. Thus, he campaigned in the runoff election a month later while still a prisoner of the marshal. "For the first time in American history," one historian observed, "a candidate for Congress conducted his campaign from a federal prison." Federalists, who needed Lyon's seat to solidify their slim congressional majority, launched unmerciful attacks from all across the country. But Lyon's constituents returned him to Congress with a substantial majority, giving him almost twice as many votes as his Federalist opponent received.[29]

Leading Republicans, including Jefferson and Madison, contributed various amounts to pay Lyon's fine. Senator George Mason of Virginia went to Vergennes to deliver the money, paid in gold, raised by the party. Lyon's constituents also collected a sufficient sum, but they deferred to Mason in order to emphasize Lyon's national support. The congressman's imprisonment had made him a national hero to Republicans.[30]

On February 9, 1799, Lyon's prison term expired. Mason paid the fine to Marshal Fitch, and arrangements were made to release the prisoner. However, Lyon took no chances. When the marshal opened the cell door that morning, Lyon announced, "I am on my way to Philadelphia." His invocation of the constitutional immunity from arrest for congressmen en route to Congress stymied any plans Fitch may have had to rearrest him for seditious comments made from jail. Lyon returned in triumph to the capital, where he reclaimed his seat in the House, unreformed and unrepentant.[31] Two years later, on March 4, 1801, Thomas Jefferson became the third president of the United

States. Exactly one week after taking office, he fired Marshal Jabez G. Fitch.

The marshals' enforcement of the Sedition Act showed the extreme limits of federal authority. It proved the danger of making the federal government too powerful at the expense of the rights of the people. The marshals had not made the law, but influenced by their own politics, they enforced it with a vengeance. Such a response was a curious and dangerous side effect of American self-government.

WAR

When Jefferson succeeded Adams as president, he immediately determined to purge the government of its Federalist influences. During his two terms eighteen U.S. marshals were dismissed, most of them Federalists whom he fired within his first two years in office. In contrast, Adams had removed only one marshal during his term, and James Madison, who succeeded Jefferson in 1809, would remove only two marshals during his two terms. Jefferson's attempt to cleanse the judiciary was hindered, however, by the lifetime appointment of judges. Because the Federalists on the bench were out of his reach, he surrounded them with Democratic-Republican marshals and attorneys.[32]

The marshals of Jefferson's day held a key power in court proceedings: They controlled the selection of juries, grand and petite. It was a simple matter for the marshals to choose jurymen according to their political sympathies. One of Matthew Lyon's complaints against Marshal Fitch, for example, was that the marshal had packed the jury with Federalists and political opponents during Lyon's sedition trial. Thus, although Jefferson could not control the federal judges, through his marshals he could at least influence the juries, and through his U.S. attorneys he could further control how cases were conducted.[33]

Indeed, Jefferson viewed the marshals and attorneys as the guardians of the judicial gates. "The courts being so decidedly federal and irremovable," he once wrote, "it is believed that republican attorneys and marshals, being the doors of entrance into the courts, are indispensably necessary as a shield to the republican part of our fellow citizens, which, I believe, is the main body of the people." By 1803, according to the calculations of Secretary of War and formal marshal Henry Dearborn, Jefferson had filled the nineteen districts with sixteen Republican marshals and seventeen Republican attorneys. Only the Federalist marshals in Rhode Island, New Hampshire, and Massachusetts survived the purge.[34]

Jefferson also began an earnest assault on the judges. In the closing weeks of the Adams administration the Federalist-controlled Congress had passed the Judiciary Act of 1801, which created sixteen new circuit courts and five new judicial districts. Adams had worked feverishly to fill the new openings for judges, marshals, and attorneys with staunch Federalists. Early in 1802, at Jefferson's insistence, Congress repealed the Judiciary Act of 1801, abolished the new courts, and thereby threw sixteen Federalist circuit judges and five Federalist district judges out of work.[35]

Yet, in his eagerness to rid the judiciary of Federalist influences, Jefferson ignored the country's urgent need for judicial reorganization. During the 1790s, Ohio, Michigan, Indiana, and Illinois were organized into territories. Presidentially appointed governors and boards of commissioners administered the regions until their growing populations could support territorial governments, the first step toward statehood. In the acts establishing the Northwest Territories, the Second Continental Congress and then the U.S. Congress granted the ruling boards of commissioners the power of subpoena and other process but failed to create an office to serve the precepts. Consequently, the boards "were then constrained to assume a constructive power to appoint a marshal to execute process." The fees of the marshals were audited and paid by the Treasury Department.[36]

In 1803 Jefferson doubled the size of the United States through the Louisiana Purchase from France. For the bargain price of $15 million, 828,000 square miles between the Mississippi River and the Rocky Mountains came to the United States, including the key port of New Orleans. Many years passed before the area was explored, populated, and organized into discrete territories, yet it nonetheless offered a new and powerful dream to the American people – the possibility of moving westward.

Before the nation could turn westward, it had to solve its problems eastward across the Atlantic. The undeclared naval war with France lasted two years, ending at the close of Adams's administration. A brief period of peace between France and Britain alleviated the strain, which was further eased by Jefferson's friendly feelings toward the French. But in 1803 Napoléon Bonaparte renewed his aggression against the rest of Europe. In response Great Britain, which controlled the seas, embarked on a policy to end all trade between neutral nations and the French. The United States, the most active neutral trader, suffered the most from this policy. On top of the constant British interference with American trade, English warships began searching American naval crews for expatriate Englishmen. French countermeasures against British trade, though largely ineffectual, aggravated the situation.

Neither Secretary of State Madison nor the president wanted war, particularly because the prospect of victory was poor, at best. Both men adopted a cautious policy toward Great Britain. In 1805 Congress passed a new law providing for "the more effectual preservation of peace in the ports and harbours of the United States and in the waters under their jurisdiction." The law specified how to handle admiralty and other lawsuits, including those arising from crimes committed by foreign seamen. Madison, in a circular letter to all the marshals, elaborated on the act by directing them to tread carefully when serving process on crewmen and officers of belligerent ships. "Previous to the execution of any warrant committed to you, you are to make known to the commanding officer of the foreign vessel of war having the offender on board, with all the usual respect and civility due to such officers, the nature of the process," Madison ordered, adding that the marshal should ask the officer to deliver the offenders over to him.

If the captain refused to surrender his men, Madison wanted the marshal to proceed, "with as much respect and delicacy" as the situation permitted, to arrest the offender. Should the captain offer resistance, Madison wanted an immediate report sent to him. If the marshal had no reason to believe the ship would set sail or the offender would escape, he was to await further orders from the president. However, if the case seemed so urgent "as to require the use of force," Madison directed the marshals to apply to their local governors for military assistance.[37]

The rather detailed instructions exemplified the Republican administration's attitude toward the belligerents. Neither Jefferson nor Madison wanted any American official to give the warring powers the slightest offense, but the administration wanted the laws enforced, even in the face of resistance.

The marshals conducted themselves well. No incidents occurred involving their enforcement of court orders or their service of process on the belligerents. However, the British and the French continued to strain relations with the United States, issuing a seemingly endless series of decrees and orders aimed at disrupting neutral trade with the enemy. Still determined to avoid war, Jefferson responded with a self-imposed embargo on American trade. Rather than risk interference with American ships, the president persuaded Congress in 1807 to pass a law prohibiting all foreign trade. It was an absurd policy, practically unenforceable, and particularly damaging to American standing in the international community. The American people, especially those in the northeastern communities, bitterly resented the embargo and actively resisted it.

The burden of enforcing the law fell on the customs collectors in each port, but the administration expected the marshals to assist them in times of trouble. And trouble was plenty. On August 14, 1808, Marshal John Willard of Vermont wrote to Madison that armed and violent insurgents had opposed the local customs collector in his efforts to enforce the embargo. The opposition continued into the next year. In April 1808, Madison advised Marshal Willard that the collector feared that forcible efforts would be made to "frustrate the execution of the Embargo laws." Madison wanted Willard to cooperate with the collector and, if necessary, raise a posse to assist him. Opposition to the law was so widespread, however, that raising a posse to enforce it was no easy matter, but Madison did not address that problem.[38]

Problems with the belligerent powers and the enforcement of the embargo plagued the Jefferson administration until the president's retirement in March 1809. Madison inherited the difficulties and at first sought the same solutions his mentor had pursued, with an equal lack of success. Finally, in June 1812, frustration with British intransigence led Congress to declare war against England.

The United States was woefully unprepared to fight, particularly to fight the most powerful nation of the time. However, the British were engaged in a two-front war, with France on the Continent and with the United States an ocean away. Nevertheless, the Americans lost most of the battles, flubbed an invasion of Canada, and surrendered their new capital to the enemy for burning.

Madison soon learned that fighting the war involved more than sending armies off to battle, especially with most of the battles occurring on American soil. Domestic opposition to the war, particularly in the Northeast, had to be circumvented. Several of the state militias had trouble filling their ranks. Many citizen-soldiers refused to respond to the order to muster out for service. Thousands of British citizens—

traders, merchantmen, and others with American interests – lived throughout the country, posing a constant threat of espionage and sabotage. Finally, each military engagement with the enemy resulted in the capture of prisoners. Guarding them drained the already weakened American armies of desperately needed soldiers. Thus, the Madison administration had an urgent need for a loyal national organization that could deal with those domestic problems.

The administration turned to the U.S. marshals. Congress had already made provision for their use in the Militia Act of 1795, which assigned them the responsibility for compelling service in the state militias. Male citizens who refused to serve were liable to fairly hefty fines levied by the marshals of each district. As soon as hostilities began, the marshals encouraged the men of their district to join their local militias or pay the penalty.

In June 1814, two years after the declaration of war, a group of disgruntled Pennsylvania militiamen sued Marshal John Smith and his deputy, Daniel Moore, for their enforcement of the Militia Act. Secretary of State James Monroe advised Smith to suspend his efforts to uphold the act until the courts could decide its constitutionality. The case dragged on until several years after the war ended. The Supreme Court decided in favor of the marshal.[39]

Marshals also helped the Madison administration respond to the widespread opposition to the war. In January 1813, Marshal James Prince of Massachusetts reported to Secretary Monroe that he was "surrounded with opposition . . . from the Bench, the Bar and the Pulpit." Although objections to the war were expressed loudly, with several states threatening to secede from the Union, little action backed up the grousing.[40]

The external enemy, the British, caused the marshals the most work and the most difficulty. Empowered by the Alien Act of 1798 as the government's agents dealing with resident enemy aliens, the marshals worked throughout the two and a half years of the war to keep track of all enemy aliens in their districts and to thwart espionage and sabotage. With the front lines of the war stretched across American territory, their work proved crucial. On July 11, 1812, less than a month after Congress declared war, Monroe ordered each marshal to appoint deputies throughout their districts to keep track of all enemy aliens. British citizens residing in the United States were required to register with the deputies and report to them monthly. Soon the State Department had lengthy lists giving the location and activities of every enemy alien.[41]

The marshals reported a total of 11,554 British aliens during the War of 1812. Pennsylvania had the largest number of enemy aliens, 3,364, but New York was close behind with 3,153. Vermont and New Hampshire reported the least number of aliens, 12 and 14, respectively. The marshals not only registered these British citizens but also spent considerable time issuing individual "licenses and passports" allowing the aliens to travel or sending them into the interior. The marshals also hired and paid the expenses of deputies whom they periodically sent to the interior locations to check on the British under their charge. Despite all their work, the marshals were neither paid nor reimbursed for their expenses until 1817, two years after the war ended. In June of that year the administration originally determined to pay them $1 for each enemy alien they reported and controlled, but the amount was subsequently lowered to 75 cents for each alien.[42]

When the military engagements shifted to American soil in early 1813, the marshals rounded up enemy aliens who lived within forty miles of the coast and ordered them to designated locations deeper in the interior. Enemy aliens in Pennsylvania, for example, were sent to Reading; those in Connecticut went to Tolland. Because war in the early nineteenth century was a gentlemanly affair, the marshals accepted each alien's promise to leave the coast. Each side assumed that a man's word was his bond, and each understood that breaking that bond would result in harsher treatment. The aliens were not guarded or put in internment camps, provided they stayed where the marshal told them to stay. Periodically, the marshals sent deputies to check on them. This trust spared the marshals the expense and trouble of hiring guards and erecting prisons, but it also posed the risk that not all enemy aliens would hold to their promises.[43]

In March 1813, Marshal John Smith of Pennsylvania accepted the word of Charles Lockington, a British citizen "resident in Philadelphia, and connected with commerce," that he would repair to Reading for the duration of the war. Lockington stayed in Reading for several months but then "violated his engagement and duty to remain there, and came to Philadelphia, at a period of considerable uneasiness." After returning to Philadelphia, Lockington apparently provided the nearby British forces with information until Smith caught up with him. When Lockington refused the marshal's polite request to return to Reading, Smith "gently laid hands" on him and took him under guard to the local debtors' prison, where all untrustworthy Englishmen were kept. The marshal kept Lockington in jail from November 1813 until the following April. Six months in prison persuaded Lockington to sign a parole (or oath) giving his word that he would return to Reading. There he resided until the end of the war, at which time he sued Marshal Smith, who was also being sued by the militiamen, for assault and battery. Supreme Court justice Bushrod Washington, sitting as circuit judge, dismissed Lockington's lawsuit.[44]

Other marshals also had problems with spies. On January 21, 1813, Marshal Thomas G. Thornton of Maine reported that one of his deputies had arrested a British spy, though no one in the district knew what do to with him. In neighboring Massachusetts, Marshal James Prince wanted to pay an informant to identify the person offering important dispatches to the British, but Prince was unsure how much the government should spend for the information. Marshal Peter Curtenius of New York City guarded that important harbor, allowing only those enemy aliens with legitimate passes to leave the country and arresting those who had been ordered to move to the interior but had failed to do so. Marshal Morton A. Waring of South Carolina suggested to Monroe in July 1813 that Waring be authorized to appoint and pay a deputy to check each ship and stagecoach for any aliens. Later that year, Secretary Monroe instructed the marshals of Rhode Island, New York, Connecticut, and Massachusetts to permit certain British subjects, whom he identified by name, to board ships to return to England. Throughout the war the marshals of coastal districts, under instructions from the secretary of state, cleared all enemy aliens and all mail for departure from the country. The marshals also disbursed the rewards to ship's crews in admiralty prize cases.[45]

On November 12, 1812, the United States and Great Britain agreed to exchange prisoners captured on the high seas by "public and private vessels of war." Designated as "general stations for British subjects" were the ports of Salem, Massachusetts; Newport, Rhode Island; Wilmington, Delaware; and Charleston, South Carolina. The marshals of neighboring districts sent any prisoners of war delivered to them to the ports, where the marshals of those districts kept them in custody until they could be exchanged.[46]

The arrangement for the exchange provided that each country

operated two "cartel vessels." Those ships sailed, "as occasion may require, between the stations established in the United States and Halifax, Jamaica, and Bermuda; the two first of which places have been fixed upon by the British authorities as their maritime stations." The marshals of the American staging points received prisoners from neighboring districts, furnishing their neighboring marshals with a receipt for each prisoner. The prisoners were kept in local jails and prisons until the regular arrival of the prison ship, at which time they were swapped for American prisoners.

When the ship arrived, the secretary of state expected the marshals "to facilitate the embarkation and departure of the prisoners in your custody; always and immediately transmitting to this department a report of the number, names, rank, etc., put on board." The secretary also wanted weekly reports on the number of prisoners each of the four marshals had in custody. Although British prisoners were under the overall superintendence of the army's commissary general of prisoners, the four marshals kept physical custody of them.[47]

Secretary Monroe established strict rules for the maintenance and supervision of the prisoners. The price of feeding them, for example, could not exceed the price of food purchased for American troops in that district. Monroe hoped that the same person who supplied the U.S. troops could also be contracted to feed the prisoners. If not, the marshal was to find "the best mode within your power . . . keeping in view the rule of expenditures." Jail space was to be rented from the state governor or from local authorities. The marshal was also expected to use army physicians to attend the prisoners. If none were available, civilian doctors could be hired, provided that their fees were not excessive.

During the actual exchange of prisoners, Monroe ordered the marshals to censor all letters. "You will, of course, observe a suitable vigilance on this head and take special care that no intelligence beneficial to the enemy finds its way thru this channel," the secretary specified. All mail was to be opened and read, then placed under seal for delivery to the American agent for prisoners of war at the ship's next destination. Similarly, as soon as the cartel docked, the marshal was to claim immediate delivery of the letter bag. Monroe further expected the marshals to "adopt the means necessary to prevent correspondence being carried on to the advantage of the enemy in any way." For that work, the marshals later received 75 cents per prisoner handled during the war. From that amount, they were to pay "the actual and reasonable expenses incurred in fulfilling this duty."[48]

By the end of the war, the marshals had firmly established themselves not only as the national government's principal law enforcers but also as its local executive officers through whom the government exercised its authority. That framework, completely decentralized and completely lacking an administrative organization, nonetheless proved extremely useful for conducting the government's routine business and responding to emergencies.

3

COUNTERFEITERS AND FILIBUSTERS
1815–1861

The fire began at night. Neither the volunteer bucket brigades nor the capital's fire department could do more than contain it. Men darted into the building and frantically began carrying documents out. Millions of pieces of paper—accounts, checks, vouchers, bonds, bank notes, and letters—fed the flames. By morning the U.S. Treasury and most of the nation's financial records were rubble. The date was March 31, 1833. No one knew how or why the fire started.

In the fall of 1835 Willis H. Blayney, a high constable in Philadelphia, stumbled upon evidence implicating "three persons of notoriously bad character" as the arsonists. Needing $400 to $500 to pursue his inquiries and hoping for an appropriate reward should he catch the guilty parties, Blayney took his evidence to H. D. Gilpin, the U.S. attorney for the eastern district of Pennsylvania. Gilpin immediately reported the conversation to Secretary of the Treasury Levi Woodbury and President Jackson.[1]

Both Woodbury and Jackson were eager "to bring to condign punishment the actual perpetrators" of the fire. After querying Blayney about his information, Secretary Woodbury authorized Gilpin to draw on Marshal Benjamin S. Bonsall for up to $500 to pay Blayney's expenses. The president promised to go to Congress for a "reasonable reward" once the arsonists were convicted. Blayney began his pursuit in earnest in December 1835. Neither he nor Gilpin had any hard evidence to support the case.[2]

Away to the west, Deputy marshal John Kelly of the district of Ohio was busily engaged "in ferreting out Counterfeiters of Coin." While working on a case, Kelly stumbled across a man named William Hicks, who knew who the arsonists were and how and why they had set the fire. Like most informants of any era, Hicks was almost as unsavory as the people he accused. Marshal John Patterson talked with him repeatedly before concluding that his story seemed plausible. But Patterson could not shake an uneasy suspicion of Hicks. The man was too convenient, his story too long delayed in the telling, his background too shady. Consequently, the investigation turned more on corroborating Hicks's testimony than on pursuing the culprits. It was a casebook criminal investigation by U.S. marshals and attorneys.

Although Hicks readily named the arsonists, he hesitated to explain his relationship to them. Patterson stubbornly pressed for the whole story. According to Hicks, Richard White, whom he had known in New York City in the early 1830s, had set the fire. White bragged to Hicks that he had been offered a considerable amount of money to destroy certain papers stored at the Treasury. White had told Hicks that it would probably be necessary "to fire the building" and that he planned to get into the building by using "false keys." Setting the fire presented no problem because White was an accomplished chemist who could easily make a "chemical preparation" that would not ignite for eight to ten hours.

White never openly confessed to the arson, but he indicated to Hicks that he had not been as successful as he and his employers had hoped. "There was so much energy displayed by the people in saving the papers," Hicks remembered White's complaining "that many were prevented from being burned that his employers intended should have been." White had not been paid as much as he had expected, receiving barely more than his expenses.[3]

Hicks's story was the first big break in the case. As U.S. Attorney Gilpin explained after Woodbury forwarded Marshal Patterson's letter, "It confirms fully the suspicions we entertained. It fixes the crime on the same parties." Gilpin believed that Richard and Henry White, along with another accomplice named Eliza Drew, were hired by a Mr. Temple of Vermont to destroy Treasury papers and other evidence implicating Temple in a pension scheme to defraud the government.

In the meantime Gilpin wanted Marshal Patterson to keep Hicks close at hand and out of trouble. It was "very important to have Hicks as an additional witness." While they waited for Constable Blayney to complete his inquiries, Gilpin cautioned the secretary of the Treasury: "The Marshal need not be informed of what is doing here. There is constant communication between these rogues, and it is unsafe to trust even those who (like Hicks), are disposed to confess their guilt or knowledge, further than is necessary." Gilpin intended to confirm Hicks's testimony himself.[4]

By February 19, 1836, Gilpin was able to verify much of Hicks's story. He also discovered that Hicks had been an accomplice of the White brothers in an "extensive forgery successfully committed on several banks" in Philadelphia. Each verification enhanced Hicks's value as a witness because it seemed clear to Gilpin that the informant was "fully acquainted with most of their desperate schemes." The prosecutor urged Secretary Woodbury to arrange for Hicks to come to Philadelphia. Hicks agreed to go to Washington and then Philadelphia, but only under Deputy Kelly's protection. The two men left in early March.[5]

Kelly and Hicks met Constable Blayney in Washington. From there the three went to Philadelphia to confer with Gilpin. Based on Hicks's evidence, Gilpin swore out arrest warrants against Richard and Henry White. He also prepared certified duplicates of each affidavit to use in obtaining warrants in the northern and southern districts of New York. (At that time, warrants from one district had no force in other districts.) He gave the papers to Kelly and Blayney, along with letters of explanation to the U.S. attorneys in both New York districts. On March 21, Kelly, Blayney, and Hicks took the mail ship for New York City to find Richard White. The plan was for Blayney to take Richard White to Washington, where the trial would take place, while Kelly continued after Henry White. By this time, Blayney had probably been deputized; otherwise he would have had no arrest powers under federal law.[6]

The three men soon found Richard White, primarily because Marshal William Waddell of New York knew him. They arrested White without incident. Within the week, Blayney escorted him to Washington. Kelly proceeded after Henry White, and Hicks went home to Stark County, Ohio, to await the trial.[7]

Hicks resumed his old pursuits. In late June the sheriff of Stark

County arrested him for passing a counterfeit bank bill. Hicks begged Marshal Patterson to come to his aid. Patterson wrote the county prosecutor to explain the importance of Hicks's testimony against the Whites, asking that Hicks be released on his own recognizance. Secretary Woodbury, dismayed that such "an important witness" was now in jail, urged the marshal to take "proper measures . . . to secure the attendance of Hicks [at the Whites' trial], as well as to prevent his conviction before that trial may take place, of an offense which will destroy his testimony."[8]

The investigation into the burning of the Treasury Building shows how the federal government handled criminal cases during the first half of the nineteenth century. The U.S. attorneys, who described themselves as the government's law enforcement officers, generally controlled the conduct of investigations. The legwork was often done by the marshals, for whom investigations were but a part of a much broader range of duties. The marshals considered themselves the government's civilian executive officers within their districts.

The marshals of this time investigated counterfeiting, bank fraud, mail robbery, neutrality violations, importation of slaves, and other federal crimes. They were not paid for how many crimes they investigated or how many cases they brought before the courts, as the U.S. attorneys were. Rather, they were paid fees for each warrant and other legal process they served. Thus, it was more financially rewarding for them to spend their time serving process than conducting investigations that might lead nowhere.

GENERAL DUTIES

George Washington, in filling the many offices of the federal government, enjoyed a luxury largely denied his successors: He knew most of the men whom he appointed. Subsequent presidents relied on advice from colleagues and friends who were familiar with each state and territory. As the system of appointments evolved, the presidents turned to their political colleagues in Congress for nomination suggestions.

Before the 1840s the entire congressional delegation—congressmen and senators who belonged to the president's party—polled themselves for nominations for the offices of federal judge, U.S. attorney, U.S.

marshal, and others available as the president's gift. This system compelled office seekers to develop close political ties by working for the election of their congressmen and senators. Thus, political patronage became the reward for service to the president's party.[9]

The system had some advantages. It ensured that the men (and it was only men during this period) appointed to offices controlled by the president sympathized with his policies. In addition, the president had a considerably easier time obtaining Senate confirmation of their nominations if he gave the senators from each state a say in who should be chosen. The system was so successful that eventually the advice of congressmen was dropped, and senators alone made suggestions for appointments.

Yet the system contained a basic flaw. The presidents had no quality control over whom the congressional delegation suggested. Many of the nominees, chosen only for their loyalty to the party within their state, turned out to be unscrupulous, dishonest, and eager to fill their own pockets at the expense of the government and the taxpayers. Thus, throughout this period marshals, attorneys, court clerks, and judges were investigated, dismissed, or arrested for crimes, usually embezzlement or theft of government property.

Because marshals handled the court's money, most of the accusations against them involved money due the government. Recouping that money meant filing suit against a marshal's bondholders. In 1805, for example, U.S. Attorney Joseph McIlwaine of New Jersey sued former marshal John Hall for $2,300 that Hall owed the government. Once he obtained a judgment against Hall, McIlwaine foreclosed on the marshal's bondholders to collect the money. The bondholders pleaded for time to pay off the debt by selling Hall's property at the highest possible price.[10]

Similarly, District Attorney George M. Bibb filed suit against Joseph Crockett and his son Robert, both former marshals in Kentucky, over money they collected during their terms but failed to turn over to the U.S. Treasury. Unfortunately, both men were insolvent, Joseph having been "ruined by his son Robert." In May 1813, Judge John Brayton of South Carolina urged Secretary of State Monroe to appoint a new marshal for his court. Marshal Robert E. Cochran, the judge reported, "in consequence of several defalcations of office, is *now in custody* and so far his functions suspended."[11]

The list of marshals against whom accusations were made could continue, but the point should be clear. One of the unpleasant aspects of the job was a constant suspicion and watchfulness, probably well founded, among administration officials over how the marshals handled government money. Nor were the marshals the only objects of such scrutiny. In May 1818, Theron Rudd, the clerk of the Court for the Northern District of New York, "absconded with nearly all the funds of the Court, amounting to about one hundred thousand dollars."[12]

Accounting for the court's money was a massive task for marshals. It involved filing detailed reports to the Treasury Department and responding to incessant demands for funds from U.S. judges, attorneys, and clerks. At the beginning of each court term, the marshals submitted estimates to the Treasury Department of how much money they would need for that term. The department required that the reports show "the specific purposes for which the money is wanted, the amount on hand unexpended, and also the date of transmitting [the marshal's] last account, with the vouchers, to the First Auditor, and stating the balance of said account, term of court, etc." The marshals divided the estimates into separate categories of fees, mainly for grand jurors, for petite jurors, for witnesses summoned on behalf of the United States, for the marshal and his deputies, for the U.S. attorney, and for the court clerk. Preparing the estimate required that the marshal find out what cases the U.S. attorney intended to file or prosecute that term and how many defendants and witnesses would be involved. The answers were not always readily forthcoming. U.S. Attorney Gilpin was not unusual in adopting a secretive attitude when preparing cases.

When the estimates from each district arrived, they were totaled and submitted to Congress for funding. Oftentimes, Congress, anxious to run a frugal government, essentially ignored the estimates and appropriated what it considered a fair amount. In the meantime the first auditor at the Treasury Department reviewed the marshal's actual expenditures during the previous court term. The law required that marshals, attorneys, and clerks individually submit "a return, embracing all the fees and emoluments of their respective offices of *every* name and character." Any discrepancies or disallowances found by the first auditor were deducted from the appropriated amounts for each district. The appropriated money was then deposited in the marshals' accounts at government-approved banks within each district. The marshals rarely received the full amounts for which they asked to administer the courts.[13]

In 1849, Congress created the Department of the Interior, transferring to it the responsibility for supervising the marshals' accounts. The marshals continued to report primarily to the secretary of state on matters of policy, and occasionally to other cabinet officers when the report concerned their department, until 1853. In that year the attorney general took over part of the supervision. The marshals sent only their accounts and vouchers to the new Interior Department. Nonetheless, the system of reporting their expenses and expenditures remained essentially unchanged. The accountants at the Interior Department proved just as merciless in auditing the marshals as their predecessors at the Treasury had been.[14]

Both the Treasury and the Interior departments held the marshals responsible for court expenditures, enjoining them to the "importance of habitual care and frugality in conducting all [their] disbursements." The Treasury Department required the marshals, and no one else, to interpret the laws controlling how the money was spent, regardless of what the judges or U.S. attorneys demanded. In 1844 a district judge in Illinois ordered Marshal Thomas M. Hope to pay jurors and witnesses a 20-cents-a-mile travel allowance. Immediately after receiving Hope's accounts showing this expenditure, the secretary of the Treasury wrote the marshal to remind him that he was "responsible for the legal and faithful disbursement of the funds" allowed the court. The law clearly provided only 5 cents a mile of actual travel for witnesses and jurors, and that was all they could be paid.[15]

In 1846, Arkansas district court clerk William Field boldly declared to the Treasury Department that "the Judge of the District Court possesses arbitrary control over the public money advanced to [the marshal], and may order its application to any purposes whether within his lawful jurisdiction or beyond it, and that it is folly in the accounting officers to call for explanations on the subject." Secretary of the Treasury R. J. Walker quickly moved to disabuse both the clerk and Marshal Elias Rector of this "extraordinary" notion. "Marshals," the secretary wrote, "cannot be rightfully ordered to disburse the public money advanced for the specific purpose of defraying the legal and ordinary expenses of courts, for any object beyond the jurisdiction of the Court." Reminding Marshal Rector that he alone was "responsible to the United States for the lawful application of public money advanced . . . for disbursement," Walker wrote: "It is therefore important for yourself, as well as for the public service, that great care be taken, not to disburse such money except for the purposes to which it has been appropriated by law."

Should the clerk and the district judge continue to insist on the judge's arbitrary power to control expenditures, Secretary Walker was prepared "to decline making advances for the expenses of the Courts of your District and let such expenses be paid only after the claims shall be duly adjusted by the accounting officers pursuant to law." The secretary offered the marshal no advice on how he was to refuse the judge. That was left to each marshal's tact and, more important, his obstinacy.[16]

Thus, the Treasury Department and Congress erected a built-in balance-of-power structure within each district. The judges and U.S. attorneys controlled the caseload within each district, including how many witnesses, jurors, and defendants they expected the marshal to haul into court. Indeed, the Treasury Department willingly bowed to the authority of the local U.S. attorneys and district judges in supervising the service of process for their courts by the marshals. But the marshals controlled how the money was to be spent, including the fees for witnesses, jurors, U.S. attorneys, and court clerks.[17]

For cases in which the United States was not a party, the marshals collected their fees and other court expenses directly from the litigants. The judge, in reaching his verdict, also determined whether the plaintiff or the defendant was responsible for court costs. Collecting the fees was frequently a problem. In one case, Marshal Andrew Hull of Connecticut complained in 1827 that he was expected to collect his fees from defendants who were in debtors' prison. "If the doctrine be Correct and after being employed by the United States to do their business and convict their debtors to prison for large sums and after all the hazard and responsibility, I am to apply to those debtors in Prison for the fees I certainly wish to be so informed, for I must of necessity relinquish the Office," Hull wrote. "I have been extremely unfortunate in accepting the office which was done with reluctance—there being no [adequate] compensation allowed for several years and little business done in the District until within the last year."[18]

The marshals also rented the places in which court was held and prisoners were housed. Generally during this period, the federal government did not build or maintain its own courthouses, preferring to lease county courtrooms or other facilities annually. The government refused to rent office space for the marshals and U.S. attorneys, though it did agree to pay for space for clerks to keep court records. Each marshal and attorney was expected to arrange and pay for his own office. In addition, the marshals and attorneys cleaned their own rooms; payments to janitors were not allowed.[19]

Jail space was rented by the week from the local sheriff. Occasionally the local jails caused the marshals problems. In October 1821, Marshal Morton Waring of South Carolina reported the escape of two federal prisoners from the county jail. "The Marshal," he complained to the secretary of state, "has no control over the Officers of the Gaol, and altho' he may notice the most glaring improprieties, and remonstrate against them, he can do no act which will remedy the evil." The county jail used by the marshals in New York City, according to Marshal Abraham T. Hillyer in 1853, was "utterly insecure." He suggested using the prison in Brooklyn to house his prisoners, despite the expense of transporting them back and forth to court.[20]

By the early 1850s, Attorney General Caleb Cushing considered the lack of adequate courthouses and prisons "a serious evil demanding the attention of the Government." He pointed out to President Franklin Pierce that "in most cases, the courts of the United States are held in buildings belonging to individuals or to the counties, cities or parishes of the respective states upon whom the United States are thus made to depend for their necessary accommodation. This dependence, in the matter of prisoners, is particularly inconvenient." On several occasions, when northern marshals tried to house fugitive slaves in local jails before extraditing them to the South, the states had refused to allow the marshals to use their prisons. Cushing believed that the time had come for the United States to build its own courthouses and prisons. "Such an application of some part of the public treasure will be perfectly constitutional and proper and the object is one of unquestionable public exigency and utility." However, construction of the facilities did not begin in earnest until after the Civil War.[21]

Fortunately, the marshals during this period were not overwhelmed with prisoners. On February 23, 1846, Secretary of the Treasury R. J. Walker polled the marshals on the number of federal prisoners housed in state prisons in their districts, the cost per day, and the names and crimes of the felons. Sixteen marshals responded to the survey, four of whom reported that they had no prisoners. Marshal Thomas Fletcher of Mississippi informed the Treasury that in fifteen years his court had never had an indictment or a conviction. The court in western Tennessee, according to Marshal Robert I. Chester, had never sentenced a defendant to prison. In Virginia no prisoner had been sentenced for a dozen years, since the spring 1834 court term. Marshal Samuel Hays of western Pennsylvania had had no prisoners during his first year as marshal.[22]

Four districts reported only one prisoner; three districts reported two prisoners. Five of the prisoners were mail robbers, two were counterfeiters, two had been convicted of manslaughter on the high seas, and one had engaged in the African slave trade. The remaining five districts reported slightly higher numbers of prisoners—four, five, six, eight, and eleven felons. Northern New York had the most prisoners, followed by its neighbor southern New York. The crimes were mail robbery or embezzlement; murder, assault, or piracy on the high seas; engaging in the African slave trade; counterfeiting and forgery; perjury; stealing federal property; and attempting to create a revolt.[23]

In most districts, marshals spent their time handling the routine business of the courts. For example, they auctioned off seized or condemned assets, such as the four Arabian horses Marshal Thomas Morris of southern New York sold in 1831. Marshals' auctions were so frequent that Marshal Chapman Coleman of Kentucky suggested using shills to raise the bids. "If the Government had an agent to attend and bid at such sales," Coleman advised the Treasury, "the property might be made to pay the debt." Because hiring shills involved yet another expense to the government, it is doubtful that the department approved the proposal.[24]

The office of marshal primarily entailed administrative work, but the routine disguised an aspect of the position that remained constant for two hundred years—its violence.

In the spring of 1839 Marshal Mott L. Crawford of southern Alabama assigned one of his deputies to execute a scire facias (a writ to show cause) and a $300 levy on some store goods owned by the Simonton family. The Simontons lived in the "suburbs" of Tuscaloosa. When the deputy tried to execute the process, he was "expelled by force from the store" by the defendants.

Several weeks later, Marshal Crawford hired several men, whom he deputized, "to act in the relevying of this stock of goods." The posse left Tuscaloosa at the end of the day, reaching the store at dusk. The store was in the central room of Simonton's house, with his living quarters and another room branching off from it at the front and the back. The posse, hoping that a "conciliatory course" would avoid further difficulty, entered the well-lit store in a group, paying little attention to the darkened doorways leading to the other rooms of the house.

As they proceeded to execute the levy, Simonton and six or seven of his fellows opened fire on them from the "perfectly dark" front and back rooms. The deputies returned fire but stood little chance against their hidden attackers. A dozen shots were exchanged within the store as the posse fought its way outside. One deputy fell dead, another had his hand shot off, and the rest of the posse, save one, were wounded before they escaped. None of Simonton's band was injured.

"Thus a second time has the mandate of the law been defied and the powers which I have been able to use proved entirely insufficient," Marshal Crawford reported in May 1839. Although local authorities arrested Simonton, the marshal determined to do everything possible to ensure "that the laws of the United States and the mandates of the courts should be vindicated." He hired a special counsel to assist in the prosecution of the case, promising the attorney $1,000 for representing the interests of the United States. Secretary of the Treasury Levi Woodbury disallowed the promised fee, pointing out to Crawford that the prosecution rested with the state of Alabama, not the federal government.[25]

CATCHING COUNTERFEITERS

Before the twentieth century, money in the United States came in an amazing array of different forms. The federal government made little effort to adopt a standardized currency. Until the Civil War the U.S. Mint concentrated its efforts on manufacturing gold and silver coins. Government paper currency was limited to "fractional currency" (denominations of less than $1), Treasury notes, and postal currency valid for the redemption of postage stamps but also used as tender. During the Civil War the government introduced greenbacks, the first national paper currency. Private bank notes and gold and silver coins continued to circulate, creating a confusing plethora of monies.

Individual banks issued their own currency, called bank notes, in all denominations. Because few banks of the period were sound, their paper currency varied in value. The situation worsened considerably when President Jackson effectively destroyed the domination of the Second

Bank of the United States in the early 1830s. Banks sprouted up across the country, each issuing its own currency, each competing for business, and none regulated or held to standard practices.

Americans took their chances with the banks, for there was no insurance on deposits, no government control over how a bank did its business. The frequent recessions and depressions of the period wiped out many fortunes, large and small, leaving in their wake a profound distrust of bankers and banks, bank notes and paper currency. Gold and silver alone retained their value, and people tended to hoard the precious metals.

Counterfeiters found their paradise, with more than a thousand banks issuing their own notes. By the 1860s an estimated one-third of the currency in circulation was counterfeit. Retailers subscribed to weekly papers showing drawings of the latest counterfeits, much like, in the late twentieth century, store clerks checked lists of bad credit card numbers.

Counterfeiters also produced fake coins. Because real coins contained the true value of silver and gold, the counterfeiters could turn a profit simply by withholding some of the gold or silver from the coin. In 1829, for example, the secretary of the Treasury alerted all U.S. marshals and attorneys to spurious silver dollars that had appeared in the West but were expected to appear soon in the East. According to the director of the U.S. Mint, the coins contained only about 40 cents' worth of silver. The counterfeits were so well made that "even an experienced eye could not detect the fraud by inspecting the external surface merely." An assay was necessary to determine the fake.[26]

The counterfeiters, called coneymen, usually specialized within the illegal trade. Printers and coiners manufactured the bogus money, which they then sold to passers, who exchanged the counterfeits for real currency or goods. Often, gangs of printers and passers worked together, infesting particular regions or sometimes branching out into other parts of the country. Detecting the fraudulent money was relatively easy compared with catching the people responsible for it.

The Treasury Department relied on the marshals to pursue the counterfeiters on a national basis. Detectives were occasionally hired as special agents of the department, usually on a case-by-case basis when the evidence warranted the expenditure. Allan Pinkerton, for example, got his start in detective work by breaking up a major counterfeiting band in Illinois. But detectives were expensive.

U.S. marshals and their deputies combatted the legions of counterfeiters by relying on informants and their own skills as detectives and by sometimes working undercover. The work of Marshal Daniel A. Robertson and his deputies in Ohio exemplified how the marshals pursued the illusive coneymen. Ohio was a breeding ground for counterfeiters. Its rural areas provided perfect hideouts for the printers; its proximity to the major cities offered convenient markets for the passers.

By the winter of 1847 Marshal Robertson had collected the names of "upwards of fifty counterfeiters in Ohio." Robertson noted that "many of them are men of property, and apparent respectability." In Robertson's view, those who made and passed counterfeit coins were "the most secret and successful perpetrators of crime in the country." Arresting them became his principal goal. One coneyman in particular, James Burns, became the object of an intense manhunt by Robertson and his deputies, especially Deputy D. K. Goodin.[27]

Burns posed as a lecturer on "Phrenology, Education, and Morals." When not lecturing, he used plaster molds to produce bogus coins, which were then passed into circulation by members of his gang. When the coins first appeared, Robertson began his investigation. Through informers and other evidence, he and his deputies identified Burns as the principal culprit, but catching him proved a different matter. Burns, "a man of much talent, education, and shrewdness," gave the deputies extensive chase, taking them from Ohio into the back country of western Virginia.

D. K. Goodin, Robertson's principal deputy in Cincinnati, coordinated the pursuit. By the time he and his men had enough evidence against Burns to warrant arrest, Burns had left his home in Sciotoville, approximately eight miles above Portsmouth, Ohio. Deputies Long and Hayman found in his house "fragments of plaster paris moulds and other implements for making coins." They hurried back to Portsmouth and telegraphed Goodin in Cincinnati that Burns was headed his way aboard the river steamer *Dolphin*. But by the time Goodin got to the Cincinnati docks, Burns and his family had already disembarked.

For the rest of the afternoon, Goodin went among the hack drivers working out of the docks, looking for the coachman whom Burns had hired. He finally found him, and for 50 cents the driver took him to the brick house "far out on Western Row" where he had delivered the Burnses. By now night had fallen. Goodin knocked at the door. "After some wrapping," he reported to Robertson, "Mrs. B. came to a window but would not let me in." The deputy pretended to be an attorney for one of Burns's fellow counterfeiters, saying that his client needed money. "She exhibited great anxiety for her husband's friends and insisted on my returning in the morning (her husband had gone out and she did not know when he would return)." Satisfied that Burns was not in the house, Goodin hired some of the Twenty-sixth Ward watchmen at $1.50 apiece. They and deputies Penderey, Colby, Seff, and Suter watched the house all night.

The next morning, with Burns still absent, Goodin and Suter went to see Mrs. Burns. "She is rather a shrewd woman and as I have since learned as deeply involved in the counterfeiting business as any of them," Goodin informed Robertson. "Of course it would not do to prosecute a woman who has young children." Mrs. Burns apparently had grown suspicious of Goodin's story, for she "played off on us pretty well," and the deputies were unable to ascertain Burns's whereabouts.

Thus stymied, Deputy Goodin turned to another ploy. One morning a few days later, Deputy Hayman called on Mrs. Burns. Hayman pretended to be a fellow coneyman and friend of the fugitive Burns. "He passed himself off as a counterfeiter so successfully," Goodin wrote, "that unless we are all greatly deceived he learned all about Burns' present location."

Hayman told the originally skeptical Mrs. Burns that her husband had stayed all night at his house in Kentucky after fleeing Fulton. Burns was an "old and intimate friend of his, and had dealt with him in bogus for 8 years." Now believing the deputy, Mrs. Burns confessed that she had tried to convince her husband's pursuers that Burns had "gone up the railroad or was out in the country, and to divert them from the bogus establishment 2 miles above the mouth of Big Sandy in Virginia or at another establishment of the same kind 5 miles back from the river." Mrs. Burns also described to Hayman how Burns had escaped the deputies "and a hundred other things which convinced Hayman that her representations were true."

That night the deputies appeared before Judge McLean and obtained a warrant "reaching into Virginia." The next day, Goodin and his team signed a promissory note to raise the necessary funds for the trip. Hayman and Long then left for Virginia.[28]

Going first to Burlington, the two deputies there raised a posse of ten men before heading for the Big Sandy. They proceeded to the home of "the notorious Mark Williams," a known associate of Burns's. After surrounding the house, the deputies called on Burns to surrender. The coneyman tried to slip out the back door but went directly into the hands of the waiting possemen, who promptly arrested him.

Hayman and Long returned to Cincinnati with the prisoner, arriving on October 16. Burns's arraignment before Judge McLean was set for October 19. He also faced seven indictments in the state court on the same charges. His wife and four young children remained at large.[29]

The deputies now relied on Marshal Robertson to persuade the Treasury Department to reimburse their expenses. None had any great expectation that they would be paid for their services. "The pursuit of Counterfeiters is a peculiar branch of police not much understood," Robertson advised the solicitor of the Treasury. His deputies in Cincinnati were "unremitting in their exertions to capture counterfeiters" and "hardly hope for compensation," Robertson wrote. "They are men who delight in that kind of excitement, which is not without its perils." Nonetheless, they were at least due their expenses.

Although Robertson had cautioned Goodin "to incur no risk in making large expenses" because they might not be reimbursed, "he (and associates) got so warm on the scent of Burns . . . that they could not forgo pursuit." Robertson asked permission to pay them the costs of the investigation, as well as a small fee for their services. "They are worthy men," the marshal explained, "and poor. They need the money." In this instance the department authorized the marshal to reimburse his deputies their out-of-pocket expenses, but it refused to pay the deputies for their time and trouble.[30]

In the mid-1860s, Congress finally recognized that the ease of counterfeiting money demanded special attention. In 1865 it created the Secret Service under the secretary of the Treasury. At first the Secret Service was too small and too disbursed, its arrest powers too limited, to cope with the problem by itself. Marshals continued to assist in investigations and in making arrests. But the creation of the Secret Service effectively transferred the responsibility for catching counterfeiters from the marshals to the new agency.

STOPPING FILIBUSTERS

Americans of the nineteenth century took an active interest in the affairs of the Western Hemisphere. Just a few generations removed from their own struggle for independence, they welcomed with spirited elation the revolt of Spain's colonies and sympathized with Canadian rebels against British rule. Foreign rebels used American soil, American supplies, and American-donated money to launch revolts against their homelands.

Frequently this interest in hemispheric affairs became too active. Bands of American mercenaries, called filibusters, organized military expeditions on American soil against foreign countries and colonies. Oftentimes the government in Washington simply looked the other way. Only the stern protests of appalled ministers whose countries were the objects of the attacks could compel the U.S. government to enforce its own neutrality laws.

The revolt of Spain's colonies in Latin America stirred many Americans to help. Pressured by Spain and the other European powers, Congress passed two neutrality laws in 1817 and 1818 forbidding American assistance. Shortly afterward President James Monroe pronounced a new doctrine prohibiting European interference in the affairs of the Western Hemisphere. Although most judicial districts encountered no violations of the new neutrality law in 1817, Rhode Island reported two cases; South Carolina prosecuted eight.[31]

In 1837 an army of self-styled Canadian "Patriots," numbering less than a thousand, determined to copy the American Revolution by wresting Canada from British control. Their plans received strong support from American citizens, particularly in western New York. The Patriots converged on Buffalo, New York, to launch the invasion of Canada.

The people of Buffalo welcomed the Patriots enthusiastically, even as the British minister in Washington protested the federal government's inactivity. The protests forced President Martin Van Buren and Secretary of State John Forsyth to order Marshal Nathaniel Garrow of northern New York to the staging area. Meanwhile the Patriot army encamped on Navy Island in the middle of the Niagara River about a mile above the great falls. The army was provisioned by sympathetic Americans who loaded the steamship *Caroline* with food and other supplies for nightly runs to the island.

Support for the Patriots extended throughout the district. The day before Marshal Garrow left for Buffalo, he reported from Rochester, "There is much excitement here—forty soldiers marching through the streets of Rochester today under drum and fife. Two pieces of cannon went off this morning." The marshal estimated that three-fourths of the people of Rochester supported the Patriots and seven-eighths of the people of Buffalo "are encouraging and supporting the thing." All along the border, American citizens were "taking strong interest in the cause of the patriots, many furnishing arms and large quantities of provisions contributed and forwarded to them and volunteers continually going on." Garrow urged U.S. Attorney N. L. Benton to meet him in Buffalo, because he could make no arrests without judicial process.[32]

Garrow arrived in Buffalo on December 23. He immediately set about investigating violations of the neutrality laws and enlisting the aid "of judges, magistrates, and other U.S. Officers to maintain vigilance along the Canadian frontier." It soon became apparent to him that he and his two deputies could do little against the Patriot army and its American supporters. On December 28, Garrow asked for military assistance.[33]

The *Caroline* continued to supply the army on Navy Island. Because the island belonged to Canada, the army was beyond the jurisdiction of the federal authorities. The British grew impatient with the Patriots. On the night of December 29 a group of Canadian militia crossed the Niagara River to the American side. After a brief scuffle with the American crew of the *Caroline*, the Canadians set fire to the ship, letting it drift out into the rapid current of the Niagara River on its way to the falls. Amos Durfee, an American aboard the *Caroline,* was killed.

Durfee's death created an immediate crisis between the United States and Great Britain. While diplomats argued the legality of the seizure of the *Caroline,* Marshal Garrow was ordered to step up his efforts to stop the Patriot army. His request for military help was denied. According to Secretary of State John Forsyth, the president "has no right to use the military force in execution of the laws, except when the civil authority has first been successfully resisted." Forsyth ordered the marshal "to arrest all offenders, calling the posse comitatus to your aid if necessary." Anyone who returned from Navy Island to the United States should be arrested immediately. "The state of affairs upon the frontiers," advised the secretary, ". . . is such as requires the utmost vigilance, and should call forth all your energies." He did not explain how the marshal could raise a posse in an area where the majority of the Americans supported the Patriot army.[34]

But the efforts of Garrow and his deputies were beginning to have an effect. "We are on our way westward," R. W. Ashley, the assistant adjutant general for the Patriot army, wrote a fellow Patriot in late

January 1838. "The Officers of the American Government give us a great deal of trouble, otherwise we would have landed at Fort Erie last week with 600 men and [been] half way to Toronto by this time." Adjutant General Donald MacLeod described the efforts to avoid the marshals as "a Game at Chess, for some time since they endeavoring to prevent our invading Canada, we to land at all events."[35]

After the burning of the *Caroline,* the Patriots took up a new position on the appropriately named Fighting Island, which was also out of Garrow's jurisdiction. On February 25, British forces invaded the island. Betrayed by their master of ordnance, who had surrendered to Marshal Garrow, the Patriots met the British with a handful of arms and ammunition. In the ensuing battle five Patriots were wounded in exchange for five British killed and fifteen wounded. The Patriots fled the field, crossing over the ice to American shores. Once across, they became the objects of an intense manhunt by U.S. marshals in New York, Ohio, and Michigan. In addition, the Van Buren administration allowed General Winfield Scott and local militiamen to assist the marshals in the capture of the Patriot leaders.[36]

To avoid arrest, the Patriot officers disbursed, agreeing to meet in Detroit as soon as possible. The commanding general, William Lyon Mackenzie, was captured by Marshal Garrow fairly quickly, but his adjutant, General MacLeod, proved more illusive. Indeed, the pursuit after MacLeod showed the difficulties encountered by United States marshals and their deputies when their fugitive was supported by numerous sympathizers.

MacLeod fled to the house of Mr. and Mrs. Spaulding in Monroe, Michigan. The ladies of the house, "the patriot soldier's true friend," dressed him in women's clothing. A deputy came to the house and began searching the premises. Poking his head in the room where MacLeod pretended to sew, the deputy saw "nothing but the back part of a supposed lovely female, busy with her needle." The courteous deputy "begged pardon and retired." That night MacLeod donned a woman's nightcap and crawled into bed with Mr. Spaulding. During the night "the marshals burst into the room, saw man and wife in bed, apologized and withdrew."[37]

The next morning, one of the men of the house dressed in MacLeod's clothes and fled in the opposite direction from which the Patriot general, still disguised as a woman, actually went. The deputy marshals gave chase to the fake MacLeod, catching up with him about eight miles from the town. When they realized that he was not their fugitive, one of the deputies complained, "The devil is in the old fellow, he has finally hoaxed us! He is like a jack o'lantern, the nearer we think we are to him the farther we are from him."[38]

MacLeod made it to Ohio, where once again he found friends to cover for him. At one point he dressed as a lumberjack, pretending to cut wood outside an inn while deputy marshals searched inside. "Notwithstanding the extensive and deep laid plans of General Scott, the vigilance and perseverance of the marshals," MacLeod later explained, "be it remembered that with the assistance of the ready wit, presence of mind, and ingenuous stratagems of the male and female friends of Canadian freedom, in the Wolverine and Buckeye states, the patriot officers were triumphantly enabled to out maneuver the whole posse of Van Buren's 'NEUTRAL LAW' preservers."[39]

MacLeod's braggadocio was slightly misplaced. Although he managed to elude the marshals, their pressing efforts to catch him and his fellows effectively disrupted the Patriot army. Further efforts to invade Canada were stopped. Neither MacLeod nor his assistant Ashley could do anything but hide from the marshals. Their preoccupation with escape stripped the army of its leadership. "I was hunted down," Ashley complained, "like a wild beast of prey by the Marshalls of the United States, and had to keep myself closetted for fear of apprehension." MacLeod later admitted that the invasion of Canada "was frustrated, not by the Colonial power [Great Britain], . . . but by the United States' Executive, by the aid of its troops and Marshals."[40]

By the spring of 1838 the Patriot army was in a shambles. Although it enjoyed a brief resurgence in the fall of that year, it never again posed any real threat to British control of Canada. Garrow and his colleagues in Ohio and Michigan kept a close eye on the remnants of the army and its American supporters. As late as 1842 a deputy marshal in Cleveland seized more than a hundred muskets belonging to the Patriots.[41]

The disruption of the Patriot army helped dissuade other expeditions against Canada, but the Western Hemisphere provided plenty of other targets for military attack. A number of factors encouraged the filibusters. The revolt of the Texans against Mexico showed how successful filibusters could be, particularly when aided by settlers. The subsequent Mexican war, with its resultant addition of vast amounts of territory to the Union, infected many Americans with the fever of expansion. Men talked about the manifest destiny of the United States to take over the continent, perhaps the whole hemisphere. Such talk encouraged action.

The motives for these expeditions were often mixed, their ultimate goals never quite specified. But they promised excitement, adventure, and wealth. For many Americans, that promise alone was enough. "Of one thing you may be assured," the U.S. attorney in New York City, J. Prescott Hall, wrote the acting secretary of the interior in August 1851, "that there are at all times in New York many hundreds of desperate men who can be induced by money to embark at any time in any cause and proceed to any point near or distant, to attack any country, Prince, or Potentate under the sun." Hall's description applied to most filibusters, whether they embarked from New York, New Orleans, or some other point.[42]

Cuba was a perennial favorite. In September 1850 the Spanish minister to the United States warned Secretary of State Daniel Webster that a filibustering expedition was again being organized against Spain's colony. Webster alerted the U.S. marshals, attorneys, and collectors throughout the country to arrest any participants who violated the neutrality laws. Six months later, Marshal Henry Tallmadge of southern New York uncovered the plot through an informant, Dr. D. Henry Burtnett.[43]

Between four and five hundred men were gathering in New York City for "the meditated invasion of Cuba." Led by Narciso López, a veteran of three previous unsuccessful invasions of Cuba, the men planned to take the steamship *Cleopatra* south to Florida for a rendezvous with other filibusters. Then they would cross the Gulf of Mexico to Cuba.[44]

Alerted by U.S. Attorney Hall, the State Department ordered him to use the available army and navy forces in the area to stop the expedition, but the local navy commander refused assistance without explicit orders from the secretary of the navy. Tallmadge "sought in vain for a single steamer" to take him after the *Cleopatra*. Fortunately, the collector of customs was more cooperative. He lent Tallmadge his revenue cutter, a sailing ship.[45]

Taking a "sufficient force" with him, Tallmadge sailed the revenue cutter to Sandy Hook, where the *Cleopatra* was docked. Neither he nor Hall had much hope to catch the filibusters once their ship got up steam, so the plan was to arrest them at anchor. However, the *Cleopatra's* engine broke down. "The accidental detention for repairs threw her into our hands," Hall later reported, "but had she once started her paddle wheels she would have left the Revenue Cutter miles behind her." Tallmadge successfully detained the *Cleopatra* on April 23. Three days later, he arrested the leaders of the expedition, lodging them in the local jail.[46]

The filibusters were out on bail by the end of the month. Throughout the summer they made new plans to invade Cuba. Picking up rumors of the renewed activity, Hall and Tallmadge dutifully reported them to Washington. At the end of August, President Millard Fillmore empowered the marshal to use U.S. land and naval powers to stop the expedition. "Every such attempt must, if possible, be arrested," the president wrote. "You may rest assured," Tallmadge responded, "that every effort will be made by the U.S. Officers in this City to suppress and arrest any expedition which may be fitted out in this City against any country at peace with the United States." On September 2 the State Department issued a general alert to the Atlantic and Gulf Coast marshals and attorneys to remain at their posts to stop the filibusters.[47]

In the meantime, the filibusters went to New Orleans. López and his American allies obtained a new steamship, the *Pampero,* to carry the expedition to Cuba. Departing the New Orleans area on August 5 with a force of 424 men, including 155 Americans, the ship reached Key West five days later. The residents greeted them with "hurrahs and waving of handkerchiefs." The ship immediately refueled and departed for Cuba.[48]

The Spanish awaited them. On August 11, after several efforts to find a landing site free of Spanish forces, López and his men launched their invasion at Morillo, a small village sixty miles from Havana. Once the *Pampero* was unloaded, López ordered it to return to the St. Johns River in Florida to retrieve the expedition's artillery pieces and to pick up new recruits. After the ship left, the filibusters moved inland. For the next few weeks they engaged in a series of brief skirmishes with Spanish troops, who kept them constantly on the run. By the end of the month the surviving filibusters were in the custody of the Spanish.

Of the 424 filibusters, well over a hundred were killed or executed. Many of those captured were imprisoned in Spain or kept in Havana's jails. Many others were unaccounted for, having deserted. On September 1, López, saying, "I die for my beloved Cuba," was publicly garroted, a primitive method of strangulation with an iron collar preferred by the Spanish, probably because they invented it.[49]

Meanwhile, the *Pampero* had arrived at Jacksonville, Florida, around August 13, taking on board "armed men and heavy ordnance." The ship then went to the sea islands of Georgia, where more recruits were added to the doomed expedition. All along the Gulf Coast, word of the López expedition's skirmishes with the Spanish troops aroused intense excitement among men eager for adventure. When news arrived of the expedition's defeat, that excitement turned to anger.[50]

Although on the lookout for the ship, the marshals and attorneys along the coast received no word of its movements until the end of the month. On August 27, U.S. Attorney Henry Williams of Georgia warned Marshal William Isaac C. Mills of the growing public excitement throughout the Gulf region. Williams urged the marshal to investigate vigorously any suspicious military formations.[51]

On September 3, Williams found out that the *Pampero* had been at Jacksonville on August 13 but had since left. On September 4 he learned that the *Pampero* had left the sea islands off the coast of Georgia bound back to Jacksonville, where "an armed expedition is ready to sail." He dispatched orders to the revenue cutter *Jackson* to sail to the mouth of the St. Johns River to block the *Pampero*'s exit to the Gulf and urged the secretary of state to send a gunboat to assist the *Jackson*.[52]

The revenue cutter arrived in time to blockade the river. On September 10 the *Jackson* fired on the *Pampero*, forcing it to flee back up the river toward Jacksonville. Fearing the armaments on the filibustering ship, the revenue cutter offered no pursuit, taking up position at the mouth of the river. "The *Pampero* is heavily armed and it is feared will attack the cutter in order to escape," Williams reported to the secretary of state. "An armed steamer is necessary. Is one cruising anywhere off the coast of Georgia or Florida?"[53]

Instead of sending a gunboat, President Fillmore turned to the marshals. The fate of the López expedition had led to attacks on Spaniards residing in the Gulf region. Afraid that volunteers would flock to López's banner, the president delegated to marshals Charles Bingham of southern Alabama and William S. Scott of eastern Louisiana the power to call out U.S. military and naval forces to stop further recruitment of filibusters. In the absence of Marshal Scott, Deputy Charles A. Labrizai in New Orleans "entered upon the discharge of the duties assigned me, appointing aids and taking other necessary steps." However, news of the executions began reaching the United States soon afterward, effectively discouraging additional volunteers.[54]

The *Pampero* remained blockaded on the St. Johns River, stationing itself near Jacksonville. On September 11, troops of the U.S. Army arrived at the city, and the crew and passengers surrendered without a fight. The revenue cutter found the abandoned *Pampero* one hundred miles upriver, hidden in a creek.[55]

During the 1850s, hardly a single year passed without filibustering expeditions' being launched against some country or colony at peace with the United States. In June 1854, President Franklin Pierce issued a proclamation urging the American people to observe the neutrality laws. The president also enjoined "the officers of the Federal Government to be vigilant in bringing to justice such as may violate" those laws. "Any such enterprise," Secretary of State William L. Marcy pointed out to the government officials responsible for prosecuting the filibusters, "could not fail to embarrass the government in its policy towards the power for the disturbance of which the expedition was intended." By the decade's end the filibusters had shamed the United States with Cuba, Mexico, Nicaragua, Ecuador, Guatemala, El Salvador, Costa Rica, Peru, and Honduras.[56]

The ease with which the López expedition slipped away from the United States pointed out the difficulties in stopping the filibustering expeditions. Despite the cooperation between the various marshals, U.S. attorneys, collectors, and naval forces in the districts concerned, the American coastline was simply too long, with too many convenient places to hide, for the small force of government officials to cover adequately. The filibusters, one historian has written, "carried on elaborate intrigues to organize their expeditions, resorted to ruses to escape the vigilance of officials directed to prevent their departure, landed on foreign soil with only a few armed men to conquer a country, and fought against defending forces, invariably losing sooner rather than later, only to return to the United States to try again—and again and again."[57]

Oftentimes the marshals succeeded in arresting suspected filibusters, only to see them acquitted for lack of evidence or because the jurors supported them. William Walker, the preeminent filibuster of his day, was arrested several times for launching expeditions against Mexico, Cuba, and Nicaragua. Each time, sympathetic juries released him, much to the marshals' chagrin. For more than a year Walker ruled Nicaragua as its conqueror and president. Even after he was overthrown in 1857, no jury would convict him. Finally, three years later, Walker was captured during an invasion of Honduras. A Honduran firing squad ended his filibustering career in 1860.

Filibustering, too, died that year. It succumbed to a far greater contest that devoured the dreams for glory and adventure that had attracted so many young men, particularly in the South. For four years, they had plenty of battles to fight within the borders of the United States. There was no need to go elsewhere.

The pursuit of counterfeiters and filibusters confirmed the U.S. marshals as the national police force responsive to the needs of the federal government. The scope of the outlawry they confronted also confirmed the need for specialized agencies, such as the Secret Service, to combat particular crimes. The marshals were ill suited to specialization. The vast scope of their duties and the abbreviated tenure of their office prohibited the development of expertise. In addition, the incentives of their position – their fees – were offered for duties other than detection.

It was typical of the federal system to combine vast authority with limited resources or, when that failed, to reverse the combination. The marshals had the authority, but rarely the resources. Secret Service operatives eventually obtained the resources necessary to combat counterfeiting, but their authority was limited. It was the American way.

4

SLAVERS AND SLAVES

1819–1861

Vermont marshal Lewis S. Partridge feared for his job. A dedicated Democrat and staunch supporter of President James Buchanan, he learned in November 1859 of a movement within his state party to oust him as U.S. marshal. Two members of the Stephen Douglas wing of the party had spread rumors against him at the last session of the state legislature. They hoped to persuade the Democratic members of the House to sign a petition to the president for Partridge's removal and for the appointment of one of their own in his place.

"The representations made to the members were that I was a disturber in the party, acted with the Republicans, etc., and would soon be found in the Black Republican ranks, etc.," Partridge explained to Secretary of the Interior Jacob Thompson. "Also that in the appointment of Deputies to assist in taking the census I would not give the Douglas wing of the Democracy any appointments." In fact, the marshal added, "every argument that could be brought to bear upon the different members was used without the least regard to truth." Partridge assured the secretary that all of the charges, except the last, were untrue.

"In relation to the charge of being a disturber I must so far plead guilty as this," the marshal began his testament of political faith, "that I have disturbed the Douglas wing 'as they term it' by my open, bold, and unflinching advocacy of the equal rights of the South, to carry their property, whether in Slaves, or any thing else, into the Territories and have it protected as other property." He opposed Douglas's view of allowing majority votes in each territory to determine the local laws on slavery. Instead, Partridge sustained the *Dred Scott* decision, which protected slaveholders' rights in the free states, and he upheld Buchanan's policy of allowing unhampered emigration of southerners and their slaves into the territories.

He was not, and would never be, Partridge assured Thompson, a member of the recently formed Republican party. He was not ready "to commit treason to our glorious Union, for their doctrines [which opposed the expansion of slavery] if carried out must lead to that." The marshal urged the secretary to support him against the libelous charges. If he could remain in office, Partridge promised to deliver "four, if not six," votes for Buchanan's renomination at the 1860 party convention.[1]

Partridge remained in office until the end of Buchanan's term, when Abraham Lincoln, a month after becoming president, replaced him with his own appointee. Yet, the attacks on Partridge showed how divided northern Democrats had become by the late 1850s. Partridge's plight also symbolized the polarization of the entire country as it moved toward the presidential election of 1860. The overriding issue in that election was not slavery but whether slaveholders should be allowed to take their property into the newly acquired regions of the expanding United States. No one in power, or with any hope of attaining political power, suggested abolishing slavery. The South, in that sense, was protected in its peculiar institution.

But southerners wanted no restrictions at all on their so-called property rights. They wanted to export slavery into the territories and beyond. Southerners rushed into the new territories of Kansas, Nebraska, and points westward, but in their hurry they did not forget to take their slaves. Many of the filibusters during this period were slaveholding southerners who saw an opportunity to establish new slave states throughout the Western Hemisphere. One of the first acts of the Tennessean William Walker, once he became president of Nicaragua in 1856, was to promulgate a law fostering slavery in the country.[2]

The issue also involved tests of political power. Which region of the country, North or South, free or slave, would control the Congress, the presidency, and the federal courts? These questions had plagued the

Union from its formation. The language as well as the act of enslavement had enshrouded the country from the beginning, blocking its vision of itself and darkening its future. The ideals of liberty and equal rights clanged against the heavy iron chains holding the slaves.

During the drafting of the Constitution, representatives from the North grudgingly accepted three sections related to slavery in order to induce southern states to accept the Union. Three-fourths of the slaves in each state were counted to determine southern representation in the House of Representatives. The Constitution also banned any law infringing the African slave trade for a twenty-year period. Finally, the Constitution called upon each state to ensure that "fugitives from labor," as escaped slaves were euphemistically called, were returned promptly to their owners.

As the Union developed, the Senate struggled to maintain an even balance between slave-state and free-state representation. The South, despite its small population, including three-fourths of its slaves, could then defend itself from any measures passed by the northern-dominated House of Representatives. A series of compromises held this precarious balance together.

As soon as the twenty-year ban on outlawing the African slave trade expired in 1808, Congress, at President Jefferson's suggestion, passed a measure prohibiting the trade. Eleven years later, the legislature passed a much stronger measure, defining the trade as piracy; merchants in it could be hung. The 1819 law also authorized the president to send the Africans back to Africa, though not specifically to their homes, and appropriated $100,000 for the repatriation. But the attack on the African slave trade was one of the few successes the North gained against slavery during the entire pre–Civil War period.

The North never achieved the unity against slavery that the South enjoyed in support of it. Many northerners, like James Buchanan, feared the threat of southern secession more than they might (or might not) have disliked slavery. They shied from any measure that even appeared to challenge the South and its institutions. Other northerners, like Stephen Douglas, willingly left the South alone within its own borders but frantically sought a compromise over the expansion of those borders. Some northerners, like Abraham Lincoln, disliked slavery in principle but recognized the practical impossibility of challenging it in its home region. They concentrated on prohibiting its spread, hoping thereby to starve it eventually into extinction. And a few vocal northerners urged the abolishment of slavery altogether.

Consequently, during the great debates over slavery, the South generally spoke with one voice, the North with many. It became fairly easy, then, for southern representatives to protect the interests of their region, although there were limits on how far those interests extended. Occasionally, and increasingly as the country headed toward mid-century, northerners found points of mutual agreement to challenge the South. At those times great constitutional crises erupted.

Compromise was then necessary. In 1820, Missouri and Maine were admitted to the Union together, one slave, the other free, in order to maintain the senatorial balance of power. Thirty years later the Compromise of 1850 admitted California as a free state and created the territories of Utah and New Mexico. The question of slavery in the two new territories was left to the "popular sovereignty" of each one's citizenry. In exchange for the disruption in the Senate's balance of power, the South received the Fugitive Slave Law, which established harsher penalties for harboring runaway slaves, created special courts to hear fugitive cases, and required, upon pain of a hefty financial penalty, the U.S. marshals to arrest accused fugitives and return those found to be slaves to their owners in the South.

The issues between North and South soon became larger than the right to own slaves. Southern advocates touted the rights of the states to determine their own destinies; northern advocates proclaimed the ascendancy of the Union. Northerners opposed the return of fugitive slaves; southerners objected to the ban on the African trade. The arguments and debates became increasingly vociferous, moving from the cold, irrecusable logic of John C. Calhoun's constitutional analyses to the bloodstained dust of Kansas, from states' rights to states in rebellion.

Like Partridge in Vermont, marshals throughout the country were among the casualties of the controversy. They became strangers in their own lands, for it was upon them to enforce the laws that their neighbors and friends most opposed. Southern marshals, most of whom, in all probability, were themselves slave owners, worked to stop the African slave trade—amid opposition throughout the South to the law prohibiting it. Northern marshals, regardless of their personal views, captured fugitive slaves and sent them back South. In doing so, they became the objects of riots and bloodshed, receiving the violent scorn of their neighbors. It was an impossible situation, a test of loyalty between region and country at a time when the states claimed as much loyalty as the Union.

When the Democrats split during the election of 1860 and fielded two candidates, their divided vote allowed Abraham Lincoln and his minority party of Republicans to come to power. The southern states, as they had threatened to do for years, began to secede. By the end of 1861, southern marshals resigned their commissions to join the Confederacy; northern marshals swapped theirs for military commissions.

One thinks of Charles Devens. As the marshal of Massachusetts in 1851, Devens risked a riot by Boston abolitionists when he returned the fugitive slave Thomas Sims to his southern owner. A decade later, Devens volunteered to fight for the Union, serving with distinction and bravery. He earned a hero's rank at the battles of Fair Oaks and Chancellorville. In 1877 Devens became attorney general, helping oversee the dismantlement of the North's Reconstruction of the South. While he was attorney general, Devens hired Thomas Sims as a messenger for the Department of Justice.[3]

AFRICAN SLAVERS

In the summer of 1820 the U.S. revenue cutter *Dallas* caught a ship engaged in the African slave trade. On board were 258 Africans bound for the South and servitude. The captain of the *Dallas* escorted the slaver to Savannah, Georgia. District Attorney Richard W. Habersham indicted the traders as pirates under the terms of the 1819 law banning the trade. The Africans were delivered to Marshal William Morel.[4]

No one knew where the traders had captured the Africans, and the Africans could not be asked because no one spoke their language. Indeed, in a group of 258 Africans, probably many dialects and languages were spoken. The law appropriated $100,000 for the president to use in returning Africans to Africa, but it did not specify where in Africa, nor did it authorize the president to establish a place. According to Attorney General William Wirt, the president could not use any part of the money to purchase land for a settlement in Africa or to buy "carpenters tools, etc., etc., for the purpose of making a settlement in Africa." Perhaps Congress hoped that the African Colonization Society would raise the funds necessary to establish a homeland for returned Africans, but the society in 1820 had not yet been able to do so.[5]

The Africans in Morel's custody, like so many who made the grueling trip aboard the slave ships, were in poor health, and many were dying. Without adequate facilities to keep them, Morel took the only expedient open to him. He farmed the Africans out to various planters in Georgia who he was sure would "treat them with kindness."[6]

Morel's quandary was not unusual for the marshals enforcing the ban on the slave trade. No one considered the Africans to be free people, and few considered them even to be human beings. They were Negroes, at best a lower species, but certainly not on the same level as Caucasians. When Marshal E. Levy received into his custody a group of Africans, he arranged to keep them in slavery with the people who had caught the traders. He realized that was not the best solution, for Congress had not intended to reward those who caught traders by allowing them to keep the Africans. Using the logic of his day and era, Levy concluded that he should dispose of the Africans as he did all other seized property: at auction, selling them to the highest bidder.[7]

The American effort to thwart the African slave trade foundered on indecision, meager resources, and lack of clear direction. Although the colony of Liberia was established on the African coast for Africans rescued from the trade, Congress never appropriated sufficient funds to take many of them there. The navy never had sufficient ships to patrol adequately the sea-lanes used in the trade. In fact, the British were far better at catching slave ships. Though the trade did not exactly flourish, it suffered little.

Throughout the 1820s and 1830s, for example, the marshals and district attorneys reported to the secretary of state only occasional captures of African slavers. Three ships were caught in 1820 and brought to Georgia; one was caught near the coast of Massachusetts. Eight years later, Marshal Waters Smith of eastern Florida wanted to know what to do with the 121 Africans brought to his deputy in Key West.[8]

In 1832 the State Department spent considerable time arranging the return of three Africans to the British authorities who had taken them. The Africans had escaped from the custody of the marshal in Alabama in 1829. How they had survived by themselves for so long in such a foreign and inhospitable place remains a mystery. They were eventually caught by Marshal John Nicholson in Louisiana, who returned them to Marshal Robert Crawford in Alabama, who in turn gave them to the British.[9]

Marshal Albert Smith of Maine arrested Sterling E. Turner in 1833 for bringing Mordo, an African whom he had enslaved, into Portland. Caleb Miller was likewise arrested in 1835 by Marshal William C. H. Waddell of New York for bringing from Africa two 5-year-old children. Two years later, Marshal Samuel H. Duval of middle Florida seized eight Africans brought into his district. As his colleagues and the marshals in other districts had done since the law banning the trade was passed, Charles S. Sibley, the U.S. attorney for middle Florida, urged the secretary of state to authorize sending the Africans back to Africa or even somewhere else. "Their support and maintenance by the Marshal will cause considerable expense in addition to what has already been incurred," warned Sibley.[10]

The surprising aspect of these scattered reports of arrests is how few Africans were involved. Where were the ships crammed with hundreds of Africans chained in rows below decks? Although the actual numbers of slaves illegally imported into the United States during the period will never be known, they can be estimated as relatively high – certainly more than the eight or two or one the marshals were getting. The memoirs of slave traders also indicate a fairly active business. Until the 1850s the government did not strongly encourage the enforcement of the prohibition of the trade. During that decade, however, the North's patience with the South began running out.[11]

Part of the problem in catching the slavers resulted from the language of the 1819 law banning the African slave trade. Although the legislation prohibited direct trade in slaves with Africa, it did not outlaw the sale of slaves within the United States nor between the United States and other countries in the Western Hemisphere. Often, slave ships returning from Africa with a full load stopped first at Cuba or some other Caribbean nation, where the Africans were unloaded for market. Americans then legally purchased them and shipped the new slaves to the United States.

Northern opposition to the slavers grew more pronounced. Abolitionists, who had for years cried out alone against slavery, suddenly found an increased sympathy for their cause. The infamous Fugitive Slave Law incensed many northerners who had hitherto taken a neutral stance. The continuing trade in slaves with Africa fueled their anger, especially because southerners seemed to sympathize with the slavers.

The two laws became points of contention, particularly because President James Buchanan determined that fairness required him to enforce both laws with equal vigor. Southerners complained angrily every time northerners resisted the Fugitive Slave Law; northerners cried foul over the continuation of the African slave trade. By the late 1850s, federal officials in the South began to feel the heat. The president insisted that they enforce the laws, but in doing so, they were criticized by their fellow southerners. Only the northern marshals who enforced the Fugitive Slave Law had a more difficult time.

U.S. Attorney James Conner of South Carolina confronted the problem of local opposition to the ban on the slave trade in September 1858. During the summer of 1858 the U.S. brig *Dolphin* captured the *Echo,* which was loaded with Africans. The *Dolphin* escorted the slaver to the nearest port–Charleston, South Carolina. The Africans were turned over to Marshal Daniel H. Hamilton; Conner indicted the captain and crew of the *Echo* for piracy.

The local sheriff began clamoring that the Africans belonged in his custody under South Carolina law. A number of Charleston citizens joined in the demand, for they saw the case of the *Echo* as a strong political issue to use in repealing the ban on the slave trade. Attorney General Jeremiah S. Black urged Conner to do his duty, regardless of the political pressures brought to bear. "If any attempt should be made," Black ordered, "no matter on what pretense, by the State authorities, to take those negroes out of the hands in which they are now placed by the federal government . . . such attempt must be resisted by all lawful and proper means." Black also informed Conner that measures were being taken to remove the Africans out of the country as soon as possible.[12]

Removing the Africans from Charleston only solved part of the problem. Conner still had to try the captain and crew of the *Echo;* he was not sure he could find an impartial judge and jury. Conner's doubts surprised Attorney General Black. "I have no doubt whatever that the prisoners are guilty," he declared in October 1858. All that was needed was a well-prepared case to take to court. "The Judges of the Circuit Court are men of eminent ability, who never have been and never will be unfaithful to their high duties in this or any other case," Black assured Conner. Nor did the attorney general believe that Conner would have much difficulty finding an impartial jury. "Public opinion is opposed to the execution of the law," Black admitted, "but that will be as nothing in the eyes of men who swear that it *shall* be executed."

Conner, Black advised, should deny the political aspects of the case, making clear that opposition to the enforcement of the law was not the way to repeal it:

There is no more reason for mingling politics in this case than any other criminal prosecution which the government demands the vindication of the law. Those who think that the slave trade with Africa ought to be reopened will have as good a chance of carrying their measure after the conviction of these men as they have now. . . . I do not however understate the difficulty of getting justice executed in a community where public opinion is strong in favor of the offenders. We have felt this very often, and the character of the government has suffered from it.

Opposition to the Fugitive Slave Law had created a number of problems, particularly in New England and the northwestern states. "Laws deemed to be necessary to the general welfare have encountered local unpopularity which sometimes defeats them," Black acknowledged. "But it is in the last degree important that the loyal State of South Carolina should not follow those evil examples."[13]

Black's lecture on good government did Conner little good. The case came to trial at the end of 1858, and despite his exertions to find an impartial jury, Conner apparently lost the case, for the Interior Department refused to pay for his services during the trial. Conner interpreted the refusal as an indication that the Buchanan administration disapproved of his course in the *Echo* case. On March 28 he tendered his resignation.[14]

The *Echo* case and others like it persuaded the Buchanan administration to redouble its efforts to enforce the laws against the African slave trade and aiding fugitive slaves. "A failure to inflict the legal punishment for importing African Negroes into the Southern States," Attorney General Black argued, "will be made an excuse in the North for trampling underfoot the laws which forbid the importation of stolen slaves to Canada." Opposition in the South to the laws, combined with the occasionally violent northern resistance to the Fugitive Slave Law, threatened the foundations of the government. "If the two sections of the Union will emulate one another in the violation of law and the impunity they give to criminals of different classes," Black asserted, "it will not be very long before we shall cease to have any law at all."[15]

The administration continued to insist "that these gross violations of the law should be stopped." At least one U.S. marshal, Daniel H. Stewart of Georgia, was fired for being "inefficient" in enforcing the slave trade laws. The failure to obtain convictions, however, reflected the degeneration of the federal government's authority throughout the South in the late 1850s. Northerners also refused to respect the laws, particularly the Fugitive Slave Law of 1850. The general breakdown in the authority of federal law was a symptom of the coming war.[16]

Southern marshals may have faced recalcitrant jurors and reluctant witnesses, but northern marshals confronted riots and bloodshed. In the end, though, it was the South, in defiant defense of its peculiar institution, that showed the greatest disrespect for the law. It ripped the Constitution, and with it the country, asunder.

FUGITIVE SLAVES

On May 27, 1857, deputy marshals Benjamin P. Churchill and John C. Elliot, accompanied by a posse of nine other deputies, went to Champaign County, Ohio, to arrest Udney H. Hyde for aiding in the escape of a fugitive slave. While looking for Hyde, the deputies were confronted by Udney's son Russell, Hiram Gutridge, and Charles and Edward Taylor. After a heated argument, the deputies arrested the four men, charging them with "having aided and abetted a fugitive slave in his escape, and having resisted and obstructed the officers of the United States in the arrest of such fugitive." They loaded their prisoners into carriages and began the trip back to Cincinnati.

As they proceeded, the probate judge of Champaign County, Samuel V. Baldwin, acted quickly to issue a writ of habeas corpus for the return of the four prisoners. The sheriff of the county, after calling out a posse, went in pursuit. Churchill's posse and its prisoners had already crossed several counties, so the sheriffs of Greene and Clark counties joined the chase. Along the way, other men joined the posse. By the time the three sheriffs caught up with the deputy marshals at South Charleston, they had "an armed posse of from one to two hundred men" to help them.

Clark County sheriff John E. Layton knew that neither reason nor argument would persuade Deputy Marshal Churchill to give up his prisoners. He decided not to identify himself or to show the writ but to surprise the federal posse and seize Gutridge and his friends forcibly. According to U.S. Attorney John H. O'Neile, the local posse attacked the deputy marshals "after the manner of highwaymen and without exhibiting any writ or making known that they were officers."

When Layton's carriage caught up with the federal caravan, Deputy

Sheriff Compton brandished his pistol at the federal possemen he passed on the way to the lead carriage. Pulling alongside Churchill's buggy, Compton grabbed the horse's bridle. Churchill pulled at the reins to shake loose Compton's hold. With the bridle in one hand and his pistol in the other, Compton waved the gun about in the general direction of the deputy marshal. Churchill hastily pulled his Colt revolver and fired at the deputy sheriff.

The shot missed Compton, but he loosened his hold on Churchill's carriage. Both buggies then pulled to a halt, forcing the other carriages to stop too. Sheriff Layton, pistol in hand, climbed down from his buggy and walked toward Churchill. He was, he later admitted, "prepared to fire, and intending to fire at Churchill." Layton, however, hesitated to shoot until he was closer to Churchill. As soon as Layton was within reach, Churchill leapt toward him, grabbing at the pistol. During the scuffle, Churchill knocked Layton's gun from his hand, then clubbed him with his Colt, severely injuring him.

The local posse surged toward the stalled carriages, seized the deputy marshals, and took them to the Clark County jail. Gutridge and the other federal prisoners were returned to Champaign County. Because neither Churchill nor his deputies were free to appear before probate judge Baldwin to show cause for the capture and detention of Gutridge and the others, Baldwin ordered the federal prisoners released.

Complaints were sworn out against the federal deputies for assault on Sheriff Layton with intent to kill and for shooting at Compton with intent to kill. After spending the night in jail, Churchill and his posse were taken to Champaign County to answer the original habeas corpus writ. Judge Baldwin released them but ordered them to return to Clark County for trial on the assault charges.

Marshal Sifford immediately applied to federal district court judge Leavitt for a writ dismissing the charges against his deputies. Judge Leavitt readily concurred. "Now," Leavitt observed, "the practical question in this case is, whether a law of the United States can be evaded and set at naught, either by direct and violent opposition, which is rebellion, or by the specious pretences of the law." The case represented a direct conflict between the power of the federal government and the state of Ohio. Which court process took precedence, the one issued to Deputy Marshal Churchill by the federal court or the one given to Sheriff Layton by the probate court? In the judge's view, the answer was simple. Within the federal government's sphere of authority, it was supreme.

Nor could the deputy marshals be held to answer to the state for actions they took in the line of duty. "Having the prisoners thus in lawful custody, they had an undoubted right to use all the force necessary to retain them in such custody," the judge declared. "And in case of an open, undisguised attempt to rescue them by force, they would be justified in killing the assailants, if that were necessary to retain the possession of their prisoner; and such killing clearly would not be a crime against the state of Ohio." The deputies were under oath to serve the arrest warrants. "It was not optional with them whether they would serve the process," Leavitt observed. Thus, the judge concluded, Sheriff Layton exceeded his authority in trying to stop the deputies; the deputies acted well within their authority in resisting him.[17]

Such challenges to U.S. marshals and their deputies threatened not merely the infamous Fugitive Slave Law but, more important, the authority and power of the federal government to enforce its laws. When fugitive slaves were rescued in Massachusetts, New York, Ohio, Pennsylvania, Illinois, and Wisconsin, the rescues were interpreted by federal officials, including the president, as direct attacks on the constitutional underpinnings of the national government. The survival of that government seemed at stake. Thus, the government responded harshly to the attacks, enforcing the Fugitive Slave Law with vigor.

On the morning of February 15, 1851, Deputy Marshal Patrick Riley of Massachusetts arrested the escaped slave Frederick Jenkins, known also as Shadrach, outside the Cornhill Coffee House in Boston, where Shadrach worked as a waiter. Because Massachusetts by statute refused to rent jail space for holding fugitive slaves, Deputy Riley tried to house his prisoner at the Boston navy yard, but the commander there also refused to help.

Riley took Shadrach to the courthouse. The courthouse, too, was owned by the state, but two rooms were rented by the marshal to hold federal court. Riley, assisted by two deputies, kept his prisoner there. The mayor of Boston refused Riley's request to assign police to guard the building.

That afternoon, Commissioner George T. Curtis opened the hearing to determine if Shadrach was an escaped slave as his purported master asserted. Five prominent Boston attorneys appeared voluntarily to defend Shadrach. They asked for a few days to prepare their case. Although the Fugitive Slave Law required only the testimony of the master or his agents as sufficient proof that the accused was a fugitive slave—the alleged

U.S. Marshal Robert Forsyth (Ga.) was the first of more than four hundred marshals killed in the line of duty. Courtesy of Carolyn Aubrey Humphries and Louise Aubrey McFarland.

From *Augusta Chronicle and Gazette of the State,* January 18, 1794.

AUGUSTA, *January* 18.

On Saturday laſt *Major* ROBERT FORSYTH Marſhall for the ſtate [diſtrict] of Georgia, was killed in the execution of his office, at the houſe of Mrs. Dixon in this place, by Beverly Allen of South-Carolina: A ſketch of the particulars is as follows; Major Forſyth being about to ſerve the foreſaid Allen with a writ;---from a principle of delicacy, aſked him out of the room, where there were ſeveral gentlemen preſent, upon buſineſs in which the ſaid Allen was intereſted;---he aſſented, and perhaps added theſe words "with pleaſure"; but inſtead of following, he aſked ſome one apart, "is not that Major Forſyth ?"---being anſwered in the affirmative, he inquired about the key of the room oppoſite, and having obtained it, he retired thither;---in the interim the Major had made ſervice of a writ on William Allen, brother to the ſaid Beverly, and had granted him ſome period of indulgence,---this, was ſpent in the room to which his brother had retired, and after being elapſed, the Major going up ſtairs, reminded William that his time was expired, (Meſſrs. Richards and Ran-

In the Circuit Court of the United States, in and for the Pennſylvania Diſtrict of the Middle Circuit.

THE GRAND INQUEST of the United States, for the Pennſylvania Diſtrict, upon their reſpective oaths and affirmations, do preſent, That David Bradford late of the county of Waſhington in the Diſtrict of Pennſylvania Eſquire being an inhabitant of, and reſiding within, the ſaid United States, to wit, in the diſtrict aforeſaid, and under the protection of the laws of the ſaid United States, and owing allegiance and fidelity to the ſame United States, not having the fear of God before his eyes, nor weighing the duty of his ſaid allegiance and fidelity, but being moved and ſeduced by the inſtigation of the devil, wickedly deviſing and intending the peace and tranquility of the ſaid United States to diſturb, on the first day of Auguſt in the year of our Lord one thouſand ſeven hundred and ninety-four, at in the county of Allegheny in the diſtrict aforeſaid, unlawfully, maliciouſly and traitorouſly did compaſs, imagine and intend to raiſe and levy war, inſurrection and rebellion againſt the ſaid United States; and to fulfil and bring to effect the ſaid traitorous compaſſings, imaginations and intentions of him the ſaid David Bradford he, the ſaid David Bradford afterwards, that is to ſay, on the ſaid first day of Auguſt in the ſaid year of our Lord one thouſand ſeven hundred and ninety-four, at the ſaid county of Allegheny in the diſtrict aforeſaid, with a great multitude of perſons, whoſe names at preſent are unknown to the Grand Inqueſt aforeſaid, to a great number, to wit, to the number of five hundred perſons and upwards, armed and arrayed in a warlike manner, that is to ſay, with guns, ſwords, clubs, ſtaves and other warlike weapons, as well offenſive as defenſive, being then and there unlawfully, maliciouſly and traitorouſly aſſembled and gathered together, did falſely and traitorouſly aſſemble and join themſelves together againſt the ſaid United States, and then and there, with force and arms, did falſely and traitorouſly, and in a warlike and hoſtile manner, array and diſpoſe themſelves againſt the ſaid United States, and then and there, with force and arms, in purſuance of ſuch their traitorous intentions and purpoſes aforeſaid, he the ſaid David Bradford with the ſaid perſons ſo as aforeſaid traitorouſly aſſembled, and armed and arrayed in manner aforeſaid, moſt wickedly, maliciouſly and traitorouſly did ordain, prepare and levy public war againſt the ſaid United States, contrary to the duty of his ſaid allegiance and fidelity, againſt the conſtitution, peace and dignity of the ſaid United States, and alſo againſt the form of the act of the Congreſs of the ſaid United States, in ſuch caſe made and provided.

Witneſſes.

David Hamilton Eſq.
Robert Calhoon
George Wallace
John Cannon
Alexander Wells
John Baldwin, affirm
Henry Hugh Brackinridge Eſq., ſworn
Beall

Beall

Attorney of the United States
for the Pennſylvania Diſtrict.

Indictment of David Bradford, a leader of the Whiskey Rebellion. Note that he was indicted for "being moved and seduced by the instigation of the devil." Courtesy of National Archives, Mid-Atlantic Region, Philadelphia.

Copper whiskey still, ca. 1790. Courtesy of Pennsylvania Historical and Museums Commission, Landis Valley Museum.

Return of Barnabas Smith appointed under Peter Curtenius Marshal of New York District to receive reports from all British subjects residing the Counties of Cayuga and Seneca from the 1st day of September to the 12 day of the same Month 1812 both days inclusive

Name	Age	Time in the United States	Family	Place of Residence	Occupation or pursuit	Dates of application to the Courts to be Naturalized	Remarks
Robert Wallace	50	33	4 Children	Scipio	Farmer	No application	... unfriendly ...
William McMillin	52	24	no Family	Scipio	Farmer	no application	a stranger however I consider him an inoffensive man
William Smith	46	17	Wife & Child	Ulysses	Farmer	no application	Friendly to the present administration
Patrick Brannon	66	12	Wife 4 Child	Scipio	Farmer	In January 1812	A respectable Subject and a good friend to the Government
John Kelley	32	6	Wife & Child	Scipio	Farmer	no application	Opposed to the present administration of the Government
Thomas Cannon	34	20	Wife 4 Child	Scipio	Farmer	no application	Friendly to the American Government
Edmund Wright	52	29	Wife & Child	Scipio	Distiller of Whisky	no application	Reputed to be a respectable family, and a good friend to the American Government
Timothy Reddy	24	15	Wife & Child	Scipio	Tailor	no application	opposed to the administration
Patrick McLaughlin	28	5	Wife & Child	Scipio	Distiller	no application	Peaceable and well disposed
Lawrence Gaffney	25	9	no Family	Scipio	Labourer	no application	a respectable young man & Friendly to the Government
John Flynn	22	9	-----	Scipio	Labourer	no application	Peaceable and inoffensive
Joseph Bird	27	1	-----	Scipio	Farmer	no application	a respectable young man and inoffensive
Samuel Brannon	22	12	-----	Scipio	Farmer	no application	The 2 young men are sons to Patrick, and friendly to government
John Brannon	18	12	-----	Scipio	Farmer	no application	
Thomas Pearson	28	5	-----	Genoa	Farmer	no application	a very industrious young man and a respectable Character
Joseph Party	55	1	Wife	Scipio	Farmer	no application	an inoffensive Subject.

List of enemy aliens compiled by U.S. marshals during the War of 1812. Courtesy of National Archives, Washington, D.C.

The Counterfeiters, by Eastman Johnson. U.S. marshals pursued counterfeiters throughout the nineteenth century. Courtesy of Collection, IBM Corporation, Armonk, N.Y.

Narciso Lopez evaded the U.S. marshals and led a filibustering expedition against Cuba. For the effort, he was garroted by the Spanish. Courtesy of Library of Congress.

U.S. marshals chased the *Pampero* and its filibustering passengers from Louisiana to Florida. From *Harper's New Monthly Magazine*, December 1852.

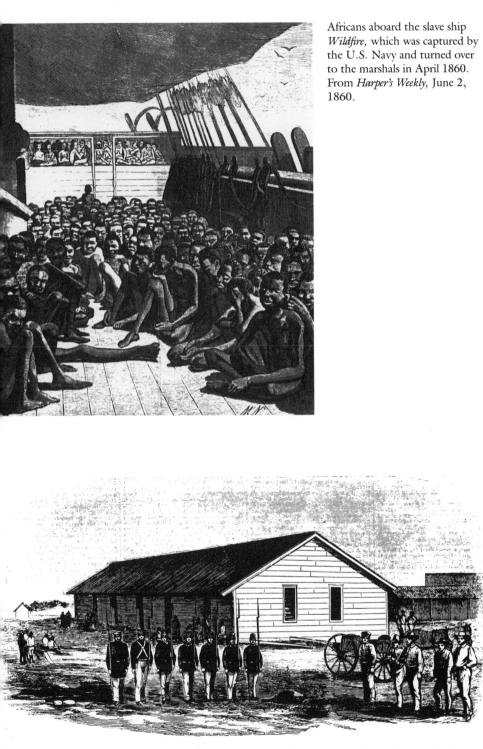

Africans aboard the slave ship *Wildfire*, which was captured by the U.S. Navy and turned over to the marshals in April 1860. From *Harper's Weekly*, June 2, 1860.

The Key West barracks where the Africans were confined by U.S. marshals. From *Harper's Weekly*, June 2, 1860.

Abolitionist cartoon, ca. 1851. Note the slave catcher, far right. Many slave catchers were marshals. Courtesy of Library Company of Philadelphia.

Warning about slave-catching marshals. Courtesy of Kansas State Historical Society, Topeka.

CITIZENS OF LAWRENCE!

☞ **L. Arms, a Deputy U. S. Marshal, has come into your midst for the avowed purpose of NEGRO HUNTING,** and is watching your houses, by his piratical minions, night and day, and will enter and search them for victims. **KNOW YOUR RIGHTS,** and **STAND TO THEM.** He has no right thus to **INVADE** your **CASTLES.** Do we live on the Guinea Coast, or in **FREE America**?

The Eldridge House is the head-quarters of the gang. — Mark them well.

U.S. Marshal Pablo de la Guerra
y Noriega, the first U.S. marshal
of southern California. Courtesy
of U.S. Marshals Service
Collections.

Abraham Lincoln confers with his generals at Antietam, October 3, 1862. Note U.S. Marshal Ward
Hill Lamon (D.C.), seated at left. Because he was as tall as Lincoln, he sat so as not to draw attention
away from the president. Courtesy of Library of Congress.

Ribbon badge for election supervisors. From 1870 to 1892, marshals deputized thousands of poll watchers during congressional elections. Courtesy of U.S. Marshals Service Collections.

From 1870 to 1892, U.S. marshals supervised every congressional election to ensure fair voting. Courtesy of Historic New Orleans Collection, Museum/Research Center, acc. no. 1959.27.19.

"Shall We Call Home Our Troops?" U.S. marshals depended on the army to help protect freedmen from recalcitrant southerners. From *Harper's Weekly*, January 9, 1875.

In "Death at the Polls, and Free from Federal Interference," Thomas Nast graphically illustrated the 1877 federal retreat from protecting the freedmen. From *Harper's Weekly*, October 18, 1879.

Photograph of a captured Ku Klux Klan member, with a contemporary description of his arrest by U.S. marshals. Courtesy of Collection of Herb Peck, Jr., Nashville.

This is a Photograph taken from life of one of the Ku Klux in the disguise worn by him, He was Captured by G Wiley Wells U.S. Dist. Atty. Northern Dist.- Miss. DH. Pierce US Marshall & John McCoy Deputy Marshall of sd'd District in the month of Sept. 1871 in the County of Tisha mingo Miss, the party turned States evidence and revealed all secrets by words, Signes, &c of the organization,

Holly Springs Miss
Dec. 20, 1871

Frederick Douglass was the U.S. marshal of the District of Columbia from 1877 to 1881. Courtesy of Library of Congress.

An assistant marshal taking the census for the last time in 1870. From *Harper's Weekly,* November 19, 1870.

Moonshiners ambushing marshals and revenuers. From *Harper's Weekly,* November 2, 1878.

U.S. Marshal George P. Foster disrupted the 1870 Fenian invasion of Canada by arresting the Fenian leader. From *Harper's Weekly,* June 11, 1870.

In this letter, General George Armstrong Custer warned U.S. Marshal J. H. Burdick that certain political elements were seeking the removal of a deputy marshal for the deputy's successful investigations of the theft of government property. Courtesy of U.S. Marshals Service Collections.

The Making of a Legend, by Don Crowley, depicts Pat Garrett at the end of his life, reflecting on the killing of Billy the Kid.

Day of Decision, by Don Crowley, depicts Virgil Earp at the end of his life, thinking about his days as town marshal of Tombstone.

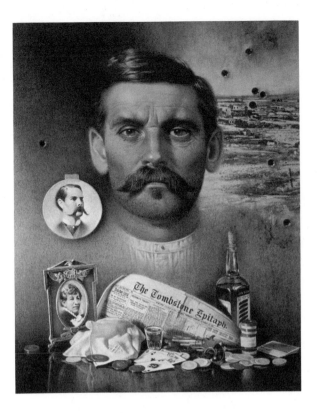

Well, I'll Be Damned! by Don Crowley, depicts Doc Holliday at the end of his short life, thinking about his days in Tombstone.

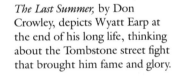

The Last Summer, by Don Crowley, depicts Wyatt Earp at the end of his long life, thinking about the Tombstone street fight that brought him fame and glory.

The Streetfight, by Don Perceval, captures the action near the end of the famous thirty-one-second gunfight. As Wyatt and Virgil Earp shoot Billy Clanton (at right), Doc Holliday and the wounded Morgan Earp kill Frank McLaury (at left). Courtesy of John D. Gilchriese, Western Americana Collection.

slave was not allowed to testify—Curtis granted the continuance. He then ordered the courtroom cleared.

As the crowd began filtering out of the courtroom, Deputy Riley and the prisoner settled down to wait. Shadrach sat quietly between two of the deputies. No shackles or handcuffs were used to hold him. Without warning, the door crashed open, and a crowd of blacks rushed into the room. Before Riley and his deputies could react, some of the blacks pushed them into the corners. As some of the group held the deputies, the others quickly grabbed Shadrach and hustled him out of the courthouse. A crowd of Bostonians formed outside to cheer them while Shadrach and his rescuers ran quickly down Court Street toward Cambridge. From there the fugitive slave made his escape to Canada. Although eight men—four blacks and four whites—were arrested for their part in the rescue, the jury refused to convict any of them.[18]

Seven months after Shadrach's escape, Edward Gorsuch of Maryland traveled to Philadelphia to retrieve four of his slaves who had escaped from his plantation in 1849. Gorsuch took with him his son Dickinson, his nephew, his cousin, and two neighbors. The six men appeared before fugitive-slave commissioner Edward D. Ingraham on September 9. Ingraham quickly issued the necessary arrest warrants for the four fugitives. Instead of delivering the warrants to Marshal Anthony E. Roberts, the commissioner handed them to Henry H. Kline, a Philadelphia policeman and part-time deputy marshal. Marshal Roberts was not informed of the process nor of the pursuit of the fugitives.[19]

After a brief hunt, Gorsuch and Kline located the escaped slaves at the home of William Parker, a free black who had been active in harboring fugitive slaves. The slave hunters arrived at Parker's house just before dawn on September 10. After a prolonged yelling match with Parker—with each side hurling biblical quotes at the other—a general fight erupted as Parker's neighbors arrived to help. Kline immediately and ignominiously fled. Gorsuch was killed; his son and several others in the posse were wounded. Parker and the fugitive slaves fled to Canada.[20]

The news of the Christiana uprising enraged Acting Secretary of State W. L. Derrick. "The resistance was a high crime against the laws of the United States and should be severely punished," he wrote U.S. Attorney John W. Ashmead on September 13, "and it is your duty, and the duty of the Marshal and every other officer, to use every exertion to bring the offenders to justice." He sent orders to the commanding officer of the marines stationed at Philadelphia and the commander of the troops at Carlisle barracks to go to the assistance of Marshal Roberts. President Millard Fillmore, Derrick advised Ashmead, insisted "that the laws must be executed, at any and every hazard and sacrifice."[21]

President Fillmore interpreted the challenges to the Fugitive Slave Law as threats to the government. "The main opposition is aimed against the Constitution itself," he informed Congress in December 1851. The issue, he averred, "involves the supremacy and even the existence of the Constitution." As the new year opened, the administration determined to see the law enforced – by the marshals throughout the North.[22]

Abolitionists and their sympathizers excused their opposition to the Fugitive Slave Law by claiming a higher authority as their justification. "If 'resistance to tyrants,' by bloody weapons, 'is obedience to God...,'" William Lloyd Garrison stated, "then every fugitive slave is justified in arming himself for protection and defence, – in taking the life of every marshal, commissioner, or other person who attempts to reduce him to bondage." The American Anti-Slavery Society summarized its view in a resolution adopted in 1851. "As for the Fugitive Slave Law, we execrate it, we spit upon it, we trample it under our feet." The marshals personified the obnoxious law; they were the ones execrated, spat upon, and trampled.[23]

In May 1854, Marshal Watson Freeman of Massachusetts became involved in an explosive situation when three of his deputies arrested Anthony Burns, a fugitive slave. Burns had escaped from his owner, Colonel Charles Suttle, in Richmond, and made his way by boat to Boston. He found employment in a secondhand clothing store until Suttle tracked him down. At eight in the evening of May 24, Freeman's deputies caught Burns on his way home from work. Freeman, still denied the use of Massachusetts jails, kept Burns under guard at the courthouse.[24]

Several attorneys, including Charles Henry Dana, volunteered to defend Burns. A series of legal actions on their part delayed the slave's return South, which also gave time for abolitionist tempers to reach a fever pitch. On May 26 a number of leading abolitionists decided to rescue Burns. Their plans were encouraged when Boston's mayor refused to give Freeman police support.[25]

The abolitionists convened a mass meeting at Faneuil Hall. Speeches by well-known and outspoken abolitionists stirred the crowd.

A call went up to attack the courthouse and free Burns. The crowd surged out of the hall and headed for the courthouse.

Freeman and his deputies heard the mob approaching. They quickly bolted the doors and prepared themselves to resist. The crowd surrounded the building. A few men tried unsuccessfully to batter the east door down. On the west side a dozen blacks used axes and a battering ram against the wooden door, smashing it down.

Rushing in, the crowd came up against Freeman and his deputies. James Batchelder, who had volunteered to help the marshal, "stood foremost at the door in repelling [the] assailants." Several shots were exchanged before the marshal repulsed the attack. "In the assault," U.S. Attorney B. F. Hallett reported to President Pierce, Batchelder "was shot and instantly killed by the rioters." Deputy Batchelder, Hallett eulogized, "fell as nobly and bravely in vindicating the supremacy of the laws as ever fell a soldier of the Union in achieving our national victories." His body lay that night in the marshal's office before Freeman turned it over to Batchelder's family for burial.[26]

After Marshal Freeman and his men forced the mob out of the courthouse that night, the Boston police, aided by a militia artillery company, arrived on the scene and restored order. The police arrested eighteen of the rioters. The next day, Freeman commandeered a small detachment of U.S. Army troops and Marines to help guard the courthouse. For his authority to do this, he relied on an 1851 order to assist the marshals from the secretary of war to the military commanders at Fort Independence and the Navy Yard. The district judge in Boston supplemented the outdated order with a certificate verifying the need for troops. Hallett considered the military forces an "armed comitatus," but he worried about the legality of using them. "I have advised the officers of their duty and powers in acting as a comitatus in aid of the civil authority," he informed the president, "and as, without their presence it would be wholly unsafe to rely upon voluntary aid, I am assured that you will approve of this course and sustain the U.S. officers in complying with the requisition of the Marshal."[27]

The questionable legality of using federal troops as a posse under the control of the marshal worried President Pierce. His concern increased after Hallett informed the administration that Burns's hearing had been postponed two days. "It will therefore be necessary to retain the U. States troops with the posse comitatus until the final disposition

of the case," Hallett stated. Pierce turned to Attorney General Caleb
Cushing for a legal opinion. After a hasty study of the issue, Cushing
determined that the marshal was empowered by the Judiciary Act of
1789 to call on all able-bodied males to form a posse, including men who
happened to be soldiers. Their organization into military units was a
mere coincidence, although clearly a fortuitous one.[28]

By May 31, Freeman had 120 marines and soldiers under his
command at the courthouse. "This force," Hallett reported, "has been
required to defend the Court House because the U.S. has only two
rooms in the building it can control, and the passage ways must be kept
open for the County Courts and offices." After the riot the Boston
authorities became more cooperative in helping preserve the peace.
"There will be no powers within the control of the Marshal left unemployed to suppress sedition and enforce the laws," Hallett promised.[29]

Burns's trial lasted until June 2, when U.S. Commissioner Edward
Greeley Loring announced his decision to return Burns to his owner.
The next day, Freeman took Burns from the courthouse to the Boston
docks. The local militia lined the route to the docks. A detachment from
the National Boston Lancers started, followed by a company of marines.
Sixty volunteers formed a marching square, with Burns in the center.
Another company of marines guarded the volunteers. Immediately
behind those men came a loaded cannon. Another company of marines
brought up the rear of the unusual procession. At the docks the marshal
loaded Burns onto a steamer to take him to the revenue cutter *Morris,*
which immediately sailed for Norfolk, Virginia, to deliver the slave to his
owner.[30]

After Burns's deportation the local courts in Boston brought the
eighteen rioters to trial. None who pleaded innocent were found guilty
by the local courts. "Fanaticism is so rampant here," Hallett reported,
"that murder of an U.S. officer is held justifiable." Hallett was determined to see justice done. He convened the federal grand jury to present
evidence that the rioters had obstructed federal officials in the performance of their duty. The grand jury, however, refused to issue any
indictments. Consequently, Hallett waited for the convening of a new
grand jury the next October.[31]

Some of the witnesses Hallett needed to prove his case lived in
Worcester. He prepared the necessary summonses. Marshal Freeman
assigned Deputy Asa O. Butman to serve the precepts. Butman left for
Worcester by train on Saturday, October 28. Unable to find the parties

named in the summonses that day and unwilling to do the court's work on a Sunday, Butman decided to check into the American House hotel and resume his search on Monday.

The opponents of the Fugitive Slave Law, however, had no qualms about working Sundays. Throughout the day they spread handbills and other literature calling on the citizens to resist the deputy. That night a mass meeting took place at the city's public hall. "Inflammatory speeches were made," Butman later swore, "and the mob came from the meeting and surround[ed] the Hotel and demand[ed] to see Butman the 'Kidnapper.'" Although Butman had arrived unarmed, the approach of the mob persuaded him to procure a pistol. Thus armed, he watched the mob from his window until the bulk of the crowd disbursed at around four o'clock Monday morning.

Later that morning the city marshal of Worcester arrived at the American House and arrested Butman for carrying a concealed weapon. The city marshal escorted the deputy back to his office, where Butman posted a $100 bond. While he was in the office, a "mob rushed in, and I received one severe blow from one of the assailants, which partially felled me," Butman recalled. "The City Marshall and his assistants finally succeeded in forcing the mob from his room." Although one black man was arrested, he promptly escaped. The crowd retreated outside, where it remained.

Butman stayed in the office until noon. Under the protection of the city marshal, a few private citizens, and five policemen, Butman walked to the railroad depot to catch the train to Boston. "On my way to the depot," he later reported, "I was struck many times by different persons in the mob, stones and missels thrown at me some of which struck me and my life in continual peril until we reached the depot." But the train had already left.

The mob outside the depot increased in size and anger. "Threats of violence were used by the excited persons who composed the crowd," Butman remembered, "and my life was with much difficulty saved by the strenuous efforts of the Marshall and his assistants." The city marshal finally succeeded in hiring a carriage, which he used to take Butman, "suffering from the effects of the blows and bruises I had received," back to Boston. Both Hallett and Butman agreed that the summonses could not be served without the support of the military. Hallett called on the president for permission to use troops.[32]

While awaiting the president's reply, Hallett presented his case to

the new grand jury. On November 25 the jury issued a dozen indictments against the Faneuil Hall rioters. Meanwhile, the citizens of
Worcester had calmed down. The city even began prosecuting some of
the men who had attacked Butman. Assured by the local authorities that
the attacks would not be repeated, Freeman decided to try again,
without military help. With some trepidation, he set off for Worcester.
The city remained true to its pledge, however, and Freeman served his
process without difficulty.[33]

The federal trial opened on April 3, 1855, with judges Curtis and
Sprague presiding. The lawyers for the defendants immediately challenged the indictments on seven specific points of objection. They and
Hallett argued those points until April 12, when Judge Curtis announced the court's decision. He agreed to quash all of the indictments,
but not for the reasons put forth by the defense. Instead, he and Judge
Sprague had found technical fault with them, which came as a surprise to
both the defense and the prosecution. According to Curtis, the indictments failed to describe adequately the power of the U.S. commissioner
to issue an arrest warrant for Anthony Burns.[34]

When Hallett offered to reconvene the October grand jury, the
judges demurred. That jury, they pointed out, had been summoned by
Marshal Freeman, "who was not an indifferent person." Hallett then
suggested that the court appoint someone to summon a new grand jury,
but again the judges declined. That would mean that two grand juries
were sitting at the same time. Finally, the judges confided to Hallett their
true objections to the case. Apparently, when the U.S. commissioner
issued his arrest warrant to the marshal to seize Burns, he had neglected
to describe the authority under which he issued it. "The difficulty,"
Hallett concluded, "therefore is inherent, and the result is that no
Indictment could be sustained . . . for resisting the process under which
Marshal Freeman held Anthony Burns." He decided to drop the proceedings against the defendants altogether.[35]

Once again, the opponents of the Fugitive Slave Law escaped
punishment for their violent efforts to rescue a fugitive slave. Although
Freeman succeeded in returning Burns to his owner, the cost was the life
of a deputy. Trying to bring the rioters to justice almost cost the life of
another.

The attacks on the marshals raised an interesting question, one that
remains unanswered under democratic and constitutional government.
In challenging the Fugitive Slave Law, the abolitionists saw themselves as

attacking one evil law. Federal officials interpreted the attacks as a serious threat to the government. It mattered not to them whether the law was good or bad; it had to be enforced because their sworn duty was to uphold all the laws passed under the Constitution. If they failed to enforce it, no law was safe.

Yet, clearly the Fugitive Slave Law was bad; the abolitionists were morally right to oppose it. But where is the demarcation that justifies those who are morally right to attack, violently and murderously, the authorities who enforce that law? And are those who enforce bad but constitutionally passed laws evil and deserving of condemnation? For generations of marshals, these were essential questions.

Many of the marshals who enforced the Fugitive Slave Law paid a terrible price within their communities. They became strangers in their homeland, hated by their neighbors because they enforced a hated law. Practically the entire state of Wisconsin, including its governor and state supreme court, challenged the marshals over the arrest of Sherman Booth, who had led a fugitive-slave rescue in 1854. After a group of Booth's supporters broke him out of jail, Booth took up a well-protected residence in the state penitentiary as the personal guest of the warden. Repeated efforts to recapture him were thwarted by prison guards. The Wisconsin Supreme Court refused to obey federal court orders. The state teetered on open rebellion against the Buchanan administration until the marshals finally managed to catch Booth.[36]

Wisconsin was not alone in ostracizing the marshals. William C. Cochran remembered walking with his cousin past Wack's Hotel on South Main Street in Oberlin, Ohio. Two or three "rough looking men" were sitting on the porch of the hotel. Cochran's cousin pointed them out as slave catchers, "the most depraved of human beings—worse than thieves, burglars or murderers." Cochran avoided walking past the hotel after that. The memory was so strong that, returning to Oberlin nearly sixty years later, in 1917, Cochran still could not bring himself to go near the hotel where slave catchers at one time had slept.[37]

Deputy Marshal A. P. Dayton, who lived in Oberlin in the 1850s, was ostracized from the local community. The townspeople suspected him "of espionage on the colored population and being in close touch with would-be captors." During the summer of 1858 Dayton attempted to arrest two fugitive slaves. Both attempts were foiled when armed men arrived to stop him. James Smith, a black stonecutter, heard a rumor that Dayton had asked Smith's former owner for a power of attorney so that he could arrest Smith and return him to North Carolina. A few days later, the two men happened to meet outside the Palmer House Hotel. Smith charged the deputy with treachery. Chasing Dayton into the hotel lobby, Smith thrashed him with his hickory cane.[38]

The area around Oberlin witnessed one of the last major slave rescues to occur before the Civil War effectively nullified the law. Late in August 1858, Anderson D. Jennings, a professional slave hunter, arrived in Oberlin, checking into Wack's Hotel. After a few days' investigation, he appeared before the U.S. commissioner, who issued a warrant for the arrest of the fugitive slave John Price. The warrant was given to Deputy Marshal Jacob K. Lowe.

Jennings, Lowe, and Deputy Dayton struck upon a plan to trick the slave into leaving Oberlin so they could arrest him without interference. The plan worked, and Lowe and two local men took Price to nearby Wellington, lodging him overnight in the Wadsworth House, a local tavern. Hearing of the arrest, many Oberlin residents took up arms and rushed to Wellington. The mob easily found the slave catchers, forcing the men and their prisoner to retreat to the attic of the tavern.

A series of conferences between the Oberlin mob and Deputy Lowe occupied some time before the mob forced itself into the attic room. Jennings was injured during the rescue. Price escaped, returning to Oberlin and then making his way to Canada.[39]

The federal grand jury indicted thirty-seven people for participating in the rescue. The Lorain County grand jury indicted Deputy Lowe and the slave catchers for kidnapping. The trials of the rescuers began first. Guilty verdicts were obtained in the first few cases, but the process moved slowly. Each trial took several weeks. Worried about the local indictments against the deputy and the slave catchers, U.S. Attorney Stanley Matthews eventually agreed to drop the prosecutions of the remaining slave rescuers if the state would forgo prosecution of the slave catchers. All of the prisoners, state and federal, were then released.[40]

Throughout the 1850s the men who served the federal government saw the Fugitive Slave Law as an important expedient for keeping the South in the Union. Presidents Fillmore, Pierce, and Buchanan each supported the law because they believed it more important to appease southerners than to appease the growing number of northern abolitionists. Those presidents appointed men who sympathized with their views, including support of the Fugitive Slave Law, to the offices of U.S.

attorney and marshal. Marshal Lewis Partridge of Vermont was not unusual.

Yet, the issue quickly went beyond the question of whether the Fugitive Slave Law was good or morally correct. For federal officials, from the presidents down to the marshals, the attacks on the law represented attacks on the government itself, and each official, sworn to uphold the law, took his oath seriously.

On March 4, 1861, Abraham Lincoln became president. He too swore to uphold the laws, and he too insisted that his marshals and attorneys vigilantly enforce the Fugitive Slave Law. Lincoln appointed his good friend and former partner, Ward Hill Lamon of Virginia, as the marshal for the District of Columbia. Lamon enforced the Fugitive Slave Law so zealously that he angered the Republican-controlled Congress. Rather than repeal the hated law, Congress punished Lamon by stripping him of his most financially rewarding duties: It created a separate marshal's office for the Supreme Court and a separate office of jailer for the District of Columbia.[41]

The Civil War eventually made the Fugitive Slave Law obsolete. The violent northern opposition to the enforcement of the law, and the less violent but almost as bitter southern opposition to the ban on the African slave trade, reflected the impending breakdown of the Union. Civil war is the ultimate failure of the law. Perhaps the marshals knew or suspected that this was their last chance to save the Union. They became more desperate and much harsher in the way they went about imposing the law on communities that bitterly opposed it. The attacks on the marshals in Massachusetts, Ohio, Wisconsin, and other states, in that sense, were the opening salvos of the Civil War.

In that sense too, Deputy James Batchelder, killed during the attempted rescue of Anthony Burns, was one of the first in a tragically long list of men killed to preserve the Union. He and those who fell in battle after him died because the South was determined to protect its strange and stultifying way of life.

2

PART ★ ★

FEDERAL CONSTITUTIONALISM

1861–1900

5

FEDERALISM FALTERS

1861–1876

They snuck into the city. Abraham Lincoln, president-elect of the collapsing Union, arrived unannounced in Washington, D.C., early on the morning of February 23, 1861, nine days before his March 4 inauguration. Ward Hill Lamon, soon to be commissioned as the U.S. marshal for the District of Columbia, accompanied him as his personal bodyguard. Allan Pinkerton and his detectives provided general security. Armed with a brace of pistols and a bowie knife, Lamon was determined to prevent any trouble from southerners. The future marshal was Lincoln's friend and business associate; they had known each other twenty years.[1]

Lamon watched with dismay as the federal experiment soured over the election of his friend. He urged the new president to distribute "circulars of appeal" to the southern people "to stand by the flag, to stand by the Union." Desperate for some way to stop the southern states from seceding, Lamon also recommended that Lincoln complete the construction of the Treasury Building. Such an action, Lamon thought, would prove to the South and most foreign nations "the confidence of the U.S. sustaining herself and will give at the same time many idlers *employment,* thereby identifying them to some extent with the government." But completing the building was hardly enough to keep the Union together. The suggestion reflected Lamon's desperation as state legislatures throughout the South passed resolutions of secession.[2]

Federalism failed.

South Carolina withdrew from the Union first. The state legislature passed its declaration of secession on December 20, 1860, less than two months after Lincoln's election. Having announced its separation from the other states, it demanded that Union forces withdraw from its territory. In the middle of Charleston harbor, Major Robert Anderson and his command refused to evacuate Fort Sumter. A stalemate ensued when South Carolinian troops besieged the island fort. At the end of March 1861, Marshal Lamon hurried from Washington to South Carolina. Although he assured Governor Thomas Pickens that he was acting privately, without charter from Lincoln, that is doubtful. The president at least knew of Lamon's intentions and probably gave his blessing to the mission.

Lamon obtained a pass from Governor Pickens allowing him to cross through the besieging forces and talk with Major Anderson. The governor sent his aide Colonel Duryea with Lamon to ensure "that every propriety is observed." Returning from Fort Sumter, Lamon again met briefly with the governor, urging him to allow Anderson and his men to evacuate the fort unharmed. Pickens decided against Lamon's advice. At 4:30 a.m. on April 12, 1861, the South Carolinian forces began bombarding the fort. After withstanding the cannonade for thirty-four hours, Major Anderson surrendered. The Civil War, the supreme test of the federal system of government, had begun.[3]

Worried that his contribution to the war as U.S. marshal would not be enough, Lamon decided to do more. On April 22, 1861, he renewed his oath to "support, protect and defend" the Constitution. In the summer of that first year of war, Lamon began enlisting army volunteers among loyal Virginians. He hoped to form a "Virginia Brigade" to fight in the Union army. Lincoln supported the plan and Secretary of War Simon Cameron authorized Lamon to draw on the Union army for arms, ammunition, and other supplies.[4]

Finding volunteers proved difficult because of the "demoralization of the people there" over Union defeats. In September 1861, Lamon traveled to Pennsylvania and Illinois to enlist recruits and returned with seven hundred men. Early in the war, the Virginia Brigade, as Lamon insisted on calling his recruits, guarded the forts along the Potomac

River. Lamon wore the rank of a brigadier general, but he also retained his commission as U.S. marshal.[5]

Lamon also took on the task of protecting Lincoln, who had no patience with security measures. One story has it that on the night of Lincoln's inauguration Lamon slept, with pistols and bowie knife, on the floor outside Lincoln's bedroom, his large body stretched in front of the door. The marshal also accompanied Lincoln on many trips. In November 1863, for example, Lamon escorted him to Gettysburg, Pennsylvania, where Lincoln dedicated the new Union cemetery.

Lincoln objected to Lamon's constant efforts to protect him. A fatalist, the president shrugged off the idea that someone would kill him. "He (the President) thought me insane upon the subject of his safety," Lamon remembered in late April 1865, "and that I had been for the past four years insanely apprehensive of his safety." Even after attempts had been made on his life, the president made little effort to protect himself.

On Thursday, April 13, 1865, Lincoln sent Lamon to Union-occupied Richmond. At their final interview before Lamon's departure, the marshal begged the president to take care. The next day, Lincoln accepted an invitation to attend Laura Keene's thousandth performance in *Our American Cousin*. John Wilkes Booth also made a brief and wholly tragic appearance at Ford's Theater that night.

"As God is my judge," Lamon lamented, "I believe if I had been in the city, it would not have happened and had it, I know, that the assassin would not have escaped the town." After Lincoln's assassination, Lamon performed one last duty for his friend. He and his deputies arranged the last rites, taking Lincoln's remains home to Springfield, Illinois, for the funeral. Less than two months later, Lamon resigned as U.S. marshal for the District of Columbia.[6]

FEDERAL COLLAPSE

In the spring of 1861 the federal system of government collapsed. The experiment inaugurated during the steamy Philadelphia summer of 1787 came a cropper as eleven states withdrew from the Union. Faced with the breakdown of federalism, Abraham Lincoln decided to hold the states together as one nation, whatever the cost. The Civil War was fought not over the issue of slavery but over the constitutional question of secession. Lincoln intended to prove the ability of the federal government to sustain itself.

With the seceding southern states went most of the U.S. marshals holding commissions in those states. "I considered that my appointment to be Marshal of this District had terminated when this state seceded," Marshal Benjamin Patteson of Alabama wrote Lincoln on April 1, 1861, "but lest you might not consider it I hereby tender my resignation." Patteson's Southern colleagues also flocked to the Confederacy, their loyalty to region and state overcoming their oath to uphold the Constitution. Marshal William H. H. Tison of Mississippi refused to "hold office under an administration that proposes to degrade the people of fifteen sovereign states to an equality with an inferior and servile race."[7]

The marshals of the western states and territories played a significant role in keeping their districts in the Union. Strong secessionist movements in California, the Arizona and New Mexico territories, and the other western areas threatened the support of those states for the war. Marshal Henry D. Barrows of southern California reported on "an extensive, secret organization" of Confederate sympathizers—or Seceshes, as they were called—as early as September 1861. "Treason is rampant here in Southern California . . . we have bold daring Secessionists who are plotting in secret; our Sheriff and nearly all our county officers just elected disavow all allegiance to our Government and say that Jeff Davis' government is the only Constitutional government! And there *must be collision.*" Seven months later, in April 1862, Barrows complained that the situation in Los Angeles was so bad, "though the valley by nature is one of the pleasantest spots to live in the world, it is no place for a *loyal* American Citizen!"[8]

Within the border states the problem of secessionists was even more pronounced. Early in the war, Confederate sympathizers in Maryland destroyed railroad bridges and rioted when Union troops passed by train through Baltimore. The government, acting principally through the military, responded with mass arrests, including the imprisonment of Baltimore's mayor and police commissioner. The U.S. attorney in St. Louis complained that the governor and a substantial number of citizens were supporting the insurrection. He indicted all of them for treason.[9]

In other border areas an active trade with the Confederates kept the rebels supplied with Northern manufactured goods and arms. Colonel John N. Foster, the commander of Union forces stationed along the

Kentucky side of the Ohio River, suspected that the rebels were receiving equipment and clothing from disloyal merchants in Evansville, Indiana. Unable to prove his suspicions, Foster hired a detective named Coffin to work undercover. Coffin posed as a Secesh and let it be known that he wanted to buy supplies for the rebels. After a few weeks he learned that the firm of L. Lowenthal and Company was actively engaged in smuggling. To prove his case, Coffin purchased a supply of coats and pants from the company and openly announced to the merchants that he intended to ship the clothing to Confederate forces in Uniontown. The company volunteered to arrange the shipment.

Coffin's investigation provided U.S. Attorney John Hanna with sufficient evidence to swear out arrest warrants for the owners and employees of the firm. Marshal David G. Rose made the arrests in early April 1863. Because the company's assets had been used in support of the rebels, Rose also confiscated the firm's inventory and supplies. The seizure took more than a week to complete. But for every company and traitor the marshals stopped, dozens more offered supplies, weapons, and hope to the Confederates.[10]

ARREST OF TRAITORS AND SUSPENSION OF HABEAS CORPUS

The marshals had two main duties related to the war effort. They arrested traitors and Confederate sympathizers, and they confiscated property used to support the rebellion. The arrests were often made without benefit of court order or even court proceedings, but at the request of local military commanders. Nor was the right of habeas corpus – the right of the accused to hear in open court the charges against him – extended to the prisoners. Both the arrests and the confiscation of property infringed on the civil rights of the citizenry; both were opposed by state and local authorities and on occasion by the federal judiciary. Yet, from the administration's point of view, the Civil War excused the trespasses. Lincoln defended his suspension of habeas corpus by asking Congress, "Are all the laws *but one* to go unexecuted and the Government itself to go to pieces lest that one be violated?"[11]

The major problem for the marshals during the war resulted from Lincoln's determination that preserving the Union required him to ignore portions of the Constitution. According to Marshal Lamon,

Lincoln believed his highest duty "was to suspend the technicalities of law and if need be, to totally disregard all law on the statute book if necessary to preserve the life of the nation." In order to defend the Constitution, Lincoln, his marshals, and his district attorneys effectively disregarded it.[12]

In the spring of 1861 Lincoln suspended the right of habeas corpus for traitors, Southern sympathizers, and active opponents of the war in selected areas of the Union. Lincoln's decision meant that people arrested for helping the South or interfering with the North's war effort could be held in prison indefinitely. Furthermore, when they were finally brought to trial, they went before military court-martials, not civilian courts. Lincoln's decision also meant that the marshals who conducted the arrests did so in response to orders from the military, not process issued by the federal courts.

Although the Constitution provided for the suspension of habeas corpus during an insurrection, it required the consent of Congress. Lincoln, however, based his action on his power as commander in chief and at first did not seek congressional approval or concurrence. The original areas covered by the orders to deny habeas corpus were those of military importance. It was not long, however, before Lincoln expanded his orders to all of the Union.

Attorney General Edward Bates advised his subordinates to proceed quietly. He wanted to avoid any official announcements that the right of habeas corpus would no longer be respected. "Words and phrases are often more influential than facts and things," Bates believed. "Men are apt to object more strenuously to the 'suspension of the writ of *habeas corpus*' than to actual imprisonment." Bates hoped that the presence of the army would dissuade those arrested from protesting, provided that no government official publicly proclaimed that habeas corpus had been suspended.[13]

In May 1861, General George Cadwallader, the commander of Fort McHenry, Maryland, ordered the arrest of John Merryman for treason and aiding the enemy. From his military prison, Merryman petitioned for a writ of habeas corpus to the chief justice of the Supreme Court, Roger B. Taney, whose circuit encompassed Maryland. Taney granted the writ, setting May 27 as the day for the hearing.

Neither Merryman nor General Cadwallader appeared at the appointed time. Instead, Cadwallader sent a message explaining his actions and the president's decree. The chief justice then ordered Marshal

Washington Bonifant to bring the general before the Court the next day. Bonifant went to Fort McHenry, but the soldiers on guard refused to admit him. Returning to Taney, the marshal reported that "there was no answer to that writ."

Chief Justice Taney believed that the marshal had the legal authority to summon a posse to arrest General Cadwallader and bring him before the Court. Taney also realized that Cadwallader's troops would resist Bonifant. Thus Taney's only recourse was to write his opinion. He filed a copy with the Court clerk and sent another copy directly to President Lincoln. Powerless to enforce his own decisions, he hoped that his words would command a presidential response.

Taney held that Lincoln acted unconstitutionally in suspending habeas corpus. Furthermore, Taney believed that the military could not arrest civilians unless the soldiers were acting under orders of a civilian court or were prepared to turn over the prisoner immediately to the U.S. marshal. In concluding his emasculated opinion, Taney called on the president to enforce the laws, particularly the process Taney had issued in the case. "This is all this court has now the power to do," Taney wrote.[14]

Taney's opinion seriously embarrassed Lincoln and his advisers. Southern sympathizers and Northern opponents of the war praised Taney as a partisan of civil liberties standing alone against military tyranny. Taney's opinion exacerbated the delicate situation in Maryland, a border state yet undecided in its commitment to the Union. According to Marshal Lamon, "after due consideration the administration determined upon the arrest of the Chief Justice." Lincoln issued a presidential arrest warrant for Taney, but "then arose the question of service." Who should make the arrest, and where should Taney be imprisoned?

"It was finally determined," Lamon remembered, "to place the order of arrest in the hands of the United States Marshal for the District of Columbia." Lincoln himself handed the warrant to his friend, instructing the marshal to "use his own discretion about making the arrest unless he should receive further orders." Lamon, availing himself of this discretionary power, decided not to arrest Chief Justice Taney. Lincoln never insisted that Lamon serve the warrant. Taney was thus spared the embarrassment of imprisonment, the country was saved from an additional constitutional crisis, and Lamon neatly avoided embroiling himself and the president in another controversy.[15]

The suspension of habeas corpus continued. In September 1862, Lincoln publicly proclaimed that traitors, Southern sympathizers, and active opponents of the war would be tried by military court-martials. Several months later, in March 1863, Congress upheld Lincoln's proclamation by statutorily granting him the authority to ignore an accused's right of habeas corpus throughout the country. The federal courts remained impotent to challenge those moves by the other two branches of government.

The military carried the burden of the war, including dealing with spies and traitors. Nevertheless, the Lincoln administration relied on its U.S. marshals and attorneys to assist in the effort. Shortly after it became clear that hostilities would be necessary, Attorney General Bates ordered the U.S. attorneys throughout the loyal states to investigate any telegrams in their districts that might "have been sent with purposes hostile to this Government, or in relation to supplies of arms and provisions purchased or forwarded to the Southern rebels." Several months later, Bates ordered Marshal Earl Bill of Ohio to cooperate with his colleagues in neighboring districts to stop all communications "between northern cities and the revolted States." The only purpose for such communications, Bates thought, was to injure the Union.[16]

Bates also urged the marshals and attorneys to move quickly and forcefully against traitors. "I would not advise the prosecution of doubtful cases," Bates told Marshal David L. Phillips of southern Illinois, "but where the proof is plain I think you ought to use the promptest action." Bates believed, as he explained to U.S. Attorney Asa S. Jones of Missouri, that "an excellent moral effect may be produced by the prosecution of some of the most 'pestilent fellows' among us." However, the attorney general worried about the effects of the government's losing a treason case, particularly in the border states. "Better let twenty of the guilty go free of public accusation," he advised Jones, "than to be defeated in a single case." Nor would it be wise to institute a large number of treason cases, as that would create a public impression of government persecution of individual civilians.[17]

Instead, Bates recommended that the best cases be tried for treason, the weaker ones for conspiracy, interfering with the mails, and other lesser charges. "A few convictions for that sort of crime," he wrote Jones, "I think would help the cause, by rubbing off the varnish from romantic treason and shewing the criminals in the homely garb of vulgar felony." Bates's concern reflected the dissension that plagued the north throughout the war. Not only were there traitors, but there were also many people who shied from committing treasonous acts but sympathized with the traitors.[18]

The reaction of the state authorities to the arrest of traitors and opponents of the war added further proof of the shallowness of the support for the war. In August 1862, Marshal Benajah Deacon of New Jersey, acting under orders issued by the War Department, arrested Jonathan P. Coddington and Charles W. Poor. Both men had been active in preventing enlistments in the Union army. On August 25, for example, Coddington and Poor "had violently disturbed a meeting held . . . to encourage enlistments." Deacon turned his prisoners over to Major L. C. Turner, the judge advocate of the local troops. Turner held the prisoners about four days, then released them.[19]

In April 1863, Coddington and Poor obtained an indictment from the Court of Oyer and Terminer of Hunterdon County against Deacon for kidnapping. U.S. Attorney A. Q. Keasbey considered appealing to the state supreme court for a dismissal of the charges. Attorney General Bates strongly urged against it because that would be an appeal "to the authority of the *State* Judiciary to enforce a national law, and that might open up anew the old vexed question between different schools of lego-politicians." Furthermore, Bates added, "the State Court might, in fact, refuse, after we had, in some sort, committed ourselves to its jurisdiction, by appealing to its power." Acting under authority of a recently passed law, Keasbey managed to transfer the case to the U.S. circuit court.[20]

Other states also entertained suits against marshals for enforcing federal orders. The Circuit Court of Edgar County, Illinois, indicted Marshal David L. Phillips for kidnapping and criminal trespass after he arrested three accused traitors in the summer of 1863. Because the marshal was acting under instructions from the secretary of war, President Lincoln authorized spending the money necessary to defend Phillips. In California a Confederate sympathizer whom Marshal Henry D. Barrows had arrested claimed false imprisonment and sued Barrows for $15,000.[21]

Indictments and other court actions against the marshals remained irritants and interferences. They showed once again that the power of the federal government, though strong, was not absolute. It was fruitless to expect that individuals would easily surrender their rights, even in time of insurrection. Nor could the administration justifiably hope that the local courts would side with it, even in the midst of civil war.

CIVIL WAR CONFISCATIONS

In the summer of 1861, Congress approved another radical action. It passed, and the president signed, two acts providing for the confiscation of property used to support or aid the Confederacy. The acts of July 13 and August 6, 1861, empowered the U.S. marshals, working with the U.S. attorneys, to carry out the confiscations. A year later, in an act of July 17, 1862, Congress further delineated the power of the federal government, acting through its marshals, to seize Confederate property.

Attorney General Bates expected the marshals to do all they could "to repress treasonable purposes and to protect the interests of the Government." Confiscations occurred whenever the marshal or attorney had reason to believe "that property of rebels is used or intended to be used for their benefit or is in transfer to them within any part of the territory held by the rebels." Property sold for cash was also liable for confiscation if the cash was used to aid the South.[22]

Under the confiscation acts, the U.S. attorney filed the libel against the property with the marshal, who then made the seizure. In practice, the marshals took physical possession of personal property only. With real property, they seized "all the right, title, interest, and estate," simply giving notice to whoever lived on the property that a seizure had been made. Intangible property such as stocks and bonds was considered seized when the marshal described the property in his return. The courts then decided how to gain possession of the assets.

Once the marshal confiscated the property, the case went before the federal courts. According to Bates, confiscation could be effected "only by judicial proceedings, in the Civil Courts." The military was not supposed to confiscate property. However, in practice, military commanders frequently ordered property confiscated.[23]

Not surprisingly, some marshals had trouble with the rather broad authority bestowed on them by the confiscation acts. The marshal for the eastern district of Virginia (essentially the city of Alexandria) was dismissed by Lincoln because of his abuse of the law. Ordered to seize the title to real property in Alexandria, Marshal James T. Close went well beyond his instructions by actually taking possession of the houses and evicting the tenants. According to Bates, Close "was removed from office, partly (and mainly) because he seized and persisted in holding, real estate (ostensibly under proceedings for confiscation) contrary to law and to my instructions." The marshals could take possession of only the title to real property, not the property itself. With the marshal holding the title, the rebel owners were prevented from selling. Because real property could not be moved, its use was thereby denied to the Confederacy. That alone was the purpose of the law.[24]

Confiscations continued for a brief time after Lee's surrender on April 9, 1865. By the end of 1865, however, Attorney General James Speed was discouraging seizures. "It is not the wish and purpose of the Government to persecute by confiscation persons who are obedient to the law, or promise to be so in good faith in the future," Speed advised one U.S. attorney in May 1866, "but persons known to you to be contumacious and still cherishing rebellious feelings may be regarded as exceptions to this rule." President Johnson's Christmas 1868 pardon of the Confederates stripped the government of its power to confiscate, because the pardon wiped away the sins of all the rebels. By that time the marshals had their hands full with other problems.[25]

FEDERALISM IN RETREAT

For the marshals and their deputies, Lee's surrender at Appomattox Courthouse signaled not the end of the Civil War but the beginning of their violent conflict with southerners. The federal government, having overcome Confederate armies, now faced the prospect of establishing its authority once again over the southern people. At the same time, the government found itself with millions of new citizens—black citizens—to defend. After passing a series of novel civil rights laws, Congress turned to the marshals and district attorneys to uphold federal authority in the South and to protect the newly freed slaves from their former owners.

The South was defeated, but its people remained undaunted. Returning from the war, the Confederate soldiers watched in despair as their former slaves tried openly to enjoy the full rights of citizenship. Blacks won election to city, county, and state offices, including state legislatures. Freedmen opened businesses, took over farms, and acted in countless other ways like free American citizens. To combat these radical, unbelievable changes, many former Confederate soldiers turned to secrecy and terror to protect their former way of life.

One December evening in 1865 a handful of Confederate veterans in Pulaski, Tennessee, started a new social club to stave off the winter boredom. They humorously dubbed it the Ku Klux Klan and gave it a complicated, almost meaningless organizational structure. Regular members were called ghouls; their officers were called genies, hydras, and turks. A structure of dens, provinces, dominions, and realms eventually formed the Klan empire.

Having had their fun creating the new fraternity, the founders soon discovered that their secret organization could be used to frighten the freed slaves and keep them in line. Klan members donned disguises—robes and hoods mimicking Halloween ghosts—and rode at night into the black communities around Pulaski. Whether the freedmen were more afraid of the ghostly appearance of the night riders or of the very real appearance of their weapons was a moot point.

The Klan and similar organizations sharing the same purpose spread rapidly throughout the South. They were known by different names—the White League, the Knights of the White Camellia, the Georgia Army, the Sons of Midnight, Pale Faces, and the White Brotherhood among them—in different states. Each group was committed to terrorizing the black community, thereby frightening any freedman who boldly chose to exercise his rights of citizenship. Marshal William H. Smythe of Georgia observed in August 1871 a "determination . . . to prevent the colored population from acquiring either knowledge or property and to either kill them, or run out all who have obtained either."[26]

Originally, President Andrew Johnson, who showed little concern with the plight of freedmen, tried to reincorporate the South into the Union through a policy of leniency and forgiveness. The policy failed for two reasons. First, southerners took advantage of Johnson's generosity, flaunting their disregard of northern expectations that the newly freed blacks would be protected. Second, the Radical Republicans who dominated Congress wanted the South punished and the freedmen protected. They passed, over Johnson's veto, three constitutional amendments and a series of enforcement acts granting citizenship and civil rights to freedmen.

Together, the new laws introduced a new concept of federalism. For the first time, Congress proposed a direct relationship between the federal government and the individual citizen. It proposed using the full extent of federal power to protect the rights of citizens from any infringements upon those rights by the states or other individuals – a radical, almost revolutionary departure from the traditional role of the federal government envisioned by the nation's founders and followed by their successors.

The Thirteenth Amendment outlawed slavery. The Civil Rights Act of 1866 extended to blacks the full range of civil rights enjoyed by U.S. citizens, including the right to vote, to enter into contracts, to sue, to give evidence, and to inherit, buy, rent, or otherwise convey real and personal property. Concerned that the act would be attacked in the courts, Congress subsequently passed the Fourteenth Amendment, defining U.S. citizenship for the first time and prohibiting the states from denying the rights of citizenship to anyone. The Fifteenth Amendment prohibited the states from abridging the right to vote on the basis of "race, color, or previous condition of servitude."

The South, relying on President Johnson's support, refused to bow before this congressional interference with its way of life. The former Confederate states voted against ratification of the Fourteenth Amendment until Congress made approval a precondition of readmittance into the Union. Johnson refused to exert much energy supporting the new laws. Attorney General Henry Stanbery, for instance, asserted on January 21, 1867, that no violations of the April 1866 Civil Rights Act had been reported to his office. The lack of reported violations reflected the laxity of the early efforts to enforce the act, not the willingness of the South to accept the freedmen as citizens.[27]

As a result of Johnson's opposition to the congressional defense of the freedmen, the early years of southern Reconstruction were absorbed in an intense power struggle between the president and Congress. Johnson pardoned individual southerners to protect them from prosection for treason and other crimes. Congress used its legislative authority to treat the entire southern region harshly. The Confederate states were denied readmittance to the Union until they fulfilled certain criteria, the South was divided into military regions and governed by the Union army, and the freedmen were supported. The president eventually lost his battle with Congress – and almost lost his job when the House of Representatives voted his impeachment. By the election of 1868, which brought General Grant to the White House, Congress had made clear its intention to deal harshly with the defeated Confederacy.

In response, southern whites went underground. Relying on terrorist organizations like the Klan, former Confederates attacked the freedmen at night, dragging them from their beds for whippings and hangings. The battle was both racist and political, for the Klan and its associated groups chose their victims from among the most politically active blacks. In general during the post–Civil War period, southern Democrats were whites, and southern Republicans were blacks, carpetbaggers (migrated northerners), and scalawags (traitorous southerners).

By 1871 white southerners had regained political control in Georgia, North Carolina, Tennessee, and Virginia. The Klan-style tactics of midnight attacks and terrorism had contributed to the victory. Whites in the remaining southern states continued the struggle to win back their homeland from the alleged graft and corruption of ignorant black legislators who were presumably manipulated by greedy and unscrupulous white northerners. Southern racism even denied the freedmen the intelligence to be dishonest by themselves.

It was a bloody power struggle. Elections became hunting seasons against politically active blacks. Voting became a statement of courage for freedmen, and running for office became foolhardy. A lengthy investigation of the Klan and its related organizations persuaded Congress to deal harshly with such groups. The Radical Republicans provided complete legislative authority to protect the freedmen by passing three Ku Klux Klan, or force, acts in 1870 and 1871.

The Klan acts prohibited individuals or states from abridging a citizen's rights to vote and to have due process of law. The new laws put elections for members of the House of Representatives–all national elections–under federal control. Henceforth, U.S. marshals and their deputies would ensure the right to vote by supervising each polling place in every large city across the country. Congress also enumerated a lengthy list of new federal crimes associated with Klan-type acts of terror, such as midnights attacks, the wearing of masks or disguises, and attacks on citizens because of their race, color, or previous condition of servitude. Violators of the laws would be tried in federal court. The laws also allowed the president to establish martial law and suspend the right of habeas corpus whenever unlawful combinations became too numerous.

The Klan acts were clearly aimed at the actions of individuals. They represented a step beyond the traditional spheres of authority between the federal government and the states. The national government had never made such a wholesale effort to protect individuals. The theory of federalism depended on the states' guarding their own citizens. Now Congress announced its intention of using the power of the federal government to ensure that the freedmen exercised their newly obtained rights without hindrance from anyone or any other authority. In the late 1860s that was a radical announcement.

The marshals were committed to the task. Marshal J. H. Pierce of Mississippi expressed the view of many of his colleagues in July 1871. "My heart," he proclaimed, "is enlisted in the cause of putting down lawlessness and restoring order by enforcing the laws that every man, even the most humble citizen of the land, may feel that his life and property are safe, and that he can express his loyalty and give his support to the gov't and its officers without fear of being deprived of his life." U.S. Attorney R. M. P. Smith of Tennessee wrote the attorney general about the need to "strike all possible terror into the midnight marauders who outrage the defenseless colored people." Prosecuting as many Klansmen as possible seemed to Smith the best way to achieve this goal.[28]

During the period of Radical Reconstruction, from the late 1860s to 1877, the marshals and deputies arrested more than 7,000 southerners for violations of the civil rights laws. In May 1871, for example, Marshal Pierce had 20 warrants against Mississippi Klansmen. The following month the grand jury indicted an additional 200 men for violating the Klan acts. U.S. Attorney D. H. Starbuck of North Carolina reported in February 1872 that he had 981 Klansmen under indictment "for conspiracies to commit deeds of violence or terror." Starbuck's evidence disclosed "the horrid facts of the taking of fathers, sons, and brothers from the bosom of their families at the hour of midnight and the infliction upon their naked flesh the torture of the lash." Deputy marshals in Alabama arrested 42 Klansmen in one day, including the sheriff of Sumter County. Eight more Klansmen surrendered the next day.[29]

The marshals could not have made these mass arrests without the help of the army. The Alabama deputies were backed up by the infantry when they went to arrest the 42 Klansmen in Sumter County. When District Attorney G. Wiley Welles of Mississippi reported "a perfect reign of terror" in Lee and Union counties, Attorney General George H. Williams arranged for two companies of cavalry to be sent there. In

February 1873, Marshal Robert W. Healy of Alabama used army troops to help arrest "upwards of one hundred of the most prominent actors in the Ku Klux outrages."[30]

Troops were stationed throughout the South to support the marshals in enforcing the law. They provided the lawmen a loyal and trained posse, something the marshals could count on from no other source. As Marshal William H. Smythe of Georgia pointed out, the use of the troops meant that "though there be few Marshals, they still have a sufficient force at their call to execute the process of the United States Courts." By September 1874 the marshals' reliance on the military had become so extensive that Attorney General Williams suggested they appoint "prudent and fearless" deputies near the places where the troops were quartered so the deputies would be available to lead the army when making arrests.[31]

"It cannot be denied," Marshal R. M. Wallace told Williams in 1872, "that there is a deep seated feeling of animosity throughout the South against the general government and particularly against the republican party." The marshals personified for southerners both the federal government and the Republican party.[32]

In Mississippi, Deputy C. H. Wisler was killed in November 1871 during a trial of Klansmen he had arrested. Less than a year later, Deputy Mitchel in South Carolina was murdered while enforcing the new civil rights laws. Deputy Burns of North Carolina was shot in the back in April 1874. When Deputy William O. Hildreth went to arrest three men in east Tennessee "for going in disguise, and whipping a collored school teacher," he too was murdered. A month later, Deputy James P. Everett of middle Tennessee was shot twice in the back of the head and once in the hand. The killers then destroyed all the arrest warrants Everett carried in his saddlebags.[33]

Other deputies were arrested by state authorities when they tried to serve process. "Every person who has acted as a United States deputy marshal and aided in the arrest of Ku Klux have been either imprisoned or are now under indictment," U.S. Attorney Welles of Mississippi wrote in September 1871. He believed the state authorities were conspiring against the deputies to keep them from arresting Klansmen and others who attacked freedmen.[34]

Originally, the Grant administration urged the marshals and district attorneys to vigilantly enforce the new civil rights laws. Attorney General Amos T. Akerman issued a circular letter in July 1871 calling on all marshals and district attorneys to use "all possible vigilance and energy" in enforcing the May 1871 Enforcement Act outlawing the Ku Klux Klan. Akerman even promised the deputies that they would be defended from arrest by the states. All he asked was for the deputies to perform their duties "in a decent and gentlemanly manner." When the number of cases against the Klan in Alabama reached toward a thousand, Akerman defended the work of his marshals and attorneys. "The Government in these matters is not vindictive, and wishes to worry no citizen unnecessarily, but it expects from all its officers the most energetic efforts to bring these marauders to justice."[35]

Despite the earnest, almost desperate efforts by U.S. marshals and attorneys to defend the freedmen, the Grant administration could not sustain the determination to protect individuals and individual rights. That job had always fallen to the states, not to the federal government. The administration, particularly the attorneys general, became increasingly uncomfortable. Neither Attorney General Akerman nor his successor, George H. Williams, could support a consistent effort by federal officials to defend the rights of the freedmen. They adopted instead a haphazard policy of responding to individual cases of southern outrages while holding back from a general policy of support for individual rights.

Federalism faltered.

Even the clear evidence of southern violence against blacks could not bring Akerman to accept federal responsibility for defending the freedmen. "I have every personal sympathy with you and those situated like you in this matter and have every disposition to enforce the law which is applicable to the case," he wrote one freedman in January 1872. "But the theory of our Government is this, that the State as a general rule shall be charged with the redress of personal wrongs." Although the Civil Rights Act protected citizens against discrimination on the basis of color or previous condition, proving such discrimination as a motive was, in Akerman's view, too difficult. He believed that such cases were best left to the states and local authorities.[36]

Attorney General Williams was hardly bolder. By late 1872 President Grant and Williams had abandoned the marshals and attorneys who were on the front lines in the war with the Klan. On the basis of scattered, overoptimistic reports of fewer Klan outrages, Williams peremptorily declared a cease-fire. U.S. Attorney D. Y. Corbin of South Carolina, for example, reported in the fall of 1872 that he had indictments outstanding against one thousand Klansmen, but he decided not to prosecute all the cases because "the Ku Klux Klan as an organization is substantially broken up, and hence a war upon it now is unnecessary for its destruction." While other districts, such as northern Mississippi, implored Williams to send military assistance to help stamp out the Klan, the attorney general embraced Corbin's optimistic – and unfounded – conclusion.[37]

In July 1873, Williams issued instructions to all the district attorneys in the South to suspend their prosecutions of the Klan. He and President Grant believed "that the Ku Klux Klan have, through [past] convictions, been almost if not altogether broken up, and that those who were concerned in, or sympathized with them have come to see the folly, wickedness, and danger of such organizations." They hoped executive clemency toward the Klansmen would "remove many causes of uneasiness and irritation now existing and conduce generally to the public peace and tranquility." Thenceforth, Williams proclaimed, only the worst cases of Klan violence would be prosecuted.[38]

The decision was premature. It had little to do with southern reality. The election of 1872 resulted in increased turmoil and violence in many districts, which culminated in the Colfax courthouse massacre in Grant Parish, Louisiana, shortly after the election. A band of white Louisianans attacked a group of blacks who were claiming victory in the election. Trapping the freedmen in the courthouse, the whites maintained a murderous rifle fire. The blacks were also armed, but they made a poor showing in the battle. By the end of the fight, between sixty-nine and one hundred blacks lay dead. Twenty blacks were taken prisoner, and that night they too were shot. The white attackers suffered few casualties.

Louisiana U.S. Attorney J. R. Beckwith wrote of the Colfax tragedy that "it has never been my fortune to be connected with the prosecution of crime so revolting and horrible in the details of its perpetration and so burdened with atrocity and barbarity." The federal grand jury issued seventy-two indictments against white Democrats for the slaughter of the black Republicans. Attorney General Williams turned down Beckwith's request for soldiers to aid Marshal Stephen B. Packard in making the arrests. Packard, fearing that "an organized resistance to arrest is probable," drew upon Louisiana governor William P. Kellogg for state militia troops. Kellogg asked Williams to obtain rations and supplies for those men from the War Department, though it is doubtful that the Grant administration complied.[39]

After a year's work and investigation, Packard arrested nine of the seventy-two men indicted. The defendants were charged with conspiring to deny the murdered blacks their civil rights. The first trial ended in a hung jury. During the second trial the defendants found a friend in U.S. Supreme Court justice Joseph P. Bradley, who sat for part of the trial with Judge W. B. Woods to compose the circuit court. Four of the nine accused were finally convicted. "The difficulty in convicting the persons participating in the Colfax massacre is indicative of the inadequacy of the courts to make law respected," U.S. Attorney Beckwith aptly concluded. The guilty defendants appealed their convictions to the Supreme Court. The style of the case carried the name of one of the defendants, William B. Cruikshank.[40]

While *U.S. v. Cruikshank et al.* made its way toward the Supreme Court, conditions in the South remained unsettled. Attorney General Williams remained optimistic that the problems were over. Williams's response to a case in Mississippi in 1873 illustrated the attitude of the administration. The actions of the local federal officials showed the risks they accepted without support from Washington.

Freed from slavery, Henry Bryant took a job as a porter in the Corinth, Mississippi, Hotel. On Sunday night, March 23, 1873, just about the time that Attorney General Williams was announcing the death of the Klan, ten men wearing white robes and crudely made masks arrived at the hotel on horseback. The Klansmen seized Bryant and dragged him outside to the street. Laughing and hooting, their curses against Bryant echoing down the street, the Klansmen beat him about the head with pistols. When Bryant was only barely conscious, the attackers tied a rope around his neck and hauled him up off the ground. He hung there, the weight of his body slowly strangling him, until he was almost dead. Then they cut him down. Leaving Bryant crumpled in the street, the Klansmen rode back into the night.[41]

Bryant fled to Holly Springs and the protection of Marshal J. H. Pierce. Despite the disguises of his assailants, he had recognized most of the men. Accompanied by the marshal and U.S. Attorney Welles, Bryant returned to Corinth to help identify his attackers. Welles prepared charges against them for violating the Ku Klux Klan acts.

When Marshal Pierce arrived in Corinth, he called on his deputy in that city, Dr. R. T. Dunn. For the next several weeks, Pierce, Dunn, and Welles investigated the attack on Bryant. Once they had sufficient evidence, Pierce and Dunn arrested the men whom Bryant identified. The prisoners were taken before the U.S. commissioner, who ordered them bound over until the grand jury could vote indictments against them at its June session. With the trial set for December 1873, Pierce and Welles returned home to Holly Springs. Deputy Dunn remained in Corinth, collecting additional evidence.

Early on the morning of August 8, at least three Klansmen rode into Corinth, pulling their horses to a stop in front of the room let by Deputy Dunn. They barged into Dunn's modest quarters. Taking him by surprise, they shot him.[42]

Attorney General Williams refused to offer a reward for the murderers of Deputy Dunn. Justice Department policy at that time prohibited such rewards, in large part because murder was not a federal offense and therefore not cognizable in U.S. courts. Williams feared that the Dunn case would create a precedent for the federal government to offer monetary rewards. He did, however, urge Marshal Pierce to "take all the means in his power to bring the parties to justice." That meant seeking justice in the Mississippi courts. For cases like this, justice was hard to find there.[43]

As the attack on Henry Bryant showed, Attorney General Williams willingly allowed his marshals and district attorneys to prosecute southerners for individual cases of violence against freedmen, but he refused to offer much help. Nor did he see any pattern in the large number of attacks on blacks. He struggled mightily to maintain the whimsical hope "that the feeling of animosity towards the freedman was passing out of the minds of the southern people." By the fall of 1873, even he was beginning to recognize that such was not the case. He was "pained to learn," he wrote the district attorney in Alabama, "that there still exists . . . such an opposition and that opposition is carried to the extent of depriving the freedmen of the means to support themselves and their families."[44]

Nonetheless, he did not change his instructions to the southern district attorneys to suspend their prosecutions. In March 1874, Williams chided U.S Attorney D. Y. Corbin of South Carolina for disregarding the instructions to stop Klan prosecutions. Corbin, who earlier had dropped charges against a majority of the one thousand Klansmen indicted in his district, defended himself by pointing out that he had asked the marshal to arrest only three men for violations of the Klan laws during the previous ten months.[45]

On April 25, 1874, Williams reiterated his instructions to cease Klan prosecutions. He ordered U.S. Attorney Virgil S. Lusk of North Carolina to drop all cases against individuals for belonging to the Klan, cooperating with it, or committing misdemeanors related to its activities. "The Government has reason to believe that its general intention in prosecuting these offenses in North Carolina hitherto have been accomplished, that the particular disorder has ceased, and that there are good grounds for hoping that it will not return," Williams wrote. "At all events, it affords the Government pleasure to make an experiment based upon these views." By any measure the suppression of the civil rights of blacks was continuing practically unabated throughout the South. Only the U.S. marshals and attorneys, unsupported by Washington, stood between the freedmen and a total denial of their newly granted but hardly used rights as American citizens.[46]

Over the course of a single week in late August 1874, six blacks were killed in Sumter County, Alabama. The next week, blacks returning from church in Lee County were fired upon by white Democrats. The whites followed the freedmen to their homes, where the blacks were "beaten and outraged in person and property." Later that night two of the churches attended by freedmen were burned to the ground. "A fearful reign of terror and death has been inaugurated," U.S. Attorney Nick S. McAfee concluded, ". . . and no man's life is safe who will not curse the Gov't of the United States."[47]

These and similar Klan-style attacks on the freedmen eventually compelled Williams to see the situation in the South as it actually was. On September 3, 1874, he unshackled his marshals and district attorneys. "Outrages of various descriptions, and in some cases atrocious murders," he wrote in a circular letter to the U.S. marshals and attorneys throughout the South, "have been committed in your district by bodies of armed men, sometimes in disguise and with the view it is believed of overawing and intimidating peaceable and law abiding citizens and depriving them of the rights guaranteed to them by the Constitution and laws of the United States." The Ku Klux Klan laws passed by Congress made "these deeds of violence and blood offenses within the jurisdiction of the General Government." Williams ordered the marshals and district attorneys "to detect, expose, arrest, and punish the perpetrators of these crimes." For this purpose, federal officials were to spare no effort or unnecessary expenses. Furthermore, U.S. troops would be at the call of the marshals to aid them in making the arrests.[48]

Despite Williams's attempt to reinvigorate the enforcement acts, the Supreme Court eventually struck them down. When the Louisiana *Cruikshank* case came before the Court in 1876, the Court found the most important portions of the Klan acts unconstitutional. The Court denied the federal government the power to protect the individual rights of citizens from the actions of other citizens. Because the Colfax courthouse massacre had been committed by private citizens, the United States could take no action against the perpetrators. The states must take up the prosecutions of such crimes. Furthermore, the Court declared, the government had not proven that the murders of the freedmen resulted from their "race, color, or previous condition of servitude." It seemed a mere coincidence, unfortunate to be sure, that the Colfax dead were all black and all former slaves. In effect, the Court told blacks in the South to look to their states for protection. In practice, the freedmen were left to fend for themselves.[49]

The presidential election of 1876 further stranded the blacks. The election resulted in a tie vote in the electoral college, but the returns from Louisiana, Georgia, and Florida were disputed. Republican candidate Rutherford B. Hayes agreed to withdraw federal troops from all the southern states in exchange for the votes of those states in the electoral college. Hayes won the election, one of many elections paid for in the currency of black rights.

The new president appointed former U.S. Marshal Charles Devens as his attorney general. As a sop to the few remaining Radical Republicans in Congress, Hayes appointed the famed black abolitionist and black activist Frederick Douglass as U.S. marshal for the District of Columbia. Then Hayes and Devens supervised the complete desertion of Douglass's cohorts throughout the South. The marshals and district attorneys were completely reined in; their protection of the freedmen was withdrawn.

In July 1877, for example, Devens requested Marshal J. H. Pierce's resignation. The attorney general cited "many accounts" as his reasons, though it was obvious that the marshal's earnest efforts to battle the Mississippi Klan and protect the rights of freedmen had stirred too much opposition against him. Devens made it clear that the request did not reflect a disapproval with Pierce personally. He offered the marshal a clerical position in the Treasury Department with a $1,200 annual salary.[50]

Both Hayes and Devens intended to end Reconstruction. Pierce and the other marshals who had "enlisted" their hearts in the cause of defending freedmen, as Pierce had vowed in 1871, were anachronisms to the new president. They were removed. In addition, Hayes and the new Congress stripped the marshals of their strongest support in the South, the U.S. Army. The appropriation act of June 18, 1878, prohibited the marshals from using any part of the U.S. military as a posse. These actions signaled the South that all was well; it could now solve its own racial problems.

Reconstruction was over. The federal government had faltered in its challenge to state authority. Although Lincoln sustained the power of the national government to hold the Union together, his successors failed to extend that lesson to show that the power of the federal government could uphold the rights of the citizens. In September 1878 a local U.S. postmaster in Tennessee reported that his ferryman, a black, had been attacked by Klansmen and severely whipped. Because the ferryman worked for the postmaster, he too was a federal official, but that status did him no good. U.S. Attorney W. W. Murray decried the crime but refused to prosecute it in federal court. "That a flagrant crime against law and order has been committed there is no doubt and that the parties engaged ought to be punished to the extent of the law is equally clear," Murray sanctimoniously proclaimed to the sympathetic Devens, "but . . . I do not think that the Federal Courts have jurisdiction of the offense committed."[51]

6

FEDERALISM RESURGENT

1866–1896

"Stop that! Stop that!" hollered Deputy Marshal David Neagle.

The deputy jumped from his seat toward David Terry, who had just slapped Supreme Court justice Stephen Field across the back of the head. Terry's right arm was raised to strike again as Field turned in his chair to face his assailant. Neagle leapt between the two men, shielding Field. The deputy, who stood just barely over five feet tall, had thrown himself within easy reach of Terry, who towered well over six feet.

"I am an officer," Neagle said in a commanding voice, loud enough to cause the sixty-odd diners in the Lathrop, California, train station's dining room to pause amid their breakfasts. Neagle had been deputized specifically to protect Field from David Terry and his wife, Sarah Terry. Both of them had repeatedly threatened to kill Field over his decision in a case involving Sarah's honor.

Neagle raised his right arm to shoulder height, palm out, in the universal police gesture of authority, a warning to Terry to keep his distance. His hand reached within six inches of Terry's massive chest. Terry stared at the deputy, recognition chasing desperation across his bearded face. A groan of deep rage escaped his throat. "He looks like an infuriated giant," thought Neagle.

Terry's right hand darted toward his vest under his left arm. Here he habitually carried his bowie knife – the knife he had used to kill David C. Broderick in their famous duel decades before, the same knife he had slashed at Neagle a year earlier. "I believed," the deputy later testified, "if I waited another two seconds I should have been cut to pieces."

With his right arm still outstretched, the left-handed deputy drew his six-shooter from his hip pocket. In one smooth motion, he cocked the hammer with his left thumb as his right hand swung over to support the pistol barrel. Using a two-handed aim, Neagle fired twice in rapid succession. "I knew it was life or death with me," he remembered, "and I wanted to be sure." The first bullet punctured Terry's heart, the second clipped his right ear as he slipped to the restaurant floor.

It was the morning of August 14, 1889, the centennial year of the United States marshals.

The diners panicked at the sound of the gunfire. Some rushed from the room; others ran toward Neagle. The deputy backed to the wall. He waved the pistol in front of him, its still-smoking barrel pointed at the ground. "Keep away," he warned the diners. "I am a United States marshal in the discharge of my duties." The crowd backed off. Seeing Justice Field, who had moved a few tables away, Neagle went over to him. "I guess we had better go in the car, Judge," the deputy said as he took the lame justice's arm. They walked slowly down the aisle formed by the rows of tables.

Neagle kept a constant watch as he and Field crossed the Lathrop station platform and boarded their Pullman car. He expected Sarah Terry to appear at any moment. After making sure that Field was comfortably seated in their room, Neagle went to each end of the railcar to warn the porters to keep Mrs. Terry from boarding. "I do not want to be compelled to hurt any woman," he told them.

Just before the shooting, Mrs. Terry had entered the dining room on her husband's arm. When she saw Justice Field sitting down to breakfast, she rushed back to the train to get her pistol, which she hid in her purse. Sarah returned to the dining room shortly after Neagle and Field had left it. She ran to her husband's body. Kneeling beside it, she cried out in anguish as she threw herself across the lifeless form.

Sarah was the first person to touch the body. With her back to the onlookers, she hugged her fallen husband. Her hands patted and moved about his still body, the final gestures of a loving wife. After a few minutes, she recovered her composure. Marching out to the station platform, she called on the other passengers to seize the murderer, to take vengeance on her fallen husband.

No bowie knife was found on David Terry's body.

Inside the train, Neagle pulled down the curtains on all the windows on the station side. Then he paced the hallway of the car. Outside, he heard a woman's voice, though the words were indistinguishable. Peeking through a curtain, he saw Mrs. Terry amid an excited crowd milling about the platform. She appeared to be haranguing the onlookers.

Sometime later, Sheriff Purvis of neighboring Stanislaus County entered the car. Neagle took him to Field's room. The three men discussed the shooting. A few minutes later, they were interrupted by Constable Walker of Lathrop township. Walker announced that he had come to arrest Neagle.

Justice Field advised Neagle to ignore the constable and to proceed on to San Francisco with Field. In the justice's view, Neagle was an officer of the federal government. Attorney General William H. H. Miller had authorized Neagle to protect Field because, for quite some time, Field had been threatened by the Terrys. The shooting had been in the line of duty.

"No, Judge," Neagle told him, nodding toward Walker, "this man is an officer, and I am willing to go with him." With that, he handed the constable his pistol. It was still warm.

Walker took Neagle off the train on the side opposite to the station. The constable wanted to avoid the crowd, so the two men walked south to nearby Tracy. When they arrived, Walker hired a buggy. Skirting Lathrop, he took his prisoner north to Stockton. Sheriff Thomas Cunningham of San Joaquin County booked Neagle into the county jail, locking the deputy in a common cell. The charge was murder.[1]

IN RE NEAGLE

Neagle's arrest culminated a long-running dispute between the federal government and the individual states concerning the power of the central government to enforce its laws through its own officials. The states frequently challenged U.S. marshals and deputies who attempted to enforce particular, and particularly unpopular, federal laws and court orders. The issue became especially acute in the North over the Fugitive Slave Law just before the Civil War and in the South over the civil rights laws and revenue laws taxing whiskey just after the war.

By arresting marshals, the states could deny federal power and disrupt federal laws. Each arrest chipped away at the structure of federalism. In September 1877, after white southern Democrats had regained political control of the South, Marshal Robert M. Wallace of South Carolina identified the heart of the problem facing federal officials. "One of the most serious difficulties with which we have to contend is the universal hostility of the democratic state officials," Wallace informed Attorney General Charles Devens. "They throw every possible obstacle in our way."[2]

Before the Civil War many federal lawyers, including most attorneys general, questioned the federal government's ability to protect its marshals from the authority of the states. For many years deputies who suffered arrest and imprisonment were essentially left on their own; the federal government offered them little help—or much solace—in challenges with the states. The theory seemed to be that the states would recognize the innocence of the marshals if they were in fact innocent. If they were guilty, of course, then the marshals deserved to suffer whatever punishment the state courts determined appropriate. The federal government expected the individual marshals and deputies to prove their own innocence, often at their own expense. Unfortunately for the marshals, the states frequently used the arrests as challenges to federal authority. If the state officials opposed a federal law, they arrested those who enforced it.

The contemporary theory of federalism failed the marshals. The attorneys general of the time could not bring themselves to the conclusion that the federal government could legitimately interfere in controversies between the states and individual marshals, even in controversies resulting from official acts of the marshal. The theories that guided the government's lawyers had no provision for such a view.

Occasionally the federal government did step in to shield marshals from the wrath of the states. Several of the northern states arrested deputy marshals for kidnapping or assault when the deputies enforced the Fugitive Slave Law by arresting runaway slaves. When deputies were arrested, the local U.S. attorney often stepped into the melee, usually filing for a writ of habeas corpus to take the case into federal court, where the judge could dismiss the charges.

Yet the Fugitive Slave Law itself represented a significant change in the relationship between the federal government and a segment of its citizenry. The law assured one class of property owners the return of lost property. That assurance represented a dramatic involvement in the lives of the citizens, not only the property owners but also those who helped the property get lost. Protecting the marshals seemed little enough to do under the circumstances.

The Civil War redefined the relationship between the federal government and the states, affirming the supremacy of the federal government in its sphere of authority. But the war failed to define the separate spheres, leaving it for later generations to mark out the boundaries. The postwar attorneys general, emboldened by the war's exertion of federal authority, offered more support to marshals who were challenged by the states. In cases that cropped up after the war, the attorney general usually authorized the local U.S. attorney or his assistants to appear in defense of the accused marshal.

Customarily, the district attorney obtained a writ of habeas corpus, transferring the case to federal circuit court. Then the issue focused on whether the marshal was acting in the line of duty and whether the actions in dispute were appropriate to the marshal's authority. If the judge decided affirmatively, the case was dismissed and the marshal freed. If the judge decided negatively, the marshal was left on his own to face the judgment of the state.

Federal judges often matched the attorney general's meekness in challenging state interference with federal authority. In July 1874, Deputy Marshal Alexander Mattison of South Carolina, who held a joint commission as a special deputy collector of the Internal Revenue, arrested two men for hauling illicit whiskey. When one of the prisoners resisted, Mattison shot him. The deputy was arrested by the local sheriff for killing the prisoner. Denied bail and held over for trial, Mattison applied to the federal judge for a writ of habeas corpus.

The judge granted the writ, and the sheriff handed Mattison over to U.S. Marshal Robert M. Wallace, the marshal under whom Mattison was working when the shooting took place. Following the orders of the court, Wallace lodged his deputy securely in the Columbia jail. There Mattison languished for more than six months while the federal judge fretted over his authority to release the deputy. Despite pleadings from U.S. Attorney D. Y. Corbin, the judge would not even let Mattison out on bail. If he had no authority to dismiss the case, the judge asserted, he probably had no authority to set bail. The question of bail could not be answered until the original, and more pressing, issue was resolved.

By the end of the year, Mattison decided to take his chances with the state court. Frustrated with the spineless, unsympathetic judge, he understood that the federal government had failed him. "I would prefer to have the case remanded back to the state court," he wrote Attorney General George H. Williams on December 28, 1874. "I would much prefer that some one else be the victim of a test-case." Although Mattison was eventually released, his case illustrated the problems facing all the marshals. What deputy could afford a six-month incarceration during which he earned no money.[3]

Congress responded to the arrests by offering very limited immunity from state prosecutions for the enforcement of specific federal laws. The Civil Rights Law of 1865 immunized the marshals from arrest for actions taken by them to uphold the provisions of the enforcement laws. However, as the government's support of those laws dramatically fell off during the mid-1870s, the protection was less needed. State interference continued, but only when the marshals enforced other federal laws, particularly the tax laws.

During the 1870s large numbers of deputies and revenuers were arrested by state authorities when they tried to enforce the federal revenue laws on whiskey. Deputy George W. Stoval was charged with murder after a battle with Tennessee moonshiners in May 1876. Marshal R. P. Baker of Alabama reported in November 1876 that his deputies were prohibited by state prosecutions from carrying out their duties. "They are harassed and indicted in the State Courts for assault to kill, assault and battery and for carrying concealed weapons, when no offence has been committed or law violated," Baker complained. Two of his deputies had been forced to flee the state to avoid trial on charges of carrying concealed weapons; another had been mortally wounded. "The spirit of resistance to federal authority remains unchanged," concluded the marshal. Less than a month later, two more of Baker's deputies, James H. Bone and Theodore A. Thurston, faced charges of assault and battery after they arrested some moonshiners.[4]

By 1878 the southern states were arresting significant numbers of Internal Revenue agents and the marshals who supported them. Deputy Marshal James Davis of Tullahoma, Tennessee, was kept "constantly under indictment for petty charges," Marshal Edward S. Wheat reported in July 1876. Over the previous two years, Davis had spent $834 of his own money defending himself against harassing suits. Davis, though, would get his revenge.[5]

Congress, concerned about its revenues, passed a law in 1877 specifically protecting revenue agents from arrest for acts taken in the discharge of their responsibility to collect taxes. The Supreme Court upheld the law in 1879 after the state of Tennessee indicted Deputy Davis, who was also commissioned as a deputy collector of internal revenue, for murder. Davis had killed J. B. Haynes after Haynes shot at him while he was chopping an illegal still to pieces.

The Supreme Court's majority opinion in *Tennessee v. Davis* aptly summarized the problem for the federal government:

> It can act only through its officers and agents, and they must act within the states. If, when thus acting, and within the scope of their authority, those officers can be arrested and brought to trial in a State court, for an alleged offence against the law of the State, yet warranted by the Federal authority they possess, and if the general government is powerless to interfere at once for their protection, – if their protection must be left to the action of the State court, – the operations of the general government may at any time be arrested at the will of one of its members.

The heart of the matter was whether the activities of the federal government could be disrupted by its member states. To further complicate the problem, as the Court pointed out, it was unwise to allow the state courts to reach decisions, then appeal the decisions to the federal courts. The federal official under state indictment, perhaps even state condemnation, would be unable to conduct his duties during the lengthy pendency of the case and its appeal. In sum, the Court observed, "We do not think such an element of weakness is to be found in the Constitution."[6]

Unfortunately for the marshals and deputies, Attorney General A. H. Garland concluded that the law protecting revenue agents from arrest did not cover marshals. He advised U.S. Attorney Andrew McLain of Tennessee in April 1885 that deputies, even when they were executing process against illicit distillers, could not be considered "officers of the revenue." Consequently, federal law offered them no immunity from prosecution by state and local courts. Nor were the attorneys general willing to reimburse the marshals the expenses of their arrests. "There is no direct and specific provision of law for the payment by the

Government of the costs its officers may incur in defending suits brought against them for executing process issued at the instance of the United States," observed Attorney General George Williams on December 4, 1874. "This Department goes to the extent of its powers in such a case when it provides for the officer legal advice and an advocate."[7]

Thus, by the 1880s, U.S. marshals and their deputies could count little on the leaky umbrella of federal protection if they were arrested by state authorities. The executive branch provided free legal advice but did not reimburse the marshals for their time or out-of-pocket expenses. The legislative branch provided limited immunity, but only if the marshals were enforcing specific laws. The judicial branch also promised relief, but only if the marshals were upholding court orders duly issued by a federal judge. The marshals remained exposed to punishment and penalty for any acts they took in the line of duty that were not covered by individual laws or court orders.

Then, on August 14, 1889, Deputy Marshal David Neagle killed David Terry. When Neagle pulled the trigger of his six-shooter, he acted according to the instructions to protect Justice Field given him by Attorney General Miller through Marshal John C. Franks. The two shots, however, lacked the color of a specific federal law or court order. They were beyond the pale outlined by Congress and the courts. Neagle's arrest and imprisonment directly challenged the federal government. Was Neagle to be tried for murder? Were marshals forever to be second-guessed by the states?

After a brief hearing before the Ninth Circuit Court, with Justice Field abstaining, Neagle was ordered released. Sheriff Thomas Cunningham of San Joaquin County, supported by the state of California, appealed the case to the Supreme Court. The Court heard the oral arguments of U.S. Attorney General Miller, opposed by California attorney general G. A. Johnson, on March 4 and 5, 1890. The justices, Field again abstaining, announced their decision a month later, on April 14. They held for Neagle.[8]

Although the Court found no specific statute requiring, or even allowing, marshals to accompany Supreme Court justices as they rode their circuits "and act as a body-guard to them, to defend them against malicious assaults against their persons," the Court determined that such specific authorization was unnecessary. To conduct his office, Justice Field needed protection; therefore, the law implied that he would be protected.

Neither the federal courts nor its judges could enforce their own decrees or protect themselves from attack. The judiciary, the Court noted, "is the weakest for the purposes of self-protection and for the enforcement of the powers which it exercises." The courts by constitutional design looked to the executive branch for protection and enforcement of their orders. The Constitution imposed upon the president the explicit duty to "take care that the laws be faithfully executed." By implication, that clause put upon the president the responsibility to protect those who interpreted the laws, that is, the members of the judicial branch.

According to the Court, "the ministerial officers through whom its commands must be executed are marshals of the United States, and belong emphatically to the executive department of the government." Through a series of delegations of authority, from the president to the attorney general to Marshal Franks to Deputy Neagle, Neagle had authority of law to defend Justice Field from attack. Furthermore, that implied authority shielded him from any legal actions taken against him.

In the Court's view, "it was the duty of Neagle, under the circumstances, a duty which could only arise under the laws of the United States, to defend Mr. Justice Field from a murderous attack upon him." The Court assumed that the need justified the act. If no law authorized Neagle to defend Field, one was well needed; its absence in no way infringed on Neagle's duty to defend the justice. The Court decided that Neagle, in killing Terry, "was acting under the authority of the law of the United States, and was justified in so doing; and that he is not liable to answer in the courts of California on account of any part in that transaction." With that, Neagle was relieved from further court proceedings against him.[9]

In re Neagle, as the case was styled, significantly strengthened the powers of the president by enhancing the authority of marshals and their deputies. Although the decision did little to discourage state authorities from arresting marshals, it provided a quick precedent for releasing them. More important, *In re Neagle* freed the executive branch from the constraint of specific statutes. Previously bound to actions explicitly permitted by the Constitution or the law, the executive – the president and his marshals – could now take actions implied by the Constitution or the law. The marshals' authority was significantly expanded to include that which was intended by the Constitution or Congress.

The decision was a triumphant victory for the federal system of government. It confirmed federalism's resurgence.

THE MOONSHINE WARS

The eight revenuers quietly dismounted three hundred yards from the stillhouse. Secrecy and surprise were essential. Illicit distillers preferred to fight from ambush, their rifles barking from unexpected places. Each of the revenuers understood the need for caution. Since leaving Greenville, South Carolina, the day before – April 18, 1878 – they had already destroyed four illegal stills across the northeastern part of the county.

The men who owned the stills refused to pay the federal tax of 90 cents per gallon of whiskey. Working at night by the light of the moon in remote parts of the mountains and hills, the moonshiners cooked their mash – corn, barley, or some other grain – to steam. Cooled by mountain water passing over the curled copper coils, the steam condensed to alcohol, which when added to water emboldened it to whiskey.

As the raiding party of revenuers well knew, stills required large amounts of wood to heat the pots of mash to boiling. The stills also used tremendous quantities of water to condense the steam. When cooking, the boiling mash gave off a distinctive stench. To hide their work, moonshiners kept their stills deep in the woods, but always close to clear mountain streams. Finding the stills was usually a matter of following a stream to the stench, and the stench to the still. The difficulty was to determine which stream on which mountain, particularly because the revenuers could count on little help from the neighbors and surrounding communities.

Now, early in the afternoon of April 19, 1878, the raiding party was ready to move against its fifth illegal still. Deputy Collector H. H. Gillson, the Internal Revenue officer in charge of the raiders, ordered three of the men to remain on guard with the horses. Gillson took the other four men, including Deputy Marshal Rufus Springs, with him to charge the stillhouse.

As the men moved through the woods, they automatically spread out, making themselves less conspicuous, more difficult targets. For most of the three hundred yards to the stillhouse, the raiders moved steadily and quietly, their rifles clenched tightly at port arms, loaded and ready. They knew that each of the four stills they had destroyed screamed out to the mountain communities that revenuers were on the prowl. Every additional still they attacked exposed them increasingly to danger.

The men watched carefully for any sign of ambush. As they got closer to the shed, they broke into a dash, rushing across the last few dozen yards. Converging at the door, the revenuers kicked it open and burst into the stillhouse. They found no still.

Barrels of mash and beer and thirty gallons of corn whiskey lined the walls. Except for the barrels, the small house was empty. The still had been removed. Left behind were warm embers in the furnace where the pot of mash had been cooking. The heat of the coals was proof that the still had been removed within the past half hour.

Knowing that the moonshiners must still be in the area, Springs insisted on looking through the woods around the house. As the deputy marshal along on the raid, Springs knew he was there to make the arrests. The Pitman brothers agreed to help him search. Deputy Collector Gillson, whose only official concern was the illegal whiskey, remained in the house. He and G. C. Moss began staving in the barrels. The moonshine streamed across the dirt floor.

Before they could finish destroying all the barrels, Springs returned, looking for the Pitmans. They had been gone too long, he said. The quiet of the mountain hollow unnerved the deputy. Springs decided to stay at the stillhouse a moment in case the Pitmans returned. With most of the barrels staved in, Gillson left to ready the horses. No one wanted to tarry. The still was too recently removed, the moonshiners yet too close.

Springs stepped outside the house to watch for the Pitman brothers. After a few minutes, Moss also came out. They stood a half dozen paces apart, their backs to the shed. Both men felt the tension. Neither man spoke.

A single rifle shot shattered the stillness.

"Lord of Mercy, I'm shot," Springs groaned. "Shot through." He slumped against the side of the stillhouse, dead. Panicked by the gunfire, Moss instinctively ran. He sprinted directly ahead into the woods, running wildly past three armed strangers. Startled by his dash, the bushwhackers had no time to fire at him. Moss kept going.

The remaining revenuers converged again on the stillhouse. Gillson galloped up with the horses. Without pause, they tied Springs's body across his saddle and fled. For several miles some men followed them, but a sudden mountain squall discouraged the chase. Gillson and his men made it back safely to Greenville. They found Moss waiting for them there.[10]

Rufus Springs was but one of perhaps three dozen casualties among the marshals in the skirmishes to enforce federal laws in the post–Civil War South. For the marshals, it was wartime again in the South. The virulent, violent reception afforded the whiskey excise and those who enforced it went beyond mere opposition to taxes. It reflected southern determination to resist the federal government, its measures, and its officers.

Opposition to the tax was not a campaign against taxation without representation. It was a cry for individual liberty free of governmental interference. The distillers simply wanted to be left alone. They wanted to make whiskey without having to pay obeisance – or taxes – to anyone. For that reason, moonshiners of the nineteenth and twentieth centuries entered American mythology as bold individualists.

The federal government never had much success imposing taxes on spirits without running into trouble – witness the Whiskey Rebellion of 1794. The particular tax enforced by Deputy Springs and his cohorts dated back to the Civil War, which, of course, further enraged southern opposition. During the war, Congress was desperate to fund the Union's military operations. To raise the money, Congress created the country's first personal income tax and established an excise on such luxuries as whiskey, tobacco, and similar items. The Supreme Court ultimately attacked the income tax; southerners took on the excise tax.

The enforcement of the excise tax dramatically differed from the federal government's eventual surrender to the South on civil rights and the treatment of freedmen. When it came to revenues and taxes, the government was just as stubborn as any recalcitrant southerner. The tax was enforced. Throughout the postwar period – indeed, until the establishment of Prohibition in 1919 – succeeding administrations combatted moonshiners with raids, arrests, and destruction of stills. The government intended to collect its due and protect its authority in doing so. On the issue of taxes, federalism never faltered.

More than any other region, the South resisted the whiskey tax with violence and vengeance. The bitter resistance made the South far more dangerous than the western territories for the U.S. marshals and particularly for their deputies. U.S. Attorney Virgil Lusk of North

Carolina reported in 1873 that "so violent has been the opposition to the law, and so frequent the resistance to the enforcement of the same, that it is with difficulty that an officer can be induced to venture into this section of the country." By 1877 two deputies in North Carolina had been killed, and several others had been seriously wounded.[11]

Other southern states offered similar opposition. Marshal Robert M. Wallace of South Carolina remarked that "firing on Deputy Collectors and Deputy Marshals in the mountain sections of this State while they are attempting to arrest illicit distillers and peddlers with contraband whiskey has become so common as to excite but little comment." South Carolina deputies regarded the shootings as "an unpleasant performance incidental to the discharge of their duties." Most of his men, Wallace told the attorney general, were prepared to return the fire.[12]

Because assaulting or killing a federal officer was not a federal offense, the marshals looked to the state and local governments to prosecute their assailants and assassins. But the local southern courts frequently showed little sympathy for them, being much more concerned for the accused than for the attacked. The moonshiners and others who were charged with attacking deputies and revenuers often went unpunished, and the state and local governments frequently used their own power and authority to hinder the revenuers and deputy marshals and to protect the distillers. In one absurd case, Deputy Marshal Will W. Deavers was indicted by the North Carolina courts for destroying personal property after he took his ax to an illegal still.[13]

Succeeding attorneys general were unrelenting. "You are to cooperate actively, vigorously, and heartily with the Collectors of your district in breaking up and putting an end to the frauds upon the revenue laws," Attorney General Charles Devens ordered in a circular letter to southern marshals in September 1877.[14]

The revenuers needed the deputy marshals because only marshals or deputies could arrest the illicit distillers. The authority of the collectors extended only to seizing illegal stills and untaxed whiskey. In addition, the deputies also provided extra manpower to the collectors' raiding parties. They were men who were good with a gun and accustomed to the dangers of pursuing lawbreakers.

Arresting moonshiners without an arrest warrant exposed the deputies to some legal problems, though the attorneys general remained unsympathetic to the difficulties. Attorney General Devens advised Marshal George Turner of Alabama that Turner's deputies could arrest illicit distillers without a warrant, provided the deputies understood that such arrests were made at the risk of subsequent disapproval by the federal government and the courts. "You can as an officer arrest for any felony without a warrant on a probable grounds of guilt," Attorney General William H. H. Miller boldly told Marshal Richard R. Farr of Virginia in 1890. However, Miller hastened to add, the risks of lawsuits for false imprisonment were "incident to the office you have assumed." The federal government would not be liable for a deputy's mistakes.[15]

Marshals earned no fees unless they had process to serve, so without an arrest warrant, the deputies could not be paid a fee. Their expenses were covered by Treasury Department funds, but that amount barely exceeded mileage. Revenue collectors often embarked on their raids without obtaining arrest warrants or other process from the federal courts. The problem was a lack of identification. The revenuers did not always know whom they would catch. They had no proof of illicit distilling until they caught the distiller at his illegal still. The deputies could then make the arrest, but they could not expect to be paid for it.[16]

When Attorney General Devens ordered the marshals to cooperate with the revenuers in their districts, he added a reminder: "Costs incurred prior to process are not to be charged in your accounts. These expenses are chargeable to the fund of the Internal Revenue Bureau." A decade later, Attorney General A. H. Garland flatly denied any payments to deputies for illicit distillers they arrested without process. Beginning with the 1889 fiscal year on July 1, 1888, Congress prohibited the expenditure of any judicial funds for revenue collection.[17]

The marshals were not particularly enthusiastic about joining revenue raids with little expectation of earning their fees. "Anything short of an ample provision to the enforcement of the law is necessarily fraught with disaster to the public good and is a possible injustice to those charged with its execution," Marshal R. P. Baker of Alabama declared in 1877. One enterprising deputy in Virginia demanded $200 from the Internal Revenue collector for information the deputy had collected on a local illicit distillery. Attorney General Garland called the deputy's attitude "disrespectful and improper."[18]

Other deputies generated their own business before the U.S. commissioners. By working up their own cases against moonshiners, the deputies could obtain arrest warrants to serve; from the warrants came fees. Revenue agent William Somerville of Georgia reported in 1879 that the deputies in his district "almost without exception have resorted to the most reckless and disreputable means to procure warrants and create fees." Acting Attorney General S. F. Phillips complained to U.S. Attorney George Thomas of Kentucky about the large number of frivolous revenue prosecutions in that district during 1884. Attorney General Miller found that deputies in Virginia had brought 1,772 revenue cases during 1891. Almost one-half of the cases were later dismissed, "but not, however, before the deputies' and commissioners' fees were charged up to the department." Before one commissioner in particular, three-fifths of the cases were subsequently dismissed after both the deputies and the commissioner collected their fees for each one. "This manifest and amazing abuse must cease at once," Miller commanded.[19]

Despite the violence, despite the high number of marshals and revenuers killed or arrested by southerners and southern states, the federal government refused to retreat. The law was almost impossible to enforce adequately. Moonshiners had too many places to hide in the mountains, they had too many friends to warn them of raiding parties, they were too resolute and too violent to give up their illegal whiskey. About all the federal government could hope to do was hold its own.

Even as the government faltered over the protection of blacks, it stood behind its revenues. The difference lay in contemporary definitions of federalism and contemporary determinations of the boundaries of constitutional authority. In certain areas, such as the collection of revenues, foreign policy, and administration, no one in Washington disputed the government's right to rule. In other areas, such as the protection of individual citizens, no one in Washington was quite sure what the government's authority was. Thus, the moonshine wars began in earnest coincidentally with the federal withdrawal of protection for the newly freed slaves.

JUSTICE DEPARTMENTALIZED

By 1861 the role of the marshals within the federal structure was well established. They were officers of the executive branch, who answered only to the president but were responsible for serving the lawful orders of all three branches of the federal government. Although the Senate could refuse to endorse a president's choice for marshal, it was powerless to revoke a marshal's commission once it had confirmed the appointment.

Although federal judges could make life miserable for a marshal, even firing his deputies, the judges could not on their own authority dismiss him. The only recourse the judges had against U.S. marshals was to complain to the executive branch. Only the president could dismiss a U.S. marshal.

Congress recognized that the attorney general had assumed general supervision over the U.S. marshals and attorneys, confirming the transfer in an act of August 2, 1861, and assigning to the attorney general full supervision over the marshals and district attorneys in their public and official duties. That supervision would no longer be shared with the secretary of state or with other cabinet officers. The Department of the Interior continued to audit the accounts of the marshals and attorneys, primarily because, in the days before the creation of the Department of Justice, the attorney general's office was so poorly staffed that the attorney general already had his hands full implementing the government's policies.[20]

Congress during this period agreed to two other substantial changes affecting the marshals. The first concerned the system of appointing marshals; the second, the establishment of the Department of Justice. The system of appointing U.S. marshals had always been time-consuming and inefficient. The president was often distracted by other issues and failed to fill vacancies for long periods of time. Political feuds frequently kept senators from making their recommendations to the president, who hesitated to make a selection without Senate endorsements. As the country expanded, communications with the distant regions took weeks, sometimes months. Consequently, districts frequently went without a U.S. marshal for considerable periods of time.

To ease the problem, Congress approved legislation in 1863 allowing local district judges to appoint temporary marshals. The court-appointed marshals enjoyed the same powers and responsibilities as the presidentially commissioned ones. They took the same oath, posted the same bond, performed the same duties. The judge could fire court-appointed marshals, as could the president. Their commission expired as soon as the men appointed by the president and confirmed by the Senate showed up to take over the office. As Congress announced in the act, the reason it wanted the courts to appoint temporary marshals was to improve the efficiency of the judicial system.[21]

In addition, Congress established the Department of Justice in 1870. The marshals came under its oversight. At first, the establishment of the department had no particular impact on the marshals. They continued to report directly to the attorney general, hire their own deputies, supply their own equipment, and work with little direct supervision from Washington. Had it not been for money, few of the marshals would have noticed much difference.

The job of marshal remained a hard way to make a living, exceeded in difficulty only by the job of deputy marshal. Because the marshals were paid a fee for each paper they served, their authority was limited strictly within the borders of their districts. They could make no arrests, nor enforce any laws or court orders, outside their own district. No marshal wanted to lose his rightful fee because a marshal from a neighboring district crossed the line to serve process.[22]

In most criminal cases, the federal government paid the marshal's fees. In civil cases involving the United States, the judge generally determined who paid the fees. In cases in which the United States was not a party, the payment of the marshal's fees followed the same procedures used by the state courts. The marshal was not allowed to demand his fees up front, nor could he refuse to serve the process for fear his fees would not be paid. "The law is imperative," Attorney General George Williams announced in March 1872, "that you shall execute throughout your District all lawful precepts directed to you and issued under the authority of the United States, without any reference whatever to the payment of your fees." Such instructions hardly promoted efficiency, though they clearly imposed economy on the marshals.[23]

Besides the fees from the process the U.S. marshal served himself, he also earned a small annual salary–about $200–and 2 percent of all the court funds passing through his hands. To discourage the marshals from creating unnecessary business, Congress limited their total annual income to $6,000. Most of the U.S. marshal's earnings, however, came from his deputies, for the U.S. marshal was allowed to keep up to one-fourth of their fees. The marshal made separate arrangements with each of his deputies, negotiating the percentage the deputy was to pay him in order to be his deputy.[24]

Because the marshals appointed their own deputies, it was not uncommon for them to select women. As early as the 1890s, women were commissioned as deputies. Deputy Marshal Ada Carnutt of the Indian Territory single-handedly arrested two perjurers in 1893. Carnutt's experience, however, seemed extraordinary, because most female deputies–like many male deputies–filled the clerical needs of the marshal's office. It would be another ninety years before President Ronald Reagan would select Faith Evans as the first presidentially appointed female U.S. marshal.[25]

Deputy marshals had the harder row. In most districts the U.S. marshal acted as general manager. He supervised the work of the deputies, made the assignments, kept the books, hobnobbed with the local power brokers. The deputies did the physical work, traveling to serve the process, make the arrests, handle the prisoners, and so forth. For that work they could keep no more—and oftentimes less-than three-fourths of the legally allowed fees. If a deputy tried but failed to make an arrest, the law allowed him $2 a day for his trouble.[26]

The deputies were also reimbursed for most of their expenses, provided their vouchers contained "every possible receipt which the deputy should procure for expenses of service in any case." Those expenses included no more than $3 a day for food when transporting a prisoner and 10 cents a mile for the trip, but only one way. "This transportation ought not to be devised as a pleasure trip for the officers, but as an onerous duty to be discharged faithfully and economically," Acting Attorney General S. F. Phillips warned Marshal George Turner of Alabama on July 14, 1877. The newly established Department of Justice worked assiduously to ensure that each such trip was more burdensome than pleasurable to the deputies.[27]

"Frugality" was the watchword, though it often proved difficult to achieve. Shortly after becoming attorney general, Edwards Pierrepont issued a common complaint to the government's district-level officials. "I find also," he announced in hurt surprise, "that in some of the Judicial Districts the expenses have been extravagant, without necessity and without honesty." Pierrepont's successors echoed him in a cacophony of calls for stricter economy, less extravagance, and no more waste. Few seemed to hear.[28]

The deputies suffered additional problems. They depended completely on the U.S. marshals to pay their fees and had no recourse if their marshal refused to pay them. The Department of Justice declined to get involved in any fee disputes, treating the deputies as officers and employees of the U.S. marshal, not as its own officers.

Deputies "are not selected by the Government, nor does the Government look to them for the discharge of public business while a marshal is in office," Attorney General A. H. Garland wrote in December 1887, adding that the fees and expenses due the deputies were paid by the marshal as "a private debt of the marshal to them." Two years later, Garland's successor took the same view. "Deputies must look to the marshal for their individual compensation," Attorney General William Miller explained.[29]

Money was always the problem. Either the marshals had too little, or they took more than properly belonged to them. As a protection to the government, Congress had always required the marshals to explain their accounts in open court and then swear to their accuracy. The U.S. attorney acted as inquisitor, questioning the marshal's expenses and claims for fees before the district judge, who certified the accounts. The marshal then sent the approved accounts to Washington, where anonymous Treasury Department officials audited each one. The auditors relied solely on the marshals for information. Seldom did anyone visit the marshal's district to investigate his reports or verify his expenditures. Seldom did anyone do more than deny the marshal specific amounts of money that he may have mistakenly – or fraudulently – claimed. It was a system ripe for abuse, and abused it was.

When Congress created the Department of Justice in 1870, it transferred to the new department the ultimate supervision over the marshals' accounts. At first the department kept the previous system essentially intact, particularly the reliance on the U.S. attorneys to review the accounts. "Such examination must not be formal and casual," Attorney General Charles Devens advised the district attorneys in 1878. Instead, Devens wanted it to be "a searching review of the accounts, with the express determination by you to allow no account to pass that is not free from all suspicion." Devens insisted that the attorneys stand "as a legal sentinel at this post of unwelcome but necessary duty." Nonetheless, the review of the marshals' accounts remained essentially a family affair, the scrutiny conducted by the U.S. attorney and the federal judge with whom the marshal worked every day.[30]

Despite frequent calls for "the severest punishment which the law can give" to government officers guilty of fraud, the cheating and abuse continued unabated, unabashedly. It soon became apparent to the new Department of Justice that the U.S. attorney's review and the judge's approval were not enough to prohibit the marshals from cheating. In fact, a number of marshals showed a startlingly inventive imagination when it came to bilking the government.[31]

The Department of Justice frequently reminded the marshals and attorneys of their responsibilities. "Deputies cannot be controlled from the Department," Attorney General Devens warned Marshal Algernon S. Gray of Virginia in January 1878, "but must be regulated by the Marshal himself." In a circular letter to all the marshals that month, Devens cautioned them that "the act of your deputy must be yours; he must be held pecuniarily responsible to you, who are in turn responsible alone to the Government for funds intrusted to you." By the 1890s the Department of Justice was asserting that a marshal was "legally responsible for the acts of his deputies." At least one marshal went to the penitentiary because he swore to fraudulent accounts submitted by his deputies. The U.S. attorney, on the other side, was expected to ferret out errant deputies. When a major case of fraud was uncovered among deputies in North Carolina in 1877, Devens reminded U.S. Attorney Virgil S. Lusk, "You are the law officer of the Government in your district." Lusk was therefore responsible for prohibiting the fraud.[32]

Eventually the number of investigations of errant district officials—marshals, attorneys, clerks, and judges—reached a level high enough to justify hiring full-time special investigators. The examiners, as the auditors were called, were hired specifically for the purpose of reviewing the government's financial accounts at the district level. At first the department had only a handful of examiners, barely enough to respond to the accusations and suspicions reported against the district officials. Within a few years, however, the department moved to systematic investigations. By the 1880s, Justice Department examiners were routinely visiting each judicial district to audit the official accounts and investigate the operations of each office.

The examiners posed the first serious threat to each marshal's autonomy within his district, for they insisted on verifying everything. During an investigation of the western district of Arkansas in 1886, which had jurisdiction over the Indian Territory, Examiner David A. Fisher interviewed not only all of the deputies but their prisoners as well. The infamous outlaw Belle Starr described her March 1886 arrest by Deputy Tyner Hughes. Fortunately for the deputy, Starr confirmed that he had furnished her with food and that he had some guards and possemen with him. Other examiners visited boardinghouses and rail stations to ensure that the costs of meals, lodging, and train tickets were actually what the deputies had claimed.[33]

The examiners soon became the most hated men in the Department of Justice, their visits to the districts dreaded, their investigations generally opposed. The hostility against them climaxed in Alabama in the spring of 1883 when examiners Joel W. Bowman and E. B. Wiegand audited the accounts of Marshal Paul Strobach and his deputies. Their investigation quickly uncovered a number of irregularities in the accounts of former deputy H. A. Wilson, who had subsequently been appointed receiver of the U.S. Land Office in Montgomery. When Examiner Wiegand chanced to meet Wilson in the street one day, he asked Wilson to come by the marshal's office so that the examiners could question him.

Wilson took offense. Calling Wiegand "a vile and vulgar name," Wilson "struck him in the face with his fist." Wiegand fell backward from the blow. As he lay stunned and helpless, Wilson drew his pistol "and endeavored to shoot him down." Several men who had witnessed the blow grabbed Wilson and wrestled the pistol from his hand before he could pull the trigger. Examiner Wiegand escaped with his life, but barely.

In his report on the attack, Examiner Bowman complained of the dangers facing the examiners when they investigated the marshals. "Deputy Marshals throughout the country, as a rule, are a rough class of men," he wrote. "Their occupation has a tendency to make them reckless of human life." Although the attack on Wiegand was an exceptional instance, Bowman pleaded with the attorney general for help. "There certainly should be some means provided to protect us in the discharge of our official duties," he complained. At the least, Bowman demanded that Wilson be fired from his post as receiver of the Land Office.[34]

The marshals were not simply greedy criminals intent on robbing the U.S. Treasury and the people. They belonged to an era when government offices were rewards for campaign work, when taking government money was merely accepting one's due for helping congressmen, senators, and even the president get elected. The small scandals that erupted in local districts across the country were only forerunners of the grander scandals of succeeding presidential administrations. If cheating the government was not a way of life in post–Civil War America, it was certainly a widespread habit.

The system itself was radically flawed. As long as the marshals continued to be paid on the fee system, they would be encouraged to fudge their reports, falsify their claims, and submit fictional accounts. Succeeding attorneys general begged the Congress at least to put the U.S. marshals on a salary so that they would have less inducement to approve the fraudulent claims of their deputies. In his annual reports in 1882 and 1883, Attorney General Benjamin Brewster estimated "that it costs the Government ten dollars expenses for every dollar's emoluments of the marshal" because of the frauds committed against the government. Brewster's successors endorsed his recommendation to change the system from fees to salaries.[35]

Congress responded slowly. For more than a decade it ignored the annual requests, seemingly unperturbed by the high costs of dishonesty. Finally, however, after more than a century of abuse, Congress passed a law putting both the U.S. marshals and their deputies on salaries. The new system began with the opening of the fiscal year on July 1, 1896.

That profound change was additional evidence of federalism's resurgence. The new system went beyond mere salaries for the marshals, for it carried with it a new responsibility for the Department of Justice. Under the fee system, each marshal had hired as many deputies as the business of his courts could support. Under the new system, with salaries paid directly from the U.S. Treasury, the department set limits on the number of deputies in each district, as well as how much they were paid. Thus, a fairly elementary aspect of the marshal's autonomy within his district was stripped away. Henceforth, the marshals had to plead with the department for more deputies, more help, and higher salaries.

7

FEDERAL FRONTIERS

1865–1900

Federal judge Frank Dale listened intently to the trial testimony. He had not understood until now just what the deputy marshals faced when they went out across the territory to make arrests. What he heard from the witnesses appalled him. Three deputies were dead, killed in the most violent shoot-out in the history of the Oklahoma Territory.

The accused killer, "Arkansas Tom" Jones, sat calmly across from the judge. He listened with "stolid indifference" as witnesses described the battle. A dozen or more heavily armed deputy marshals guarded the doorways and surrounded the courthouse. Most people assumed that Arkansas Tom's confederates would try to rescue him. The outlaws, led by the notorious Bill Doolin, had established an impressive record of killings and violent robberies across Oklahoma, Kansas, and the Indian Territory. Successors to the Dalton gang, Doolin and his men usually stuck together. They had little left to lose.[1]

During the trial, Judge Dale learned how informants had alerted Deputy Marshal John Hixon in late August 1893 that Bill Doolin and five of his gang were comfortably ensconced in the small town of Ingalls, Oklahoma Territory. The marshals had been chasing Doolin and his men for more than a year. Rewards totaling thousands of dollars had been put on the outlaws' heads, but no one had yet been able to collect the money. Hixon saw his chance.

The deputy called out a posse. He planned to hide his men in two covered wagons, then drive the wagons into Ingalls and take the outlaws by surprise. With two wagons and a dozen deputies, Hixon left for Ingalls late on the night of August 31. Delays en route kept them from the town until midmorning, too late to sneak the wagons into town. Abandoning his plan, Hixon stopped just outside Ingalls and divided his posse in half. He assumed that Doolin and his men were still at the O.K. Hotel, so he directed the posse to converge there.

Hixon brought his wagon and half the men in from the south, stopping at a grove of trees on the edge of town. The possemen, each armed with rifles and pistols, dropped quietly from the wagon. They fanned out and entered the town on foot, moving carefully from house to house, building to building, toward the hotel. Deputy Ham Hueston and the other half of the posse came in from the southwest. At the edge of town they slipped from their wagon to move on foot toward the hotel. Posseman Dick Speed drove the wagon through town to the Pierce and Hostetter feed barn. On the way the wagon rattled past Ransom's saloon, where Doolin and his men passed the morning dealing poker.

The outlaws were cautious men. As soon as Hueston's wagon passed the saloon, George "Bitter Creek" Newcomb left the poker game to investigate. With his Winchester in one hand, he mounted his horse and slowly walked it down the street. Peering from the barn door, posseman Speed watched the outlaw's approach.

When Bitter Creek got close enough to see into the shadows, he recognized Speed. Reacting instantly, he slapped the butt of his rifle to his shoulder as Speed threw up his Winchester. The posseman was the faster. His shot hit Bitter Creek's rifle, throwing off the outlaw's aim, then ricocheted downward into his right leg. Gasping in pain, Bitter Creek reined his horse about in order to flee the town.

Arkansas Tom was resting in his room in the attic of the O.K. Hotel when he heard the shots. Leaping for his rifle, he darted to the window just in time to see Speed step from the barn to fire again at the fleeing Bitter Creek. Arkansas Tom popped off his first shot. The slug caught Speed in the shoulder, spun him around, and drove him staggering back toward the wagon. Arkansas Tom's second shot killed him.

The deputies had not quite positioned themselves when the shooting began. As Doolin and his men opened a withering fire from the saloon to protect Bitter Creek's escape, the deputies darted forward to find the best places to shoot back. They took cover where they found it, slipping in and out of doorways and ducking behind water troughs. Within moments the deputies poured shots into the front, the rear, and one side of the small bar. Deputy Hixon called out for the outlaws to surrender. "Go to hell!" Doolin hollered between shots.

A young boy named Simmons stepped out of a nearby building. Arkansas Tom, mistaking him for a deputy, mortally wounded the boy. None of the lawmen yet realized that Arkansas Tom was well placed above them in the attic of the O.K. Hotel. Instead the posse concentrated its fire on Ransom's saloon. A horse skittered nervously in front of the bar. One of Hueston's men dropped it with a quick shot. The horse fell broadside to the front door.

The posse's bullets riddled the plank walls of the saloon and screamed through the air around the outlaws. George Ransom, the barkeep, was wounded in the leg, but the outlaws were not hit. Doolin decided to leave. The gang moved quickly to the side door, then covered each other in a race to the stables.

Neil Murray, who tended bar for Ransom, stood just inside the front door. He raised his Winchester to fire at the posse. Before he could squeeze the trigger, three of the possemen fired simultaneously. Two of the shots caught Murray in the ribs, the third broke his right arm in two places. Murray pitched forward into the street, dropping his rifle across the threshold of the bar. He survived to sue the federal government for his wounds.

Doolin and his men made it to the stables before the deputies realized they had left the bar. Doolin and "Dynamite Dick" Clifton hurriedly saddled the horses while Bill Dalton, "Red Buck" Waightman, and "Tulsa Jack" Blake opened up on the posse. Outflanked, Deputy Hueston's men shifted position to return fire on the stables. Hueston moved from behind a pile of lumber to cover the rear of the barn. Inside the O.K. Hotel attic, Arkansas Tom frantically punched a hole in the roof large enough for his head and shoulders. Standing on a chair, he pumped two shots into Hueston's left side and bowels.

Their horses ready, Doolin and Dynamite Dick raced from the front door of the barn. The other outlaws galloped from the rear. Deputy Hixon managed a quick shot that caught Dalton's horse in the jaw. The injured animal reared and spun about, but Dalton managed to stay in the saddle and forced the horse to head down the street out of town. Some distance off, Deputy Lafe Shadley fired. The bullet hit the luckless horse in the leg. Dalton dropped from the saddle but used his limping, frightened mount to cover him. Another shot from Shadley forced Dalton to dive into the ravine bordering the town.

The other outlaws raced from Ingalls. They headed straight toward a wire fence stretched across the Oklahoma prairie.

Convinced that he had hit Dalton, Shadley ran after the fleeing outlaws. Crossing through the backyards of Ingalls, he climbed a fence, but his coat caught on a picket. He tripped forward, his coattails tangled in the fence. As Shadley frantically extricated himself, Arkansas Tom turned his deadly Winchester toward the exposed deputy. Shadley's hip shattered from the impact as the bullet bounced up through his gut to lodge in his right breast. The deputy freed his coat and staggered to the nearest house. He pounded on the door until Mrs. Ransom opened it, but she refused him help. As soon as the deputy moved from the shadows of the house, Arkansas Tom caught him again with three more shots to the chest. Knocked to the ground, Shadley began crawling away.

While Arkansas Tom was shooting Shadley, Dalton raced back to his horse to retrieve the gang's only pair of wire cutters. He shot the horse in the head, grabbed the cutters from his saddlebags, and ran back to the fence. The lawmen followed carefully, with Deputy Jim Masterson several yards in the lead. Masterson reached the cover of a blackjack tree and began shooting. The outlaws, stalled before the fence, returned the fire. Their bullets chewed the bark and twigs off the tree. Within a few moments, Masterson was out of ammunition. He dashed back to the wagon and filled his pockets with rifle cartridges before racing back to his tree.

The pause in the shooting gave Dalton time to cut through the fence. He jumped up behind one of the riders as the outlaws galloped through the break. "Hell, fellers," Masterson called to the other deputies, "they're getting away." Adjusting his rifle sights to five hundred yards, he shot after them. Dynamite Dick fell from his saddle as the bullet creased his neck. His friends stopped long enough to lift him back on his horse, then raced away. At the top of a small Oklahoma hill, Doolin and the others paused for parting shots at the posse. Frank Briggs, a teenager too intent on the fight to worry about taking cover, was hit in the shoulder. The gang turned their horses toward freedom and galloped away.

The deputies fired back briefly but offered no pursuit. They had brought no saddle horses with them. Besides, the lawmen had suddenly realized that the deadliest fire against them had come from the attic of the O.K. Hotel.

Deputy Hixon ordered his men back toward the hotel. They surrounded the small building while Hixon ordered the occupants to evacuate. Everyone left but Arkansas Tom, who hastily knocked another hole on the east side of the roof. He now commanded the town. When Hixon called on the outlaw to surrender, Arkansas Tom admitted that "he would be taken finally, but in the meantime he would kill at least seven men, whom he had range on." The deputies opened an almost continuous fire on the attic room.

Chief Deputy John M. Hale arrived with reinforcements. The new posse took up Doolin's trail while Hixon and his men kept up the battle with Arkansas Tom. The shooting continued until shortly after two o'clock that afternoon, when Arkansas Tom surrendered. The deputies handcuffed him and loaded him aboard a spring wagon for the trip to the Payne County jail. Dick Speed's body and the wounded Shadley and Hueston were put aboard the wagon that had brought them to Ingalls. Although Shadley and Hueston survived the hour-long trip back to Stillwater, Hueston died the next day, and Shadley the day after.[2]

Arkansas Tom was charged with murder in the first degree for the death of Ham Hueston. Marshal E. D. Nix assigned forty deputies to guard the Payne County jail in case Doolin and his men tried to free their friend. The trial finally opened in the spring of 1894. After hearing the testimony of the various witnesses, the jury returned a verdict of manslaughter in the first degree. The next day, Judge Dale sentenced Arkansas Tom to fifty years in jail. Several weeks later, Marshal Nix's deputies delivered the outlaw to the Lansing, Michigan, federal penitentiary.[3]

After the trial, Judge Dale called Marshal Nix to his chambers. The evidence before the bar had shocked him. The judge realized that, by necessity, he and the marshal relied on men who had no combat experience to go after desperate outlaws like the Doolin gang. The possemen were townsmen, farmers, or ranchers. Too young for service in the Civil War, their experience was limited to hunting meat for the table or killing coyotes and other varmints. Most had families who needed their support.

Doolin and his men were hardened fighters who challenged death each time they robbed a bank or held up a train. They were combat veterans too, for their robberies differed little from battles. The outlaws had nothing to lose; they faced a violent death, jail, or the gallows.

Marshal Nix took the seat across from the judge's desk. Dale looked at him for a few moments, his expression troubled. "Marshal," the judge finally said, "this is serious. I have reached the conclusion that the only good outlaw is a dead one. I hope you will instruct your deputies in the future to bring them in dead."[4]

WESTERING

Restlessness defined the New World. For centuries Europeans risked everything to come to America. Some were fleeing, some searching. All were restless. They sailed their small ships against the howling Atlantic without knowing what they wanted nor what they would find. In the New World, they, their children, and their children's children continued to wander westward, always searching, always restless.

John Steinbeck called it westering, the irresistible impulse to breach the frontiers and challenge the unknown. The challengers conquered the land, the weather, and the natives to build log cabins and sod houses. They erected small hamlets of civilization as testaments to the power of community. As more people trudged westward, the hamlets grew to villages, then towns and cities.

The issues of expansion preceded the Constitution. Questions of how to incorporate new communities into those that already existed arose every time settlers headed farther westward. Conquering the wilderness meant more than chasing out the Indians, chopping down the trees, and tilling the soil. The settlers also erected local and state governments based on legal charters. Finding a legal method to induct those governments into the Union of former colonies posed difficult administrative and procedural problems.

The congress that was spawned by the unworkable Articles of Confederation first defined a territorial system of sorts for the fledgling country. It approved the Northwest Ordinance in the summer of 1787, defining the step-by-step method by which territories evolved into states. The ordinance delineated territorial boundaries, provided for the appointment of territorial governors, secretaries, and judges, and established territorial laws. Two years later, the new Constitution and its Congress of the United States accepted, with occasional refinements, the system defined by the Northwest Ordinance.

The territorial system moved in stages. In the beginning, when the population was low, each frontier area was defined as an unorganized territory. Boundaries were surveyed, and territories were established and named. Federal law prevailed, with little provision for local laws or structures. The president appointed the governor, judges, and other officials, whose authority emanated directly from the national government. They ruled over the territories without provision for local self-government.

When the population of free white males reached five thousand, the territory was organized, a bicameral legislature elected, and territorial laws promulgated. The organization of a territory signaled a shift in the power structure from national to local. As it matured, the territory acquired more and more of the duties and responsibilities assumed by states. When the population reached sixty thousand free residents, the territory was nominated for statehood. After proof was presented of the republican nature of the territorial government, Congress determined whether the individual territory could be admitted to the Union. Once admitted, the former territory was automatically transformed into a state, equal in all respects to its fellow states.

The relationship between the federal government (and its officials) and the territories (and their residents) depended entirely on what stage of development the territory had reached. The territories ranged from total dependence on federal governance to reliance on their own officers and local governments. Territorial evolution mimicked – minus a revolution – the national government's growth from colony to nation, from foreign rule to self-government.

In the unorganized territories, the courts established by Congress sat as federal district or circuit courts to hear cases involving federal law, which covered all issues that arose in the unorganized territories. Once the territory was organized, however, the courts acted in twin capacities. They continued to sit as federal courts, hearing cases involving federal law. With the rap of the judge's gavel, they transformed themselves into territorial supreme or district courts to hear cases on appeal involving territorial law.

The role of the marshals corresponded with the role of the federal courts. In the unorganized territories the marshals were the only lawmen. They pursued all the outlaws because all criminal activities were by definition a violation of federal law. As the individual territory passed through the organized stage toward statehood, the marshals surrendered more and more of their authority to territorial lawmen. By the time the territory was on the brink of statehood, the marshals were usually concerned solely with the federal courts, laws, and violators.

Once the territory was organized, the territorial legislature could choose whom it wanted to execute territorial court orders and to uphold territorial law. The legislature could call on the U.S. marshal to act as an officer of the territorial court, or it could establish its own office of sheriff for each county. If the legislature chose the latter course, the marshals were concerned only with federal law, and in that respect the territory resembled a state. Territorial sheriffs administered territorial laws; federal marshals executed federal laws.

Most territories chose to create their own law officers as they moved closer to statehood. For example, by the 1870s – forty years before statehood – the Arizona territorial legislature had provided sheriffs for each of its counties. Most of its cities and towns had chiefs of police or town marshals. Conversely, until Alaska achieved statehood in 1959, it provided territorial lawmen only in its few cities. U.S. marshals upheld territorial law throughout the rest of the territory.

The relationship between territorial and federal lawmen in each territory was further confused by the practice of obtaining joint or concurrent commissions. Many sheriffs and town marshals throughout the American frontier also held commissions as federal deputy marshals. The double office gave the lawmen considerable authority, as well as the chance to earn extra fees. As a result, the lines of authority between territorial and federal lawmen, who were often the same man, were frequently confused and laxly respected.

Often the marshals clashed with local sheriffs, each taking a different side in local disputes. In 1878 and 1879, for example, cattleman James J. Dolan challenged cattle baron John S. Chisum for political and economic control of Lincoln County, New Mexico. Dolan's men, hiding under the authority of the sheriff, killed an associate of Chisum's, an Englishman named John H. Tunstall, on February 18, 1878. Because

Marshal John Sherman already had warrants outstanding for previous crimes against several of Tunstall's suspected killers, he instructed his deputy in Lincoln County, Robert Widenmann, to arrest them.

Deputy Widenmann sided with the Chisum faction. He allowed Chisum to fund a posse for him, selecting the possemen from among the cattleman's ranch hands. One of the men, barely more than a boy, was named William Bonney. He also went by the names "Henry McCarty," "William Antrim," and "Billy the Kid." For the next several months, Deputy Widenmann and his men, supported occasionally by the U.S. Cavalry, scoured the county supposedly hunting the murderers of the Englishman Tunstall. Shoot-outs with the Dolan cattle faction were frequent. A number of men were killed, including Deputy Marshal William Brady. Marshal Sherman, uncertain of what to do, unadvised from Washington, and unwilling to take personal control, stood by helplessly.

The situation grew so bad and so complicated that the Justice Department finally dispatched a special agent to investigate. The results of the inquiry convinced President Rutherford B. Hayes that he should order the army to pacify the county. The president also fired the territorial governor, Samuel Axtell, who had allied himself with the Dolan faction. Deputy Widenmann left New Mexico for his father's home in Michigan. The county, for the most part, calmed down, except for Billy the Kid. After a three-year spree of killings that included three deputy marshals, Billy was finally gunned down by Deputy Marshal Pat Garrett.[5]

Episodes like the Lincoln County War further complicated a system that was already complex and inefficient, yet strangely compatible with the needs of the expanding country. One famous case illustrated the unique system of federal frontiers. In 1876 Jack McCall stepped into a bar in Deadwood, Dakota Territory, and shot James Butler Hickok, who was better known by the sobriquet "Wild Bill." The citizens of Deadwood hastily convened a court, convicted McCall, and sentenced him to hang.

McCall's attorneys pointed out on appeal that Deadwood was in the unorganized portion of the Dakota Territory. The citizens had no power to form a court or try McCall, much less hang him. Consequently, a year after the shooting, federal officials convened a federal court, obtained a federal conviction, and sentenced McCall to a federal hanging. Federal deputy marshals conducted his execution.

Upholding the laws protecting the Indians, government property, and the U.S. mails caused the frontier marshals the most problems. A complex construction of federal statutes insulated the Indians from unscrupulous whites and isolated them, unarmed and sober, on their reservations. Stealing government property, particularly cutting timber on government lands, was a popular offense, especially on the Great Plains, where houses were built of sod, and buffalo droppings were burned for warmth and cooking. Rifling the mails, a federal offense, seemed an inevitable adjunct to train and stagecoach holdups, which were local crimes.

Theft of government property was a common occurrence, particularly at army posts. In the spring of 1874 Marshal J. H. Burdick of the Dakota Territory cited the theft of government property as one of the major problems in his district. The year before, several mules had been stolen just as General George Armstrong Custer was about to launch his spring campaign against the Indians. Although one of Burdick's deputies successfully investigated the crime, thefts continued to plague Custer's Seventh Cavalry. "There is a great amount of stealing of Horses, Mules, and Cattle belonging to the Government at points along the upper Missouri River," Burdick reiterated in early August 1874 when he reported the recent theft of eight mules.[6]

Timber was a precious commodity throughout much of the frontier. Its theft from government lands was another crime that plagued the marshals. In July 1873, for example, the commander of Fort Hayes, Kansas, awarded a contract to two men to furnish the post with wood. Six months later, Marshal William S. Tough developed several witnesses who asserted that the lumbermen were cutting trees on government reservations to resell to the army. One hundred fifty cords, all of it stolen government timber, had already been cut for delivery to the quartermaster. Tough seized the wood and, under court order, offered it at auction. The quartermaster at Fort Hayes was the highest bidder.[7]

Robbing the U.S. mails, particularly in association with train and stagecoach robberies, was a perennial favorite among outlaws. Jesse and Frank James refined the art of train robbery. For more than a dozen years the brothers eluded arrest, though local authorities, U.S. marshals, and Pinkerton detectives pursued them throughout Missouri. Frequent shoot-outs decimated the gang, but Jesse and Frank were never caught. Frank finally turned himself in to local authorities after one of their gang members, Bob Ford, shot Jesse from behind, killing him.

Few other outlaw gangs were as successful, though certainly not for lack of trying. Between November 1875 and mid-April 1876 the North Western Stage Company was robbed five times carrying the mail across Idaho. Throughout that winter the U.S. marshal and his deputies, working with local officials and Wells Fargo detectives, "labored indefatigably" to catch five of the seven suspected outlaws. Similarly, frontier Texas was plagued with train and stage robberies. In August 1878 the general superintendent and the superintendent of the Texas Express Company applauded Marshal Stillwell H. Russell for stopping a series of train robberies after local officials had refused to act.[8]

The Black Hills coach company in Wyoming was robbed three nights in a row in June 1877. Thefts became so common in Wyoming that by the end of 1878 the governor was calling for military assistance. "Robberies of the worst character, both of the U.S. Mails and of private citizens, are still of frequent occurrence in Wyoming," Governor John W. Hoyt advised Attorney General Charles Devens, "and they are committed at places so remote from the more settled portions of the Territory, as well as by bands so large and desperate that the civil authorities are unequal to the work of breaking them up."[9]

Toward the end of the century the Hole-in-the-Wall gang plundered trains and post offices throughout Wyoming. After each robbery the gang retreated to its hideout, from which it got its name, in the Wyoming mountains. Marshal Frank A. Hadsell worked closely with Pinkerton detectives to track the outlaws down, but neither was successful. The most Hadsell and his posses could do was chase the outlaws out of Wyoming. Butch Cassidy and Harry Longbaugh, better known as the Sundance Kid, fled to Bolivia. Other members of their gang headed east to Tennessee and elsewhere. Each of them kept to the trade of robbery; each met a violent death.[10]

The New Mexico Black Jack gang rivaled any other group of outlaws for brazenness and brutality, robbing and killing almost with impunity. In New Mexico alone (where death was the penalty for train robbery) the outlaws held up two trains in 1896, three in 1897, three in 1898, and two in 1899. "They never will be taken alive," Marshal Edward L. Hall reported, adding that "they have lots of friends in the country, who will give them information, provisions and arms."[11]

During the last half of 1896 the Black Jack gang robbed the post office at Separ in August, then easily eluded the posse raised by Chief Deputy Horace W. Loomis. In October, gang members tried to hold up the Arizona and Pacific train when it stopped at the Rio Puerco depot forty miles west of Albuquerque. Loomis happened to be a passenger on the train. Grabbing his shotgun, he jumped from his coach and hid in the scrub until he got a good shot at that night's leader, Cole Young, killing him with two rounds of buckshot. The rest of the gang fled in panic. The next morning Loomis raised a posse to follow them, but the outlaws once again outrode them.[12]

The following month Marshal Hall fielded a posse of six men to keep up the pressure on the gang. On November 19 they caught up with one segment of the band. A brief skirmish left one outlaw dead, one dying, and the rest in flight. Black Jack and his men wintered that year in Mexico, beyond the reach of the marshals.[13]

The gang, led by William "Black Jack" Christian, crossed the border back into New Mexico in March 1897. They announced their return by robbing the Cliff post office. Other robberies followed at a rapid clip. Marshal Hall sent out a number of posses in the hope that he could catch the outlaws. The plan, though expensive, worked. Deputy Fred Higgins arranged for two informants to guide his posse to the outlaw camp eighteen miles east of Clifton on the morning of April 28, 1897. During the ensuing skirmish Black Jack was killed. Marshal Hall, convinced now that the troubles in New Mexico were over, recalled his posses.[14]

Tom Ketchum assumed the name "Black Jack" and the leadership of the gang. Chased that spring into Arizona, the gang continued to rob trains and post offices until Marshal W. M. Griffith ran them across the border into Mexico. Throughout the rest of the year and into 1898, the new Black Jack and his men crisscrossed the border, raiding New Mexico and Arizona and then retreating back across the line. Marshal Griffith and the new appointee for marshal in New Mexico, Creighton M. Foraker, worked with agents of Wells Fargo Express to coordinate the pursuit of the outlaws.[15]

In August 1898, Deputy Jeff Milton of Arizona finally caught up with "Bronco Bill" Walters, "Kid" Johnson, and "Red" Pitkin. He and his posse of Wells Fargo agents had been pursuing the outlaws across Arizona into New Mexico and back, following them from one robbery to the next. After sneaking into the mountains, traveling only at night, and forgoing the purchase of supplies, Milton and his men crept up on the outlaws. "A fight," Marshal Griffith reported, "commenced by the desperadoes, ensued which resulted in the death of Wm. Johnson, the capture of 'Bronco Bill,' desperately wounded, and the escape of 'Red'

Pitkin into the heavy undergrowth on the mountain." Milton handed over his prisoner to Marshal Foraker of New Mexico because most of the crimes had been committed there.[16]

By September 1898, Foraker was bragging to the attorney general that he had eight of the Black Jack outlaws in custody, with three more killed in shoot-outs with his deputies. He was optimistic about getting the rest of the gang, including the new leader. The new Black Jack, however, headed the remnants of the gang south across the border. They kept to themselves over the next year, venturing out only occasionally to rob post offices and trains.

In the summer of 1899 the long spree of robberies and hold-ups ended. The Black Jack gang held up a train on July 13, and Marshal Foraker took a posse after them. Outside Cimarron they caught up with the outlaws, who chose to fight rather than surrender. Two of the possemen, Sheriff Farr of Huerfano County, Colorado, and William Love were killed, and F. H. Smith was shot through the leg. Among the outlaws, Sam Ketchum, Black Jack's brother, was killed, and W. M. McGinniss was wounded. He escaped but was subsequently captured.[17]

On August 24, Black Jack held up a train outside Trinidad. He shot the railway mail clerk through the face but was badly wounded himself. Stumbling from the mail car, Black Jack collapsed beside the tracks. When Foraker and a sheriff's posse arrived several hours later, they found him still there.

U.S. Attorney W. B. Childers agreed with the territorial officials of New Mexico that Black Jack should be tried under local law. New Mexico imposed the death sentence for train robbery; federal law provided only a jail sentence for mail robbery.

Black Jack was the first man convicted under the New Mexico death penalty, and the first to be executed for train robbery. The territory's lack of experience resulted in a gruesome spectacle. The hangman overestimated the length of drop necessary to break the condemned man's neck. When the trap was sprung, Black Jack plummeted downward with increasing speed. The rope around his neck caught him with a jerk, popping his head off. The body fell to one side, the head rolled a few feet away.[18]

In pursuing mail robbers, the marshals received encouragement, but little support, from the Department of Justice. The post office frequently offered cash rewards, which were a strong inducement for informers, but the Justice Department shied from any cash outlays.

During 1879, Congress and President Rutherford B. Hayes wrangled over the budget, which left the marshals with no appropriated funds. When Marshal Crowley P. Dake of Arizona inquired about covering his expenses in pursuing mail robbers, Attorney General Devens advised him that the post office had sufficient funds to cover most of the expenses, but the marshal's fees could not be paid. Devens still expected Marshal Dake to go after the outlaws.[19]

Attorney General A. H. Garland urged his marshals to pursue train robbers but to keep their expenses down. "Use economy but enforce the law against train robbers," he telegraphed Marshal W. A. Cabell of Texas on June 25, 1887. Two days later, Garland reiterated that the marshal "should keep economy in view." The constant reminders to stay "within reasonable economic limits" helped tie the lawmen hand and foot in worries over spending money. The advice seemed to hinder more than help them.[20]

Indeed, the federal government seldom gave the marshals adequate guidance. No general guide to the work of the marshals was published until the late 1890s. Before that, newly appointed marshals were referred to the relevant statutes written over the past century. Seldom did any lawyer within the Department of Justice actually sit down and explain, in detail and in layman's terms, exactly what the government expected of its marshals.[21]

The result was frequent confusion. One newly hired deputy in the Washington Territory heard that the job required uniforms. No one, including his marshal, knew for sure. The deputy wrote the attorney general in February 1868 to find out when he would receive his uniform. "Your credulity has been imposed upon," Assistant Attorney General John N. Hinckley responded. "The laws and judicial orders regulating the service of process do not require that the officers should wear any uniforms." The department did not even furnish badges, the great symbol of frontier authority. Marshals who wanted to pin on a badge did so at their own expense, using badges of their own design. About all the government offered a new U.S. marshal was a large, fancily worded commission signed by the president.[22]

"When I came into office no books, papers or anything else were left for guides to me in the discharge of my duties," complained Marshal Smith O. Scofield of Missouri in 1865. "I have been forced to travel a new and very difficult way alone with no chart except statutes covering a period of nearly one hundred years to guide me." Marshal Isaac Q.

Dickason had similar problems in the Arizona Territory. "Up to the present time I have been unable to ascertain what my annual salary is or what fees are allowed," he observed in 1871, four months after he received his commission. After M. C. Hillyer assumed the newly created office of marshal in the Alaska Territory in 1884, he complained to the attorney general that "none of the Government Officers here have received any instructions or laws." Hillyer was even unsure if he was to provide the courtroom, fuel, lights, and other office supplies to the U.S. commissioners. Nor had he received any instructions to take over the operation of the jails, even though the law defining the Alaska Territory specified that he should.[23]

On one exceptional occasion, Attorney General Ebenezer R. Hoar explained the duties of a U.S. marshal in the territories. The letter, written to newly appointed U.S. Marshal Church Howe of the Wyoming Territory on June 15, 1869, indicated the complicated relationship between federal and territorial authority. After referring to the various statutes that defined the office of marshal, Hoar observed:

> You are to serve all processes directed to you as Marshal by the courts. I do not know what the Territorial laws may be, or whether there are any but the Territorial Legislature may provide that all processes issuing from the courts in suits arising under the Territorial laws shall be directed to, and be served by the Sheriff of the county, or his deputy; or it may provide that such processes shall be directed to, and be served by, the Marshal of the United States or his deputy. It is competent, I think, for a Territorial Legislature to enact laws either way. But the duties of the Marshal which are beyond the control of the Territorial Legislature, are, to execute all processes issuing from the Supreme or District Courts, while exercising their jurisdiction as Circuit and District Courts of the United States; and he is also to perform substantially the same duties, and be subject to the same regulations and penalties, and be entitled to the same fees, as Marshals of the U.S. in the States.

Hoar went on to explain that the courts, when acting in their federal capacity, had jurisdiction "over all cases arising under the Constitution and laws of the United States." Those were the cases of most concern to the marshals, who became involved in territorial cases in the organized territories only if the legislature invited them.[24]

The vast distances separating officials in the Department of Justice from their frontier marshals exacerbated the difficulties between them.

The telegraph provided a quick, effective, albeit abbreviated link between Washington and the field, but its use was limited by its expense. The charge per word made telegraph messages cryptic and incomplete. The real problem was the failure to communicate. Department officials seemed consistently incapable of understanding the problems confronting the frontier marshals. For their part, the marshals were never particularly adept at explaining or even describing the problems they faced. When they tried, the message seldom got through to Washington. The Department of Justice wrapped itself in a blissful ignorance of the problems its frontier marshals faced.

INDIAN TERRITORY

The messenger chased the dawn to Guthrie, Oklahoma Territory. Edith Doolin, the wife of the notorious outlaw Bill Doolin, was on the move. The day before, August 22, 1896, she had packed a covered wagon with household effects, a plow, and a coop of chickens. She was obviously leaving her father's house in Lawson. While she loaded the wagon, Tom and Charlie Noble watched from hiding. That night they sent a messenger racing to Guthrie with the warning for Deputy Marshal Heck Thomas: Edith Doolin was on the move.

Once before, tracking Edith Doolin had led the marshals to her husband. In January 1896 she had received a postcard. Deputy Bill Tilghman learned from the postmaster that it came from Eureka Springs, Arkansas. The message, the nosy postman remembered, told of how soothing the mineral waters were for "Mr. Wilson's" rheumatic left leg. Tilghman went alone to the health resort, caught Doolin by surprise, and brought him back to Oklahoma. Six months later, Doolin escaped from the territorial jail to rob trains, banks, and post offices throughout the territory.[25]

Since the fight in Ingalls three years before, most of Doolin's gang had been killed. The so-called Three Guardsmen of Oklahoma—deputy marshals Bill Tilghman, Chris Madsen, and Heck Thomas—played major roles in ridding the territory of the notorious desperadoes. In June 1894 deputy marshals trapped Bill Dalton in a house and killed him as he fled through a bedroom window. In April 1895 a posse led by Madsen shot down Tulsa Jack Blake after he robbed a train just across the district line in Texas. That same month, Bitter Creek Newcomb died in a shoot-out with a posse led by Heck Thomas. In March 1896, Madsen cornered Red Buck Waightman, killing him when he resisted. By August 1896, Arkansas Tom Jones was doing fifty years in the federal penitentiary; most of the other gang members were dead. Only Doolin and Dynamite Dick Clifton remained free.[26]

Heck Thomas suspected that Mrs. Doolin's departure from her father's house meant one of two things: Either she was going to her husband, or he was already with her. Taking his son Albert and one other man with him, Thomas rushed to Lawson. They arrived in the middle of the afternoon on August 24. The Noble brothers reported that Bill Doolin's horse was tethered in the back shed.

Thomas hastily organized a small posse. He lent his Winchester to one of the men but kept for himself a cumbersome Number 8 shotgun. Just after dusk the possemen crawled through the brush along the single-lane dirt road leading to the house. When they got as close as they safely could, the men hid in the tall grass. Half of them were on one side of the road, half on the other side. Thomas kept watch on the house with field glasses.

Close to midnight, Bill Doolin came out of his father-in-law's house. Leading his horse, he started down the lane. His Winchester was cradled in his arms, ready to fire. To the hidden deputies, the outlaw acted as though he was looking for something or someone. Silhouetted by the moon, the possemen could see him easily. "He was walking slow," Thomas remembered, "looking first to one side and then the other." When he got between the divided posse, Thomas called out for him to surrender. Doolin fired at the sound of the voice.

Thomas swung his shotgun toward the outlaw. "It was too long in the breech and I couldn't handle it quick," the deputy later reported, "so he got another shot with his Winchester." Doolin had no clear sight of the posse, though, and none of his shots scored. One of the possemen fired, hitting Doolin's Winchester and jarring the rifle from his hands. The outlaw quickly drew his pistol while Thomas struggled with the ungainly shotgun. As Doolin fired his six-shooter, Thomas blasted him with a single round of buckshot. Doolin flipped backward several feet to land in a bloody heap on the dirt road. The fight lasted barely a few seconds. The undertaker later counted twenty-one buckshot holes in Doolin's body.[27]

More than a year later, in November 1897, deputy marshals George

Lawson and W. H. Bussey killed Dynamite Dick Clifton near Muskogee, Oklahoma. The Doolin gang was at last accounted for.[28]

Doolin's death ended an era. Doolin and his men were the last of the midwestern locust gangs—the Doolin, Cook, Dalton, Younger, James, and other outlaw bands that swept through the Midwest to strip its banks, railroads, and post offices of cash and negotiables. They stole at pleasure, murdered at will. Many of the gangs, like Doolin's, evaded the law and its lawmen for a surprisingly long time. Most of the outlaws, like Doolin, lost their lives in bloody gunfights, victims of their own way of life.

The Indian Territory and the northern fifty-mile strip adjacent to it known as No Man's Land were the most violent of the American territories. They lay roughly between Arkansas and north Texas, Kansas and south Texas—essentially the area composing present-day Oklahoma. Congress originally set the Indian Territory aside in 1834 as the place to resettle the Indians whose land had been stolen by westering whites. The Cherokee Trail of Tears ended here, as did the trails, equally tearful, of other tribes.

The law creating the Indian Territory established strict regulations on trade and intercourse with the Indians, such as the prohibition on selling them liquor or weapons. The intent was to protect the Indians from unscrupulous whites. At the same time, the Indian Territory relieved whites from the savagery of Indians who were defending their tribal lands.[29]

But the Indian Territory was in the way of the westering nation. Established at a time when the southern United States essentially ended at the Mississippi River, Congress showed little foresight when it planted Indians directly in the path of future expansion. The Indian Territory straddled the route to Texas and the Southwest. Once the massive population shift began, Americans who turned westward found a huge section of the country blocked to them. That island in the midst of the westering stream could neither be ignored nor resisted. It was simply a question of time before land-hungry whites began clamoring for parcels of the Indian Territory.

The whites who drifted into the territory lived in lonely outposts, scratching farms out of the dusty soil or fleeing the laws of neighboring states. The territory remained completely unorganized until the 1889 Oklahoma land rush. No territorial legislature was established; no territorial officials were appointed. With the exception of tribal self-government, law in the Indian Territory was entirely federal, upheld solely by federal marshals. Crimes among Indians were resolved by Indians, but crimes involving whites, even whites and Indians, were dealt with by the marshals working for the federal court in Fort Smith, Arkansas.

The Western District Court of Arkansas had jurisdiction over the Indian Territory. Headquartered in Fort Smith on the Arkansas River, the U.S. marshal for the western district dispatched his deputies across the river to enforce the law. "You have authority as a peace officer in all [the] Indian Territory," Attorney General William H. H. Miller instructed the marshals. A force of two hundred deputies rode over the seventy-four thousand square miles of the territory. In an unprecedented decision the Department of Justice also allowed the marshals to hire up to three possemen without first obtaining departmental permission.[30]

In late 1874 Marshal James F. Fagan detailed the offenses and crimes that came under the jurisdiction of his deputies. The list totaled twenty-one crimes ranging from first-degree murder to escape and including assault, larceny, arson, bribery, and manslaughter. "But deputies are not called upon to hunt after every violation of the law under these several heads," Fagan wrote. Deputies did not earn their three-quarters of the fee, nor Fagan his quarter, without process to serve. The deputies were "to serve the warrants and other process in their hands," Fagan admonished. "This is their first and chief duty." He continued:

> As officers of the United States it is also meet and proper they should make every reasonable effort to discover and bring to justice persons guilty of murder, assault with deadly weapons with intent to kill or maim, where the injured party is disabled from appearing before the commissioner in person, robbing the mail, stealing government property, resisting or obstructing the administration of justice, and substantial violation of the intercourse law. Prosecutions for offenses against the property of individuals should not be instituted by Deputies having no personal knowledge of the facts, but in such cases the injured party should be referred to the Commissioner.

The marshal understood that his deputies had their hands full in the Indian Territory. They had enough business, enough warrants against murderers, thieves, and other outlaws to serve, without drumming up more.[31]

President Ulysses S. Grant appointed a former congressman from

Missouri as the new federal judge for the western district. Isaac C. Parker arrived at Fort Smith on May 2, 1875. For the next twenty-one years, Parker dispensed federal justice over the Indian Territory. Under his direction, the marshals challenged some of the worst criminals in American history, savage men like Sam Starr, Rufus Buck, Crawford Goldsby (better known as Cherokee Bill), and Ned Christy. Judge Parker sent hundreds of outlaws to prison; he sentenced 160 of them to die. After appeals and commutations, the marshals hung 79 of the condemned men. The hangings earned Parker the chilling nickname "the Hanging Judge." The court's executioner was known as the Prince of Hangmen.

The crimes ranged from murder, rape, and robbery to assault, theft, and fraud. On December 3, 1880, the brothers Amos and Abner Manley took refuge from the cold in the home of Ellis McVay. While their host slept, the brothers killed him with a bullet to the brain. They shot and axed the farm's hired man, William Burnett, cutting off his right hand and gashing him across the neck before stealing what little they could find and fleeing. Caught by the marshals, the brothers were hanged from the Fort Smith gallows.[32]

On October 12, 1875, Aaron Wilson, a twenty-year old freedman, invited himself to dinner on the prairie with James Harris and his twelve-year-old son, who were westering their way to Texas. Wilson waited for the two to camp down for the night before he killed the father with an ax, the son with a load of buckshot from a double-barreled shotgun. A squad of U.S. troops caught Wilson several days later. After Judge Parker condemned Wilson's crime and sentenced him to the gallows, the prisoner calmly returned with his guards to his cell. "By God," Wilson exclaimed to his escort, "that is nothing when you get used to it!"[33]

Such becalmed depravity infested the Indian Territory. Life was valued at the pocketknife and pocket change that Silas Hampton killed Abner Lloyd to obtain. It was worth no more than the saddle that Malachi Allen murdered two men to take, nor more than the whiskey that Harris Austin killed Thomas Elliott over.[34]

Yet civilization through settlement could not long be denied. Neither outlaws nor Indians could forestall the advance of westering whites. By 1889 the pressures against the Indian Territory compelled Congress to open large portions of it to whites. On April 22, 1889, Deputy Ransome Payne signaled high noon. The rush for land began. As the boomers darted across the Oklahoma plain, they hurried into a series of camps already established. The night before, a number of sooners, many using purchased or forged deputy marshal commissions, had crossed the Cimarron River to stake their claim to the best parcels of land.[35]

The 1889 land rush and the 1893 rush across the Cherokee strip established Oklahoma as a territory. With white settlement came white government. The Indian Territory simply shrank; it did not disappear. The marshals continued to police the wide Oklahoma prairie. Frequently the budding towns hired the deputies to serve as local lawmen as well. The joint commissions enhanced the lawmen's authority, as well as their annual earnings.

The outlaws, however, continued to prowl. The Dalton brothers waited until the late 1880s to retire as deputy marshals in favor of the more profitable career as outlaws. The Buck and Doolin gangs rampaged across the area during the 1890s, as did other notables such as Ned Christy, a Cherokee who waged a personal war on white settlement. The closing decade of the nineteenth century seemed to spawn more famous – and more desperate – outlaws than ever before. It was, in a way, a last gasp of lawlessness drowning amid the great diluvial wash of westering whites.

INDIAN TROUBLES

Throughout the frontier, U.S. marshals and their deputies acted as a buffer between the native Indian population and the westering whites. The army contained the Indians on reservations and selected lands, restricting nomadic movements and subduing any uprisings. The marshals enforced the laws related to the Indians, such as the prohibitions on selling them liquor, guns, and other items. Federal lawmen also protected Indian lands from encroachments by whites. Crimes between Indians and whites were handled by the marshals, though crimes among Indians were treated as internal Indian affairs.

The legal relations among Indians and between whites and Indians were muddled. One particularly tragic case in the Indian Territory illustrated both the confusion and the danger. In 1872 a Cherokee named Proctor shot a white man named Kecterson in the head, seriously wounding him. Then Proctor turned his weapon on the white man's Indian wife, killing her. The murder was apparently part of a feud between Proctor's family and Mrs. Kecterson's family.

The Cherokee court charged Proctor with murdering the wife (an affair between Indians cognizable by Indian courts). Kecterson worried that the Indian court would acquit his assailant. He applied to the U.S. commissioner for a federal warrant against Proctor for assaulting him (an affair between a white and an Indian cognizable by federal courts). The commissioner issued an arrest warrant to deputy marshals Jacob Owens and Joseph Peavy with instructions to serve it only if the Cherokee court failed to convict the Indian defendant. Owens and Peavy raised a posse of ten men, including two of the murdered woman's brothers and two of her cousins. The deputies and their posse rode to the Going Snake Cherokee district court, fifty miles west of Fort Smith.

The lawmen reached the Going Snake district on April 15, 1872. The court had moved from its usual place to the local schoolhouse, which stood alone in a prairie clearing. The school commanded a full view of all its surroundings. As the possemen rode into the clearing, they saw several armed Indians dart around to the back of the building.

Deputy Owens ordered his men to dismount and hitch their horses some thirty yards from the building. Although later accounts conflicted, Owens probably cautioned the possemen to avoid any overt hostility. He wanted them simply to take their seats at the back of the court and await its verdict. If Proctor was acquitted, they were to arrest him on the assault charge.

The marshals may have approached the courthouse with weapons drawn, though that too is unclear. Undoubtedly, whether they carried their weapons in hand or not, the approach of armed men toward the schoolhouse would have made the Indians within it uneasy. The relatives of the murdered woman were well known to the Cherokees; their presence clearly branded the posse as unfriendly, perhaps even hostile, toward Proctor. Because the Indians had moved the court to a more defensible position and brought their weapons with them, they possibly expected or even wanted trouble. But that is only conjecture, based largely on what happened next.

The marshals crossed the clearing toward the front of the school-house. As they approached, several Cherokees came out the front door. Without hesitation, the Indians shouldered their rifles and fired into the posse.

The possemen had no place to hide. Inside the schoolhouse, according to a later report, the "guards, Jury, lawyers for defense, and prisoner participated in the fight." The deputies hastily retreated toward their horses, pausing only to take quick aim. The lawmen killed three Indians and wounded six others.

Seven deputies were killed outright as they retreated. Deputy Owens was wounded and died several hours later. It was the worst slaughter of marshals in history.

The next day, the Cherokee jury acquitted Proctor of the murder of Mrs. Kecterson.[36]

The Going Snake massacre was an exceptional occurrence in the Indian Territory. The marshals generally enjoyed a peaceful, if not altogether friendly relationship with the five Indian tribes. The Indians understood that the marshals helped protect them from westering and unscrupulous whites. Because the Indians policed themselves, the U.S. marshals and their deputies had little interest in internal Indian affairs.

Illegal trading with the Indians in liquor, guns, and game was one of the most widespread and enduring law enforcement problems for the marshals. The volatile combination of liquor and weapons contributed to the frequent outbreak of bloody Indian insurrections. The brief, brutal wars were then viciously subdued by the U.S. Army. Investigating the illegal trade was especially difficult. The wide expanse of territory, the ingenuity of the peddlers, and the inability of the Justice Department to fund the investigations adequately all worked against the marshals. Neither the U.S. marshal nor his deputies had time to conduct the frequently lengthy investigations. Consequently, once the marshals suspected illegal trade, they requested permission from the department to hire detectives, who were specially deputized before the marshals sent them out to patrol the local Indian reservations and report any evidence of illicit trading. If sufficient evidence was collected, warrants could be sworn and arrests made.

The nature of the offense contributed to the difficulties in stopping the trade. The Indians were both victims of the crime and participants in it. The strained relations between federal officials and their supposed Indian wards prohibited any easy cooperation between the marshals and the tribesmen. Defeated in war and denied their traditional way of life, the Indians had been stripped of their freedom and imprisoned on reservations. For many Indians, whiskey was the only escape. They sought it as eagerly as the peddlers sought them.

Life on the reservations added more inducement to turn to drink. Corruption within the Indian bureau reached legendary proportions. The Indians paid the toll for it. Their food was usually spoiled and rancid, their rations were shaved for graft, and the other entitlements due them by law and treaty were withheld or corrupted. Because federal officials committed the crimes, it was little wonder that the Indians learned to distrust anyone working for the government, including the marshals.

Keeping liquor out of the Indian Territory was a constant battle for the marshals. The problem was immensely compounded during the early 1870s when the railroad was built through the territory. The crews were rough men who held the law in little regard. Their camp followers showed even less respect. The end of each day's line became temporary cities of sin. "The construction of Railroads brings a most lawless turbulent floating population," Marshal Logan H. Roots reported to the attorney general on February 2, 1872. "The terminal Railroad Depot is perhaps today the wickedest place on earth . . . in numerous places citizens are murdered without redress and Deputies who endeavor to bring the villains to justice are subject to assault and assassination."[37]

The Justice Department repeatedly urged its lawmen to put a stop to the "illicit intercourse" with the Indians throughout the frontier. As usual, the department hesitated to support its instructions with adequate resources. Attorney General George Williams typified that attitude when he wrote Kansas marshal William S. Tough in March 1874: "It is my wish that this illicit traffic with the Indians be broken up. At the same time I wish to incur as little expense as possible."[38]

Federal lawmen in Montana suffered similar problems enforcing the laws. In December 1870, Marshal William F. Wheeler reported that one of his deputies had seized two wagons, four mules, three horses, and one hundred gallons of whiskey from white traders on the Blackfoot reservation north of Fort Benton. With Deputy Charles D. Hand, who held a joint commission as a special detective for the Indian bureau, Wheeler worked up cases allowing the government to seize a steamboat on the Missouri River, a trading post twenty miles south of Canada, and $3,000 worth of buffalo robes.[39]

In 1875 the Royal Canadian Mountain Police stepped up its pursuit of illicit traders, forcing them to slip south into Marshal Wheeler's district. "I have more business arising from violations of the Indian Intercourse laws than in any of the six years while I have been Marshal of Montana," Wheeler wrote Attorney General Edwards Pierrepont in June 1875. During the fiscal year ending in that month, he handled nearly $4,000 in forfeitures and penalties. That month alone, Wheeler conducted two seizures involving $6,000 to $10,000 in goods. "The contest with [the illicit traders] is a constant warfare," Wheeler continued, "and considering the very limited means and force at my disposal I have made the business expensive to them."[40]

Those cases paled before events in Minnesota that rang out the nineteenth century. In October 1898 the last of the nineteenth-century-style Indian uprisings, and the last victory for the Indians, closed the era. When federal marshals tried to arrest some Chippewas for dealing in illicit whiskey, the frustrations of the ill-treated Indians finally exploded.

For several decades whiskey traders had been a problem in Minnesota. In June 1881, Attorney General Wayne MacVeagh, after learning of liquor traffic between St. Vincent and the White Earth reservation, ordered Marshal Robert N. McLaren "to take vigorous measures to detect and punish these violators of the law." McLaren responded in fairly typical fashion: He hired a detective named James B. Blanchard.[41]

In less than a month Blanchard, the former sheriff of Clay County, had accumulated enough evidence against J. B. Fairbanks's saloon in Audubon to warrant arrest. Other arrests followed as Blanchard worked assiduously, but the volume of trade worked against him. The construction of the railroad through Minnesota, as well as various engineering projects, created fertile fields for the illegal trade. "The selling of liquor to Indians seems to be more general now than for some time past and is particularly a source of great evil and annoyance at the Government Works and along the line of Railroads now being built," U.S. Attorney D. B. Searle noted in September 1883, two years after Blanchard was hired.[42]

By the 1890s, signs of frustration began to show in the Minnesota marshals. The treatment of the Indians by the lawmen became something less than friendly. Relations with one particular Indian, a Chippewa chief named Bugonaygeshig, were particularly troublesome. On one occasion the marshals summoned Bugonaygeshig to Duluth to testify as a witness. When the chief failed to tell all that he obviously knew, the marshals refused to pay his witness fees. Stranded far from home with no money, Bugonaygeshig made his own way back to the reservation on the shores of Leech Lake in northern Minnesota.

In April 1895, marshals arrested Bugonaygeshig for selling whiskey to his tribesmen. Because the evidence against him could not sustain the case, the chief was released within a few days. Two months later, he and several other Indians were subpoenaed to testify in yet another case.

Each of them failed to appear at the appointed hour, so the court issued bench warrants against them. Although deputies immediately arrested Bugonaygeshig and his colleagues, the Indians were rescued from the marshals' custody before they could be taken from the reservation. Several days later, most of the fugitive witnesses surrendered. Bugonaygeshig and two others, however, refused to give up. In the fall of 1899 they were still fugitives from the bench warrants.[43]

The Indians had their own complaints. Federal law protected their trees and lumber, the most important cash crop for the reservation, but only lumber from live trees. Wood from dead and fallen timber was free for the taking, but the law did not define how long the trees needed to be dead before the wood became open to all. White speculators and uncaring lumbermen helped the trees along by cutting them down, then claiming the timber. Although the Chippewas repeatedly expressed their opposition, including sending a petition to President William McKinley, they got little relief from federal authorities.[44]

In September 1898 fresh warrants were sworn against Chief Bugonaygeshig and another Indian for again selling liquor on the Leech Lake reservation. Deputy marshals entered the reservation on September 15 and arrested them. As the deputies escorted the two men off the reservation, a band of fifty drunken Indians surrounded them and freed the prisoners. Although no one was hurt, the marshals could not allow the challenge to federal authority to go unanswered. Twenty-two new warrants were sworn against the known participants in the escape. Minnesota marshal Richard T. O'Connor asked the U.S. Army, fresh from its victory over Spain in Cuba, to help subdue the minor uprising at Leech Lake.[45]

O'Connor handed the arrest warrants to Deputy Timothy J. Sheehan with instructions to accompany the troops. A veteran of the Civil War and the Sioux outbreak of 1862, Sheehan had four scars to prove his bravery under fire. He had ended the war a lieutenant colonel and returned to Minnesota. For twelve years he was sheriff of Freeborn County, then accepted an appointment as Indian agent at the White Earth agency. In 1890 Sheehan took the oath of a deputy U.S. marshal.[46]

Sheehan asked Brigadier General John M. Bacon, the commanding officer of the department of Dakota, to send 150 men to the Leech Lake reservation. Bacon sent only 20. The small detachment, commanded by Lieutenant Chauncey B. Humphreys, left St. Paul with Sheehan on

September 30, 1898. The next day, Sheehan, Humphreys, and several officials from the Indian agency crossed into the reservation, where they served subpoenas summoning several Indians to the Leech Lake agency on October 3. That evening Marshal O'Connor and an additional half dozen deputies arrived.[47]

On the appointed day not a single Indian showed up at the agency. O'Connor went to the reservation to consult with tribal leaders. They confirmed that the Indians would not attend a conference with him at the agency nor would the leaders surrender the Indians wanted by the courts. Sheehan was "disgusted with Indian promises." He warned that the Indians "were bound to fight." Marshal O'Connor agreed that the Indian attitude meant "war is on." Lieutenant Humphreys urgently telegraphed General Bacon for more troops. The next day, October 4, 1898, eighty more soldiers of the Third Infantry, commanded by Brevet Major Melville C. Wilkinson and accompanied by General Bacon himself, arrived at Leech Lake.[48]

Early on the morning of October 5, O'Connor, six deputies, and seventy-seven soldiers boarded two lake steamers and crossed Leech Lake to the north shore, where a small peninsula jutted into the water. The men marched directly to Chief Bugonaygeshig's small house, which stood in a clearing. Thick woods bordered the property on three sides.

A small group of Indians watched the federal forces approach. Deputy Sheehan recognized Mahqua, one of the Indians wanted for the September 15 rescue of Bugonaygeshig. When he tried to handcuff Mahqua, the Indian twisted the iron cuffs from Sheehan's grasp and lashed out at the deputy with them. Sheehan warded the blow with his hands, then grabbed Mahqua. The two men wrestled to the ground, striking and hitting each other as several deputies and soldiers rushed forward to help. The soldiers quickly overpowered the Indian while the deputies cuffed his hands behind him.[49]

For the next two hours the soldiers and deputies crisscrossed the peninsula looking for fugitive Indians. No more were seen, except one Indian who surrendered and was put in custody with Mahqua aboard the steamboats. The lawmen and troops regrouped in the clearing outside Bugonaygeshig's house. O'Connor and several deputies returned to the boats while the soldiers stacked their arms and prepared for lunch.[50]

A rifle fired.

Everyone jumped. The trooper who was stacking the smoking rifle looked startled at first, then embarrassed at his own carelessness for keeping a round in the chamber. Realizing it was an accident, the soldiers relaxed slightly. The sound of the shot echoed through the woods.

Two quick shots answered the echo. A thunderous volley of fire followed immediately. From three sides, the Indians hidden in the woods shot at the soldiers. Without waiting for orders, the troopers leapt for their rifles. They quickly organized themselves into three loose defensive lines. Deputy Sheehan took command on the right, Major Wilkinson on the center, and Second Lieutenant Tenny Ross on the left. With their backs to the lake, the soldiers sought what cover they could find.

Major Wilkinson answered the eerie war cries of the Indians by exhorting the troopers, "Give it to them, boys; give 'em hell!" Sheehan charged his men toward the Indians firing from the right. The charge drove the Indians deeper into the woods, but Sheehan did not force the pursuit. He returned with his men to their cover in the clearing.

The initial intense skirmish lasted almost half an hour. For the rest of the afternoon, the soldiers and Indians traded shots, but neither side seemed incline to push to victory. As dusk fell, the Indians slipped away. During the fight Sheehan, his hands already bruised from the scuffle with Mahqua, was again wounded. Ten of the soldiers also suffered gunshot wounds.

Six of the troopers were killed, including Major Wilkinson. Wounded twice, he caught a third bullet in his gut while striding openly among his men challenging them with shouts of "Give 'em hell, give 'em hell."

The next morning, General Bacon began taking the wounded back to the steamboats. Another burst of fire from the Indians pinned the force down. Finally, late that morning, the wounded were put aboard the ships, and the excursion force returned to safety.[51]

As word of the fight spread, reinforcements were sent to General Bacon in case the uprising spread. The Indians, however, had had enough. They accepted a negotiated settlement. By mid-October, all the fugitives were in the custody of the marshals. Tried and found guilty, they received sentences ranging from sixty days in jail and $25 fines to ten months in jail and $100 fines. In December 1898, upon the recommendation of the Indian agency, the sentences were commuted to two months' imprisonment, and the fines were dropped.

The Leech Lake uprising was the last serious Indian disturbance for more than seventy years. Liquor continued to be a problem, and the marshals continued to work against its sale, but the violence abated as the Indians accepted defeat and tried to adjust to the poverty of life on their reservations. During the 1970s the American Indian Movement (AIM) would rekindle Indian pride and chauvinism. Through a series of demonstrations and occupations, AIM would protest the treatment of Indians and try to recapture the spirit of their lost heritage. Once again, the U.S. marshals and their deputies would be caught in the middle.

8

FEDERAL BORDERS

1867–1900

United States Marshal Fred Pinder understood loyalty, particularly loyalty to friends. In the summer of 1863, when General H. A. Burgevine was wounded, dismissed from the army, and then refused his back pay, Marshal Pinder shared his friend's outrage. When Burgevine joined a band of rebels that same summer, Pinder empathized with him and volunteered to help. Burgevine asked for supplies, especially rifles.

On Saturday afternoon, September 19, 1863, Marshal Pinder and another friend, J. W. Butler, chartered a small boat named the *Rose*. Throughout the afternoon, they loaded the lorcha with 110 rifles, 28 pairs of boots, 40 blankets, several cases of cigars, 4 cases of champagne, and 16 cases of various liquors.

Late that evening, as the small boat headed downriver, someone watched from hiding. When the *Rose* was well away, the spy hastened in search of Commander Solway, a British naval officer in command of the gunboat *Amoy*. The open animosity between the British and the Americans over Britain's support of the Confederacy was no secret. The spy knew that the British would dearly love—and dearly pay for—information implicating an official of the U.S. government in illegally supporting a rebellion.

Commander Solway dispatched his lieutenant, Samuel Ridge, in their small boat while he headed overland to the *Amoy,* which was docked some distance downstream. By dawn, Solway had reached his gunboat. Lieutenant Ridge and his crew arrived minutes later. Neither group had seen anything untoward along the river. Suspecting that the *Rose* had found sanctuary in one of the hundreds of inlets along the way, Commander Solway headed the *Amoy* back upstream.

Within a few miles he and his men spied the *Rose* beating downriver. After hailing the boat to a stop, Commander Solway accompanied his boarding party onto the lorcha. A brief look about the ship convinced him that he had been right to seize her. The rifles and other supplies, he knew, were proof enough to convict the Americans.

Pinder protested. He was, he said, the U.S. marshal. He had seized the *Rose* and arrested its crew for smuggling. Where are the prisoners? Solway smugly inquired. They jumped overboard, Pinder lamely told him. Solway asked for the marshal's warrant, but Pinder had none. Why were they headed downstream, Solway asked, away from Pinder's court? To get provisions, Pinder replied weakly. Smirking, Solway asked for proof, some kind of identification, that Pinder was a U.S. marshal. Pinder had none. Solway then announced that the *Rose,* its crew, and its passengers were under arrest. The British sailors turned the *Rose* about, taking their prize and their prisoners upriver.

They sailed less than a mile before they saw another small boat flying the American flag. The *Amoy's* sudden appearance created a commotion aboard the smaller vessel. As Solway put his spyglass to the smaller craft, he saw General Burgevine darting below deck. The British hailed to the boat to come about and prepare for boarding, but the smaller craft turned toward the shallows. The *Amoy* gave chase, but it drew too deep a draft for the inlets and tributaries where Burgevine's boat headed. After waiting twenty minutes for the small boat to reappear along the river, the British commander gave up the search.

Commander Solway turned the *Amoy* and its prize back up the Yangtze River toward Shanghai, China. As the gunboat headed home, Solway smiled in anticipation. He looked forward to turning his prisoners over to the U.S. consulate in Shanghai for trial in the American consular court.[1]

Three years earlier, in June 1860, the U.S. Congress passed legislation putting the terms of treaties with China, Japan, and other Far Eastern countries into effect. The treaties established the principle of extraterritoriality, a system employed by all the Western powers with interests in the Far East to protect their nationals. The European powers, including the United States, refused to recognize the right of the non-Christian oriental countries to judge European and American nationals according to seemingly primitive laws applied by inequitable courts. Extraterritoriality guaranteed Western traders, merchants, and visitors immunity from the laws of the host countries. Instead, Westerners lived according to the laws of their homeland, their disputes heard in their own courts.

The law passed by Congress in June 1860 erected a system of consular courts, creating one court each in Japan and Siam and four courts in China. Almost as an afterthought, similar courts were provided for Persia, Tripoli, Tunis, Morocco, and Muscat.

Specific legations and consulates were given judicial authority to hear civil and criminal cases in their districts. The consular courts had jurisdiction over all legal issues and disputes, civil and criminal, involving American citizens. The decisions on those issues, the law prescribed, would, "in all cases, be exercised and enforced in conformity with the laws of the United States." The courts were empowered to sentence convicted criminals, even to pronounce the death sentence, and funds were appropriated to rent jails and prison buildings.

Congress also created the office of U.S. marshal to serve the consular courts and authorized the president to appoint marshals to the new courts, though it limited the number of such positions to seven. The law specified one marshal each for Japan, Siam, and Turkey (which had surrendered extraterritoriality in its 1830 treaty with the United States), and four marshals for China. Like their counterparts in the United States, the consular marshals earned fees for performing specific services. Unlike their counterparts, the consular marshals also received an annual salary of $1,000. The consular marshals, too, were bonded, though at only half the amount—$10,000—expected of their colleagues in the United States.

Succeeding presidents tended to appoint Americans already resident in the foreign country as the marshals of the consular courts. On occasion, presumably when no American was readily available, the president selected a European national for the position, but that was rare. The duties of the consular marshals were essentially the same as those of the marshals in the United States and its territories. They served the process of the consular courts, arrested people accused of crimes, kept custody of prisoners, and executed the orders of the courts.[2]

President Lincoln appointed Fred Pinder as the first U.S. marshal for the consular court in Shanghai. Pinder, of course, was not acting as the marshal when he tried to smuggle supplies to his friend and fellow American General Burgevine. Burgevine had been in the employ of the Chinese emperor until his poor treatment by the government persuaded him to join one of the many bands of insurgents. Marshal Pinder's effort to bring him supplies was illegal, an embarrassingly clear violation of American neutrality. The only aspect of the situation that saved the marshal was his arrest by British officers, particularly because American consular authorities would try him.

Pinder's trial for aiding and abetting the insurgents opened on September 25, 1863, in the Shanghai consular court, Consul George Seward presiding. Seward, the nephew of Secretary of State William H. Seward, was a fierce patriot, a fiercer Anglophobe. The testimony of Commander Solway, Lieutenant Ridge, and several other witnesses clearly established Pinder's guilt. The marshal refused to testify in his own defense. No explanation was given for his trip down the Yangtze River, for the rifles and supplies he carried aboard the *Rose,* or for General Burgevine's presence in the area. Despite the overwhelming evidence against the marshal, Consul Seward dismissed the charges. The British officers, he announced, had not proved their case. To add further insult to the British, Seward refused to accept Pinder's tendered resignation. Pinder continued to enjoy, Seward wrote, his full confidence and support.

Eventually, however, General Burgevine tired of the rebellion. He surrendered to American authorities in the late fall of 1863. In a private conversation with Seward, Burgevine confirmed Marshal Pinder's guilt. Because sufficient time had elapsed to show American spite toward the British, Seward demanded Pinder's resignation. Pinder unhappily complied.[3]

Other consular marshals, whether in the four courts in China or in the courts in Japan, Siam, and Turkey, were neither as belligerent nor as unfriendly to their hosts as Pinder had been. Instead, those marshals devoted their time to performing the same duties as their cohorts at home. Marshal Pinder, however, epitomized the complete disregard for Chinese sovereignty that the system of extraterritoriality entailed. By aiding and abetting a rebellion against the lawful Chinese government,

Pinder simply followed the system to its logical conclusion. Despite intense opposition and outrage from the Chinese people – the famous Boxer Rebellion of 1900 was essentially a violent protest against foreigners and their insistence on extraterritoriality – neither the United States nor the other Western powers were willing to surrender their nationals to face Chinese courts and laws.

The system of American consular courts remained intact for varying lengths of time, depending largely on the Western view of each Far Eastern country's progress toward modernity. Japan and Turkey, for example, extricated themselves from the embarrassing treaties by the end of the nineteenth century. China endured them the longest, from 1860 until 1943. In 1907 the United States transformed the four consular courts into one U.S. district court with four divisions. Federal judges and attorneys were appointed in place of the consular officials, and the consular marshals took up the duty of serving the district court.

The consular courts illustrated the federal government's determined efforts to have complete control over U.S. foreign policy. Although the government wavered on other issues, never quite confident of its own power or authority, it reigned supreme over relations with other nations.

THE FENIANS

The potato famine in Ireland forced large numbers of Irish men and women to emigrate to the United States. Like many immigrants, they never forgot their homeland; they never quite accepted the United States as their new nation. Drafted into the Union army during the Civil War, many Irishmen gained experience in fighting and military organization. Returning home after Appomattox, they used their wartime experiences in planning ways to achieve Ireland's independence.

The plan they struck upon was wild and impractical, almost nonsensical, yet all the more dangerous because they took it so seriously. Calling themselves Fenians after the pre-Christian Irish army Fianna Eirann, they decided to free Ireland by invading Canada. The Fenians never quite made it clear just what they would do with Canada once it was in their possession, whether they would hold it hostage in return for a free Ireland or they would launch their final invasion of the British Isles from Canadian shores. But that did not stop the recruits from flocking to join the Fenian army, it did not stop the money coming into the Fenian coffers, and it did not stop the Fenian army from launching its invasion of Canada in the early summer of 1866.[4]

Buffalo, New York, hosted the Fenian army as it prepared for the invasion in the spring of 1866. The preparations included sending large shipments of arms and munitions to Buffalo, nightly military drills in the city, nationwide meetings to raise funds, and published requests for money "to aid us in establishing a Republican form of government in Ireland." Warned by Secretary of State William H. Seward, Attorney General James Speed finally took notice of the Fenian activity in early April 1866. Speed instructed Marshal Edward Dodd and U.S. Attorney William A. Dart to repair to Buffalo to stop the invasion. "If upon investigation," he told Dodd, "you should be satisfied that there is a probability of an infraction of our neutrality laws, you are hereby instructed to take the necessary steps against the party or parties contemplating such infraction." Speed asked the marshal to be "active and prompt, and at the same time as quiet as possible." He wanted to avoid giving the Fenians more notoriety, which always attracted more recruits.[5]

Very early on the morning of June 1, 1866, John O'Neill and his army of six hundred men crossed the Niagara River on canal boats and entered Canada at Waterloo. Marching across the countryside, the Fenians engaged the Canadian militia in two separate skirmishes on June 2. The first battle took place at seven in the morning outside Ridgeway. The Canadian force numbered about fourteen hundred militiamen and British soldiers. The Fenians routed them and chased them through the town.

Cut off from communications with the rest of the Fenians, O'Neill took his troops to Fort Erie. Late that afternoon the Canadians again attacked. Again the Fenians drove them off, taking forty prisoners. Thirty Canadians were killed during the two battles; about a hundred were wounded. The Fenians suffered eight dead, fifteen wounded. That evening O'Neill took his stand at the old Fort Erie. He vowed, if necessary, to turn it into a "slaughterpen."

The Fenian victories, however, were indications of Canadian surprise rather than Fenian might. O'Neill and his small army stood no chance of winning. On the night of June 2 the general learned that no other Fenian forces had crossed the Niagara River. U.S. Attorney Dart, Marshal Dodd, and Collector Norton had finally taken decisive action against the Fenians. While O'Neill was fighting his way along Canadian shores, the federal officials seized the arms and munitions the Fenians depended on for resupply. They also blocked all reinforcements from joining the invaders.

Realizing his predicament, O'Neill ordered his command home to the United States on the morning of June 3. The men boarded a scow, which a tug pulled out into the Niagara River. As the tugboat headed the scow toward American shores, the USS *Michigan* intercepted it. Commander Andrew Bryson fired the ship's twelve-pounder across the tug's bow, bringing it to a rapid halt. The Fenians surrendered. O'Neill and his officers were put in custody aboard the *Michigan*. Their troops were imprisoned aboard the open scow.[6]

Marshal Dodd made no arrests on June 3, although the Fenians were held aboard the *Michigan* and the scow without benefit of legal process. The next day, O'Neill and his men applied to the local justice of the New York Supreme Court for a writ of habeas corpus. When Sheriff G. W. Clinton served the writ on Bryson, the commander denied having custody of the Fenians, despite their obvious presence aboard his ship. They were "in the hands of the U.S. Marshal," he replied on the writ, "and the writ should be served on him." In response to that effort to free the Fenians, U.S. Attorney Dart appealed to U.S. Commissioner Perry G. Parker for arrest warrants against the Fenians. Parker issued the warrants on June 5. The state's writ of habeas corpus was dismissed.[7]

Attorney General Speed adamantly insisted that the Fenians "must be taught to respect and fear the law." By August, however, Dart was not sure he could successfully prosecute the invaders of Canada. He believed that any jury drawn from the Buffalo and Erie County area would by sympathetic with the Irishmen. Their lawyers would have no difficulty "in packing the jury for their acquittal." Although Dart disliked "to be beaten where I think I ought to succeed," he also feared "that such a result would bring the Government and its laws into contempt." The new attorney general, Henry Stanbery, agreed. He allowed Dart to dismiss the charges. O'Neill and his Fenians went free.[8]

The Fenians immediately began planning another invasion of Canada. For the next several years the marshals in northern New York investigated sporadic reports of their activity. In July 1869 the attorney general put out a general alert to the marshals and district attorneys along the Canadian border. Deputy Marshal William Hildreth learned in August 1869 that the Fenian army had more than fifty thousand breech-loading rifles ready for another invasion. Acting Attorney General W. A. Field hesitated to spend money for further investigations. "A quiet watchfulness on the part of the Marshal or his deputies . . . will detect whatever is being done," he explained to U.S. Attorney William Dorsheimer of northern New York.[9]

Federal officials dared hope that the Fenians had given up their wild scheme to take Canada. Acting Attorney General Field called off the July alert in September 1869. This optimism, however, did not take into account John O'Neill's Irish stubbornness. Instead of repeating the foray into Canada from northern New York, O'Neill looked northeast to where Vermont touched Canada. He took his army of Irishmen to that small state in the spring of 1870.[10]

Vermont's U.S. attorney, B. F. Fifield, reported increased Fenian activity to the new attorney general, Ebenezer R. Hoar, in mid-April. Hoar, however, did not believe his force of civilian officials could stop an invasion of Canada. "I do not know that the District Attorney can lawfully do any thing that will really prevent an invasion of the Canada frontier, if one should be attempted," he told Secretary of State Hamilton Fish. "If such an invasion is attempted, it can I think be prevented only by military force. Indictments would not, I think, prove effectual." Despite his pessimism, Hoar instructed Marshal George P. Foster to do all in his power to enforce the neutrality laws against the Fenians.[11]

Foster, a former general in the Civil War, visited O'Neill's camp at midmorning on May 25, just as the Fenians were preparing to launch their invasion of Canada. Foster took with him Deputy Thomas Failey and a small posse of Vermont citizens. Seeing them approach, O'Neill called his men to line "with the intention of resisting arrest in case the marshal attempted it." O'Neill was prepared to take Foster prisoner if necessary.

One of the Fenian officers met the marshal's carriage as it pulled into the camp. Realizing that he was vastly outnumbered by armed troops, Foster made no attempt to arrest any of the Fenians. He simply requested that they keep the roads clear. O'Neill readily agreed to the request, and Foster left the camp. After a brief inspection across the border, where Canadian forces were gathering to resist the invasion, Foster headed back toward Franklin, or so O'Neill thought. In fact, the marshal and his posse went a short distance away, stopping at the home of a Mr. Vincent.

O'Neill launched the invasion. Unlike his troops of four years before, however, young boys who had never tasted the fear of battle made up most of the new army. The invasion stammered. Many Fenian soldiers retreated as soon as the Canadian troops opened fire. Compounding the confusion, O'Neill's reinforcements did not arrive.

O'Neill decided to return to camp to speed up his reinforcements. Chancing upon one of his men lying wounded in front of the Vincent house, the general stopped to see to him. Marshal Foster and Deputy Failey emerged from behind the house. Desperate to avoid arrest, O'Neill grabbed for his saber, but Foster and Deputy Failey pinioned his arms to his sides. The marshal's posse surrounded O'Neill as he was taken to the marshal's carriage. The officers put him in the backseat, Marshal Foster taking the seat beside him. Deputy Failey clambered aboard the front seat with the driver.

The invasion collapsed. "The arrest of O'Neill broke the back of the whole thing," U.S Attorney Fifield wrote to Attorney General Hoar, "and I cannot well tell you how miserable and pitiable the failure is." The defeated army disintegrated into small groups, each making its own way home from Canada. As the remaining Fenian officers slipped across the American border, Marshal Foster's deputies arrested them.

Marshal Foster took General O'Neill before U.S. Commissioner Smalley in St. Albans. They charged him with violating the neutrality laws. The commissioner set bail at $20,000, an amount well beyond O'Neill's reach. Fifield feared that the defeated Fenians would attempt a rescue, so he asked Marshal Foster to take O'Neill to the jail in Burlington, about thirty miles away.[12]

Two days later, Attorney General Hoar put the U.S. military forces in the area under Foster's command. He instructed the marshal to seize all Fenian arms and munitions and to arrest anyone who tried another invasion. "Your prompt action in arresting the leader of these misguided men gives great satisfaction," Hoar congratulated the marshal.[13]

General O'Neill remained in the Burlington jail for two months. A group of sympathizers, including former attorney general William M. Evarts and Congressman Benjamin Franklin Butler, raised money to provide for his family. At trial, the Fenian was found guilty and sentenced to two years in jail. Hardly had he begun to serve his time before President Ulysses S. Grant pardoned him and his fellow officers.[14]

Although the defeat of the Fenians did not end the dream of an independent Ireland, it effectively discouraged further efforts to take Canada from Britain. Even General O'Neill answered questions about another invasion with "No! emphatically no." With the exception of a small raiding party into Manitoba from the Dakota Territory in 1872, the Fenians caused no more real difficulty, though they continued to make a considerable amount of noise. Vermont enjoyed a brief scare again in the fall of 1876, but it turned out to be nothing. In February 1877, Marshal Foster reported that he was unable to find any evidence that the Fenians were moving along his frontier.[15]

Throughout this period and beyond, the marshals were also troubled by considerable activity among Cuban patriots to bring supplies and recruits to their island home. During the first Cuban revolution of 1868–78, Cubans turned to the United States for sympathy and help. From New Orleans to New York, the marshals found themselves trying to block smuggled weapons and supplies, a difficult, sometimes fruitless task. Eventually the Spanish ruthlessly subdued the rebellion. It would not be until the late 1890s that Cuba would taste the freedom it sought.

THE HEATHEN CHINESE

While the Fenians and Cubans launched invasions from American shores, the American people identified another group of foreigners as invaders of the United States. Between 1854 and 1868, roughly seventy-five thousand Chinese came to the United States. Arriving on American shores, the immigrants hardly found a warm reception awaiting them. American laws and American courts offered them precious little protection. Anti-Chinese prejudice, expressed in frequent riots, further marred their welcome.

Known disparagingly as coolies, the Chinese came to America primarily to build the transcontinental railroad. Many came as indentured servants, a system that dangerously bordered on outright slavery or peonage. In 1864, Congress, for example, established the office of commissioner of immigration. The commissioner had authority to admit contract laborers who exchanged twelve months' labor for passage to the United States. That was the formal practice.

Many Chinese suffered informal arrangements. Private companies spotted their tickets to the United States in exchange for considerably more of their life than one year's labor. Once in the country, it was relatively easy to increase the coolies' debt by charging them exorbitant, fraudulent prices for food and shelter. Southerners used a similar system of peonage – debt slavery – to subjugate theoretically free blacks.[16]

Once the Union Pacific linked up with the Central Pacific at Promontory, Utah, in 1869, most of the coolies lost their jobs. They migrated across the country, finding employment with mining companies, ranches, and industries and establishing their own communities within the larger cities and towns. Over the next fourteen years, between 1868 and 1882, 160,000 Chinese came to America, more than double the number of immigrants in the previous period. Chinese immigration peaked in 1882, when almost 40,000 Chinese arrived. Because the railroad companies no longer needed them for the brutal work of laying the track, the flood of Chinese immigrants was channeled into the cities along the western coast. The rapidly expanding Chinatowns were easily noticeable, and just as easily targeted, by the local citizenry. The tidal wave of immigration exacerbated the already deep-seated prejudice against the Chinese.

Sporadic anti-Chinese riots along the west coast evidenced the prejudice the Chinese confronted in the United States. Riots in Tacoma, Washington, in 1885 ended with the mayor a prisoner of the U.S. marshal and indicted on federal charges for inciting the violence. The willingness of the Chinese to work for low – almost starvation – wages earned them no friends among American workers.[17]

After approving a new treaty with China in 1880 that allowed the United States to "regulate, limit or suspend" but not prohibit Chinese immigration, Congress passed a law in May 1882 prohibiting all immigration of Chinese laborers for a decade. Fearing that "the coming of Chinese laborers to this country endangers the good order of certain localities," Congress restricted immigration for the first time in American history.

The law required all Chinese coming to the United States to carry certificates from the Chinese government verifying that they were not laborers, whether skilled or unskilled. Chinese laborers already in the United States were allowed to remain, and were even granted the right to return if they decided to leave, but Congress made clear its desire to see them off forever by denying them the opportunity to become American citizens. The law also called on the president to ferret out all illegal or uncertified Chinese in the country and deport them.[18]

In 1886, four years after Congress passed the Chinese exclusion law, the Statue of Liberty lifted her torch to beckon the tired, the poor, and the hungry to American shores. But Liberty faced eastward toward the Atlantic and Europe. She purposefully turned her back on the Chinese.

The burden of enforcing the Chinese exclusion law fell on the customs collectors, who handled the actual deportation of the illegal Chinese. The collectors, stationed at the U.S. ports of entry–both land and sea–were not well placed to search for all the Chinese who did not belong. The U.S. marshals and their deputies, however, were well situated to find uncertified Chinese. The president turned to them to enforce the congressional injunction to rid the country of all illegal Chinese.

Originally, the executive interpreted the exclusion law to mean that Chinese smuggled into the country by land routes, either through Mexico or Canada, would be returned to the country from which they entered. In 1887 Acting Attorney General G. A. Jenks explained that the marshals were authorized to arrest any Chinese laborer known personally by a marshal to have entered the United States by land or whom a customs collector or other official swore a warrant against. Laborers who were unable to produce the certificate required by the act were taken before a U.S. commissioner for a hearing. The burden of proof fell on the arresting officer to show that the Chinese was in fact a laborer and had entered the United States by land. The marshal also had to specify from which country the Chinese had entered.[19]

The law proved immensely difficult and time-consuming to enforce. Marshals in every district soon found themselves enmeshed in Chinese laborers; thousands of them were sneaking into the country illegally, aided by unscrupulous merchants in Chinese labor. Deputy Marshal W. H. Van Riper of the western district of Texas complained at the end of July 1887 that the Chinese exclusion law was "violated almost every day along the Rio Grande River; from the character and lay of the country, it being very near impossible to prevent them from crossing into the United States." The situation along the Canadian border was the same.[20]

A sampling of district reports shows how extensive the problem of deportation was at the local level. During the fall and winter of 1887–88, U.S. Attorney W. H. White of Washington Territory reported the arrest of thirty-four Chinese who had crossed into the United States from British Columbia. In 1894 the district of southern Florida arranged the deportation of twenty-three Chinese at one time. New Mexico marshal Edward L. Hall suspected the existence of "a regular business in 'certificates of registration' being carried on in El Paso, Texas," during the early 1890s. Smuggling Chinese into the country was both profitable and relatively safe.[21]

By the early 1890s the attorney general dropped the stipulation that the Chinese be sent back to the country through which they had entered the United States. Neither Mexico nor Canada would agreeably take them, and the deportations had strained relations with America's neighbors. Instead, the attorney general issued new instructions that the Chinese be shipped back to China as expeditiously as possible.

The normal procedure for the marshals in districts across the country was to round up the illegal Chinese laborers and escort them to the West Coast for deportation. The vast majority of deportations went through San Francisco, though Seattle and Tacoma, Washington, were also used as ports of exit. The collector of customs handled the actual deportation, but the laborers remained jailed in the marshals' legal custody until they boarded the ship for China. The Customs agent paid all the costs, including the expenses of the marshals.

San Francisco received so many Chinese that on January 24, 1890, Attorney General William H. H. Miller appointed George W. Schell as a special assistant to the U.S. attorney for northern California with the sole responsibility to handle the tremendous number of Chinese deportation and immigration cases. Many Chinese immigrants asserted that they were born in the United States, which entitled them to unrestricted readmission into the country. The assertion was extremely difficult to disprove. Miller urged the new assistant attorney to make "a zealous and searching examination" of all applications for admission into the United States, carefully questioning each individual about his birthplace, people he knew, and any indications that he was lying.[22]

In 1894 a new treaty between China and the United States extended the ban on Chinese immigration another ten years. Congress established the office of Chinese inspector to help enforce the ban. The inspectors, who worked for the Department of the Treasury, were stationed in various cities across the country to search out illegal Chinese. The illegals were turned over to the marshals, who took them to San Francisco. The creation of this new office indicated how serious the problem had grown.[23]

By 1897 the Treasury Department, worried as always about expenses, arranged special rates for conveying illegal Chinese to the West Coast for deportation. Several of the railroads agreed to take the Chinese at discounted fares. The companies also offered to provide guards, whom the U.S. marshal was expected to deputize. The marshals, then, would have to send only one deputy to San Francisco with the Chinese to guard them until their departure. Because the deputies were paid mileage and expenses for the trips, the railroad guards and discounted tickets promised the government a significant savings.[24]

Many marshals objected to the arrangement. In a typical complaint, Marshal J. Shelby Williams of eastern Texas maintained that he could not "consent to deputize parties named by the transportation company and become responsible for their acts and of whom I know nothing." The arrangement also seemed to Williams to be impractical because it imposed upon a single deputy the duty of guarding the Chinese prisoners once the train arrived in San Francisco. Williams conveniently forgot that he had a colleague in San Francisco who could help his deputy. The marshals' real objection went unmentioned. They stood to lose a considerable amount of money in fees and expenses if the railroad companies provided guards.[25]

Although premised on racial prejudice, the Chinese exclusion acts offered some protection to the large number of coolies who were, in effect, sold into a modern style of slavery. When appointing George W. Schell as the special assistant attorney in San Francisco, Attorney General Miller warned him to be on the alert for Chinese women imported for prostitution. "The necessity for the enforcement of the exclusion acts appears to be more important now than ever, if it be true as represented that the law is being evaded in the importation of Chinese women into the United States for immoral purposes," Miller explained. "This evil must be stopped."[26]

In May 1896, Inspector J. Thomas Scharf of New York City uncovered an abusive scheme to import young Chinese boys into the United States. The Reverend Hui Kin, an ordained Presbyterian minister, used his ministry and church mission school as a cover. Before making his annual mission to China, Kin visited upwards of twenty merchants and laundrymen throughout New York City's Chinatown, soliciting orders for young boys to be put to work. While in China, Kin filled the orders. He demanded $200 to $250 to be paid up front by the boys' families, plus an additional $60 "tuition" a year for two years. Kin asserted that the boys were students coming to the United States for an education.[27]

The Chinese exclusion laws illustrated the federal government's determination to maintain its authority, at least in certain well-defined spheres. No one challenged its power to restrict immigration, even though the laws represented the first time Congress ever tried to stop anyone from coming to the country.

VIVA MEXICO!

Neither the Mexican government nor its people ever forgave the United States for helping Texas in its fight for independence. Texans, for their part, never forgot the Alamo as a symbol of their own bravery and of Mexican brutality. After the Mexican War of 1846–48, when the United States stole enough land to form half a dozen new states, Mexicans felt justly aggrieved. Most people in the United States almost innocently assumed that the continent belonged to them, a destiny that should have been manifest to all. An imaginary line and a shallow river were all that kept the two countries apart. They were never enough.

Relations between the two countries deteriorated even further when France took advantage of the American Civil War to install a new government in Mexico. The opposition of the United States to Emperor Maximilian and the lovely Carlota helped bring the French puppet before a firing squad in 1867. Secretary of State William H. Seward, backed by fifty thousand U.S. Army troops on the border, persuaded the French not to interfere with the toppling of the Maximilian government by revolutionaries under the command of Benito Juárez. Yet the Mexicans were not entirely happy with Seward's help, which was motivated by his desire to uphold the Monroe Doctrine against European interference in the Western Hemisphere. Mexicans, like most Latin Americans, were never quite sure how much the protection would ultimately cost them.

After the Civil War, thousands of U.S. citizens flocked to the western territories looking for land, gold, and silver. The incidents of violence between Mexico and the United States increased almost in direct proportion to the increases in population along the border. As early as November 1865, Marshal Milton B. Duffield of Arizona reported the murder of three U.S. citizens by Mexican soldiers. The "imperialist troops under Col. Salvador . . . boasted of killing more Americans," Duffield wrote Attorney General James Speed, adding that "the peace of the Country is endangered by their depredations, which they are perpetrating on every occasion." For a score of years after the war, raids from both sides across the international boundary were frequent and bloody. The incursions reflected a deep animosity between the two countries, with neither government fully able to control the violence of its own citizens.[28]

Border raids went in both directions. Virgil Earp's tenure as deputy marshal in Tombstone, Arizona, during the early 1880s was continually troubled by a gang called the Cowboys, who made almost nightly forays into Mexico to rustle cattle and kill or rob Mexicans they found along the way. The problem was just as bad from the other side. "Mexican officers and soldiers make regular raids into Texas, stealing, robbing and murdering," U.S. Attorney D. J. Baldwin of Texas wrote to Attorney General George Williams in March 1872. The complaint regularly echoed back and forth across the border over the next decade.[29]

Each side, too, bemoaned the other side's inability to prevent marauders from crossing the line. District Attorney Baldwin persuaded the federal grand jury in Brownsville to indict General Juan Nepomuceno Cortina of the Mexican army and his men for "holding a saturnalia of crime, violence, and rapine upon the soil of Texas." The charges against the Mexicans covered a seven-year spree of raids north across the Rio Grande. "The settlement of that country from which so much was greatly expected in the raising of sugar, has been stopped," Baldwin concluded, "and that whole region, among the most valuable in the world as a sugar producing country, is in the way of being rapidly depopulated and that, too, caused by depredations from the Mexican side of the river." The indictments remained outstanding. The Mexican soldiers were never arrested, never tried in U.S. courts, never punished by Mexican authorities.[30]

U.S. officials scored little better. Federal control of the marshals generally permitted a more energetic pursuit of outlaws than Mexico's infirm system of national government allowed. But even when arrests were made, it still was immensely difficult to bring the ruffians, killers, and raiders to justice. Juries were unwilling to convict a man for crossing the international line and murdering or robbing a Mexican, particularly because the violations were federal crimes, not state crimes. Even though the marshals arrested more raiders than their Mexican counterparts caught, the conviction rate was generally as poor as Mexico's, a reflection of the continued hostile feelings toward that country.

In many instances, protecting the border took a backseat to the private concerns of the deputies and their petty feuds with local officials. Deputy Marshal Kirkpatrick of Texas flatly refused to investigate possible border violations in early 1878 because such investigations offered no payment for the deputies. Although Kirkpatrick believed that "something is in the air" along the border, he had no firm proof of a military expedition against Mexico. Nor was he willing to search very hard for confirmation. "My compensation does not justify me in devoting my time to detective service in which there is not the least remuneration and which is necessarily expensive," Kirkpatrick explained to U.S. Attorney Baldwin in February 1878.[31]

Furthermore, the marshals received little help, and sometimes considerable interference, from the local governments along the border. "The state government is totally inadequate to the protection of life and property in Texas all the way from the San Jacinto to the Rio Grande," Baldwin confirmed in November 1876. Most private citizens disliked Mexicans, in large part because the Americans lusted so heartily after Mexican land. No one along the border was terribly concerned about the niceties of neutrality laws or about diplomatic relations with the government in faraway Mexico City. Those were federal worries.[32]

In addition to the resistance from citizens and local officials and the lack of adequate fees for enforcing the neutrality laws, Congress eventually added to the marshals' problems. The 1878 Posse Comitatus Law prohibited the marshals from calling on the army for assistance. When the so-called Cowboy gang began raiding the border into Mexico, the Justice Department urged Marshal Crowley P. Dake of Arizona to take firm action against the outlaws. The Cowboys, as Dake well knew, were rough, violent men. They were hardly likely to comply peacefully to an arrest, but Attorney General Wayne MacVeagh could promise little help. If the Cowboy gang resisted arrest, he once hinted to Dake, and if the U.S. Army happened to be nearby, the marshal and his posse could avail themselves of their protection.[33]

Dake's troubled tenure as marshal of Arizona during the late 1870s and early 1880s amply illustrated the problems besetting the marshals who protected the border. Dake was a man of courage and experience, hardly someone who trifled with the duties of his office. He served as a Union officer during the Civil War, commanding a company of Michigan volunteers that he had raised. Dake fought at Gettysburg and other battles before a debilitating leg wound abruptly retired him from the war. The injury gave him a lifetime of pain and discomfort. After the war, Dake worked in a number of public and government offices, even running unsuccessfully for a Michigan congressional seat. Eventually he accepted the job of chief deputy marshal in Detroit under Marshal Salmon S. Matthews. In June 1878, President Rutherford B. Hayes commissioned Dake as the U.S. marshal for the Arizona Territory. Dake left immediately for his new office in Prescott.[34]

Arizona, especially southern Arizona, epitomized the wild frontier during the late 1870s and early 1880s. The acting governor, John J. Gosper, ascribed the lawlessness around Tombstone to the insane rush for quick riches that mining for silver promised but seldom delivered. "The underlying cause of all the disturbances of the peace, and the taking of property unlawfully," Gosper stated, "is the fact that *all men* of every shade of character in that new and rapidly developed section of mineral wealth, in their mad career after money, have grossly neglected local self government, until the more lazy and lawless elements have undertaken to prey upon the more industrious and honorable classes for their subsistence and gains."[35]

If mining failed a man, money was still to be made stealing cattle or holding up stagecoaches. The Cowboy gang engaged in frequent raids in and out of Sonora, Mexico. They operated on both sides of the border, rustling cattle, robbing Wells Fargo stages, and killing anyone who got in their way. Attorney General MacVeagh pressured Marshal Dake to stop the lawlessness along the border, though typically the department was agonizingly slow to forward the marshal money. Eventually, however, the Cowboy troubles overcame the department's habitual parsimony. When Dake's expenditures on posses, witnesses, and travel exceeded his $20,000 bond, MacVeagh approved a new $20,000 bond for him. The unique authorization allowed Dake to expend up to $40,000 of the government's money in the pursuit of the Cowboys. All the department asked in return was that he keep good a account of his expenditures.[36]

Dake made an honest, persevering effort to stop the Cowboy raids and other illegal activities in his district. By September 1878, just three months after his appointment, he reported to Acting Attorney General S. F. Phillips that he had "organized a corps of deputies throughout the Territory at points where I think they will be the most valuable for the detection and capture of 'road agents' and other criminals." Already, he added sadly, two of his deputies—J. H. Adams and Cornelius Finley— had been murdered by the Cowboys.[37]

For months at a time, Dake and his posses tracked the bandits, chasing them across the border into Mexico beyond the marshal's jurisdiction and authority. He made arrests, obtained convictions, and, with the cooperation of Arizona territorial officials, even saw some of the outlaws executed. Yet the lawlessness endemic to southern Arizona overwhelmed him. The outlaws were too well organized, too well armed, and too dangerous for Dake and his men.[38]

Deputy J. W. Evans, stationed in Tucson, originally estimated that the Cowboys numbered 380 strong. "They are constantly raiding into Sonora driving out stock and killing the Mexicans," Evans wrote on the last day of June 1881. Six weeks later, he revised his estimate to 75 to 100 members. But, he hastened to point out to Dake, "they are thoroughly armed and will no doubt fight desperately." U.S. Attorney E. B. Pomroy agreed with Evans's assessment. The Cowboys, he informed Attorney General MacVeagh in June 1881, "subsist by rapine, plunder, and highway robbery," and they amused themselves with "drunken orgies and murder." Pomroy warned, "The evil is one that feeding upon itself does not exhaust it, but causes it to thrive. It is now assuming alarming proportions."[39]

The Cowboy troubles peaked in 1881. Throughout the year the Wells Fargo stage between Tucson and Tombstone was repeatedly held up, the passengers robbed, the U.S. mail stolen. In between robberies, the Cowboys raided Mexico. In January they slaughtered forty Mexicans in Sonora. The following June, Mexican officials caught and killed four of the Cowboys on their side of the border. Several weeks later, Mexican soldiers killed the Cowboy leader, Newman H. Clanton, better known as Old Man Clanton, during one of his raids across the boundary. Three of his men died with him. In early August, members of the gang raided Mexico, ambushed and killed four Mexicans, and robbed other Mexicans of $4,000. The Mexican ambassador to the United States, M. de Zamacona, complained several times to Secretary of State James G. Blaine of the continued depredations. Blaine passed the protests to Attorney General MacVeagh.[40]

MacVeagh ordered Dake to arrest the Cowboys. Dake looked to his deputy in Tombstone for help, but Deputy Virgil Earp had more pressing concerns. He and his brothers James, Wyatt, and Morgan had caught the money fever raging through Tombstone. Unpracticed in the art of mining, the brothers sought their fortunes in mine speculations, gambling, and riding shotgun for Wells Fargo.[41]

Virgil branched into law enforcement. He received a commission as deputy marshal from Dake in November 1879, then got himself hired as town marshal of Tombstone. He made a good living from the percentage he took for collecting the city taxes and licensing fees from the town's store owners, professionals, and prostitutes. To those earnings he added his fees for serving federal warrants. Chasing gangs of outlaw Cowboys held no real appeal to him: It promised so little money for the effort and the danger.

Wyatt longed to be the sheriff of Cochise County, a position that earned substantial fees for collecting county taxes. His campaign to defeat Sheriff Johnny Behan for election hardly set the tone for friendly cooperation between Virgil and Behan. Wyatt further strained their relations by courting Behan's common-law wife, Josephine. The private feud between the Earps and Behan completely overshadowed the Department of Justice's concerns about the Cowboy raids.

The feud reached its peak when Behan watched the Earp brothers and their friend Dr. John Holliday coldly gun down Billy Clanton and the McLaury brothers, Frank and Tom, on the afternoon of October 26, 1881. Although Marshal Dake leapt to the conclusion that the gunfight just down the street from the O.K. Corral resulted from Virgil's efforts to stop the Cowboy raids, the marshal was flat wrong. The Earps had no real evidence of any complicity by either the Clantons or the McLaurys in Mexican cattle rustling or stagecoach holdups. Both sets of brothers probably were members of the Cowboy gang. Old Man Clanton, the Cowboy leader killed by Mexican soldiers, was Ike and Billy's father. But that was not why the Earps went after them that fall afternoon.

The gunfight escalated from an argument between Wyatt and Ike Clanton, a Behan ally, over who broke a promise between them. Wyatt had asked Ike for help in identifying the men who had taken part in a recent stagecoach robbery. Wyatt wanted the credit for arresting the robbers, which would help him in his campaign for Sheriff Behan's job. Wyatt promised Ike the reward. When Ike hesitated to commit himself to the deal, the two men agreed to keep their talk a secret. Rumors immediately swept Tombstone's saloons that Ike had turned traitor. Each man accused the other of breaking the vow.[42]

On the morning of October 26, a chance encounter between Wyatt and Ike turned violent. Wyatt clobbered Ike over the head with his pistol. Virgil then arrested the groggy cowboy for disturbing the peace, apparently his brother's peace. Fined and released, Ike met up with his brother, Billy, and their friends Frank and Tom McLaury. After bragging to anyone who would listen what he would do to the Earps, Ike and his companions decided to leave town.

They saddled their horses in the vacant lot next to Fly's photography studio on Fremont Street. Behan happened to walk by, and Ike stopped him a moment to gripe about the rough treatment the Earps had given him earlier that morning. The story outraged Billy and the McLaurys, but the telling of it to Behan delayed their leaving town. It cost Billy and the McLaurys their lives.

Town gossips made sure that the Earp brothers knew of Ike's threats. The brothers decided to put an end to Ike's braggadocio. "It was a *street fight* between my brothers, Doc, and myself and those who believed they could shoot down the Earps," Wyatt would explain repeatedly in later years. Virgil deputized his brothers Wyatt and Morgan and their friend Holliday as they strode purposefully down Fremont Street, past the O.K. Corral, to the vacant lot where the Clantons and McLaurys were complaining to Behan. In making the deputations, Virgil used his authority as town marshal of Tombstone, not his authority as a federal deputy marshal. Virgil had no evidence, nor any concern, that Ike had broken any federal law. He intended to charge him and possibly his brother, Billy, with carrying weapons within the city limits. Had Wyatt given Virgil time to check before he opened fire, the town marshal and his deputies would have found Ike Clanton and Tom McLaury unarmed.[43]

Behan was just leaving the south end of the lot when the Earps came up on the north side. "Throw up your hands," Virgil commanded, but his brother did not give them the chance to do it. Wyatt, who had taken his Smith and Wesson .44 out of his coat pocket before they reached the vacant lot, saw Frank McLaury reaching for his holstered pistol. Wyatt lifted his pistol and fired. The bullet tore into Frank's lower abdomen, twisting him around and sending his responding shot wild.

Ike Clanton, unarmed and helpless, fled into Fly's studio. Doc, using the shotgun Virgil had lent him, blew a hole in Tom McLaury's side, then tossed the gun aside to draw his Colt revolver. Virgil and Morgan both fired at Billy Clanton. One bullet hit Billy in the right wrist, the other in the chest. He was knocked backward against the wall of the neighboring house. Billy slumped to the ground and switched his pistol to his left hand.

Tom McLaury staggered down the street, collapsing dead around a telegraph pole half a block away at the corner of Fremont and Third. His brother, Frank, wanting now only to escape, stumbled after his startled horse. With one hand pressed to the hole in his gut, he crossed north on Fremont, going past the Earps. Doc Holliday turned after Frank, his pistol tracking the wounded man. Billy Clanton, firing left-handed, shot Morgan in the shoulder. The impact of the bullet sprawled Morgan over a half-buried water pipe. Rising to one knee, he turned toward Frank McLaury just as Frank reached for his bucking horse. Both Morgan and Doc fired simultaneously; Morgan's bullet took off the top of Frank's head.

Billy Clanton fired next at Doc, who was standing in the street off to Billy's right. The bullet hit Doc's holster, causing him only a bruise. Billy, however, did not waste time watching the effect of his shots. He turned slightly to his left and fired at Virgil, hitting him in the leg. Simultaneous shots from Wyatt and Virgil mortally wounded the spunky Billy. Still, he refused to quit shooting until his pistol ran out of ammunition. Billy used the last of his sapping strength to crawl out to Fremont Street, begging for someone to reload his pistol. But the thirty-one-second fight was over. Billy died moments later.[44]

Aside from the deaths of Frank and Tom McLaury and Billy Clanton, the street fight had no effect on the Cowboy raids nor on the violence in Tombstone. Dake's unfounded assertion that "my deputies"—only Virgil was a deputy—"have rid Tombstone and neighborhood of the presence of this outlaw element" simply underscored how out of touch the marshal was with the strained affairs in Tombstone. Far away in Washington, Acting Attorney General S. F. Phillips discounted Marshal Dake's conclusion that the fight signaled an end to the Cowboy troubles. Phillips understood enough of the situation to caution his marshal about Deputy Virgil Earp's tendency "rather to quarrel with the Territorial authorities than to cooperate with them." He sternly warned Dake that "there must be no rivalry between the officers of the United States and those of the Territory." Unfortunately for Dake, the feud between his deputy and the territorial officials increased in intensity after the Tombstone street fight.[45]

City officials fired Virgil as town marshal after the gunfight. They hired in his place a young man named David Neagle, who would find his own destiny as a deputy marshal in a gunfight eight years later. On the evening of December 28, 1881, shortly after Virgil's leg healed from Billy's bullet, he was ambushed as he crossed a darkened Tombstone street. Several rounds of buckshot tore out most of the bone in his left arm, leaving it floppy and lame but unparalyzed.

Wyatt hastily telegraphed Marshal Dake the next day, December 29, 1881, begging for a commission as a deputy marshal. Although no record exists of the commission, Dake probably issued it in a subsequent telegram. The marshal clearly hoped that Wyatt would go after the Cowboy gang, which was causing him so much trouble with Washington. The next month, Dake visited Tombstone, bringing with him $3,000 for Wyatt to use tracking the Cowboys. Wyatt used both his commission and the money to go after the men who attacked his brother. It was only a coincidence if some of them happened to belong to the Cowboy gang.[46]

Two months later, on March 18, 1882, Morgan Earp exercised his wounded shoulder at a game of billiards with Wyatt. As he bent over, cue stick in hand, two or three gunmen fired their pistols through the back door of the pool hall. Wyatt, his remarkable luck holding true, escaped unscathed. Morgan did not. One slug tore into his back, severing his spine. His cue stick clattered to the floor as he collapsed onto the billiard table. He died moments later.[47]

Wyatt went on the rampage. Protected by his friend Holliday and a "posse" of six others, he killed three more men, Frank Stillwell, "Indian Charley" Florentio, and "Curly Bill" Brocius, avenging Virgil and Morgan. Although the three men undoubtedly deserved punishment for crimes committed, Wyatt had no evidence against them, no warrant to arrest them, and no legal cause to murder them. Sheriff Behan formed a posse and rode after Earp and his alcoholic, consumptive friend Holliday. Wyatt and Doc, their vengeance apparently satiated, fled to Colorado.[48]

Earp, though, tried to have the last laugh on both Marshal Dake and Sheriff Behan. Despite numerous pleas from Dake, he never offered an account of the money the marshal had advanced him. For the rest of their lives, Dake and his bondsmen were hounded by the Justice Department for the $3,000 advanced against the $40,000 bond Attorney General MacVeagh had authorized to pursue the Cowboys. Like most of his bondsmen, Dake died in poverty, a victim of Arizona's unstable silver economy. The department never recovered the money it advanced against Dake's two bonds.[49]

Behan may have had the final revenge on Wyatt Earp. Behan's common-law wife, pursued by the handsome Wyatt during their days in

Tombstone, deserted the sheriff to follow Wyatt to Colorado. For the rest of Wyatt's long life, Josephine Earp's quick temper and gratingly shrill voice tormented his peace of mind.

The Cowboy troubles continued after Wyatt's flight to Colorado. In April 1882, General William Tecumseh Sherman inspected the Arizona border while on his way to California. Sherman noted that the outlaws "make use of the boundary line to escape pursuit first on the one side and then on the other." The ease with which the criminals evaded arrest by stepping south across the line, he observed, threatened to compromise U.S. relations with Mexico. He recommended that the army take over the task of subduing the Cowboys, despite the restrictions of the Posse Comitatus Law. "The Civil Officers," Sherman reported to Attorney General Benjamin Brewster, "have not sufficient forces to make arrests, to hold prisoners for trial or punish when convicted."[50]

On May 31, 1882, President Chester A. Arthur proclaimed the areas in which the Cowboys operated to be in a state of rebellion. The proclamation gave Dake the power and resources he needed, including the use of the army against the Cowboys, because the Posse Comitatus Law did not apply in areas of rebellion. The suspension of the act allowed the marshals to field troops against the Cowboys. Within a few months, law and order had been restored to the area between Tombstone and the Mexican border.[51]

President Arthur dismissed Dake in August 1882, replacing him with Z. L. Tidball. For the few years remaining to him, Dake fended off departmental examiners who hounded him for receipts and accounts. Virgil Earp took Morgan's body to their parents in California. Virgil's dangling left arm did not prohibit him from again pinning on a badge, this time as chief of police in the small town of Colton, California. Wyatt and Josephine wandered the West in search of that one lucky strike. They headed north to Alaska when gold was discovered there in the 1890s, then drifted back to California. San Francisco finally became their home base, though the couple seldom stayed there for long. Although Wyatt never found the riches he so desperately sought, he stumbled into American myth and legend. The bullet he fired into Frank McLaury carried him into the romantic, unreal realm of the frontier hero. The remembrance was as undeserved as it was enduring.

Outlaws continued to prey along the border with Mexico, but by the turn of the century they were anachronistic. The new century brought new problems for the marshals. The outbreak of revolution south of the border changed their work from keeping outlaws out of Mexico to keeping revolutionaries in Mexico. The problem of revolution, particularly the Mexican revolution, was a twentieth-century phenomenon that reflected social and economic discontent brought on by industrialization. The clumsy efforts of the Fenians to free their homeland paled before the intensity of Mexico's upheaval.

3

PART

CONSTITUTIONAL CHALLENGES AND CHANGES

1894–1983

9

RAILROADS, REVOLUTION, AND WAR

1894–1919

Indiana stumbled early into the twentieth century. In July 1877 the circuit court ordered U.S. Marshal Benjamin Spooner to challenge striking railroad workers and get the trains running. Spooner's frightened response portended the labor wars that rocked the country as it moved closer to the next century, as it achieved an industrial economy, as it balanced capitalism's drive for profits against labor's demand for jobs and wages. The trauma of twentieth-century economics came early to Indiana.

A financial panic in 1873 threw the economy into a severe depression. For the next four years workers were regularly fired, and fortunes regularly collapsed. Although the railroads had conquered the continent by 1869, eight years later they were struggling to survive. Many were bankrupt. United States marshals took custody of their assets, and court-appointed receivers managed their operations. Discontent and uncertainty permeated the country. The great industrial boom that followed the Civil War seemed at an end.

In a foretaste of management's general insensitivity to labor, the surviving roads followed the Baltimore and Ohio's lead by slashing workers' wages 10 to 20 percent in June 1877. At the same time, many of those roads continued to pay healthy dividends to their stockholders. Cornelius Vanderbilt's New York Central, for example, managed to pay 8 percent dividends on stock capitalized at double its true value. A slight cutback in dividends would easily have obviated the need to cut workers' pay, but such a choice was foreign to management strategies. Labor needed the power to make wage cuts expensive.[1]

In July 1877 the Brotherhood of Locomotive Engineers refused to work until the companies restored their wages. Railroad workers across the nation joined the strike. Riots in Pittsburgh, Baltimore, Reading, and Chicago intensified the disruption of rail operations. The bankrupt roads were not immediately threatened by the strike—their workers remained on the job—but it was clear they would have difficulty operating trains through the striking yards. The court-appointed receivers sought writs of assistance from the circuit courts to keep the trains moving. The courts issued the precepts to their U.S. marshals.

Marshal Ben Spooner feared the worst. By July 24 he knew that the court would command him to assist the running of the Indianapolis, Bloomington, and Western trains through the striking railyards of Indianapolis. A thousand angry strikers milled about the yards to keep their companies stalled. Spooner was certain they would not let other trains roll.

The marshal panicked. Before he received the writ of assistance, Spooner pleaded with Attorney General Charles Devens for permission to raise a posse of a thousand men. "The strikers at the Depot number near if not quite that number," he explained on the morning of July 24. Circuit court judge W. Q. Gresham also worried about Spooner's ability to enforce the writ. In an uncommon, rather questionable move, Gresham cabled Devens before issuing his writ. "Will and can the government furnish troops to sustain the marshal?" he asked. The inquiry presaged the incestuous relations that developed between the judicial and executive branches when they confronted strikes. The constitutional separation of powers between the courts and the executive was blurred.[2]

On the afternoon of July 24, Spooner received a writ of assistance from Gresham ordering him "to aid, assist, and defend George B. Wright, receiver of the Indianapolis, Bloomington, and Western Railroad Company in executing the orders of the said and in operating said railroad now prevented by violence and intimidation." Spooner immediately asked Attorney General Devens for military support because "an organized mob too powerful for ordinary force is preventing the execution of legal process in the premise." Thus far, of course, no effort had been made to roll the trains through the strikers. The marshal based his request on what he feared would happen.[3]

The pleas for help were premature. Devens was unable to get troops to Indianapolis before July 27. Unwilling to delay the train schedule for three days, Marshal Spooner risked talking to the striking workers. The workers willingly agreed to let the I,B&W trains out of the yard. On the morning of July 25, I,B&W freight and passenger trains resumed their normal runs.[4]

Marshal Spooner remained unsatisfied. "I regard the situation here dangerous and critical," he reported to Devens. "A large majority of the laborers are in strong sympathy with the strikers and there is an element which is anxious to rob and murder." Although the I,B&W trains were running without incident, the marshal again requested troops. He expected to receive arrest warrants against the leading strikers for contempt of court for maintaining the strike and thereby interfering with the operation of the lines in receivership.

The marshal wanted "a sufficient force to enable me promptly to make these arrests." Spooner added, "We need regular soldiers more than anything else and a full force of deputies armed." He assured Devens, "We do not overrate the danger nor the amount of force needed if we are to clean the mob out at once and avoid a prolonged fight and its consequences." Once again, Judge Gresham endorsed the marshal's report.[5]

The I,B&W trains continued to run on schedule out of Indianapolis. The Indiana strikers respected the orders of the circuit court. When the trains reached Urbana, Illinois, however, strikers there forced them to halt, creating a backup all along the line. Still panicked, Judge Gresham complained that Indiana authorities were doing nothing to assist Marshal Spooner. The judge was not specific about what he expected the local officials to do. "It is still perfectly clear to my mind," the judge admonished Attorney General Devens, "that several hundred of regulars is needed at once. There is constant danger of an outbreak and the moral effect of the presence of such a force would certainly prevent the loss of life and destruction of property."[6]

Attorney General Devens promised that troops would arrive by July 27 to act as the marshal's posse. "Act with prudence as well as courage," Devens ordered Spooner, "and execute the processes issued to you by the

United States Court." Concerned by the apprehensions of the judge and the marshal, Devens advised Spooner to delay executing any arrest warrants against the strikers until the troops arrived, even if that meant waiting until July 28. However, the court orders issuing from Indiana and other districts across the country had essentially broken the strike by July 27. "It is a mere shell," Judge Gresham crowed. With the danger past, the judge grew impatient for the marshal to arrest the leaders. In obedience to Devens's instructions, though, Spooner stalled until the troops arrived.[7]

Judge Gresham's eagerness to imprison the strike leaders meant little to Devens. In his mind, the most important task was to get the trains running. On July 27 he ordered Marshal Spooner to postpone any arrests until after the marshal made sure the freight trains were rolling. "This is the first duty," Devens announced. He authorized Spooner to cooperate with the marshals in neighboring districts to protect the trains and to put special deputies on each train to ensure that they got through to their destination. "Have full confidence in your courage and discretion," the attorney general assured his marshal.[8]

By the end of the month, the strike was clearly broken nationwide. The trains were running without disturbance, the strikers either fired or compelled to accept the drastic wage cuts. Although other districts had faced more compelling problems, the reaction of federal officials in Indiana exemplified the government's excessive defense of the railroads and its insensitivity to labor. Judge Gresham's clear sympathy with the property rights of the railroad corporations hardly assured the strikers a fair hearing. He gave them a foretaste of what was to come in their struggle to obtain decent wages and decent working conditions.[9]

THE PULLMAN STRIKE

Expansion and explosion defined the nineteenth century; trauma and turmoil distinguished the twentieth. Americans of the 1800s looked westward. From thirteen states and territories in 1789, the country grew to forty-nine states and territories by 1889. The great issues of the era dealt with the incorporation of new territories and new peoples into the blossoming country. Even the controversy over slavery, which eventually exploded into Civil War, was most hotly debated in terms of its expansion, not its existence.

By 1890 the frontier was closed. With the exception of Hawaii, the areas that would eventually compose the fifty states had been obtained, their boundaries marked, and their status as state or territory defined. The procedures for inducting new states into the Union were well established and well used. Slavery had been abolished. Blacks were segregated socially and economically; Indians were segregated physically on reservations. For well or ill, the systems for expanding geographically and incorporating different peoples into society had been defined and tested. They would remain intact for the next seventy years.

The economy shifted from an agricultural to an industrial base, pointing the way to the twentieth century. By 1920 more people lived in towns than in rural areas, and more people worked in business and industry than in agriculture. Industrialization wrought profound changes economically and socially. The economy grew more complex and interdependent, capable of stupendous bursts of energy and profit, yet more susceptible to crash and collapse. Large industries generated smaller, specialized industries. A falter in one sent tremors through all.

A severe depression during the early 1890s, for example, was touched off by the failure of a single bank – the Baring Brothers House in Great Britain. The bank failure pushed other elements of the economy over like dominoes, pitching the United States into one of its worst financial collapses. Although the nineteenth-century economy was never stable, it had been blessed with simplicity. Its periodic collapses caused inconvenience and uncertainty, primarily through currency shortages, but little more. The twentieth-century economy combined complexity with instability, a mixture as volatile as it was powerful. Its crashes caused massive unemployment and general unrest.

Socially, Americans shifted their faith from the rugged individual who conquered the wilderness alone to the corporate man who united men and machines to a single goal. Henry Ford and Samuel Gompers replaced Davy Crockett and Daniel Boone as the new heroes. Horatio Alger, the all-American boy in dozens of children's books, succeeded by scaling corporate heights, not taming frontiers.

It was the golden age of associations and societies, trusts and monopolies, unions and brotherhoods. Standard Oil took over the petroleum industry; Carnegie monopolized steel. In 1886 the twenty-four railroads with terminals in Chicago formed the General Managers' Association to address common problems. By 1894 its members controlled 41,000 miles of track and employed 221,000 workers. Membership in labor unions tripled between 1896 and 1910. The American Federation of Labor grew from 150,000 members in 1886 to more than 2,000,000 by 1914. In 1893 Eugene Debs founded the American Railway Union. Within a year it had a membership of 150,000 railroad workers.[10]

Like any revolution, the industrial transformation of America purchased its dramatic changes in the currency of trauma and turmoil. Neither the Constitution nor the federal courts that interpreted it or the marshals who enforced it adapted easily to the transition. Each belonged to a time of individuals and independence. The new age of collectives and interdependence took getting used to, took a wrenching constitutional adaptation that wrought its own turbulence.

It was the springtime of reform. Populists, concentrated mainly in the South and the West, demanded the reincorporation of silver into the currency system, which was based entirely on the gold standard. They also urged the protection of agricultural interests, the eight-hour day for labor, income tax, and a number of other reforms intended to give individuals more say over their own destiny. The Progressive Movement, which won more national acceptance than Populism, embraced reforms to protect individuals, break up trusts, and improve society by abolishing child labor, prohibiting alcohol, and regulating industry and commerce.

The original response of the federal government was reactionary. Reforms were resisted and, when finally accepted, largely diluted when passed into law. The labor movement in particular was opposed by government action. Federal officials practically dismissed out of hand the rights of workers to negotiate collectively with management and to strike when negotiations failed. The government embraced management's view that labor strikes posed a serious threat to American society, government, and the economy. The disturbances were interpreted in the most calamitous terms, described as great national disasters of momentous portent. Strikes were seen as gross challenges to federal authority, not simply as disputes with corporate management.

Federal judges colluded among themselves, with their U.S. attorneys and marshals and, more disturbingly, with the attorney general and the Justice Department to suppress strikes. To break most strikes, they relied on their power to punish anyone summarily for contempt of court. During railroad strikes, they also relied on interference with the U.S. mails and on violation of the Sherman Antitrust Act as their legal excuses to assault labor. The judges simply ordered the marshals to arrest labor leaders or to protect the vested property rights of management.

Though eager to comply with court orders to break the strikes, the marshals were ill equipped for the job. Having special deputies was an uncomfortable solution to facing strikers. Frequently, like Marshal Ben Spooner of Indiana, the marshals panicked in the face of labor unrest and called for troops to help them.

Labor unrest peaked during 1894. The industrial economy collapsed; society itself seemed to teeter on the edge. During 1893 alone, 642 banks failed. The amount of railway that went into federal receivership totaled 22,500 miles. Unemployment reached into the millions; the wages of those still with jobs were drastically cut as corporations and industries struggled to cope with the collapsing economy.[11]

In the spring of 1894 Jacob Coxey led a ragtag army of the unemployed that marched on Washington to demand an ambitious public works program. Nationwide, as many as ten thousand people joined the Commonwealth of Christ army. Away to the west, the Commonwealers, faced with thousands of miles of marching, frequently resorted to stealing trains, many of which were bankrupt and under federal receivership. When that happened, U.S. marshals went after the train thieves.[12]

Coxey's march panicked federal officials and judges. Attorney General Richard Olney, a railroad lawyer in private practice, saw the march as the opening scene of revolution. He moved quickly to suppress it. Federal judges readily concurred. Judge H. W. Smith advised one of his colleagues on the Utah district bench, "It is all-important that [the Coxeyites] be found guilty and held for contempt." When the marshals proved incapable of overcoming the large numbers of Coxeyites, Olney persuaded President Grover Cleveland to send out the army. That lesson would not be forgotten in July 1894 when the American Railway Union refused to move Pullman cars.[13]

The Pullman Palace Car Company strike began in May 1894 in the small town of Pullman, Illinois, just south of Chicago. The immediate and most pressing cause was a series of wage cuts imposed on the workers as the company tried to adjust to the economic slump. The crisis was exacerbated by a festering resentment among the workers over their general treatment by the corporation. The company exercised a debilitating paternalism on its work force, defining where the workers would live, how they would live, and how much they would pay for it.

Grieving the wage cuts, the Pullman workers went on strike on May

11, 1894. In response the company locked its doors against the workers. For a month the Pullman employees stood alone against the company. Then, at the June convention of the American Railway Union in Chicago, they reported their plight. The union members hastily approved a resolution calling on the entire union to boycott Pullman cars if the company continued its refusal to negotiate. The resolution set June 26 as the day for the sympathy strike to begin.[14]

Privately, Debs questioned the union's ability to stand up to Pullman and its supporters. Nevertheless, once the union accepted the boycott, Debs took the lead in designing its strategy. On June 22 he outlined to the convention how the members should proceed. Workers should continue to do their jobs as usual, except that Pullman cars were to be completely isolated. Car inspectors should refuse to inspect Pullman cars, switchmen should refuse to switch them onto trains, and engineers and brakemen should refuse to pull them. If any member of the union was fired because of his participation in the boycott, then the other members would immediately go on strike against that railroad.[15]

Four days later the boycott began. Union members continued to work the roads. Mail, freight, and passenger cars were inspected, switched, and hauled. Only the Pullman cars stood untouched. The general managers of the various railroads sided with Pullman, largely because they saw an opportunity to crush the American Railway Union. Most of the railroads were under contract to the Pullman Company to haul the palace cars as part of their trains. The general managers pointed to that obligation when they insisted that their workers end the boycott. The managers refused to let a train leave the station without its normal complement of cars, including Pullman sleeper, dining, and parlor cars.[16]

When the workers refused to handle Pullman cars, they were fired. As planned, the other employees immediately went on strike. By June 28, two days after the boycott began, eighteen thousand workers were on strike. Rail operations in the midwestern and western regions of the country came to an abrupt halt. The eastern section of the country escaped much of the strike, primarily because neither the American Railway Union nor the Pullman Company were strong there.[17]

All sections of the country suffered from the stoppage in the shipment of goods and produce. Among the stalled freight and passenger cars, amidst the rotting produce and reprieved livestock, stood the cars that carried the United States mails. The interference with the mail gave Olney the legal rationale he wanted to break the strike. He called on the U.S. marshals and attorneys "to employ necessary force" to ensure that the mail trains kept running. "See that the passage of regular trains carrying United States mails in the usual and ordinary way, as contemplated by the act of Congress and directed by the Postmaster General, is not obstructed," Olney ordered his attorneys on June 29, three days after the boycott began. "Procure warrants or any other available process from United States courts against any and all persons engaged in such obstruction and direct Marshal to execute the same by such number of deputies or such posse as may be necessary," he added.[18]

The American Railway Union repeatedly offered to move the mail, provided no Pullman car was attached to the train. Neither Olney nor the general managers agreed to the arrangement. Government officials apparently gave no thought to compelling the railroads to exclude Pullman cars from mail trains. Olney willingly accepted management's interpretation that mail trains contained the full and regular complement of cars, including Pullman cars.[19]

Attorney General Olney interpreted the strike as a direct assault on federal authority. "We have been brought to the ragged edge of anarchy," he stated on July 4, 1894, "and it is time to see whether the law is sufficiently strong to prevent this condition of affairs." The government developed its general strategy toward the strike in Chicago, where it all began. On June 30, Olney authorized Marshal John Arnold to hire as many deputies as he needed "to prevent obstruction of United States mails and to arrest all persons who may attempt such obstruction." The attorney general also urged U.S. attorney Thomas Milchrist to help the marshal by obtaining the necessary injunctions and court orders. "Action," Olney wired Milchrist, "ought to be prompt and vigorous."[20]

Once Olney and his subordinates took up the battle, the General Managers' Association deferred all action to the federal government. By the time the national strike was barely a week old, the association exultantly announced, "So far as the railroads are concerned with this fight, they are out of it. It has become a fight between the United States Government and the American Railway Union, and we shall leave them to fight it out."[21]

More important, on June 30, Olney obliged the request of the General Managers Association by appointing Edwin Walker a special U.S. attorney. Throughout the course of the strike, Walker claimed to have a "thorough understanding" with circuit court judge Peter S.

Grosscup. Both men believed that the government "should proceed with a firm hand, not only by bill in equity, but also by criminal procedure," to break the strike. Working with Walker, Milchrist drafted an omnibus injunction that Judge Grosscup and his colleague Judge William A. Woods signed without hesitation on July 2.[22]

The injunction defined Pullman cars as indispensable to the operation of trains. Consequently, the refusal of the strikers to move trains containing Pullman cars was an interruption in the carriage of the mails and a disruption of interstate commerce. The court ordered the strikers not to interfere with the trains. They were to stay away from the rail-yards and to cease all efforts, either through coercion, threat, or persuasion, to entice any railroad employee to leave his job. The injunction even forbade the use of telegrams to encourage employees to quit.[23]

The omnibus injunction, which other court jurisdictions adopted, stripped Debs and the railway union not only of their sole weapon, the strike, but also of their ammunition – persuading railroad employees to quit. The *New York Times* called it a "Gatling gun on paper." Deputy marshals personally served the injunction on Debs and other union officials on July 2. Public notice was obtained by publishing it in the newspapers the next day. The court order left Debs and the union no escape. Debs not only guided the strike locally in Chicago but also used the telegraph lines voraciously to coordinate it nationwide. After July 2 every wire he sent became evidence against him.[24]

Marshal Arnold had sworn in almost six hundred deputies by the time the omnibus injunction was ready for service. "The situation here is desperate," he explained to Olney. In hiring the deputies, he paid little attention to the backgrounds of the men, nor did he check into their experience, aptitude, or coolness under fire. Anyone in reasonable health who presented himself at the marshal's office was given the oath and the star.[25]

Many of the new deputies were thugs hired by the railroads. More than two-thirds of the five thousand deputies eventually sworn in by Arnold worked for the railroads. The names of the deputies were scrutinized by the General Managers' Association. Marshal Arnold followed its recommendations, appointing anyone it wanted. The association members armed the special deputies and sent them back to work on the trains. Arnold never heard from them again.[26]

Neither the marshal's desperation nor his mass hirings instilled confidence in Walker, his friend Judge Grosscup, or Olney. "I do not believe that the Marshal and his deputies can protect the railroad companies in moving their trains, either freight or passenger, including of course the trains carrying United States mail," Walker advised Olney, who allowed the mass hirings because the marshals had to fail before he could justify sending in troops.[27]

Marshal Arnold and his men amply justified the need for troops on the afternoon of July 2. With Grosscup's injunction in hand, Arnold went to the railyards in Blue Island, southwest of Chicago. Thousands of strikers and their sympathizers had so overrun the yard that the Rock Island Railroad abandoned all its trains there. Accompanied by his new deputies, some local police, and a few railroad officials, Arnold tried to read the injunction to the strikers. He was greeted with jeers and catcalls by those who paid any attention. A few strikers shoved him as he tried to read the process a second time, and his chief deputy was injured.[28]

"The deputies sworn in yesterday were of no possible value," Walker cabled Olney. "They were men taken from a crowd that applied for employment, and in character were scarcely any improvement upon the strikers themselves." It was time, Walker believed, to call in troops. Marshal Arnold endorsed the request. "We have had a desperate time with [the strikers]," he wired Olney from Blue Island. "Our force is inadequate and in my judgement it is impossible to move trains here without having the 15th infantry from Fort Sheridan ordered here at once. There are over two thousand rioters here now and more are coming. Mail trains in great danger." As if to prove the point, the strikers overturned three boxcars the night of July 2, creating a huge roadblock across the tracks.[29]

Olney seized the chance. During the daily emergency cabinet meeting with President Cleveland on July 3, the attorney general obtained the orders to send the army to Chicago. Troops began arriving the next day. By July 10 almost two thousand soldiers were in the Chicago area. "While action should be prompt and decisive," Olney warned U.S. Attorney Milchrist for the record, "it should, of course, be kept within limits prescribed by the Constitution and laws." Milchrist and Walker were to ensure that those prescriptions were followed. Olney continued to rely on Arnold "as Marshal and Chief Executive Officer of the United States Court . . . to execute every process of the Court," but he rested easier knowing that now the army would be behind the precepts.[30]

Independence Day witnessed an escalation in the level of violence in

Chicago. That night mobs of strikers roamed the Blue Island yards, turning over railcars and destroying property. The vandalism and violence continued into the next day. Even the troops seemed powerless to stop it, and their very presence further incensed the strikers. On the night of July 5 the World's Columbian Exposition at Jackson Park caught fire, consuming seven buildings. The next day, mobs of strikers wrecked railroad property worth $340,000, mostly by fire in the railyards. Someone shot at a group of deputies, and two rioters were killed.[31]

Illinois governor John P. Altgeld had generally opposed the federal government's policy during the strike. The governor was committed to preserving order, not upholding the railroads in their labor disputes. President Cleveland had not even bothered to consult with Altgeld when he ordered the army to Chicago. By July 6, however, it was clear that the situation was out of hand. Altgeld sent in the state militia; Cleveland ordered army reinforcements.

As the troops and deputies fought the strikers, Special Attorney Edwin Walker stepped up his legal efforts to end the strike. "We are after the leaders," he announced at one point. On July 6 he reported to Olney that he hoped soon to indict Debs and other officials of the American Railway Union. Once they were indicted, he would ask for a high bail, then conviction. "I firmly believe that the result of these trials, and the punishment of the leaders, will be so serious, that a general strike upon any railroad will not again occur for a series of years." The stakes, Walker knew, were high. In the balance hung the railroad's ability to manage its affairs without threat from its employees.[32]

Marshal Arnold continued to swear in deputies wholesale, regardless of the quality or intentions of the men. "The marshal is appointing a mob of deputies that are worse than useless," Walker noted. Some evidence suggests that special deputies were responsible for starting some of the railroad fires; the fires and violence kept them employed at $4 a day. Olney challenged Arnold about the mass hirings. "Under the circumstances, what is the use of the great mob of deputies which you seem to be employing?" he asked. "Are not a large proportion wholly unreliable?" Arnold had no sufficient explanation, other than his own fear of confronting several thousand angry strikers. The quality of the deputies was so poor that, of the 190 arrests they made during the strike, only 71 resulted in indictments.[33]

The violence peaked on July 7. Strikers attacked a squad of state

On August 14, 1889, Deputy Marshal David Neagle killed David Terry to protect Supreme Court justice Stephen Field. Neagle was promptly arrested for murder by the local sheriff. From *Life of David S. Terry* by A. E. Wagstaff (San Francisco, 1892).

Neagle being visited in jail by friends. The Supreme Court decided that Neagle acted within his authority as a deputy marshal when he killed Terry. From *Daily Alta,* 1889.

"Run of 1893." U.S. marshals supervised the various land runs. Courtesy of Archives and Manuscripts Division, Oklahoma Historical Society.

The Three Guardsmen of Oklahoma: deputy marshals Bill Tilghman, Chris Madsen, and Heck Thomas. Tilghman courtesy of Archives and Manuscripts Division, Oklahoma Historical Society; Madsen and Thomas courtesy of Western History Collections, University of Oklahoma Library.

Ned Christy (5) and the marshal's posse that killed him. Courtesy of Western History Collections, University of Oklahoma Library.

Marshals taking Cherokee Bill (3) to Fort Smith. Courtesy of Western History Collections, University of Oklahoma Library.

U.S. marshals enforced U.S. law in China from 1866 to 1942. Photo by Jim A. Esquivel, courtesy of U.S. Marshals Service Collections.

In 1882, Congress excluded Chinese workers from emigration to America. U.S. marshals enforced the exclusion act. From *Harper's Weekly,* May 8, 1876.

During the 1894 Pullman strike, marshals enforced the omnibus injunction against the strikers by hiring thousands of special deputies. From *Harper's Weekly*.

Deputies try to move an engine and a car on the Chicago, Rock Island, and Pacific Railroad at Blue Island, July 2, 1894. From *Harper's Weekly*.

During World War I, U.S. marshals registered 11,554 German aliens. Courtesy of National Archives, Washington, D.C.

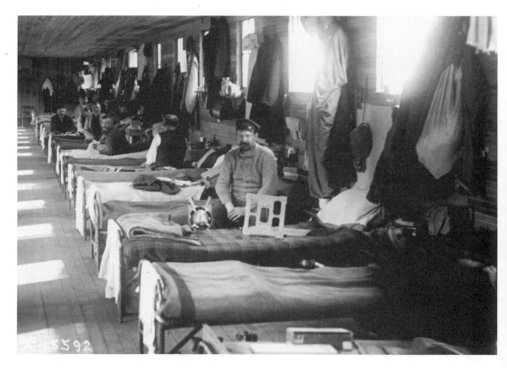

Enemy aliens suspected of espionage were confined by U.S. marshals in prison camps run by the U.S. Army. Courtesy of National Archives, Washington, D.C.

During Prohibition, marshals seized the speakeasies, trucks, warehouses, and other properties and equipment used by bootleggers. Permission granted by *Detroit News,* a Gannett Newspaper, © 1929.

Al Capone in the custody of U.S. marshals. He is using his hat to hide the handcuffs. Courtesy of National Archives, Washington, D.C.

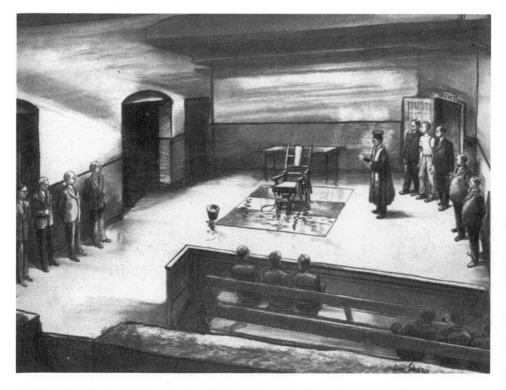

In 1954, U.S. Marshal William A. Carroll (fourth from left along wall opposite Julius Rosenberg)
arranged the executions of Julius and Ethel Rosenberg. Reprinted with the permission of Ruth Sharp.

State and federal authorities clash on September 26, 1962, at Ole Miss, as Lieutenant Governor Paul Johnson confronts Chief U.S. Marshal James J. P. McShane and James Meredith and denies them entry onto campus. Photo © Flip Schulke, Black Star.

Deputy Al Butler and his squad of deputies arriving at Oxford, Mississippi, September 30, 1962, to compel James Meredith's enrollment at the University of Mississippi. Courtesy of Al Butler.

U.S. marshals holding the Lyceum at Ole Miss. Photo © Flip Schulke, Black Star.

After the riot, Chief Marshal James J. P. McShane and John Doar escort James Meredith to his first class. Photo © Fred Ward, Black Star.

In October 1967, U.S. marshals protected the Pentagon during an anti-Vietnam demonstration. Courtesy of U.S. Marshals Service Collections.

When arrested, the demonstrators went limp, forcing the marshals to drag them to the prison vans. Courtesy of U.S. Marshals Service Collections.

On May 8, 1973, the takeover of Wounded Knee, South Dakota, by the American Indian Movement ended. Courtesy of U.S. Marshals Service Collections.

The arrest of Christopher "the Falcon" Boyce proved the marshals' prowess as fugitive hunters. Photo by Bruce McKim, *Seattle Times*. .

Deputy U.S. Marshal Thomas P. Spillane disguised as the San Diego chicken. This now famous Washington, D.C., operation resulted in the arrest of one hundred fugitives who thought they were going to a Redskins football game. Photo © 1985 *Los Angeles Times*. Reprinted by permission.

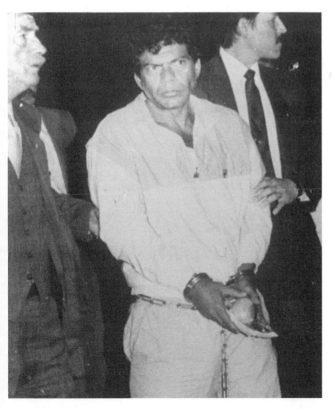

Juan Matta Ballesteros, a notorious drug trafficker, under arrest by U.S. Marshal Charles E. Healey and Deputy Roberto Escober. Courtesy of AP/Wide World News.

A hooded organized-crime informant testifies in exchange for a new identity and the opportunity to begin a new life. Photo by Edward N. Stiso, courtesy of U.S. Marshals Service Collections.

U.S. marshals also protect federal courts. Deputy Lydia Blakely provided security at the trial of drug trafficker Carlos Lehder Rivas. Photo © David Walters, *Miami Herald*.

The Special Operations Group of specially trained deputies assists in handling particularly dangerous arrests or difficult operations. Photo © 1989 Walter P. Calahan.

The Marshals Service operates the National Prisoner Transportation System, which uses two Boeing 727s to move 90,000 prisoners a year. Photo by Rich Sugg.

U.S. marshals seize the ill-gotten gains of drug dealers. Since 1984, marshals have seized more than $1 billion from drug dealers, including this $8 million in cash that was buried in one dealer's backyard. Courtesy of U.S. Marshals Service Collections.

On January 4, 1990, Manuel Noriega was booked into the custody of the U.S. marshals on charges of drug trafficking. Two weeks earlier, twenty thousand U.S. troops invaded Panama to depose Noriega and install a democratically elected government. Courtesy of U.S. Marshals Service Collections.

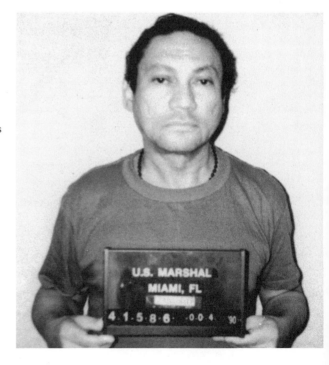

militia guarding a wrecking train at Forty-ninth and Loomis streets. The mob pelted the troops with rocks, and a few shots were fired. The command "Fix bayonets" earned the militia a brief respite, but the crowd returned to the attack moments later. After several such attacks, the militia returned the fire, killing four rioters and wounding twenty. Afterward, President Cleveland ordered in more troops. On July 8 he issued a proclamation calling on the citizens to obey the law.[34]

The strike followed a similar course in other sections of the country, except in the East, where neither the American Railway Union nor the Pullman Palace Car Company had made many inroads. Most other areas escaped the violence that racked Chicago. In railyards across the Midwest and the West, members of the union refused to touch Pullman cars. The train companies insisted that the trains could not leave without them, and federal circuit court judges issued omnibus injunctions and other orders to protect the mails.

Throughout the regions affected by the strike, Olney insisted that the marshals enforce the omnibus injunctions protecting the mail trains. He allowed the marshals to hire as many deputies as they wanted. Federal troops were dispatched only after the marshals were overwhelmed by the strikers. Although Olney would probably have preferred to send out the army, he realized that the marshals were the legitimate enforcers of federal court orders. The army could be used only in their support.[35]

Strike breaking was an onerous occupation for the marshals. Marshal George M. Humphrey of Nevada wrote the attorney general on August 30, 1894, long after the strike had been quelled. He described the problems confronted by his special deputies, who had not yet been paid by the Department of Justice:

> I used my utmost efforts during the strike to preserve the peace and prevent the destruction of lives and property. I labored under many disadvantages. It was an unpopular duty and it was with great difficulty that I secured men to act as deputies, as it required more than ordinary courage, both moral and physical, to stem the tide of public feeling, and to face the actual perils of the position. They are mostly poor men, many of them with families, and they sorely need their money.

Although accurate estimates of the numbers of special deputies hired across the country are impossible to make, the total reached well into the thousands. The final cost to the government, paying each deputy no more than $5 a day, came to $750,000. For most of the men hired, taking the oath as special deputy offered a welcome escape from unemployment. They, like the Pullman strikers, were victims of the vagaries of twentieth-century economics.[36]

The decisive battle was won in the federal courtroom in Chicago. The war was won in the Supreme Court. On July 10, Special Attorney Edwin Walker obtained the long-sought indictments against Debs and other officials of the American Railway Union. To Walker, Debs and the others personified the evils of unionism. The attorney placed the sole blame for the strike and its violence on them. Appearing before the grand jury, Walker asked for a series of indictments against the union officials for conspiracy to disrupt the mails and conspiracy to commit violence. The jury complied. Walker also instituted contempt proceedings against Debs and the others for violation of the omnibus injunction.

Warrants were promptly issued, and the union officials were as promptly arrested. Although bond was set at $10,000 each, Debs and his colleagues managed to raise it. After a few hours in jail, the men were released.

While Debs and the others were in custody, deputy marshals raided the union's headquarters. Records were seized as evidence, and every office was ransacked in the search. However, the process carried by the deputies did not justify the seizures. All they had was a subpoena requiring Debs's secretaries to appear before the grand jury with the union's books and records. Even Judge Grosscup, as friendly as he was to the government's efforts to defeat the union, could not sustain the deputies. The papers were returned to the American Railway Union.[37]

Judge Woods conducted the hearing on the contempt charges. The brilliant attorney Clarence Darrow appeared for Debs and the other union officers, but his talents were wasted before Woods. On January 8, 1895, Woods sentenced Debs to six months in prison, the other officers to three months.[38]

On appeal to the Supreme Court, Woods's decision was affirmed. In *U.S. v. Debs* the Court endorsed the government's authority to use all the power at its command to protect the mails and interstate commerce. It confirmed that federal court injunctions, federal marshals, and federal troops were appropriate weapons for that purpose. The affirmation gave Olney everything he wanted to protect management from the willfulness of labor unions. It was a stunning setback for organized labor.[39]

Debs returned to circuit court to face a jury on the conspiracy indictments. After several weeks Darrow felt confident that a majority of the jury accepted his arguments. Then, in February 1895, one of the jurors fell ill. Rather than impanel another jury, Walker and Milchrist agreed to drop the charges. They too had seen the direction the case was taking.[40]

Eventually the federal government backed away from its unquestioning support of management. Under Woodrow Wilson the government first recognized the right of unions to exist. During the New Deal the Roosevelt administration adopted a neutral stance toward labor-management difficulties. As the government came to see itself more as arbiter, the marshals were given more reasonable tasks. But all of that took a wrenching war by labor to achieve.

MEXICO'S REVOLUTION

The social upheavals of the twentieth century were international phenomena. The industrial revolution spawned worldwide demands for radical social, economic, and political transformations. Throughout the Western world, undercurrents of discontent disturbed the entrenched order of things. The campaign to transfer power from the traditional ruling classes to the people had clearly begun by the turn of the century.

The first of the great twentieth-century social revolutions erupted not in Europe but in Mexico. The country was ripe for radical social change. Increasingly, pockets of trouble plagued the thirty-one-year regime of President Porfirio Díaz, and various disjointed groups tried independently to gain some measure of power and autonomy. Many of the problems cropped up along the long, unprotected border with the United States. A steady flow of munitions from the north kept southern dreams of rebellion alive and well armed.

Policing the border originally fell to the U.S. marshals and their deputies. They enforced U.S. neutrality laws prohibiting military attacks on friendly governments from U.S. soil. The marshals also tried to contain the violence of revolution within Mexico's borders. They were consistently hampered in those tasks by the inadequacy of U.S. laws and by a growing sympathy for Mexico within the United States.

Throughout 1909 and 1910 the border hosted a motley group of radicals, socialists, and Mexican revolutionaries. American socialists like John Murray of the Political Refugee Defense League and the famed Mother Jones journeyed to the Texas border to address mass meetings and call for the overthrow of Díaz. Marshal Eugene Nolte of West Texas and his deputies generally attended the meetings to monitor the discontent, though it was clearly beyond their power to prevent border crossings and smuggling completely.[41]

The marshals' occasional successes in making arrests were more than offset by the difficulty of obtaining convictions. Extraditing the accused to Mexico and proving neutrality violations were almost as difficult as protecting the border. Even when the government obtained sufficient evidence to prove the defendant's involvement in a military raid on Mexico, extraditions were prohibited by an 1899 treaty with Mexico. Article III of the treaty expressly denied extraditions for offenses "of a purely political character."

"Violations of the neutrality laws that have occurred along the border in recent years have practically all arisen in connection with movements conducted under the color and guise of 'political movements,'" U.S. Attorney Charles A. Boynton wrote. Although Marshal Nolte and his deputies arrested Colonel José M. Rangel, the leader of an attack on Las Vacas, in August 1909, Boynton doubted the rebel could be extradited to Mexico, where the crime occurred. Rangel could too easily prove that his attack had been politically motivated and that his punishment by Mexican authorities would be equally political.[42]

Then, on November 20, 1910, Francisco Madero led a band of Mexican insurgents across the border into Chihuahua, Mexico. Madero was a visionary and an idealist, a spiritualist whose management of his family's hacienda in Coahuila both turned a profit and improved the living conditions of the workers. His movement, which he defined in 1910 as the San Luis Potosí plan, promised to broaden political power, introduce parliamentary democracy, and restrict the rights of foreigners to exploit Mexico's economy and resources. Mexico had found its savior.

The San Luis Potosí program was in essence a mild transformation from dictatorship to democracy. It fully satisfied few, yet it rallied to its banner the opposition against Díaz. Madero attracted such oddly incompatible lieutenants as the wealthy Venustiano Carranza, the bandit Francisco "Pancho" Villa, the peasant Emiliano Zapata, and the rancher-general Alvaro Obregón.[43]

Although Nolte and his deputies noticed some activity along the border as Madero prepared to cross, nothing extraordinary gave them cause to interfere. Reports of large purchases of guns and ammunition and of gatherings of Mexicans along the line were so commonplace, and the laws to stop such activity so incompetent, that Nolte could do little but watch. Even after Madero entered Mexico, the marshal reported that he had no evidence of a violation of U.S. neutrality laws.[44]

"My representatives along the border are alert, closely in touch with the situation, investigate all rumors of gatherings of supposed revolutionists," Nolte asserted as late as December 31, 1910. He added, "We have found no evidence of any violation of neutrality. There is good reason to believe that many Mexicans have crossed the border from this side, but not in large bands." Nolte's colleague in New Mexico, Marshal Creighton M. Foraker, concurred with Nolte's assessment, though he expected the rate of neutrality violations to increase. To prepare for that contingency, the federal government beefed up its border patrols. Marshal Charles A. Overlock of Arizona deputized thirteen customs collectors to supplement his deputies. As frequently as possible along the long, open border, deputy marshals rode patrol.[45]

The border was Madero's most benign ally. Madero's supporters flowed steadily into Mexico, taking with them the supplies of war. In California, U.S. Attorney A. I. McCormick registered his suspicions that the neutrality laws had been repeatedly violated by local leaders of the revolution based at Colexico, but he had no proof. Although Attorney General George Wickersham increased the number of Bureau of Investigation agents along the border and urged the marshals to cooperate with them, little proof and few prosecutions resulted.[46]

William Howard Taft called out the army to enhance the marshals' patrols. Brigadier General J. W. Duncan, the commander of the department of Texas, estimated in a "conservative census" dated February 21, 1911, that 80 percent of the Mexicans on both sides of the river and a majority of Americans along the border were insurgent sympathizers. Because the military was on a peacetime footing, without the authority of martial law, deputy marshals accompanied the cavalry patrols to make the arrests. Attorney General Wickersham instructed the U.S. marshals and their deputies:

> Perform, in conjunction with the military forces stationed along the Mexican border, such patrol duty as may be necessary to prevent violations of the neutrality laws, and in proper cases to arrest persons caught

in the act of violating such laws, or whose apprehension is otherwise requested, in proper manner. It is also apparent that under certain circumstances, especially when there is no investigating officer of the Department present to perform the work, it is proper for your deputies and the military forces to make appropriate inquiry in connection with the arrest of persons engaged in violating the law, or where it is believed that the law is being violated at or near the places where such deputies or military forces are operating.

Despite that broad grant of authority and the aid of the military, protecting the border was nearly impossible.[47]

Marshal Calvin G. Brewster, after originally denying any problem in his district, eventually enhanced his force of deputies by swearing in twenty customs inspectors. His men acted as scouts for the army patrols, "co-operating with the military in the capacity of guides, and continually working as an independent body patrolling the river front from its mouth." The patrols covered a distance of almost six hundred miles over rough, hilly country. The men "were kept constantly on the alert by wild rumors of frightened people," most of which turned out to be unfounded.[48]

Both marshals Nolte and Brewster of Texas believed that fully 90 percent of the people living along the border shared a "universal sentiment" of sympathy for Madero's revolt, resulting in considerable assistance for the rebels. "It approaches well nigh the impossible for any officer, or any number of officers, to procure the evidence necessary to afford affirmative proof," Nolte wrote the attorney general in the spring of 1911.[49]

With his supply lines stretched securely into the United States and with his rear protected, Madero advanced rapidly across Mexico. Long years of corruption had left the Mexican army weak and flaccid; it crumpled. By the spring of 1911 Madero was clearly triumphing. In May the rebels captured Ciudad Juárez in a decisive victory. On May 21, Madero and Díaz signed the Treaty of Ciudad Juárez, ending the rebellion and Díaz's thirty-one years in power. The revolution was just beginning.[50]

The United States looked to Madero to bring peace to the border. In the fall of 1911, at the suggestion of Acting Secretary of State Huntington Wilson, Attorney General George Wickersham agreed to drop all prosecutions of Maderistos for violations of U.S. neutrality laws. President Taft's long-standing policy remained in effect. The marshals and the army were to "prevent the territory of the United States being used as a base for a military expedition against the established government in Mexico."[51]

In March 1912, Congress resolved and President Taft proclaimed a prohibition on the exportation of arms or munitions of war to Mexico. According to Attorney General Wickersham, Taft's proclamation broadly encompassed "those articles which are primarily and ordinarily used for military purposes." The proclamation significantly enhanced the legal authority of federal officials along the border. They now needed to prove only smuggling, not an intent to violate the neutrality of the United States.[52]

Yet, as Marshal Overlock of Arizona hastily pointed out, the proclamation alone was not enough. "The exporting of any arms or ammunition of war from the United States into the Republic of Mexico is not generally done through any port of entry, but is generally carried over by small parties miles away from the towns and where there is no deputy stationed." Throughout 1912 the marshals, supported by cavalry patrols, continued to guard the border. The increasing volume of smuggling testified to the problems Madero faced in establishing control over the revolution-racked country.[53]

Madero's collapse came from within. Throughout his seventeen months as president of Mexico, he was beset repeatedly with attempted coups, open rebellions, and other attacks. For the most part the army upheld him, even against individual generals and commands that rose to challenge him. Then, in February 1913, General Victoriano Huerta saw his opportunity. Over a tragic ten-day period, Huerta arranged Madero's assassination and took control of Mexico. Madero's bloody death foretold Mexico's future.

Huerta's violent coup occurred just less than a month before a gentler transfer of power in the United States. On March 4, 1913, Woodrow Wilson succeeded William Howard Taft as president. The murder of Madero shocked the new president. Promising to teach Mexicans how to elect good men, Wilson embarked on a vicious diplomatic war against the usurper. He dispatched a number of special emissaries to negotiate Huerta's retirement and to establish contact with Venustiano Carranza, Emiliano Zapata, and Pancho Villa, the principal leaders of the constitutionalist rebellion against Huerta. The president also tried to isolate Huerta internationally by pressuring Germany and England to leave Mexico to him.[54]

Under Wilson, the military assumed most of the responsibility for sealing the border against the Mexican revolution. Taft's arms embargo remained in effect, but Wilson expected the army to carry the principal burden of enforcing it. General Tasker H. Bliss, commander of the southern department, found patrolling the border to be just as frustrating as the marshals had. In April 1913 he proposed establishing a neutral zone along the Mexican side to stop the smuggling and contain the fighting, but the proposal never gained acceptance.[55]

Wilson's diplomacy failed to unseat Huerta. In February 1914 the president lifted the arms embargo to allow Carranza and Villa to purchase all the weapons they could afford. Two months later, Wilson ordered the navy to seize the port of Veracruz as a reprisal for a national insult to the American flag when Mexican soldiers forced American sailors off a U.S. whaleboat in Tampico. The occupation was timed to block delivery of a shipload of German munitions to Huerta.

As soon as the bluejackets and marines landed on Mexican soil, General Bliss declared a new embargo on arms to Mexico. The president, after a brief hesitation, allowed the embargo to stand. It never had the sanction of a presidential proclamation, which meant, as Bliss pointed out, that "we have no law to back us up." Finally, on September 8 the War Department lifted the embargo because the lack of a proclamation exposed the soldiers to personal liability.[56]

The occupation of Veracruz emboldened Huerta's internal opponents while denying him supplies and revenues. Confronted by the attacks from without and within and effectively isolated internationally by Wilson's diplomatic initiatives, Huerta resigned in July 1914. He fled Mexico before the advancing armies of Carranza and Villa. The constitutionalists seized Mexico City—and national power—in the fall of 1914.

United in opposition, the alliance of Carranza and Villa collapsed in victory. Within months of taking control of Mexico, their forces were in open combat. Once again, Pancho Villa took to rebellion against the government of Mexico. Throughout 1915 he fought a losing battle with Carranza, steadily retreating to his home base in northern Mexico. The revolution in Mexico continued. In March 1916, Villa crossed the border to attack Columbus, New Mexico. Wilson, frustrated in all his efforts to influence the course of the revolution, sent General John J. Pershing and more than ten thousand troops on a punitive expedition against the bandit general. Although elements of Pershing's command penetrated four hundred miles into Mexico, Villa escaped. The expedition remained in Mexico almost a year before Wilson withdrew it in early 1917.

By the time the expedition entered Mexico, the role of the marshals in protecting the border had been fully taken over by the military. The limited force of marshals was no match for the fury of Mexico's revolution.

WILSON'S WAR

While revolution consumed Mexico, war ravaged Europe. On June 28, 1914, a Bosnian nationalist watched a motorcade drive through the streets of Sarajevo, the capital of the Bosnian province within the Austro-Hungarian empire. As the cars pulled past him, the young man fired several shots at Archduke Franz Ferdinand and his wife, royal heirs to the decadent empire. Their deaths stepped off a macabre waltz to war as the European balance of power twirled and tripped. A month later, Germany and Austria were at war against the Triple Entente of Russia, France, and Great Britain. Eventually Italy and Japan joined the alliance against the Teuton powers. President Woodrow Wilson declared America's neutrality from the devastating conflagration, then spent the next two and a half years defending that neutrality from belligerent encroachments.

On the last day of January 1917 the German government officially informed the United States that it would immediately resume its wartime policy of unrestricted submarine warfare. No ship, neutral or belligerent, would be safe from German U-boats on the high seas. The announcement was tantamount to a declaration of war against the United States. During the years that Europe had been at war, Wilson had repeatedly protested German violations of America's neutrality. Submarine attacks had been at the crux of the issue. Although the rules of war did not comprehend submarines, Wilson insisted that the law reigned supreme over new technology.

The United States broke off diplomatic relations with Germany on February 3. But in one of the great moments of indecision in American history, Wilson shied from war. For two full months, February and March, he waited. Unwilling to accept Germany's decision, Wilson seemed equally unable to ask Congress for a declaration of war. Meanwhile, Germany embarked on an ambitious effort to disrupt Allied supply lines to the United States. Sunken ships, many of them of U.S. registry, littered the Atlantic trade routes.[57]

Wilson feared the effect of twentieth-century world war on the American people. "It required illiberalism at home to reinforce the men at the front," the president supposedly told Frank I. Cobb, editor of the *New York World*. "We couldn't fight Germany and maintain the ideals of Government that all thinking men shared." The president knew his people. "Once lead this people into war and they'll forget there ever was such a thing as tolerance," he asserted. "To fight you must be brutal and ruthless and the spirit of ruthless brutality will enter into the very fiber of our national life, infecting Congress, the courts, the policeman on the beat, the man in the street." Not the Constitution, free speech, nor right of assembly could survive the national effort required to defeat Germany. "Conformity would be the only virtue," Wilson concluded.[58]

Assistant Attorney General Charles Warren researched the statutes of war to find the antique Alien Act of 1798 still in force. Although "unsatisfactory and probably not fully suited to the present conditions," Warren concluded on March 23 that the law's provisions "for the apprehension and removal of alien enemies out of the United States or their restraint according to Presidential proclamation" were sufficient until Congress could pass new legislation. His main objection to the old law was its requirement that the marshals needed an order from the courts to arrest enemy aliens. That requirement was, Warren told Attorney General Thomas W. Gregory, "an entirely inadequate way of dealing with the problem." New legislation was needed to empower the marshals to act solely at the direction of the president.[59]

Fearful "that Germans and German sympathizers in the United States intend to commit widespread crimes of violence at the very outbreak of war," Warren urged Gregory to issue a presidential proclamation on enemy aliens immediately. At the least, Warren wanted to be ready with a proclamation as soon as war was declared. Warren advised that once one was promulgated, the government should arrest "all Germans in this country who, from our investigations during the past two and a half years, are known to have been leaders, or particularly dangerous or able men, in the German propaganda." The point, he explained, was "to break up the German plans at the very outset and in the first two days after war is declared."[60]

Warren's principal concern was the internment of Germans who threatened the United States. Alarmed by his assistant's uneasiness, Attorney General Gregory alerted the marshals to use "constant vigilance" against hostile acts by Germans. Gregory also alerted the chiefs of police in major cities across the United States to take special care to search for hidden stores of arms and ammunition and to monitor meetings of alien enemies.[61]

The department also prepared a proclamation for Wilson's signature authorizing the internment or deportation of alien enemies who, by word or act, posed a risk to U.S. security. The marshals making the arrests were not required to obtain a court order. Instead, they were to make "summary arrests" under presidential warrant. Despite Warren's original interpretation that new legislation was needed, the department decided to act on the Alien Act of 1798, the same law that guided the marshals during the War of 1812.

The department's proclamation also established strict regulations on the movement, possessions, and actions of enemy aliens. They were not allowed to own weapons, radios, or ciphers; they were prohibited from approaching within half a mile of any forts, arsenals, ships, navy yards, factories that made war material, or other prohibited areas; and they were cautioned against aiding the enemy by word or act. Arrangements for interning dangerous enemy aliens were negotiated with the War Department. By the end of March 1917 the Justice Department was ready for the domestic exigencies of war.[62]

On April 2, Wilson addressed a joint session of Congress. He called for a declaration of war against Germany "to vindicate the principles of peace and justice in the life of the world as against selfish and autocratic power." Congress debated the request for four days, finally declaring war on April 6, 1917. Wilson immediately promulgated the department's proclamation on enemy aliens.[63]

That same day, Attorney General Gregory bluntly summarized the enemy alien proclamation in a cover letter to U.S. attorneys and marshals across the country: "No German alien enemy in this country, who has not hitherto been implicated in plots against the interests of the United State, need have any fear of action by the Department of Justice as long as he observes the following warning: Obey the law: keep your mouth shut." While the proclamation was being distributed, U.S. marshals arrested upwards of sixty-three Germans whom departmental investigations had identified as dangerous to the peace and safety of the United States.[64]

The Department of Justice and the American people went beyond Gregory's simple warning. Germany, Germans, and German products became objects of scorn. Sauerkraut was renamed "liberty cabbage"; hamburgers became "liberty sandwiches." The governor of Iowa forbade the use of German on streetcars, on telephones, or in public places. German aliens, even naturalized Americans of German descent, were frequently mobbed at the slightest sign of disrespect, and several were lynched. After the war, Wilson summarized the country's attitude toward German-Americans, the so-called hyphenated citizens. "Any man," the president explained, "who carries a hyphen about with him carries a dagger that he is ready to plunge into the vitals of this Republic."[65]

The Wilson administration sheathed the dagger. Throughout the war, federal officials, particularly the marshals, maintained an intense scrutiny of the activities of enemy aliens. As soon as war was declared, the Justice Department issued a broad definition of restricted areas that German aliens were prohibited from entering without a pass issued by a U.S. marshal, including docks, factories, military forts, sewers that emptied into the sea near public harbors, Milwaukee, the District of Columbia, and other sensitive areas. Special passes issued by the marshals were required for any enemy alien to pass within half a mile of a restricted area.[66]

The continuing, gnawing concern that not all enemy aliens had applied for permits and passes finally persuaded the department to invoke Article 11 of the president's April 6 proclamation requiring the registration of all German males resident in the United States. In December, when the United States finally declared war on Austro-Hungary, the regulations were applied to those aliens as well. Preliminary instructions on the registration were issued to the marshals in December 1917, followed by detailed regulations a month later. February 4, 1918, was set as the day of registration.[67]

The registration was effected by dividing the country into urban areas (cities with a population greater than five thousand) and nonurban areas. In urban areas, the local police conducted the registration of each male enemy alien. In nonurban areas, male enemy aliens reported to the local post offices to register. The registration consisted of an affidavit, filed in triplicate, of information including residence, occupation, description, and fingerprints. One copy was filed with the local marshal, one was forwarded to the Department of Justice, and one was kept by the registrar. In return, each enemy alien was issued a registration card. Thenceforth, it was unlawful for a male enemy alien to be caught without his registration card.

On the appointed day, more than 260,000 male enemy aliens registered. Four months later, in June 1918, the registration was expanded to include females. For ten days, a total of 220,000 enemy alien females registered.[68]

Enemy aliens whom federal officials suspected of being "dangerous to the peace and safety of the United States" or of deliberately violating the president's proclamation were arrested and interned in prison camps operated by the army at Fort Oglethorpe and Fort McPherson, Georgia. The Department of Justice insisted that the arrests could be made solely on the authority of the president and, through his delegation, the attorney general, without a court order, hearing, or trial.

By June 30, 1917, the marshals had arrested 295 enemy aliens. Over the next four months, an additional 600 were sent to the internment camps for the duration of the war. By war's end, more than 6,300 had been arrested under presidential warrant.[69]

The Wilson administration allowed normal constitutional procedures to take a holiday. Early in May 1917, just over a month after the declaration of war, U.S. Attorney J. Virgil Bourland of Fort Smith, Arkansas, reported that Marshal John H. Parker had arrested Jo Zin, a German alien who had in his possession an unloaded pistol and a sword hidden in a cane. Hauled before the district judge, Zin averred his loyalty to the United States. The judge condemned the pistol and cane to the marshal's custody and ordered Zin to report to the marshal once a week for the rest of the war.[70]

Assistant Attorney General Warren objected to the handling of the case. "If a person comes within the terms of the Proclamation, the authority of the Attorney General to arrest and detain him is plenary and no recourse to the courts is necessary," he bluntly informed U.S. Attorney Bourland, adding that "there is no reason why the alien enemy need appear before a court." In the future the local marshal or attorney should telegraph the department for authority to arrest the enemy alien.[71]

Through a memorandum of understanding with the army, the Department of Justice worked out procedures for arresting enemy aliens. The arrests were accomplished under the "specific authority" of the attorney general, which meant that the department approved each arrest individually. Once the marshal had the internee in his custody, he arranged for transportation to the place of detention and delivery to the army. Detailed physical descriptions of each enemy alien were completed by the marshals in case one escaped. Several who did try to escape were treated like all fugitives, complete with wanted posters and manhunts.[72]

Shortly after war was declared, Congress passed the Espionage Act, making it a crime for anyone "to cause insubordination, disloyalty, mutiny, or refusal of duty in the military or naval forces of the United States, or [to] willfully obstruct the recruiting or enlistment into the service of the United States." A separate Sedition Act outlawed "any disloyal, profane, scurrilous, or abusive language about the form of government of the United States, or the Constitution of the United States, or the flag of the United States, or the uniform of the Army or Navy." Both laws were used effectively to stifle discontent about the war.[73]

"What I am opposed to is not the feeling of the pacifists, but their stupidity," Wilson explained in November 1917. "My heart is with them, but my mind has a contempt for them." Attorney General Gregory adopted a harsher view. "May God have mercy on them," he said of opponents of the war, "for they need expect none from an outraged people and an avenging Government." According to one account, the Sedition Act alone anointed each U.S. attorney as "an angel of life and death clothed with the power to walk up and down in his district, saying 'This one I will spare, and that one I will smite.'"[74]

Both laws were interpreted with astonishing breadth. The Reverend Clarence H. Waldron, a Pentecostal minister in Windsor, Vermont, was sentenced to fifteen years in the federal penitentiary in Atlanta for preaching that the war was contrary to the teachings of Christ. "Surely," the minister wrote in one pamphlet, "if Christians were forbidden to fight to preserve the Person of their Lord and Master, they may not fight to preserve themselves, or any city they should happen to dwell in. Christ has no kingdom here. His servants must not fight." Attorney General Gregory considered the verdict in Waldron's case an "effective deterrent against a very dangerous type of antiwar propaganda."[75]

The U.S. marshals and their deputies also participated in the massive wartime suppression of free speech. Most of the investigations of suspected traitors and seditionists were conducted by local police officers or agents of the Bureau of Investigation. The marshals, though, made all federal arrests.

Wilson's prediction came true: Illiberalism and intolerance infected the nation. Marshals enforced the Selective Service laws, arresting anyone who opposed the draft or dodged it. They worked with Bureau of Investigation agents and private vigilantes to ensure a united home front in support of the war. The spirit of ruthless brutality guided the treatment of enemy aliens, and illiberalism allowed the suppression of free speech and free thought.[76]

In the fall of 1918 Wilson negotiated an armistice with Germany, ending hostilities at the eleventh hour of the eleventh month. A month later, Attorney General Gregory proposed rescinding enemy alien regulations on Christmas Day 1918. Wilson approved the suggestion. In the spring of 1919 the German prisoners interned at the army's camps were repatriated to their fatherland through Switzerland.[77]

Intolerance lingered. The new attorney general, A. Mitchell Palmer, embarked on a vicious attack against socialists, communists, and immigrants from eastern Europe. Marshals provided some of the manpower for Palmer's raids during the Red Scare of 1919. With no clear focus on what they were looking for, government agents scoured the slums and neighborhoods where new immigrants first tasted American life. Midnight raids on suspected communist and socialist cells uncovered enough evidence – but barely – to fuel Palmer's steamroller tactics. When the revolution that Palmer predicted for May 1 failed to appear, the Red Scare largely faded to memory. Its scars remained.

In response to the turmoil of the new century, the federal government had explored new ways to exercise its power, novel methods to suppress dissent, control labor, and wage war. They were awkward solutions awkwardly implemented by the U.S. marshals and their deputies. The search for the right balance between individual rights and governmental power would continue for the next six decades.

10

PROCESS, PROHIBITION, AND PROFESSIONALISM

1919–1953

"I make this statement knowing I am about to die," Deputy Marshal J. Herbert Ray began.

U.S. Attorney Mac Swinford sat in the sterile hospital room quietly recording the deputy's dying statement. Through the window, Swinford could hear the bustle of midmorning traffic, of life itself, along the streets of Lexington, Kentucky. It was February 2, 1935.

The night before, Ray had eaten dinner alone on Rand Street before setting out to find Clay Crowe. He had an arrest warrant against Crowe for bootlegging and failure to pay federal taxes on whiskey. The deputy left the diner at 6:20 and drove west on Fifth Street. Just after he crossed Upper Street into the black section of Lexington, Ray noticed a car parked on Campbell Street across from one of the city's more popular speakeasies. The car looked like the one owned by Clay Crowe.

Deputy Ray turned onto Campbell, slowing to a stop behind the car. He got out, crossed over to the curb, and walked up on the right-hand side of the other car. Ray did not recognize either of the two men in the car; neither was Clay Crowe. Reaching the front passenger door, Ray flashed his badge. He told the men that he was a government officer and wanted to talk to them. With his free hand, he opened the car door and motioned the men to get out. The driver fired a pistol across his passenger's lap.

"It hit me in the stomach, and I fell to the ground unable to get up," Ray remembered later. "I continued to lie on the ground. I shot six times." The car sped away. Ray lay bleeding by the side of the road. Across the street, a few faces peeked out from the speakeasy. No one called the police. Ten hours after giving his statement, Ray died.[1]

In May 1934, Congress had made killing a federal officer a federal offense. U.S. Attorney Swinford called in an agent of the newly renamed Federal Bureau of Investigation to assist the Lexington police in finding Ray's killers. The detectives checked with nearby hospitals in case one of Ray's shots had hit the mark. The hospital in Covington, Kentucky, about a hundred miles away, reported a gunshot case.

The patient, Joe Hackworth, had been shot in the arm. After a brief interview with detectives, he confessed that he had been the passenger. Clay Crowe's brother William was the driver and had shot the deputy. After they sped from the scene, the two men had picked up another Crowe brother, Chester Crowe, before rushing Hackworth to the hospital in Covington. The Crowes had left him there.

Hackworth's confession gave the prosecution an open-and-shut case. Still, Swinford hesitated to bring charges under the new statute punishing assaults on federal officers. "Due to the fact that the Act of May 18, 1934, provides that the deceased must be in the performance of his official duties, there is, in my opinion, some danger attached to a prosecution of this case in Federal court," Swinford advised the Department of Justice on February 13, 1935. He preferred to rely on state authorities to try the defendants "on a straight murder charge." The county prosecutor was capable, and Kentucky provided the death penalty for murder convictions.

Swinford's approach to the case reflected the single most important trend aborning with the twentieth century: the reliance on experts. By the 1920s the marshals were understood to be the experts on executing process and serving court papers. To act beyond that expertise flouted the twentieth century.

Ray had been armed with a warrant and was in search of the man named thereon. He was acting on the justifiable suspicion that the car belonged to the Crowe family and might contain Clay Crowe or information leading to his whereabouts. Despite those facts the U.S. attorney doubted he could prove that the deputy was on official business under the terms of the Act of May 18, 1934. "Ray had no warrant for either of the occupants of the car, the door of which he opened and from which he was shot," Swinford concluded. Without specific process, the marshals apparently could hope for no official protection. They were process servers strictly limited to the terms of their precept.[2]

The transformation from a rural to an industrial society resulted in a phenomenal explosion of detail and information in the twentieth century. In every field of human endeavor, knowledge burgeoned. The boundaries of the known far surpassed the ability of any single individual to comprehend. Knowledge exceeded the limits of the individually knowable. Thus, American society developed experts who mastered a single field and who depended on experts in other fields beyond their ken.[3]

The government, too, wholeheartedly embraced the compelling infatuation with experts. During the first third of the century, government departments, divisions, bureaus, and agencies sprang up like mushrooms of a summer morning. Two world wars and a world economic collapse contributed to the boom in government, but the rapid growth actually reflected the drive toward expertise. No other period witnessed such a rapid growth in the size, scope, and interests of the federal government. No other period saw such an increase in federal experts.

The Department of Justice began its own process of subdivision. Departments and bureaus were established to deal with specific aspects of federal law and regulations. By 1937 the department consisted of six divisions, all but one of which were established during the twentieth century: claims by and against the United States (1870), trade and commerce (1903), customs (1909), public lands (1910), internal revenue (1919), and crimes (1919). Each was headed by an assistant attorney general.[4]

Within the Department of Justice, Attorney General George Wickersham created the Bureau of Investigation in 1908 for the detection of crime and criminals. By 1917 more than half a dozen federal investigatory agencies existed. In June of that year Attorney General Thomas W. Gregory sent a reminder to the various U.S. attorneys and marshals across the country:

> The Department of Labor maintains a force to handle violations of the
> Chinese Exclusion laws, immigration and naturalization matters, matters

arising under Section 6 of the white slave traffic act, steamboat inspection laws, alien contract labor laws, etc.; the Department of Agriculture employs agents that enforce the pure food laws, meat inspection act, etc.; the Interior Department has forces to handle the investigations of violations of the land laws, pension laws, Indian laws, etc.; the Post Office Department employs inspectors to investigate generally matters relating to that Department, including depredations upon the mail; the Treasury Department employs secret service agents to deal with violations of the counterfeiting laws and for the protection of the person of the President, a customs force to enforce the customs laws, a force under the Commissioner of Internal Revenue to enforce the internal revenue laws, etc.; and the Interstate Commerce Commission has agents to make investigations coming under certain acts regulating interstate commerce.

Over the next several decades the trend continued. Income tax laws led to tax investigators. The Volstead Act resulted in Prohibition agents. Trouble along the international boundaries led to the establishment of the Border Patrol. The continued building of federal penitentiaries meant the creation of the Bureau of Prisons. It was the age of experts.[5]

During that age, the Department of Justice categorized the marshals as experts on serving the orders of the federal courts. Officials considered serving process and conducting investigations to be two categories that were mutually exclusive yet inclusive of all aspects of law enforcement. "The marshals and their deputies are process serving as distinguished from investigating officers," Assistant Attorney General Rush L. Holland warned Marshal James E. McClure of southern Illinois in July 1923. Little thought was given to the need for investigations when serving warrants or for culminating an investigation by making an arrest.[6]

The comptroller of the Treasury, in a series of decisions, concurred with the assessment. "The duty of making preliminary investigations of violations of law is one which does not devolve upon a United States marshal, and such marshal, or deputy marshal, while so engaged is not traveling upon official business and is not entitled to traveling expenses," one decision concluded.[7]

The distinction was an unfortunate misunderstanding of the age-old duty of the marshals "to execute all lawful precepts issued under the authority of the United States." The key was not in the term "precept," which means "written order," but in the meaning of the phrase "authority of the United States." Those words went beyond the federal courts to encompass all three branches of the federal government. During World War I, for example, the marshals had executed presidential arrest warrants against enemy aliens. Officials within the Department of Justice had insisted that the marshals keep the arrests away from the federal courts. Before the age of experts, the marshals had never been restricted to the execution of court-ordered process.

Other agencies were confined by law and regulations to specific tasks and authorities, but the marshals could do anything, providing only that they had instructions from one of the three legitimate branches of government. The charter was breathtaking in its scope, a grant of power so general in character that only the Constitution of the United States could prescribe it.

But the age of experts introduced specialization, which meant restriction to an expertise. Forcing the marshals into the limited specialty of process serving for the federal courts condemned them to a decreasing relevancy within the federal judicial system and the Department of Justice. Serving process, as an expertise, required little talent and no special skills. The marshals lacked, too, a national organization to represent them within the Department of Justice. Hence, they had no one to promote them at budget time nor to defend them against bureaucratic infighting. Their description as process servers increasingly became a sneering diminutive.

The system of appointing U.S. marshals enhanced the problem. Filling the office of marshal imposed no special qualifications, no professional criteria or standards. As the department and other law enforcement agencies within it became more specialized and professional, they looked down on the politicians who were appointed marshal. By 1950 the strengths that had carried the marshals through the nineteenth century strangled them.

PROCESS AND PATRONAGE

The decline of the marshals began in the mid-1890s. Under the fee system of payment, the federal government managed the work of the marshals by refusing to pay for anything save the service of process, except when specific work was requested or authorized. Although frequently admonished not to investigate crimes, the marshals were almost as often called upon to make such investigations. The difference was in the control.

Marshals who independently made inquiries into violations of the law were, in effect, creating business for themselves. Their investigations led to the issuance of court process. Serving the process earned them fees. The temptation to fudge the investigation existed. A marshal might move quickly or fraudulently to convince the courts to issue a warrant, subpoena, summons, or other precept so he could then pocket the fees. Consequently, succeeding attorneys general adopted as standing policy that marshals were not to conduct investigations.

The policy was honored in its repudiation. Violations of the law were not always simple affairs; investigations were needed to identify the suspects, locate them, and prove their complicity in the crime. In theory, those were duties of the U.S. attorneys, but it was hard for them to conduct inquiries and represent the government's legal interests at the same time. Succeeding attorneys general frequently found themselves calling on the marshals to investigate cases, but those calls were always treated as exceptions. That way, the marshals were kept on a tight leash.

The crying need for some investigative organization at the federal level resulted in the establishment of the Bureau of Investigation in 1908. The nucleus of the new bureau came from the examiner's department. Its members had gained some detective experience in conducting their frequent audits and examinations of the marshals' accounts and records. The most immediate effect of the new bureau was to further restrict the marshals to an administrative sphere. According to the department's division of authority, the Bureau of Investigation's special agents justified the issuance of court process through their investigations. The marshals executed the process.

It was a typically American solution. The bureau's special agents had no arrest powers; the marshals had no authority to conduct investigations. Thus, those who worked up evidence in a case had no part in apprehending the suspects. Those who arrested the suspects had nothing to do with collecting the evidence against them. The intention was to make the investigations more complete. The marshal who culminated a case by making an arrest would need detailed information from the Bureau of Investigation to catch the suspect. At the same time, the arresting marshal would have no individual stake in the case, no pride or personal involvement, to influence him.

However, the effect of dividing federal law enforcement into exclusive spheres of investigation and execution was devastating to the marshals. The glamor and the respect went to the investigators, for theirs was the harder part, the mysterious part, the fun part. The marshals became simple executors. They were process servers.

As the age of experts evolved, the distinction between investigator and executor was especially destructive within the Department of Justice. From the department's perspective, the special agents were the experts on crime and law enforcement. The marshals were simpletons who merely carried out orders. Practically from its inception, the Bureau of Investigation was an organized, cohesive bureaucracy within the department. Time and experience allowed it to become more organized, more cohesive, more bureaucratic. At their best, the marshals comprised a loose confederation of independent judicial districts. At their worst, they were a collection of private fiefdoms concerned only with affairs in their own area. They had no central representation in Washington, no spokesman or defender, and, ultimately, no J. Edgar Hoover.

Increasingly, the marshals were shunted aside while the bureau grew in size and power. As the government expanded its interests, the bureau received new types of crimes to investigate. Espionage, interstate car theft, kidnapping, bank robbery, and unlawful flight to avoid state and local prosecutions were all added to its jurisdiction within its first three decades.

Oddly, the bureau's authority expanded at a much slower rate. It was exclusively confined to the investigation of crimes. New authority was rarely granted beyond that sphere. In 1924 the bureau's identification division became the repository of all fingerprints collected by federal agencies. Four years later, the bureau assumed the task of tracking down escaped federal prisoners. In 1934 special agents were granted arrest powers and allowed to carry weapons. Although each of those duties represented an expansion of authority, they were tied tightly to the bureau's responsibility to investigate federal crimes.[8]

While bureau agents concentrated on solving crimes, the marshals retained their twin duties to act as lawmen in making arrests and as executives in running the courts. That duality of purpose had been a problem since 1789, for at no time was it ever made clear just what the intent and purpose of the marshals' office was. Were the marshals a national police force or a national administrative organization? During the age of experts, that split personality was detrimental. The overriding concern of the age was to define in precise terms that which had always been vague. Although the marshals held the broadest law enforcement jurisdiction, they were less frequently called upon to use it.

As the emphasis on experts developed, department officials focused on the various administrative functions assigned the office of marshal. The new Bureau of Investigation offered a tempting replacement as a national police force. By 1916, official instructions defined the marshals as "the executive officers of the Federal courts" and "the local disbursing officers of the courts and the Department of Justice." The description harked back to a century earlier when the marshals described themselves as executive officers of the courts. But in that earlier time, the marshals meant that they executed the law; by the twentieth century, department officials meant that the marshals simply served process and paid bills. The difference was profound.[9]

By defining the marshals as executive and disbursing officers, the department arbitrarily restricted the scope of authority inherent in the position. The process of restriction coincided with the growing influence of the Bureau of Investigation. Officials within the department began to disparage the marshals by confining them exclusively to the service of court process and the handling of its money, ignoring the traditional flexibility inherent in the position. Flexibility was not a keystone of expertise.

In late 1917 Commander L. McCauley, the assistant director of naval intelligence, requested that four of his lieutenants in New York be sworn in as special deputies to enhance their authority to ferret out Navy spies. John L. O'Brian, the special assistant to the attorney general, denied the request. His rationale illustrated the restricted view the department had by then adopted toward its marshals:

> Any individual, including a United States Marshal, has the power of arresting a person caught in the act of committing a violation of the Federal Penal Statute. Nobody, whether a United States Marshal or other person, has the power of arresting any person not caught in the act of committing the crime, except upon warrant of arrest duly issued by the United States Commissioner or other Federal or State official authorized to issue warrants of arrest.
>
> Furthermore, deputy marshals have powers only within the district of the Marshal appointing them and being subordinates of such marshal are subject to his orders and instructions and responsible to him.

O'Brian's definition of the marshals' authority was correct, though unnecessarily restrictive. As representatives of the federal executive within their districts, considerable power and authority inhered in the office of marshal. The Supreme Court's *In re Neagle* decision of 1890 had defined the marshals as federal peace officers with broad powers to preserve the peace and enforce the laws. But that went for little once the Department of Justice determined to proscribe the authority of the marshals.[10]

"Deputy United States Marshals have only limited police powers," Assistant Attorney General Rush Holland confirmed in May 1923. He opposed commissioning special deputies to conduct particular investigations. "They serve no purpose and very often prove embarrassing," he explained in July 1923. "In any event, it is not the duty of the United States Marshal to secure evidence regarding alleged violations of the Federal laws as the marshals and their deputies are process serving as distinguished from investigating officers. The work incident to securing necessary evidence is handled by the Bureau of Investigation of this Department, the Bureau of Internal Revenue, and other government organizations."[11]

The hiring practices for deputies reflected the marshals' diminishment. In 1896 the marshals and most of their deputies were placed on salaries. Although that was the first step in the professionalization of the position, the second step was so long in coming that any immediate impact of the first was soon negated. Once the marshals and deputies were on a salary, the Department of Justice began to take an interest, not necessarily in whom the marshal hired, but in how many deputies he employed.

After 1896 deputies came in two types. Office deputies were fulltime, salaried employees usually stationed in the district's main office. Field deputies were part-time employees paid on the fee system and stationed at convenient points throughout the district. They served the process and other court orders in areas distant from the main district office. Departmental regulations specified that "field deputies must be located at various places throughout the district, with a view to economy and efficiency in the conduct of the public business." They were paid three-fourths of the gross fees established by law, including mileage, but only up to $1,500 a year. Although the marshals retained complete discretion in hiring field deputies, the department reserved the right to cancel "inexpedient" appointments.[12]

The marshals also hired their own office deputies, primarily because deputies were covered by the marshal's personal bond. As Attorney General Harry M. Daugherty explained in July 1921,

> It has been the uniform practice to permit Marshals to make their own selections of deputies, subject, of course, to the approval of the Attorney General. This practice is doubtless based on the ground that the Marshals are liable on their bonds for the acts of their deputies, so that it has not been the practice of this Office even to suggest the names of prospective appointees. Such a policy, it seems to me, is well founded.

Department officials asked only that the marshal inform them of the candidate's name, age, residence, previous occupation, qualifications, proposed salary, and proposed work assignments. Each deputy's commission expired when the marshal who hired him went out of office. When the office deputies went on salary, the Department of Justice assumed control of how many deputies were hired in each district and how much they were paid.[13]

The Department of Justice had a far more difficult time shielding the marshals from their patrons, the politicians who got them their jobs. As the government's civil service regulations tightened, the opportunities for patronage rewards dwindled apace. The marshal's office remained one of the last plums, and politicians used it to pay off political debts, reward loyal followers, and earn future favors. Patronage became a major impediment to the professionalism of marshals.

In 1920 the Republican party regained the White House under the leadership of the bourbon-swilling, girl-chasing Warren G. Harding. After eight years out of power, the Republicans, in time-honored American tradition, were anxious to claim their patronage. Barely had Harding completed his oath of office on March 4, 1921, before newly appointed Republican administrators moved to purge the government of its Democrat holdovers. Of the eighty-eight federal judicial districts existing in 1921, thirty-four had new marshals by December 1921. Many of those marshals in turn cleansed their districts of Democrats by refusing to recommission their office deputies. As the Democrats had before them, the new marshals rewarded members of their own party with commissions as office deputies.

When William C. Hecht became U.S. marshal in the southern district of New York, he soon "reorganized" his staff of forty-eight deputies. The Republican party in New York, however, was split. Congressman Hamilton Fish, Jr., headed one faction against a coalition of local county party chairmen. Hecht sided with the county chairmen against Fish, although Fish's Twenty-sixth Congressional District—

Putnam County—was the only solidly Republican county in southern New York.

Anxious to appease his patrons, Hecht invited recommendations from the Republican county chairmen of Manhattan, the Bronx, and Westchester County. Squeezed out of the action, Fish applied to Attorney General Daugherty for three of the deputy positions. Daugherty promised him two, but Hecht offered only one. Then, in the rush to fill the commissions, Hecht's pledge to Fish was overlooked.[14]

The oversight infuriated Fish. In a letter to Assistant Attorney General Holland on December 13, 1922, Fish insisted on two deputies for the district, "especially in view of the fact that we have none of the judges, clerks, etc., in proportion to our vote." The county chairmen whom Hecht had consulted had nothing to do "with the dispensation of patronage in my district," Fish complained. He reminded Rush that the attorney general himself had promised him two positions. "This controversy is a small matter to you, but it has become one of real importance to me," Fish wrote. "As I have already half promised the positions, the continued attempt upon the part of Marshal Hecht to ignore the instructions of the Attorney General is preposterous."[15]

The department was eager to favor Fish, but Holland could not compel Marshal Hecht to hire anyone, because deputies were covered by the marshal's bond. "To take away from him the privilege of naming his own deputies and, at the same time, hold him responsible for the proper performance of his functions as a court official, would be manifestly improper," Holland replied to the congressman. The department had never tried to dictate to the marshals whom to hire. All the attorney general could do was veto the marshal's selections. He could not impose choices upon the marshal.[16]

"I would like to have justice and not sympathy," Congressman Fish responded. He pointed out to Holland that Hecht had admitted that he did not make his own selections for deputies but had consulted with the Republican county chairmen. The department, Fish suggested, should veto all subsequent applicants until the promise to him was fulfilled. "I am not trying to dictate anything to Marshal Hecht," Fish advised, "but as a matter of justice I hope word can be conveyed to him that out of the forty-eight appointments that have been made my district has none, and that no new deputies will be appointed until my district has received two."[17]

Unsatisfied with Holland's response, Fish went over his head to

Warren F. Martin, the special assistant to the attorney general. Fish was important enough to the administration that Martin took Holland to lunch to work out a deal. Holland remained adamant that the department could not dictate the hiring of deputies to the marshals, but Martin called his bluff. Returning from lunch, he sent Holland a note asking for a memorandum to the attorney general explaining why Fish could not have two New York deputies, now that there were four or five vacancies in Hecht's district.[18]

Trapped, Holland admitted that he intended to allow three new deputies for Marshal Hecht, but he had been waiting to settle the controversy with Fish before making the assignments. "It may be that Marshal Hecht is a little stubborn in his attitude, but nevertheless I have exhausted all my resources in the matter," he wrote to Attorney General Daugherty. Eleven days later, probably under Daugherty's instructions, Holland explained to Fish that Marshal Hecht was soon to get three new deputies. The department, Holland wrote, "put the matter before the Marshal and has indicated to him that it would look with favor" upon a nomination of Fish's choice. Holland urged the congressman to take the matter up with the marshal.[19]

Fish immediately applied to Marshal Hecht, but he was barely appeased. "Inasmuch as there are only to be three I feel that although I am entitled to two that it is the better part of wisdom to accept one at this time, and I trust that I can persuade you to increase the number later on," he wrote Holland. "However, I earnestly request that your Department withhold authorizing these appointments until I have heard from Marshal Hecht regarding the matter." Hecht agreed to the deal. One new appointment went to Fish, two to New York County. Later in the year, southern New York was allowed six more permanent deputies and four temporary appointments of six months. Of those, Fish got one permanent appointment, New York County got three permanent and two temporary, and the Bronx and Westchester County each got one permanent and one temporary.[20]

Political squabbles like those further diminished the marshals in the eyes of the department's growing pool of professionals. When it came time to assign budgets, apply to Congress for supplemental appropriations, modernize offices, purchase new equipment, establish training programs, or divvy up the department's myriad other resources, the marshals gradually were left out. They were politicians, after all, at a time when that title was said by professionals with a sneer of distaste.

PROHIBITION

The Volstead Act was the last gasp of the progressive reforms. Passed over President Wilson's veto on October 27, 1919, the Volstead Act animated the Eighteenth Amendment's prohibition on the sale of intoxicating beverages, defined as containing more than 0.5 percent alcohol. The law established its own enforcement experts under the commissioner of Prohibition. The new agency was placed under the commissioner of Internal Revenue in the Department of the Treasury.

The Justice and Treasury departments shared the enforcement responsibilities. Congressional appropriations, however, assigned more money to the Treasury's Bureau of Internal Revenue. According to the Justice Department, obtaining the lion's share of the resources imposed on Internal Revenue the principal responsibility for enforcement. Assistant Attorney General Guy D. Goff explained the breakdown to Marshal Henry F. Cooper of Oklahoma on August 26, 1921:

> While the duty generally of enforcing all Federal laws is placed upon the Department of Justice, whenever Congress has signified to impose the administrative enforcement of a particular law upon some other branch of the Government, and has furnished such branch sufficient appropriation, this Department feels that the duty of enforcing such act should rest primarily on that Department. The duty of enforcing the National Prohibition Act has been placed jointly upon the Commissioner of Internal Revenue and the Attorney General, and a much larger appropriation for its enforcement granted to the Treasury Department than to the Department of Justice. The policy of this Department has therefore been to assist and cooperate with the Prohibition unit in every possible way in the enforcement of the National Prohibition Act, but to expect the greater part of the work to be handled by their force. While the Department desires to give all assistance possible to the Prohibition enforcement officers in their work against violators of the Prohibition laws, it feels that you should not neglect the duties of your office to do so.

Consequently, from 1920, when Prohibition went into effect, until its repeal in 1933, the Department of Justice took a backseat to the Treasury in enforcing what proved to be an unenforceable law.[21]

In practice, the division of responsibility meant that Prohibition agents conducted the investigations, and marshals made the arrests. "Under the National Prohibition Act and the Internal Revenue Statutes, it is the duty of the Commissioner of Internal Revenue and the Agents and Inspectors working under his direction, to investigate alleged violations of the liquor laws," Assistant Attorney General Holland stated in November 1923. "It is, however, the duty of the United States Marshal to serve all process issued under the authority of the United States and directed to him." The marshals did not need to go with Prohibition agents when conducting investigations. They needed only to serve whatever process issued from those investigations.[22]

The growth in the number of investigatory agencies during the age of experts, combined with the vast increase in criminal investigations growing out of the Volstead Act, imposed a tremendous workload on the marshals. "Since we are being constantly driven by the United States Commissioner; the District Attorney's Office; the Corps of Special Intelligence Officers; and the Federal Prohibition Forces to *arrest, arrest,* and keep on *arresting,* we are just about to run over ourselves making arrests," Marshal John W. Van Heuvel of southern Alabama complained to the attorney general in 1923.[23]

Even when prohibition agents were assisted on their raids by the local police rather than deputy marshals, the workload on the marshals was hardly relieved. The police could detain Prohibition violators on state charges, but the marshals still had to pick the prisoners up and return them to the district court to stand trial for federal violations. "Prohibition and other government officers making raids in various parts of the District, place their prisoners in the nearest available jail," Marshal Frederick L. Esola of northern California observed in December 1924. "This practice requires me to send deputies to distant points to bring the prisoners before the Courts and the Commissioners."[24]

In addition to making federal arrests, the marshals also seized all the illicit breweries and distilleries and took into custody the cars, trucks, and other equipment used by bootleggers. Once a facility was seized, the marshals hired guards to protect it, then began the sometimes lengthy process of inventorying the property. Based on the inventory, the U.S. attorney filed a libel with the court condemning the property to federal possession and disposal. After public notice of the condemnation and sufficient proof presented to the court, the marshals disposed of the property under court order, destroying the distillery and brewing equipment and selling the other property.[25]

In some districts the administrative burden on the marshals was especially onerous. During June 1925 the marshal's office in Chicago daily averaged forty-nine writs served and eighteen arrests made. On July 1, 1926, the marshals had in custody forty-nine seized distilleries and breweries. More than two hundred guards had been hired to protect the properties.

The major racketeering trials of the period further drained district manpower. In 1931 the Internal Revenue Service completed its income tax evasion case against the most famous of the mobsters, Al Capone. Capone had fled to Florida to avoid arrest warrants issuing out of the northern district of Illinois, but a pair of deputies, one of whom was Norma Haugan, caught up with him and effected the arrest. Fearing that the trial would overwhelm the Chicago marshal's office, the Department of Justice made an exception to its normal rules by allowing the deputation of agents of the intelligence unit of the Treasury Department who had worked up the case against Capone. The commissions would allow them to assist the marshals in subpoenaing the great number of witnesses involved in the case.[26]

Normally, the Department of Justice denied requests to commission Prohibition agents as deputy marshals. The principal concern was money. "There are many objections to such appointments, one of which is the fact that those agents would probably incur expenses as deputy marshals which we would be obliged to pay," General Agent John W. Gardner explained on July 29, 1927. The commissioner of Prohibition, R. A. Haynes, thought the idea of commissioning his agents so attractive that he even contemplated some way to arrange for the Treasury Department to pick up their expenses. Justice regulations, however, were insurmountable.[27]

Nor was the Department of Justice particularly willing to commission the guards hired to protect the properties seized under Prohibition laws. Departmental attorney John G. Harlan thought deputizing the guards would "lend a much higher moral tone to their presence on the premises and command a much greater respect from gunmen, bootleggers, etc., who now consider the guards as mere watchmen from whom they do not have much to fear." Officials in the department, however, remained unconvinced. They saw no savings accruing from the deputations. According to one departmental opinion, "Should a court in passing judgment order the costs assessed against the defendant, it is highly doubtful whether salaries of Deputy Marshals could be included as costs, while it is possible that guard hire might be covered in such assessment."[28]

The enforcement of Prohibition broke down largely because the law itself was so grandly unenforceable and, for the average citizen, so fun and exciting to break. Overwhelmed by the disregard for the law, the federal government returned to the revenue and customs laws to bring forth its prosecutions. Capone, for example, was charged with income tax violations, not rum-running. The revenue and customs laws "had been developing from the earliest days and carried adequate penalties which the courts had grown accustomed to impose upon offenders," explained Attorney General Homer Cummings. The government relied more and more on state and local authorities to uphold the Prohibition laws within the interior of the country, but the locals were no better than the federals at enforcing the laws.[29]

Congress, also discouraged, began to hold back adequate funding. "Nothing can be imagined which would tend more to create disrespect than to leave criminal statutes in force but relax the effort to enforce them," pleaded Attorney General William D. Mitchell. President Herbert Hoover responded by appointing a commission of experts to study the body of federal laws and their enforcement. Headed by former attorney general Wickersham, the commission made a number of suggestions, the most important of which was the adoption of a code of federal criminal procedure. "Reform of procedure, however, was old straw," Cummings pointed out.[30]

Under Cummings's encouragement, Congress approved a number of laws attacking racketeering and extortion through the mails or interstate commerce, receipt or passage of ransom money, robbery of banks covered under the Federal Reserve System, and transportation of $5,000 or more. Cummings also established regulations on firearms, funds appropriated for rewards, and federal permits for the expanding body of federal agents to carry arms and make arrests.[31]

It was the beginning of a revolution in federal law enforcement. Suddenly federal lawmen were investigating almost all aspects of life in America, from kidnapping to bank fraud, from stolen cars to having a drink after work. Prohibition's repeal in 1933 relieved much of the wasted work on unenforceable laws, thereby allowing the newly empowered federal agents to spend their time more productively. Among all the agencies, the Federal Bureau of Investigation under J. Edgar Hoover enjoyed most the boom. In a series of arrests played to the hilt for their publicity, the FBI captured the public's imagination and established itself as the preeminent expert on law enforcement.

PROFESSIONALISM

For a while, the marshals seemed destined to be the government's professional strikebreakers. The Pullman strike established a pattern that subsequent courts followed readily. The federal government sided with the rights of property when labor tried to assert its rights to influence working conditions. Yet the alliance was an uncomfortable one. The inevitable clashes between labor and management were frequently violent and always bitter, leaving the marshals with an odd expertise that finally became insupportable. The federal government had no interest or purpose in defending one side against the other. It served far better as a neutral arbitrator. Eventually, that was the role it accepted.

In 1914 the Clayton Act offered labor some protections. It established the legal right for unions to exist, protected them from lawsuits under the antitrust laws, and promised jury trials for people accused of contempt for ignoring court injunctions during strikes and disturbances. Samuel Gompers called the Clayton Act "the industrial Magna Carta." Soothing as it was, the new law did not fully resolve the conflicts between management and workers.

The election of Warren G. Harding in 1920 allowed a return to the principle that the government had a vested interest in protecting property from labor. The administration's philosophy was summed up by one assistant attorney general who observed, "Men have a right to strike and men have a right to work. In my judgment we must be careful that the idea does not prevail that striking is a right and that working is a wrong." According to that view, the government could employ thousands of special deputy marshals to protect men who wanted to work, even if working meant crossing strike lines and challenging the wrath of striking workers.[32]

The 1922 strike by railroad shopworkers grieving cuts in pay allowed Attorney General Harry Daugherty to assert the right of strikebreakers to work. Arguing that he intended to ensure the transportation of the mails and to protect interstate transportation, Daugherty allowed marshals across the country to hire upwards of three thousand special deputies to keep the rails open. The department looked back to *In re Neagle* to justify the mass hirings, asserting, in an oddly specious distortion of the Supreme Court opinion, that the marshals were entitled to maintain the peace of the United States. Protecting railroads from striking labor seemed a part of that peace.[33]

Strikebreaking was an expensive expertise to maintain. During the 1922 railroad strike, the department spent as much as $15,000 a day on special deputies. Although the strike was nationwide and therefore somewhat unusual, the department was never comfortable expending that amount of money on marshals. When the Great Depression hit in 1929, it became even less willing to foot the bill. As a result, department officials reversed themselves to argue that the marshals had no business establishing an expertise on strikebreaking.[34]

In 1932 a milk war in Chicago escalated to violence when rival mobs attacked each other's dairy trucks. The dispute crossed state lines, so the case went before the northern district of Illinois, which put the Crescent Dairy Products Company under federal receivership. In late November one dairy truck was destroyed, another attacked. The three owners of the company, after arming themselves, began trailing their trucks. Because that caused a problem with the various local jurisdictions along the route, the federal receiver petitioned the court to order the men deputized, thereby legitimizing their armed escort of the milk.

The Department of Justice balked at the suggestion, but not because of its obvious absurdity. It relied, instead, on the definition of marshals that evolved out of the age of experts. Rather than point out the obvious danger of legally arming half of the interested parties in the dairy war, department officials denied the authority of the marshals. "It should be noted at once," one opinion concluded, "that [marshals] are distinctly process serving officials with no general police powers and that they cannot make an arrest or detain a person without a warrant issued by the proper officers, unless they personally observe a violation of the law." Consequently, the marshals were relieved from duty in the dairy war.[35]

The election of 1932 confirmed the trend. Franklin Delano Roosevelt depended on labor's participation in his newly formed coalition to win the presidency. The new administration was much more sympathetic to labor and certainly not eager to oppose such a large block of supporters. Strikes would continue to cause problems, but henceforth the government would take a neutral stance.

By late 1935 the Chicago milk wars had devolved into a more traditional strike. The federal judge in eastern Illinois ordered the marshals to protect the milk trains rolling into Chicago, but attorneys in the Department of Justice objected. Attorney Alexander Holtzoff had established himself as something of an expert on marshals by drafting legislation authorizing marshals to make arrests without warrant when crimes were committed in their presence. Now he penned a lengthy legal brief denying to the marshals the powers they had typically exercised in labor strikes and thereby stripping them of much of their power to enforce the law and execute court orders.

"The United States Marshal occupies an anomalous position," Holtzoff observed. "He is appointed by the President. He is an officer of the United States District Court, and is under a duty to serve its process and carry out certain of its orders. . . . The Attorney General is given by express statutory provision superintendence and direction over the United States Marshals and control over the appointment of deputies." A marshal, Holtzoff noted, was not a police officer: "He is primarily an officer whose duties are to serve process. His duties as a policeman are limited to the court room and its immediate vicinity." Although marshals were expressly empowered to execute the laws of the United States, Holtzoff maintained that the laws the marshal was to execute were simply the service of process and no more.

A marshal could not question the process delivered to him by the court if it appeared regular on its face. However, because the attorney general was authorized to supervise the marshals and to control their expenditure of public funds, Holtzoff wrote, "it is entirely proper for the Department to make informal representations to a judge, if an order given by him to the Marshal appears to be unauthorized or even improvident." Holtzoff also believed that "in extreme cases it is proper for the Department to decline to authorize the Marshal to employ additional deputies required to execute an order of the court which the Department deems illegal or improvident."

By restricting the powers of the marshals, Holtzoff hoped "to prevent the Federal Government from being unnecessarily, and possibly unjustifiedly, catapulted into labor disputes." He wanted to avoid making the marshal a chief of police and making the U.S. district court a police court trying breaches of injunctions issued against strikers. Rather than use marshals to protect the property, the courts should order the federal receivers to hire special guards, armed with a badge inscribed "Receiver's Guard" to impress the public.[36]

Confined now to the service of process that the Department of Justice accepted as legal or proper, the marshals no longer had any flexibility or broad authority. They were policemen in the courtroom, process servers on the streets. It was a misunderstanding that officials in the Department of Justice would come to regret but would have trouble shaking.

Coincident with the effort to neutralize the marshals during strikes, the Department of Justice also began to allow deputies to act as bailiffs in courtrooms. The result was to tie the marshals even more closely to the federal courts and judges, further diminishing their standing as lawmen. The marshals came to be seen as sleepy old men whose sole duty was to wait on the judges.

Since 1789, bailiffs had been hired by the marshals under separate appropriations from deputies. Traditionally, the bailiffs were not deputy marshals and had none of a deputy's authority to make arrests or serve process. They merely served the court by assisting the judges and maintaining order in the courtroom. They were paid only for the days court was in session.

In 1916 the Department of Justice tried to do away with bailiffs and replace them with deputies. Some marshals applauded the attempt. Marshal Herman O'Connor of western Michigan saw it as a way to increase the number of his deputies. Those who acted as bailiff could help serve process in between sessions of court. "The change," he informed the attorney general, "would simply result in additional help in a time of emergency without increasing the number of employees."[37]

However, using deputies as bailiffs violated the law by using one appropriation (pay of bailiffs) to supplement another (pay of deputies). The problem was not discovered until 1928, when the department tried to restore the previous system and encountered the opposition of judges and marshals. The judges objected because their bailiffs threatened to quit if they were paid only when court was in session and then only $3 a day. The marshals objected because it meant they lost deputies, even if many of those deputies were treated as "personal attaches" of the individual federal judges.[38]

In 1937 the department obtained new legislation from Congress giving marshals the option of replacing bailiffs with deputies. In 1944 Congress went a step further by appropriating funds for judges to hire bailiffs but also expressly permitting them to use the money to hire an additional law clerk instead of a bailiff. Given the choice, especially when the judges could easily arrange for the marshal to provide one of his deputies to act as bailiff, the judges naturally chose the clerk. The marshals dutifully supplied the bailiffs.[39]

The system further tied the marshals to the courts and further distanced them from the specialists within the department. It created an almost indelible impression, particularly on the attorneys who ran the Department of Justice, that marshals acted solely as bailiffs. The FBI acted as policemen. Appropriations and resources were divided accordingly. The marshals accepted their new lot, and the job of deputy began attracting retired policemen and soldiers, men who sought only calm in their waning years.

Despite the decline in the authority and general uses of the marshals, the age of experts brought a few glimmerings of professionalism, most of them fostered by the Department of Justice. By the late 1930s the department had become sufficiently bureaucratized to insist on levels of bureaucracy on all its elements. That insistence translated into the imposition of specific standards and regulations, which pointed the way to professionalism.

In 1937 officials within the department issued a new regulation requiring the marshals to investigate the reputation, character, and general qualifications of all applicants to the position of deputy marshal. Two years later, Attorney General Frank Murphy raised the standards among deputies by requiring deputies to be from twenty-three to fifty years old, to have a high school education or its equivalent, to be physically fit, and preferably to have some law enforcement experience. "United States Marshals and Deputies," Murphy declared, "are law enforcement officers of the United States." Murphy also increased the minimum annual salary to $1,800.[40]

The marshals acquiesced in the new standards, although the changes cut into a marshal's power to hire whomever he wanted as a deputy. The new regulations, combined with the spirit of the age of experts, encouraged the marshals to look to their own professional development. In response to a request from Attorney General Murphy, they convened for the first time, in Washington in 1939, to discuss the standards for deputies.[41]

On January 1, 1942, classified civil service procedures and regulations were extended to deputy marshals, despite widespread and surprisingly vocal opposition from the marshals. In January 1941, Marshal John Logan of Oklahoma organized a Washington conference of his colleagues to lobby their senators and thwart the extension of civil service to the deputies. Several weeks after the meeting, Logan returned to the capital to continue the effort.[42]

The central objection was the requisite written examination. "I heartily agree with you in regard to the training and experience being the best qualifications for a Deputy Marshal," Marshal Benjamin McKinney of Arizona wrote Logan. "Regardless of how high a rating a deputy gets passing an examination, it takes from three to six months actual performance of duties before he can be classed as a first class deputy. . . . Some of my deputies who would be in the lower brackets in a mental or written examination, are very valuable." During the 1941 conference Logan's plan of "having the examination of deputies made upon training and experience entirely" was adopted by the marshals.[43]

In late 1941 the department announced that it reserved to itself the power to appoint all deputies. The civil service regulations went into effect the next month. Deputies now had certain protections they had never had before. The effect of the protections was to shield the deputies from the marshals. Among other things, it meant that deputies hired by one marshal no longer automatically left office when their marshal left.[44]

The U.S. marshals' loss was only temporary. The civil service system of examining applicants, making selections based on nationally described written standards, and then sending the deputies to meet their U.S. marshal for the first time after they had been hired, proved unworkable. In April 1944 the department exempted the marshals from the civil service exams and allowed each marshal to recruit deputies directly. The deputies retained their job protection beyond the term of their marshal, thereby extending their longevity in office. For the first time, it became possible to see the job as a career, as a profession.[45]

The department helped foster that view by publishing the *United States Marshals Bulletin*. The first issue was sent to the districts in November 1946. "It is our purpose to issue an informative bulletin to United States marshals at irregular intervals as the needs of the service may require," S. A. Andretta, the administrative assistant to the attorney general, noted in the first issue. "It will contain general information and will be an attempt to keep you posted on all the latest developments, decisions, interpretations, and other matters of interest."[46]

The early issues of the *Bulletin* focused on administrative matters. The first issue, for example, contained articles on travel regulations, driver responsibility, post office boxes, the marshal's manual, and the purchase of cars. A regular theme was the need for close economy in all district affairs.

The importance of the *Bulletin* lay not in the dullness of its information but in the fact that it was the first regular attempt to communicate nationally with all marshals. It implied a national standardization of procedures. The first issue, for example, promised that a manual for the office was being prepared, as well as a handbook for deputies. The fortress walls around each district were beginning to crumble.

The age of experts was finally encroaching on the last bastion of local federalism. Since 1789 the U.S. marshals had represented the national government by relying on local people, local methods, local traditions. The dependence on the familiar helped make the national government more palatable. But the cost was the retardation of the development of the office of marshal as a profession. By 1950, however, the marshals were beginning to awaken from their slumber. The full awakening would take two decades and several nightmares to accomplish.

11

CIVIL RIGHTS AND CIVIL REFORMS
1953–1968

The Alabama bootblack furiously whipped his buff across the stranger's shoes. The man's suggestion infuriated him. He personally knew Governor George Wallace, had shined Wallace's shoes whenever the governor stayed at Birmingham's Roosevelt Hotel, had polished them just recently in fact. "Them marshals ain't going to get Governor Wallace," he said with finality. "He's on his way to New York. He's going to go up there and meet the press and tell the world what they're doing to him."

Like the bootblack, most Alabamians were outraged at federal judge Frank Johnson's summons to haul George Wallace into court to explain the state's opposition to court-ordered desegregation. To their delight, Wallace had gone into hiding—the marshals had been unable to find him to serve the summons. Without personal service on him, Wallace asserted, he had never been officially notified of the summons. Without personal service, he did not have to obey it.

"Good for George," the stranger said. "I wonder how he's going to get out of Alabama and beat them guys?"

"He's going to fly out," the bootblack announced importantly. He had overheard the governor and his aides discussing the plans a few days before.

"How the hell's he ever going to get on an airplane?"

"He ain't going to use his name," the bootblack said with the pride of an insider's knowledge.

After the stranger left, he made a brief phone call before heading for the airport. One by one, he visited each airline. Airline representatives, alerted by a phone call, nervously waited to hustle him to the back offices. The stranger took his time checking the passenger manifests, seemingly unconcerned by the unease his presence caused. He was not sure what name he would find; he just hoped he would recognize it when he saw it.

At United Airlines, he did. Earl Morgan and a party of twelve were booked on a flight originating in Mobile, with a brief stop in Birmingham before heading on to New York. Morgan, the stranger knew, was the name of Governor Wallace's executive secretary. After another phone call, the stranger caught the next flight to Mobile.

Shortly before the scheduled departure of the United flight from Mobile, airline officials escorted the stranger onto the plane. He took the jump seat just behind the pilot. Right on schedule, the plane lifted off and took the stranger back to Birmingham.

Once the plane landed at Birmingham, the stranger slipped on the copilot's hat and jacket. The steps rolled up, a few passengers dismounted, and several more joined the flight. Once everyone was settled, a National Guard army plane landed, then taxied up close to the United plane. Al Lingo, the director of the Alabama Highway Patrol, boarded the plane. He checked the crew and passenger manifest, then strode through the aisle looking at each passenger. Returning to the front of the plane, Lingo stuck his head in the cockpit door. Reassured by the crew's uniforms, he signaled across to the National Guard plane.

Governor George Wallace jogged easily down the steps and across the Tarmac to the United plane. The stranger watched through the open door. When Wallace reached the bottom of the ramp, the stranger pulled something from each back pocket. He kept both hands inconspicuously behind him. Wallace, followed by his aides, bounded up the steps.

The governor turned to the pilot with his hand out. They shook, and Wallace turned slightly toward the stranger.

The stranger handed a folded piece of paper toward Wallace's outstretched hand. He lifted his left hand. The badge cupped inside flashed against the cabin light.

"Governor," the stranger said, "my name is Deputy Marshal Don

Forsht. This is your subpoena. Please don't leave town, because you are due in Judge Johnson's court tomorrow morning."[1]

Forsht's story—true or not—perfectly illustrates the quixotic redemption of the U.S. marshals. By the end of the 1940s the marshals were mired in their own history of independence and generality. They clearly could not compete with such specialized bureaucracies as the FBI, the Bureau of Prisons, the Border Patrol, the Secret Service, the Bureau of Alcohol, Tobacco, and Firearms, or the dozens of other agencies that populated the executive branch. Officials viewed the marshals as archaic holdovers from the frontier. No one knew quite what to do with them in a modern world.

Their salvation began during the 1950s. At mid-decade, officials in the Justice Department finally devised an organizational scheme to provide the marshals some centralization and consistent direction. More important, in 1954 the Supreme Court destroyed the legal basis of racial segregation. The court ordered the states to move "with all deliberate speed" to desegregate their schools, but the process was slow and bitter. By 1960 the department needed an organization that had the authority and the flexibility to execute court-ordered desegregation. The FBI had neither, even if Director J. Edgar Hoover had been sympathetic to the task. Nor did any of the other specialized bureaus. But the marshals did.

McSHANE'S BOYS

During the early 1950s the marshals continued to flounder. Leaderless and decentralized, they had no representatives at the Department of Justice, no protection at budget time. And they were considered politicians, a title that was distasteful among departmental lawyers and specialists. The FBI, fresh from its triumphs against gangsters in the 1930s and German spies during World War II, continued to grow in size, stature, and power. By the 1950s Hoover was strong enough to take on communism wherever he could find or conjure it.

Politics consumed the marshals. In June 1953, Marshal William A. Carroll supervised the execution of Julius and Ethel Rosenberg, who had been convicted in federal court of conspiring to sell wartime atomic secrets to Russia. Proclaiming their innocence to the end, the couple became—and remain—a cause célèbre. Thousands protested their conviction. By the time of their execution, their case had become politically loaded.

Marshal Carroll was a Truman appointee, a thirty-year veteran of Tammany politics. Although Dwight D. Eisenhower's 1952 election to the presidency gave the Republicans control over federal patronage for the first time in twenty years, no one in the new administration tried to dump Carroll. The Republicans saw no point in letting one of their own marshals carry the onus of the Rosenberg executions. Rather than replace Carroll immediately, the Republicans allowed him to remain at his post more than two years, just long enough to rent the electric chair at Sing Sing and manage the couple's court-ordered death on June 19, 1953. The next day an official from the department called Carroll to ask for his resignation. Carroll refused.

"I've done a dirty job for you," Carroll told the Republicans through the *New York Times,* "and now you want my resignation. Well, you're not getting it."[2]

Carroll was a politician. He knew how the game was played. His objection was not to his dismissal but to its timing. He had been "done out" of a month's accumulated vacation time to arrange the execution, he claimed. All he wanted was the time due him. Suddenly, however, the Republicans could not wait to get their own nominee in office. On July 14, Carroll received a special delivery letter from President Eisenhower dismissing him from his post. The marshal promptly surrendered his office and went fishing.[3]

In 1956 department officials recommended the establishment of the Executive Office for U.S. Marshals. A similar office had been created to manage the U.S. attorneys three years before. As Deputy Attorney General William P. Rogers pointed out to Attorney General Herbert Brownell, Jr., in August 1956, the deputy attorney general was traditionally responsible for the line supervision of the marshals. However, Rogers and his predecessors had generally confined themselves to disciplining marshals who got in trouble. Few of the officials had the time – and fewer the inclination – to provide effective day-to-day supervision.[4]

Brownell, a student of governmental efficiency, approved the proposed Executive Office for U.S. Marshals. On November 30, 1956, Rogers announced its creation effective December 17. Placed under the supervision of the deputy attorney general, the new office was charged with providing "general executive assistance, direction, and supervision" of the marshals, maintaining a check on their performance, serving as a liaison between the marshals and the department, and facilitating the exchange of information and ideas among the marshals.[5]

Clive W. Palmer, the executive assistant to the deputy attorney general, was put in charge. The office was staffed with six full-time professionals: Palmer, three assistants, an editor of publications, and a training officer. Nine field examiners reported their audits to the office, and three secretaries and two typists supported the work.

Palmer described his office as one that "provides executive assistance, direction, and supervision to the United States Marshals; maintains a check on the conduct of business; serves as liaison, coordinator, and expediter between the Marshals' offices and all offices in the Department, and develops programs to improve and promote more efficient and economical operations." The description was more ambitious than accurate. The office was too small to have much effect. Palmer and the staff concentrated on training, compiling periodic reports, supervising the marshals' expenditure of money, and keeping the field informed through bulletins, an ever-growing Marshals Manual, and circulars.[6]

Efforts to centralize the marshals or focus their work were clearly beyond the capabilities of the Executive Office, even if such an effort would have occurred to Palmer. Indeed, Palmer did not consider himself a marshal. Rather than assume that title, he remained as executive assistant to the deputy attorney general. The new office ensured that the routines were followed, the forms were correctly filled out, and the proper procedures implemented. Other than add more forms and a layer of bureaucracy, the Executive Office for U.S. Marshals had little immediate effect.[7]

The marshals continued to work largely in isolation. Each district transported its own prisoners to federal penitentiaries, with little coordination or sharing of resources with other districts. A marshal's authority stretched only to the boundaries of his own district, not a foot beyond. Each marshal hired his own deputies, although firing a previous marshal's choice was difficult.

But the Executive Office was a beginning. It provided an infrastructure upon which a centralized organization could be fleshed out. It also gave the marshals a voice, albeit barely a whisper, within the department.

At about the same time, a new breed of deputy marshal was evolving within the districts. In 1954 President Eisenhower appointed Carlton G. Beall, the sheriff of Prince Georges County, Maryland, as

U.S. marshal for the District of Columbia. Beall looked back to his old sheriff's department for deputies. He hired a small group of young men – Al Butler, Ellis Duley, Don Forsht, Bob Haislip, Frank Vandegrift, and a few others – who brought to the job a youthful strength and brashness. When interviewing Al Butler, Beall expressed concern over Butler's reputation for being fast with his fists. "Well, I'll tell you, Marshal," Butler replied with characteristic cockiness, "I never hit a man in my life that didn't ripple his muscles at me first." These Young Turks reinvested the job with a sense of adventure. They reenergized the marshals.[8]

Beall's new breed of deputy marshal consisted of men, all in their early to mid-thirties, who looked for challenge and accepted its danger because they wanted most the excitement. Butler and Forsht in particular, the others to a lesser extent, were not organization men, though they helped reorganize the marshals. Nor did they play by the rules, a trait that got some of them in trouble later in their careers after their work had culminated in a strong, centralized, rule-infested Marshals Service. Butler, Forsht, and the others were mavericks at a tumultuous time. Together they changed the history of the marshals and, in no small part, the history of the United States.

To maintain the interest of the new deputies, Marshal Beall organized a warrant squad for the D.C. office under Ellis Duley. Rather than waste their energy waiting on judges or serving simple process, the squad members made arrests, pursued fugitives, and acted like real cops. Because the marshals for the District of Columbia also acted as the sheriff for the district, there were plenty of criminal cases to keep the young men happy.

Clive Palmer solicited the Bureau of Prisons to organize a training class for a select number of deputies. Butler, Forsht, and Duley attended the class and attracted the attention of the instructors, who recommended that the three take charge of training all deputies nationwide. For the next several years Butler, Forsht, and Duley held a series of two-week training seminars. John Cameron, a young lawyer who had joined the Executive Office, supervised the program for Palmer. By the end of the decade, the four men had met – and trained – just about every deputy marshal in the United States.

The new breed of deputy found its natural leader in James J. P. McShane. Known as Shifty by his intimates, and later as Uncle Jim by his deputies, McShane was a New York City homicide detective; a heavy-drinking, tough Irish cop; a former Golden Gloves boxer; and for two weeks every year, the replacement chauffeur for the Shakel family. During one of those two-week stints, McShane met a skinny rich kid who was married to one of the Shakel daughters. His name was Robert Kennedy. The men took an immediate liking to each other. McShane personified the Hemingwayesque image of a policeman, the kind of man that Bobby Kennedy admired. He persuaded McShane to quit the police department and join the staff of the Senate racketeering committee. When Jack Kennedy ran for president, Bobby nominated McShane for chief of security. During the frantic campaign of 1960, McShane was the Democratic nominee's personal bodyguard.[9]

On May 10, 1961, the Kennedy brothers—one president, the other attorney general—rewarded McShane with an appointment as U.S. marshal for the District of Columbia. There he met Butler, Forsht, Duley, Vandegrift, and Haislip. A year later, on May 8, 1962, the Kennedys appointed McShane to succeed Clive W. Palmer, who was retiring as head of the Executive Office for U.S. Marshals. Unlike Palmer, McShane took the new title of chief U.S. marshal. The Kennedy brothers depended on him to take the brunt of southern resistance to court-ordered desegregation. McShane's immediate task was to spearhead the administration's commitment to enforce the court orders.[10]

For the deputies, McShane was a man to admire, a leader they willingly followed. He invested the office of chief marshal with two assets—excitement and access—that kept them on the job. McShane skillfully guided their natural confidence against the odds. He allowed them considerable leeway for their egos and their independence. Desegregating the South made them feel like they were changing the world single-handedly. It was a heady feeling.

The chief marshal also had access to the attorney general and the president. He could enter Bobby Kennedy's office anytime, without an appointment, without even knocking. McShane put the deputies near the seat of power, awed them by the shadow of the throne. Many of McShane's boys remember nights they gathered in hotel rooms in the South, drinking and listening to McShane tell his White House, Kennedy-brother stories. If this were Camelot, they were among the knights around the table. That, too, was heady stuff.

In return for the excitement and the access, the boys gave McShane their utter loyalty. Ultimately, he let them down.

But that came later, after everything had changed and the Kennedy brothers were gone. In the beginning McShane channeled the energy of his deputies into an amazingly effective force that swept across the South. McShane accomplished the seemingly impossible. He kept control of his unruly deputies and succeeded in the job at hand – the desegregation of the South.

Frank Vandegrift remembers a story, probably apocryphal – so many of the stories are – that illustrates the approach of McShane and his boys. During one of their stints in Alabama, when they were in Birmingham, Tuscaloosa, or perhaps Montgomery, McShane and some of the boys went one evening to a local bar. After downing a round, McShane turned with his back to the bar and looked out at the rednecks about him. In his loud Brooklyn voice, he announced, "Fellows, we're the guys that have been bringing all those niggers down here."[11]

"WITH ALL DELIBERATE SPEED"

"At times history and fate meet at a single place to shape a turning point in man's unending search for freedom." President Lyndon Johnson looked briefly from his text to the members of Congress gathered before him. "So it was at Lexington and Concord," Johnson continued, his Texas twang jarring the eloquence. Words and accent combined to damn the past and to challenge the future. "So it was at Appomattox. So it was last week in Selma, Alabama."[12]

As Johnson spoke that Monday night, March 15, 1965, the Reverend Martin Luther King, Jr., and four thousand blacks waited in Selma, Alabama. They hoped to march the fifty-four miles to Montgomery to protest the state's refusal to register blacks to vote. Twice before, they had tried to cross the Edmund Pettus Bridge on the road to Montgomery. On the first occasion, Alabama state troopers rioted against them, beating them back across the bridge, whipping them with batons, and burning them with tear gas. One marcher later died from the police beating. On the second attempt, King turned the marchers back in the face of yet more violence threatened by the Alabama state troopers.

"Their cause," the president concluded, "must be our cause, too. Because it's not just Negroes, but it's really all of us who must overcome the crippling legacy of bigotry and injustice. And we shall overcome."[13]

Only a southern president could adopt the battle cry "We shall overcome" to dramatize federal support of the civil rights movement. Or perhaps the drama inhered in the times, in that decade or so between 1954 and 1965 when America purged itself of legally sanctioned color distinctions. It was a violent cleansing. Not since the Civil War had the federal government been so at odds with the states. Simply to ensure that the marchers would be safe, Johnson sent a hundred deputy marshals, almost four thousand soldiers, and a hundred FBI agents to Selma. The army protected the route, the FBI investigated the risks, and the deputies joined King and his cohorts on the walk to Montgomery.

By 1965 the events in Selma seemed strikingly typical of the tumultuous decade. Johnson used the Selma crisis to call on Congress to approve a liberally designed voting rights bill. During the civil rights movement, the president and Congress cranked out new laws protecting civil rights, voting rights, school rights, and citizen rights. By March 1965 three major civil rights acts had been promulgated, Johnson had declared war on poverty, and the Supreme Court had destroyed the constitutional foundation for "separate but equal" schools, public places, and voting booths. The Department of Justice's civil rights division had filed more than fifty lawsuits in federal court to protect the rights of blacks. Deputy marshals descended on the South. From Little Rock, Arkansas, to New Orleans, Louisiana, from Tuscaloosa, Alabama, to Oxford, Mississippi, the deputies enforced court-ordered desegregation.

They met resistance at every turn. Southerners saw themselves protecting their traditional way of life, upholding standards established by generations of their forefathers. They were not just subduing unruly blacks but defending ideological concepts of states' rights.

Besides, fundamentally, white southerners hated blacks. Even the most genteel southerner shuddered at the thought of eating in the same restaurant, riding on the same bus, or sending his children to the same school with people who were only one step out of bondage. They accepted blacks into their homes, but only to clean. Blacks were the servant class, the untouchables. To elevate them to equality seemed a cruel, misguided joke.

So southerners fought back. They resisted, just as, a century before, their great-grandfathers had donned the gray to protect their way of life. Once again the South took on the nation and took great pride in the challenge. Southerners leapt to the defense of an ugly system with ugly words and ugly actions.

Consequently, McShane, Cameron, and the deputies went from one southern hot spot to another, serving process, escorting blacks, and protecting Freedom Riders who crisscrossed the South, challenging segregation. Rather than use marshals from the districts involved, McShane and Cameron brought in deputies from other districts to enforce the court orders. They realized that the local marshals had to live in their districts. Compelling them to enforce unpopular court orders put them at risk in their own homes. There was also the possibility that the local marshals would refuse to support the courts.

The confrontations began just across the western border of the South, in Topeka, Kansas. In 1954 the Supreme Court's *Brown v. Board of Education of Topeka* struck down the principle underpinning legally sanctioned segregation, finding "separate but equal" unconstitutional. But the *Brown* decision simply called on the states to move "with all deliberate speed" to desegregate. Most ignored the order. The delays forced the National Association for the Advancement of Colored People (NAACP), which spearheaded the legal side of the civil rights movement, to file individual lawsuits challenging specific segregationist systems. It was a slow, expensive, and painful process.

Three years after *Brown,* in the fall of 1957, the NAACP won a court order for nine black students to attend Central High, the white high school in Little Rock, Arkansas. Governor Orval Faubus took a political stand against the desegregation of Central High. In defiance of the federal court, he ringed the schoolyard with the Arkansas National Guard, who managed to keep the students out of school. After a riot by white citizens on September 23, Eisenhower federalized the guard and dispatched one thousand paratroopers from the 101st Airborne to Central High. On September 25 the nine new students spent their first day at the formerly all-white high school. "We are now an occupied territory," Governor Faubus announced on television. For the entire school year paratroopers patrolled the halls of Central High.[14]

The marshals were not involved at Little Rock. Faubus had immediately escalated the crisis by calling out the National Guard, which forced Eisenhower to nationalize it and send in the army. The next year, 1958, Marshal Richard Beal Kidd painstakingly prepared to take over from the 101st Airborne. With help from the Executive Office for U.S. Marshals, Kidd hired more than a hundred special deputies, drew up a detailed plan of action, and equipped his men to protect the black students. Then Governor Faubus closed Central High for the school year.

Nonetheless, the Little Rock crisis had a profound effect on the marshals. The presence of heavily armed paratroopers monitoring the halls of a local high school deeply embarrassed the Eisenhower administration. Images of M1s stacked in the schoolyard conjured up similar scenes of the Soviet Union's brutal crushing of the Hungarian revolt. As long as the paratroopers remained at Central High, the difference between the United States and the Soviet Union could be portrayed by America's enemies as one of degree, not of kind. The American message of freedom and democracy was belied by southern officials and politicians preaching the purity of segregation while U.S. Army troops again occupied the South.

After Little Rock, Eisenhower and his successors turned first to the marshals to enforce the orders of the federal courts. The marshals, as they had from the beginning, personified the principle of civilian control. Using them first represented a return to the age-old tradition of relying originally on civilian officials to enforce the law and resorting to the military only after the civilians failed or were overwhelmed.

Although the Little Rock incident was an aberration from the federal side, it established the pattern of resistance for the South. Southern officials—senators, governors, mayors, policemen—manned the barriers. Whites lined the streets, yelled obscenities, threw bricks. They rioted against federal officials and blacks who dared challenge their system of segregation. During the early 1960s, white and black Freedom Riders swept through the South by the busload, purposefully flaunting segregationist traditions and regulations. Hand in hand, black on white, they invaded lunch counters and waiting rooms, eating and sitting together in open defiance of "whites only" and "colored only" policies. They were arrested—and almost as frequently beaten—by the southern police. Several of the Freedom Riders, black and white, were killed.

When the marshals went South, they went up against the entire southern establishment. Their opponents were not outlaws, but governors, mayors, and police chiefs. On June 11, 1963, Governor George Wallace blocked the front entrance to the University of Alabama in Tuscaloosa. While Deputy Attorney General Nicholas Katzenbach and a group of deputy marshals waited patiently, Wallace lectured against the stultifying power of the federal government. "It is important that the people of this state and nation understand that this action is in violation of rights reserved for the state by the Constitution of the United States and the Constitution of the state of Alabama," Wallace proclaimed. As soon as he finished his speech, the marshals escorted James Hood and Vivian Malone into school. The university was integrated.[15]

Deputies escorted black first-graders to school in New Orleans in 1960. Crowds of whites taunted the children, slurring them with foul language, to the disgust of the deputies. Later, the deputies went to small towns throughout Louisiana to ensure that the orders of the court were implemented. Often they simply provided a federal presence without having to take any action. They spent their days pitching pennies outside schools, waiting in case something happened.

Frequently things did happen. In the spring of 1961 a group of deputies protected Martin Luther King, Jr., when he spoke at a church in Montgomery. A crowd of whites gathered in the park across from the church and began pelting the deputies with rocks. A pickup truck loaded with rubble pulled up, giving the crowd plenty of ammunition. After enduring the rock storm for as long as they could take it, the deputies charged across the street, their riot batons flashing in the streetlights. With some violence, they chased the whites away from the church.

One of the whites pulled a knife on Deputy Jesse W. Grider, slashing at his throat. Infuriated, Grider chased the man down the street, whacking him hard with a nightstick. Afterward, Grider, who hailed from Glasgow, Kentucky, stood catching his breath. Joe Bennett, a deputy from Aberdeen, Mississippi, came up to him. "Goddamn, fella," Bennett said. "You shouldn't hit a white man over one of them niggers."

"I'm not hitting that son of a bitch over niggers," Grider shot back. "I'm hitting him over me."[16]

Deputies like Bennett were the exception. They were rarely used again once they were found out. Grider, himself a southerner, developed a profound sympathy for integration after he watched Bull Connor, the chief of police in Birmingham, let loose police dogs against the civil rights workers. "After some of the stuff you saw there, I really became an integrationist, I guess you'd call it," Grider later remembered. "Because that, that was awful."[17]

A NIGHT IN MISSISSIPPI

In the evenings, the deputies gathered in front of the television in the barracks dayroom at Millington Naval Air Station just outside Memphis to watch themselves on the nightly news. James Meredith, the only black among them, always took the easy chair directly in front of the set. John Doar, the only practicing attorney among them, took its mate. McShane and the deputies buddied up on the sofa or stood behind the chairs.

Meredith wanted to be the first black admitted to the University of Mississippi at Oxford—Ole Miss. Doar was the deputy director of the Department of Justice's civil rights division. During that September in 1962 Doar, Meredith and the deputies watched the news reports on the state's efforts to thwart Meredith's enrollment at Ole Miss. One night they saw themselves meeting Governor Ross Barnett outside his office in Jackson. "Which one of you is Meredith?" the deputies would later laughingly remember Barnett's saying, just before he denied any black admission to the school.

On Wednesday evening, September 26, the deputies watched as the cameras picked up their caravan as it turned onto the main entrance to the university earlier that day. The cars slowed to a stop in front of Lieutenant Governor Paul Johnson, who stood with arms folded to block their entry. Flanking Johnson were troopers from the Mississippi Highway Patrol lined shoulder to shoulder in a barricade. McShane, Meredith, and Doar approached.

"We want to take him in," Doar told Johnson.

"I am going to have to refuse on the same grounds the Governor did. I refuse because of imminent breach of the peace," Johnson answered.

Suddenly McShane shoved his shoulder against Johnson, forcing him back a step to regain his balance. The state troopers immediately closed the gap, squeezing McShane out. He moved along the troopers, randomly trying to shoulder his way through the line. Each time, the state troopers held firm.

"You are senseless," Johnson said, "in trying to show off in front of television cameras for the rest of the nation to see."

"I'm not showing off," McShane answered, "but doing my duty."

After the third or fourth shove, McShane knew he would have to slug his way onto the university. He and Attorney General Bobby Kennedy had agreed that a symbolic use of federal force—McShane's shoulder—might allow the Mississippi officials to retire gracefully from their opposition. The firm line of troopers proved the theory wrong.

McShane, Meredith, Doar, and their escort of deputies returned to the cars and drove back to Millington.[18]

The newscaster summed up the situation. For the second time, Meredith had been refused entry to the University of Mississippi by the highest state officials. Governor Barnett and Lieutenant Governor Johnson stood in open defiance of an order from the Fifth Circuit Court of Appeals to register Meredith. The federal government had been stymied again.

Deputy Dick Holsom stood leaning his elbows on the back of Meredith's chair. As the news ended, Holsom mimed a sad shake of his head. He looked down at the dejected student. "Jimmy," he said mournfully, "did it ever occur to you that they don't want your black ass in there?"[19]

Whether Ole Miss wanted Meredith or not, the Kennedy administration had committed itself to getting him into school. The NAACP represented Meredith in court; the Justice Department filed as amicus curiae on his behalf. Although the local district court sided with the university, the Fifth Circuit Court of Appeals in New Orleans had overturned the lower decision and ordered Meredith admitted. During the last week of September, Bobby Kennedy talked daily, sometimes several times a day, with Governor Barnett. Kennedy was searching for some formula that would save the governor face, yet get Meredith into school. Barnett, however, inevitably broke his deals with the Kennedy brothers.

The Mississippi stalemate culminated southern frustrations and federal determination. No other incident better illustrated the challenge that court-ordered desegregation created, or better showed the marshals' role in ending legal segregation. During a single night southern anger coalesced into a bubbling, violent riot against federal interference. The violence and the anger were aimed directly at U.S. marshals.

Frustrated by Barnett's refusal to keep his word, Bobby Kennedy decided to act. After learning that Barnett had made an impassioned plea for Mississippi, her people, and her customs at an Ole Miss football game the previous evening, Kennedy ordered the deputies to Oxford early Sunday afternoon, September 30. He wanted the deputies to seize the Lyceum, a beautiful, white-columned antebellum building that housed the university's administrative offices, including its registrar. By jumping in before the state could react, Kennedy hoped to avoid more entryway confrontations with state officials and troopers. Once the deputies controlled the Lyceum, Meredith would be brought in and registered for school.

After Sunday dinner at Millington, McShane told Butler, Forsht, and Duley to load their men onto the army transport planes waiting on the Navy runways. They were to tell the deputies that it was a practice drill to see how well they and their equipment, such as it was, fit on the planes. Although many of the men wore their normal business suits, quite a few appeared for the drill in T-shirts and sport shirts. None were properly attired for a night in Mississippi.[20]

Their equipment was meager. The army had supplied vintage World War II steel helmets. The deputies painted them white, then stenciled "U.S. Marshal" on the front. The army also gave them excess 1.5 tear gas guns and gas masks, all left over from the war. The federal prison industries supplied custom-made canvas vests with special pockets to hold the tubes of tear gas. Each man supplied his own riot baton; many were homemade. Under the vests, each man wore his service revolver.

McShane was also short of men. Although he was the chief marshal, his authority was limited. He could only borrow deputies from the districts. If a local marshal refused the request, McShane had no real recourse against him. Cameron, who handled the details during most of these operations, spent hours contacting the districts and begging men. To bolster the small force of deputies, Attorney General Kennedy assigned men from the Bureau of Prisons and the Border Patrol. Of the 536 men who went to Oxford that night, 123 were full-time deputies, 316 were border patrolmen, and 97 were prison guards. Each was sworn in as a special deputy marshal.

The Border Patrol also supplied a few government cars, radios, and a small airplane to move Meredith. The rest of the cars were rented from Hertz. No extra radios were supplied.

Confused by the order to practice boarding the planes, the men shrugged into their canvas vests, put on their steel helmets, and clambered aboard. Cases of tear gas were also loaded. No food, tents, sleeping bags, or medical supplies were taken, because Cameron had arranged for the men to camp at a national park just outside Oxford. After waiting about thirty minutes, the planes took off. Within the hour, they touched down at the grassy airfield near Oxford. Army trucks, driven by black soldiers, waited to carry them onto the campus.[21]

Meredith stayed in Millington watching television. Deputy Cecil Miller sat beside him. They were scheduled to leave for Oxford after the marshals secured the Lyceum. McShane had assigned Miller, who helped train deputies in jujitsu and self-defense, as Meredith's personal bodyguard. From that Sunday morning on, they would not leave each other's side until Meredith stepped into his first classroom at the University of Mississippi.[22]

The deputies unloaded at the Lyceum. Butler's group took position in front of the white columns of the stately building. Forsht took his group to Butler's right, Duley took the left. Because another building adjoined the Lyceum, the deputies had no need to protect their rear. A single-lane circular drive passed in front of the Lyceum. Across the drive was a large grove populated with beautiful Mississippi oak trees. The grove was several football fields in size and sloped downward to the main entrance of the campus. At the bottom, a bronze statue of a Confederate soldier greeted visitors and students.

Katzenbach and the Justice Department contingent established a command center inside the Lyceum. They immediately called the attorney general, using the pay phone in the main hall. Throughout the night, that phone was their only link to the outside. The two intersecting hallways became their hospital, the basement their jail. The half-ring of deputies outside was their only barricade.

At first, Katzenbach frantically searched for someplace—a nearby gym or auditorium—where he could station the deputies out of sight. He realized that their presence in front of the Lyceum was an open challenge to the people of Oxford and the students at Ole Miss. The Lyceum was the principal, endearing architectural structure on the campus. Its history stretched back to the Civil War, back to when brave southerners resisted federal interference with the southern way of life. But no one was on campus to unlock the gym or point the way to any lecture halls. The deputies remained outside the Lyceum.[23]

Shortly after the deputies arrived, state troopers appeared. They stationed themselves just outside the perimeter of deputies. About five o'clock the students who had been in Jackson for the Ole Miss football game the night before began returning. The deputies in their white helmets and canvas vests, their gas masks hanging in bulky bags on their hips, immediately attracted a crowd.

It began friendly enough. The students jeered the deputies while Butler strode back and forth, smiling broadly to show he had no malice. The crowd began calling him "Smiley"; the jeers slowly became vulgar taunts. A few of the students threw pennies and coins, then rocks.

Butler tried to calm his men, always smiling, his teeth gritted. As the news traveled across the campus, through the town, and across the state, others began descending on Oxford and Ole Miss. Commercial and ham radios spread the word that the Yankees had occupied Oxford. The rednecks headed for Ole Miss.

By dusk the crowd was vicious. Someone broke into the chemistry building and began supplying the crowd with vials of acid. Butler was hit on the arm. The acid burned through his suit into his skin. Cameron was splattered on the neck; other deputies were also burned. Rocks, bricks, and rubble were launched at the deputies and the black army drivers. A state trooper taught a student how to let the air out of the truck tires. The other troopers made no effort to control the crowd. Just before dark, Governor Barnett ordered them off the campus. The deputies were left alone in front of a crowd of about three thousand angry students and outsiders.

Several times between 7 and 8 p.m., Butler and Forsht begged McShane to allow their men to use tear gas to drive the crowd away. McShane hesitated, unwilling to escalate the conflict. By 8 p.m., however, as President Kennedy went on national television to urge peace on Oxford, McShane decided he had run out of time. He gave the order to load the gas guns and fire.

Shortly after dark, Meredith, Miller, and Doar flew to Oxford in a small Cessna. They were met at the airport by Katzenbach and a squad of deputies. They drove immediately to Baxter Hall, Meredith's dormitory for the next year. Meredith, Miller, and a dozen deputies raced into the dorm. From the Lyceum about a mile away, they could hear the noise of the riot. Meredith's suite consisted of two rooms. He took the interior one, the deputies the outer room. Miller posted his dozen men outside the dorm and in the halls. Each deputy carried a baton, a pistol, a gas gun, and a supply of tear gas.

At the Lyceum the deputies used tear gas to hold back the crowd. With their gas guns, they could shoot a stream of gas reaching more than twenty feet. The gas grenades exploded in a more localized puff. Smoke grenades held the gas down, shrouding the immediate area in a hellish, noxious mist. That night even the wind was against the marshals. A steady breeze blew the gas back against them.

The rioters bombarded the marshals with rocks, bricks, and rubble from a nearby construction site. A few of the rioters were armed. Throughout the night, snipers fired on the deputies with rifles, pistols, and at least one shotgun. The Lyceum's stately columns were pockmarked by bullets. Deputy Gene Same from Indiana was stung in the neck with shotgun pellets. One of the pellets nicked his carotid artery. Carried inside to the Lyceum hallway, Same was kept alive by a border patrolman who maintained pressure on the wound, stanching the flow of blood. No medical assistance arrived until well after midnight, nor were the deputies able to get Same through the rioters to a hospital until early the next morning. While Same lay bleeding, word spread among the deputies that he was dead.

Other deputies sat or lay up and down the hallways, exhausted. They had been injured by rocks or rubble or overcome by their own tear gas. They had no where to go, no relief, no medical assistance. Periodically, those that could returned to the front lines to join battle once again.

Outside, some of the deputies crouched behind the cars lining the roadway in front of the Lyceum. Most, though, had no protection. They relied on tear gas to keep the rioters at bay. Deputy Hershel Garner, who served in Forsht's group on the right flank, remembered throwing rocks and rubble back at the rioters. The gas grenades also made effective missiles. Although Butler and Forsht asked permission to return fire on the rioters, the Kennedy brothers absolutely refused. The deputies obeyed the orders. They kept their pistols holstered.[24]

Two men, a French reporter named Paul Guihard and an Oxford resident named Ray Gunter, were killed by unknown assailants in the mob. Guihard was shot from behind at close range; Gunter was struck by a stray bullet that killed him instantly. Throughout the night the news reporters were as much an object of the riot as the deputies were. Most stayed within the protective perimeter of deputies.

At any one time the rioters numbered around three thousand, but that figure was misleading because the rioters were constantly reinforced. Most of the students left fairly early but were replaced by outsiders. The continued influx of people kept the rioters fresh with energy and anger. The deputies had no such relief.

The riot went in waves. The rioters rushed forward to throw their bricks and rocks, then retreated from the tear gas. Someone broke into the campus fire station and stole a fire truck. It careered down the single lane road toward the Lyceum. As it passed, Butler and a few of the other deputies leapt aboard. At the next curve, Butler was thrown rolling into the grove. One deputy managed to stop the driver, and others incapacitated the truck. The driver was handcuffed and taken to the Lyceum basement, where all the people arrested that night were confined. By midnight the basement was full.

Shortly afterward, the deputies were attacked by a bulldozer driven by a drunken sailor. Once again, they managed to board it, arrest the driver, and stop the engine. The bulldozer was placed protectively in front of the Lyceum.

Occasionally, Forsht or Butler led a squad into the grove, their riot batons swinging at anyone in their way. The rioters would retreat farther down the grove, out of reach of the deputies. McShane did not have enough men to clear the area, so the deputies remained in front of the Lyceum. There they were easy targets, forced to take the defensive, unable to move out in a line or wedge formation to break up the riot.

At the Confederate statue at the entrance to the school, retired army general Edwin A. Walker, who had commanded the 101st Airborne during the integration of Little Rock before he decided integration was wrong, directed the rioters. He divided them into two forces, sending them to attack the flanks. Shouting encouragement, Walker timed several of the attacks to give the deputies as little relief as possible.

By 10 p.m. Katzenbach was convinced that the deputies could hold out no longer. They had run dangerously low on tear gas. Border patrolman Charles Chamblee had taken one of the trucks to pick up another load of gas at the airplanes. On the way back, he was stopped by a Mississippi state trooper who tried to arrest him. Chamblee reached out the truck window with his riot baton and slammed the trooper across the forearm. He gunned the truck back to the Lyceum.

Katzenbach asked the president to send in the army. Kennedy immediately gave the order to Secretary of the Army Cyrus Vance, then spent the next several hours cajoling the army to move. A small unit of seventy-five national guardsmen, which Kennedy had nationalized earlier that day, arrived at the Lyceum just before 10:30. On their way to the Lyceum, a dozen of the men were injured. The unit's commander, Captain Murray Falkner, raised his arm protectively when someone threw a brick at his jeep. The brick shattered the windshield before striking Falkner on the wrist, crushing three bones. Rescued by a squad of deputies, the guardsmen proved to be largely ineffectual. They had no gas masks or tear gas. They did, however, take their share of abuse.[25] Meanwhile, it took five hours for regular army troops to drive from Millington to Oxford, a distance of less than a hundred miles.

At Baxter Hall, Miller and his men had contended with their own, smaller version of the Lyceum troubles. Students and others worn out by the Lyceum rioting passed by Baxter Hall. When they noticed the deputies there, they started throwing rocks and causing trouble. Miller and his men were able to keep them away from Meredith's suite with tear gas.

Then the deputies ran out of gas. Miller alerted McShane that he was out, then withdrew the deputies from their posts around Baxter Hall into Meredith's suite. He went into Meredith's room and quickly shoved Meredith into the closet, covered him with a mattress, and ordered him to stay there until Miller gave the okay. Going back to the adjoining room, Miller posted his men near the windows and the door. He explained that he would shoot the first person who tried to get into the suite. After that the men were to fire at will.[26]

It took more than thirty minutes for McShane to resupply Miller with gas. While they waited, a few people made noises outside the dorm, but no one tried to enter. As soon as the deputies disappeared from sight, the crowd seemed to lose interest. Apparently no one realized that before Meredith would become the first black to register at the University of Mississippi, he would become the first black to live in an Ole Miss dorm.[27]

The army finally began arriving after 2 a.m., Monday, October 1. The first contingent consisted of 160 MPs flown in from Millington by helicopter. The troops donned their gas masks, loaded their rifles, fixed their bayonets, and marched in line across the campus to the Lyceum. Several hours later, just before dawn, truckloads of troops arrived. The troops swept the campus clean of rioters, moving them inexorably into the town. There the rioters damaged some stores and buildings, but the fury of the night before had dissipated.[28]

At 7:30 a.m. a heavily guarded caravan pulled up to the Lyceum. Meredith, under the protective escort of deputies, entered the building and went to the registrar's office. There he filled out all the paperwork required of new students, including a late registration form. Within the hour he was a full-time registered student at the University of Mississippi. A team of deputies led by Doar and McShane escorted him to his first class, a course in American colonial history. As they would throughout the coming year that they protected him, the deputies let him enter the classroom alone, then remained in the halls outside, ready to escort him at the end of the lesson.

One hundred sixty marshals lay injured, twenty-eight seriously. Two men were dead. Two hundred rioters, less than a fourth of them university students, were under arrest. The campus was a wreck. Meredith's afternoon class was canceled because of lingering tear gas. Gas canisters, rocks, rubble, and the other detritus of a riot littered the beautiful grove. Burned-out cars, victims of Molotov cocktails, smoldered on the street and neighboring parking lot. A fire truck and a bulldozer remained on guard in front of the Lyceum. And Meredith was a student.[29]

A YEAR IN MISSISSIPPI

The deputies who spent that night in Mississippi were sent home within the first few days of October. For several years they were warned by department officials to avoid the state for fear that they might be arrested. A few weeks after the riot, Mississippi prosecutors indicted McShane and Katzenbach. The charge was inciting the riot. Later, one of the rioters and a state trooper sued both men for personal injuries sustained that night. All the cases were transferred under habeas corpus to federal court and dismissed. Some of the deputies—Hershel Garner was one—felt so bitter that they avoided the state for years afterward. Although he lived in neighboring Arkansas, Garner refused to stop or spend any money in Mississippi.[30]

The riotous opposition by the state convinced McShane and other officials at the Department of Justice that the marshals could not withdraw their protection of the new student after he was registered. During the year that Meredith, a transfer student, attended Ole Miss, teams of deputy marshals protected him twenty-four hours a day. The army, which remained in force on campus, maintained the peace.

McShane put Frank Vandegrift in charge of Meredith's protection. Eventually Bob Haislip and Chester Smith rotated with Vandegrift as the detail supervisors. Vandegrift established a schedule of three-week shifts for the deputies. Wherever Meredith went on campus, deputies accompanied him, stopping only at the classroom door to wait for his lessons to end. Four deputies worked undercover posing as students. They reported to Vandegrift on the campus mood, rumors of demonstrations, and threats of violence. Although three of the undercover deputies were phased out by January, Deputy Leon Davis stayed undercover all year.[31]

Attorney General Kennedy established the policy of no steps backward. The intent was to move steadily toward making Meredith's life as much like that of a typical student as possible. The process was divided into stages. Once a stage was reached, there would be no retreat from it. Once Meredith ate at the cafeteria, then he would always eat there. Once he began walking to class instead of driving, then he would always walk.

Every week, Vandegrift decided how close the four deputies with Meredith would walk around him. During the first couple of months, they crowded, two in front, two behind, quite close to him. As the campus calmed down and began, if not quite to accept Meredith, then at least to tolerate his presence, the deputies gave him more room. At first, the follow car crept just behind Meredith and his escorts, but slowly it, too, pulled back to give Meredith more room, more illusion that he was an ordinary student.[32]

October and November were the worst months. The school administration did little to discipline the campus. The local chapter of the White Citizens' Council supplied students with fireworks to bombard Meredith's dorm or to throw at him and the deputies as they walked to class. That first month of school it was not uncommon for Meredith and the deputies to be doused with water or spat upon. Students heckled and cursed them wherever they went on campus. Sometimes students filled balloons and condoms with paint to splatter on them or tossed cherry bombs at the entourage as it passed.[33]

Throughout the fall, nightly demonstrations disturbed Meredith's studies. Cherry bombs hurtled through the air toward Baxter Hall. Frequently, three cherry bombs were wrapped together in aluminum foil, covered with glue, then rolled in crushed glass from Coca-Cola bottles. Slingshots made from surgical rubber gave the students considerable range to launch the fragmentation bombs from hiding. The deputies could do little but take cover and watch the bombardment.

The demonstrations culminated on October 30, 1962. Throughout the night, Baxter Hall was steadily rained upon with cherry bombs. Students gathered in the street to shriek their hatred of Meredith. The campus verged on another riot. Although Meredith remained safely ensconced in his suite with the deputies on guard, the bombardment was a signal that something had to change.[34]

The university administration and faculty finally awoke to the problem. After that night, faculty members began patrolling the campus, and the administration threatened to expel any student who caused problems. The students ceased their violent demonstrations in favor of more passive resistance. They simply ignored Meredith. Meredith had integrated Ole Miss, but by January 1963 he found himself far more segregated than he had ever been.[35]

By the second semester the students seemed resigned to Meredith's presence. The campus calmed down, but during the spring a number of practical jokes reaffirmed the continued opposition to Meredith. The pranks were relatively harmless, yet all the more irritating. Someone stole his glasses, someone put a dead raccoon—or coon, in southern parlance—on his car, someone let the air out of his tires. Campus graffiti artists made him their favorite topic.

Through it all, Meredith maintained a tenacious dignity, what Cecil Miller described as a quiet courage. Alone, ostracized, hated, with deputy marshals to protect, not befriend him, Meredith reached desperately for the routine of going to school. He attended class, ate at the cafeteria, ran errands, and otherwise stretched for some pretense of normality. But always, bodyguards protected him on a campus occupied by federal troops, amid a student population that repeatedly, vociferously rejected him.

Most weekends, Meredith and his entourage of deputies left the campus to visit his wife and family, but that was but a brief respite. He also received voluminous quantities of mail, which perhaps sustained him. The deputies especially remembered his daily trips to the post office, the one part of his routine he never seemed to vary. Yet even his mail engendered bitter feelings. Many of the letters contained cash, token expressions of support from other blacks who saw in Meredith a champion. A number of the deputies recalled with resentment Meredith sitting on his bed, open envelopes littering the room, tidy piles of money beside him.[36]

On August 18, 1963, under the protection of a reinforced team of deputies, Meredith received his bachelor of arts degree in political science. After the graduation ceremony, Meredith and a friend, Robert L. T. Smith, drove from the campus toward home. The deputies escorted him in a caravan for the last time. Looking at the carloads of deputies in front and behind them, Smith asked incredulously, "J, was it like this all of the time? Man, I don't see how you stood it! I just don't see how you could take it!"[37]

After Meredith, students of both color passed freely, if not entirely easily, through the bullet-scarred columns of the Lyceum. Although southern opposition remained strong, it had peaked in Mississippi the night of October 30, 1962. Wallace was yet to block the entry to the University of Alabama, but when he did, it was only to deliver an angry speech, not to spark a violent riot. Bull Connor was yet to loose police dogs on black demonstrators in Birmingham, and James Chaney, Andrew Goodman, and Michael Schwerner were yet to find their graves in an earthen Mississippi dam, but that violence was the death throes of segregation. The mortal wound was self-inflicted that night in Mississippi when five hundred deputy marshals endured the violent hatred of an aroused South. After Meredith, state-defended segregation was in full retreat.

For the marshals their year in Mississippi represented a historic turning point. Their desegregation of the South illustrated the enormous flexibility of their authority; their competence in keeping Meredith alive verified their professionalism. McShane's influence within the Kennedy administration guaranteed that the marshals would now be taken seriously. During the Ole Miss riot, Attorney General Kennedy joked that the deputies had signed on as sleepy courtroom sitters, but now to their chagrin they were risking their lives enforcing the orders of the court. After their year in Mississippi, such jokes became antiquated. The marshals had gained new stature.[38]

CENTRALIZATION

While the marshals desegregated the South, the Justice Department also assigned them such other difficult tasks as protecting the participants in the trials of James Hoffa. The war on organized crime began again in earnest. The Crime Control Act of 1969 established the witness protection program, which assigned the marshals to protect witnesses against organized crime. The marshals established the program and procedures for establishing new identities, new lives, and new jobs for witnesses. The deputies became social workers with guns.

The trend was toward centralization. Just after McShane became chief marshal in 1962, the Department of Justice issued a statement of organization, order 271-62. The order specified that the Executive Office for U.S. Marshals was to "provide general executive assistance and supervision to the offices of the United States marshals, coordinate and direct the relationship of agencies of the Department with such offices, and approve the staffing requirements of the offices of the United States Marshals." The order reflected some modification of the Executive Office's original charter, particularly the authority to approve staffing requirements for each district.[39]

That same year, deputies Joseph Wasielewski and Earl Brown established a national prisoner transportation network, which saved considerable money, time, and effort. The system was simple in design, yet difficult to execute. It required each district to report those prisoners it had in custody and those it needed from other districts. Instead of sending deputies on one-way trips to deliver or pick up a prisoner, Wasielewski and Brown coordinated the trips to ensure that the deputies escorted prisoners both ways.

The new system met some resistance from the districts and the deputies. A few of the districts opposed it because it threatened their autonomy, although it offered a rational process for moving prisoners. Many of the deputies objected because increased efficiency decreased the amount of money they earned transporting prisoners, for which they received 10 cents a mile when they used their own cars.

McShane encouraged other reforms pointing toward increased professionalism. In 1966 the selection of deputies was taken from the U.S. marshals and put under competitive civil service regulations. Over the next two years the Executive Office gained control over the staffing of each marshal's office. Although the local districts continued to choose the individual deputies, civil service imposed national standards on the selection. The Executive Office also regularly reviewed the budgets and expenditures of each district.[40]

In addition the two-week training sessions given by Cameron, Butler, Forsht, and Duley reached every deputy in the country. Newsletters, bulletins, a quarterly magazine, and an association of deputy marshals gnawed away at the independence of the districts. Innumerable special assignments took the deputies out of their districts and introduced them to their colleagues from other parts of the country, and an informal network grew among the deputies. Based on mutual experiences and shared risks, it stretched across district lines to form the foundation for a primitive national organization.

Still, the U.S. marshals retained considerable independence. The Executive Office served largely as an advisory unit. As late as September 1968 it had a staff of only ten people, hardly enough to give adequate guidance to such a disparate national organization. McShane had no power to compel a U.S. marshal to obey him. Cameron, for example, had no authority to force a marshal to send his deputies on special assignments. Reduced to begging for men, Cameron depended on the goodwill of individual marshals. Many refused to cooperate. Their presidential commissions put them out of reach of the chief marshal.[41]

And there McShane let his boys down. Although he had desegregated the South, he was incapable of integrating the marshals into a centralized national organization. He had immediate access to the attorney general, but he failed to use it for any larger purpose than the crisis of the moment. He had the opportunity and the influence but not the vision.

Early in the year Meredith was in school, Vandegrift made a special trip back to Washington to complain. The deputies' lack of radios made the protective detail extremely difficult. He could not keep in touch with his men; they had no way to alert him when they were in trouble. With Vandegrift in tow, McShane marched into Bobby Kennedy's office. Making a single phone call, the attorney general arranged to borrow walkie-talkies from the White House. Within hours, Vandegrift remembered, he was on a White House plane loaded with radios and headed back to Mississippi. He sat in awe of his chief marshal.[42]

The larger issue—that the marshals had no radios as standard equipment—remained unchanged. McShane made no real effort to introduce the nineteenth-century-bound marshals to twentieth-century technology. The deputies continued to drive their own cars on government business just as, a century before, their predecessors had ridden their own horses. Office storerooms housed the vintage World War II steel pots, the homemade batons, and the antique tear-gas guns excessed by the military. For the rest of McShane's tenure, the marshals relied on outmoded office equipment, accounting systems, and techniques to perform their jobs.

The assassination of President Kennedy in November 1963 and Bobby Kennedy's resignation months later left McShane floundering amid the department's heartless bureaucracy. With his mentor gone, McShane found himself isolated within the department, excluded from decision making. By many accounts, personal problems consumed him. The steps toward centralization came to a halt.

During the rest of the sixties, during the ghetto riots and the anti–Vietnam War demonstrations, the marshals were usually only tangentially involved. By 1965 their work in desegregating the South was largely done. They had no role in cooling the long, hot summers of riots in black ghettos that sporadically erupted across the country. During the various people's marches on Washington, deputies frequently took station around the Department of Justice, but that was generally all they did.

Except in October 1967. In response to the nationwide call for a march on Washington to protest the war in Vietnam, officials at the Department of Justice ordered McShane to bring in deputies to support the military. The demonstrators, estimated at more than fifty thousand strong, threatened to take over the Pentagon in order to disrupt the war effort. Jack Cameron again contacted districts across the country to organize a force of about 250 deputy marshals. Equipped again with their antiquated white helmets, homemade riot batons, and pistols, the deputies provided the civilian arrest power. Soldiers and military police composed the manpower.

Deputy Robert Christman later remembered driving all night from Rochester, New York. He arrived in Washington early Saturday morning, October 26, in time to attend a briefing given to the deputies by McShane and Cameron. The deputies were told to arrest any protesters who trespassed too close to the Pentagon or otherwise threatened the building or its occupants. Bused to the Pentagon, the deputies found several thousand soldiers posted around the five-sided building. The lawmen quickly formed a single-file, wide-gapped line of their own.[43]

Late that Saturday afternoon, the marchers left the speeches and antiwar chanting in front of the Lincoln Memorial, crossing the Potomac toward the Pentagon. As they approached the ungainly building, several hundred of them broke into a sprint. Screaming out the sixties refrain of antiwar slogans, they tried to run the gauntlet of soldiers and deputies and break into the Pentagon.

Worn down by their day-long vigil and unnerved at the sight of the charging mob, the soldiers and deputies roughly repelled the demonstrators who broke through the perimeter. In the first clash the marchers were equally rough. Deputy James O'Toole from Connecticut was briefly trapped in a group of angry protesters. Someone stabbed him in the thigh; others tried to push him to the ground. Frank Vandegrift and a few other deputies waded into the mob to rescue O'Toole. They pulled him back to safety behind the soldiers, who closed ranks against the demonstrators.[44]

A couple of dozen or so protesters reached one of the Pentagon doorways. A handful of deputies, led by the ubiquitous Al Butler, counterattacked. They pushed through the mob, pulling and shoving people from the door. Swinging their riot batons, they forced the demonstrators back from the building outside the protective perimeter of soldiers. Butler was surprised at how little resistance the protesters offered; it was nothing compared with that night in Mississippi.[45]

After the initial scuffle and a few score arrests, the demonstration settled down to a sit-in. The protesters simply sat in front of the soldiers, chanting slogans and screaming objections to the war but making no more attempts to force through the line. Exhausted by their vigil, the deputies waited nervously for the next attack. None came. Instead, protesters slipped flowers into the soldiers' rifle barrels. McShane made no arrangements to relieve, feed, or refresh his men. The deputies stayed on the front line outside the Pentagon.

The demonstration permit expired at midnight, Saturday night. As the deadline approached, the deputies began warning the protesters to disperse. Anyone caught touching one of the soldiers, who were lined shoulder to shoulder around the building, would be arrested for trespassing. Near midnight, the soldiers began inching their way forward, pushing themselves up against the seated demonstrators. Protesters were immediately arrested once contact was made.[46]

A long process of contact and arrest began. The protesters soon learned not to move, no matter what. Most of them fell limp as soon as the deputies came to arrest them, forcing the deputies to carry or drag them to the waiting trucks, buses, and vans headed for jail. Hundreds of people were hauled away. Soon the deputies' arms and backs ached with the effort. On duty for more than sixteen hours, they continued to pull the demonstrators to the staging area where they were loaded on the vehicles. As the effort robbed the men of patience and sympathy, their handling of the protesters grew rougher.

By dawn the demonstration was over. Hundreds of protesters had been arrested, and most others had left. A few remained huddled in groups to ward off the October morning chill. Rubble and trash littered the sloping grounds of the Pentagon. The deputies and soldiers maintained their protective perimeter. For some of the lawmen, especially those who had been at Oxford five years before, it seemed that the marshals had become the government's experts at protecting buildings.

A little more than a year after the Pentagon riot, in December 1968,

James J. P. McShane died. During his tenure as chief marshal, the confluence of national events and his access to the Kennedys rescued the marshals from the burden of their past. Through the orders of the courts, the marshals became involved in the most dramatic domestic changes of the twentieth century. They had not seen such action, nor been involved in such important tumult, since the settlement of the West a century before. Their desegregation of the South reawoke officials in Washington to the complex flexibility and authority that inhered in the office of marshal.

McShane supervised the transformation of the marshals from bailiffs to full-fledged officers of the courts. But he was incapable of bringing them fully into the twentieth century or pushing them into mainstream law enforcement. The basic organization changed little under his tenure. The Executive Office remained a handful of individuals; the U.S. marshals reigned supreme in their districts. Bureaucratic organization and expertise, the measures of professionalism, eluded the marshals.

The marshals also remained dependent on the courts for work and jurisdiction. Until they could strengthen their headquarters and find some independence from the judiciary, they would be unable to establish themselves as equals among the other federal law enforcement agencies.

12

THE UNITED STATES MARSHALS SERVICE
1969–1983

Commander Gavilan waited impatiently. For more than a year, and more than twenty-seven visits to Honduras, plus side trips to the Dominican Republic, he had begged and cajoled local officials to help him. During that year, escaped federal prisoner Juan Matta Ballesteros had squired around Tegucigalpa acting like a modern-day Robin Hood. With the millions he made smuggling cocaine into the United States, he generously passed a few bucks to one neighbor, picked up another man's hospital bills, or paid the education of another's children. His neighbors knew him for his generosity. Honduran officials feared him for his ruthlessness.

The marshals wanted Matta for his drug running and his murders. They used his 1971 escape from the Eglin, Florida, federal prison as their excuse to catch him. In 1979 the marshals had essentially stolen federal jurisdiction to recapture fugitives from the Federal Bureau of Investigation. The new arrangement distanced the marshals from the federal courts just enough to enhance their stature as cops. They were no longer bailiffs but investigators. Their investigations took them around the world, from Libya and the arrest of the ex-CIA gun smuggler Edmund Wilson to the Los Angeles section of Tegucigalpa. There, Commander

Gavilan and the other deputies waited impatiently in their rental cars for the Hondurans to boot Matta out of the country.

Since Carlos Ledher's arrest the year before, Matta had taken over the sprawling Mettelin-family cocaine business. His tentacles stretched throughout the Western Hemisphere, from Colombian poppy fields to U.S. street corners where crack, cocaine, heroin, and other drugs were sold in volume. Although illiterate and uneducated, Matta had modernized the drug business by introducing the use of computers to maintain his illicit inventories and radar to track the smuggling. He was one of the richest men in the world—and among the most dangerous.

U.S. officials suspected Matta of complicity in the 1985 murder of U.S. drug enforcement agent Camarena Salazar. Matta was also implicated in thirteen murders in Colombia and in a decade-old drug partnership with Panamanian strongman Manuel Noriega. No one doubted that he could easily kill again. Even the marshals, though backed by the full authority of the United States, moved carefully against him. In the drug war, no one questioned the strength of the enemy.

Stanley E. Morris, the director of the Marshals Service, wanted badly to get Matta. Catching drug leaders like him and Ledher helped disrupt the billion-dollar drug industry, if only temporarily. More important, Morris realized, arresting the drug kingpins proved that they could not operate with international impunity. Taking Matta would not end the drug war, nor would it be the beginning of the end, nor even the end of the beginning. But it would illustrate the U.S. government's commitment to fighting back. In a war in which the enemy had more money, better weapons, and more incentive than the police, symbols were crucial to the battle.

The marshals needed to get Matta to American territory to effect his arrest. Then he could be tried for the murders and the drug violations. First, they had to get Matta out of Honduras. The Honduran constitution forbade extraditions of any kind, regardless of the crime. Consequently, Commander Gavilan—the code name used by the deputy marshal in charge of the operation—and associate director for operations Howard Safir had campaigned quietly but earnestly with Honduran military and police officials to find some way to expel Matta. After a year of negotiations, the Hondurans agreed to kick Matta out.

Now, on April 5, 1988, Commander Gavilan and a handful of other deputies, who had also adopted odd code names like Tarzan, Ponce, Pollow, Parque, and Yunque, waited in the early Honduran morning. A force of 120 Honduran police and soldiers had swooped down on Matta's estate by helicopter and car, but the Honduran constitution forbade the execution of search warrants before 6 a.m. They had arrived just before 5:30. Because form was equal in importance to action, everybody waited.

Matta, followed as usual by a carload of bodyguards, had gone for his regular morning jog. After a run of a mile or two, he stopped for his habitual cup of coffee with his lawyer, who lived only a block or two away. When Matta's sister called to tell him of the commotion outside his house, he decided to return home. With his money and the power it bestowed on him, he felt immune from the danger of simple policemen.

Commander Gavilan saw him first. He yelled to the Hondurans, "There he is." Two officers approached Matta to take him into custody, but he resisted their efforts to get him into the marshals' rental car. As the deputies watched, Matta kicked and punched. He knocked one of the Hondurans to the ground before other officers overwhelmed him. As Matta, who feared he was on his way to his execution, struggled, the Hondurans put a hood over his head and pushed him to the floorboard of the marshals' car.

Matta's resistance allowed the Hondurans to search his house fifteen minutes early. Almost immediately, they found a bag of cocaine sitting on his kitchen table. It was reason enough to expel him from the country. Two Honduran officers scrambled into the back with Matta. With one deputy driving and one riding shotgun, the car pulled out toward the airport. Commander Gavilan and another deputy followed in a second car.

No one spoke—except Matta. He offered $1 million cash if they would release him. When no one answered, he raised his offer to $2 million, then $3 million. During the forty-minute car ride, he upped the price several more times, finally promising $20 million in cash if only they would let him go. His captors maintained their silence. None of them doubted the seriousness of Matta's offer nor his ability to pay them immediately—or kill them later.

When they reached the airport, the guards pulled Matta from the car and bundled him onto a plane bound for the Dominican Republic. Matta repeated his offer of $20 million cash, no waiting. The deputies, who with salary and overtime might make $30,000 to $40,000 a year, remained silent. Later, Commander Gavilan reported the bribe offers to Safir. "Boss," he said with a laugh, "he was getting close."

The plane flew to the Dominican Republic, which refused Matta entry because he had no passport. He was now a stateless person, unprotected and unwanted. As usual in such cases, the Dominicans put Matta on the next plane out, which happened to be going to Puerto Rico. It also so happened that the only available seat on the plane was a middle one. Deputy U.S. marshals occupied the adjoining aisle and window seats. As soon as the plane entered U.S. airspace, the deputies arrested Matta for his prison escape. They caught the next plane to New York City, where they put Matta aboard a Marshals Service airplane and delivered him straight away to the maximum security prison in Marion, Illinois.

Morris called it a creative arrest, an innovative response to the international drug problem. Honduran students showed somewhat less creativity when they demonstrated against the arrest by pulling a typical anti-American trick. They burned down the American embassy's annex. Honduran President José Azcona Hoya promised to investigate the charge that the Honduran constitution had been violated.

Federal courts in the United States, though, were unsympathetic to Matta's assertion that his rights under the Honduran constitution had been violated. As in previous decisions, the courts refused to examine the method of his capture in a foreign country. Matta remained in federal prison. U.S. attorneys prepared to prosecute him for illegal drug operations and for the murder of drug enforcement agent Salazar. Commander Gavilan and the other deputies returned to their districts. The war against drugs continued.

In that war the marshals relied on the talents that two centuries of experience had bequeathed them: creativity and innovation. Morris knew that computers, radar, AWACS, and fleets of Coast Guard cutters alone could not win the war against Matta and his cohorts. The drug dealers, too, had computers, radar, and fast ships. And they had lots and lots of money. Matta himself probably had more money in his checking account than the annual budget of the marshals. The $20 million he offered Morris's deputies was hardly pocket change to him. He made that much in a single cocaine deal.

To win the war, Morris believed, the lawmen had to rely on their ability to outwit the drug lords. They could not match the resources that drug sales generated, nor should they compete with the ruthlessness that drug dealing fostered. Morris promoted innovative arrests like Matta's because they were his best weapon.

Between 1969 and 1989 the U.S. marshals and their deputies experienced a revolution. The Department of Justice imposed a centralized, powerful headquarters establishment upon them, forcing the disparate districts to accept regulation and routine. The challenge, as Morris well knew, was to enforce the bureaucratic requirements that centralization demanded without stifling the independence and innovation on which the marshals had always depended. The effort to achieve that balance defined the last two decades of the U.S. marshals' first two centuries.

THE HEADQUARTERS REVOLUTION, 1969–1974

In one of the great ironies of American history, Richard M. Nixon based his 1968 domestic platform for the presidency in considerable part on the restoration of law and order. Events would show that he insisted on order to the law's detriment, but originally that emphasis redounded to the advantage of the marshals. The Nixon administration oversaw a dramatic transformation in the organization, authority, and responsibilities of the marshals. The revolution took place in the name of enhanced law enforcement and increased governmental efficiency, the twin principles Nixon pronounced for his presidency.

The Democrats under Kennedy and Johnson relied on McShane and the marshals to respond to particular emergencies and court orders. No one suggested any need to reorganize the Executive Office for U.S. Marshals or to increase its authority over the districts. What the Democrats required was a coordinator, not a director. McShane admirably filled that bill. Neither ambition nor bureaucratic aggrandizement drove him to expand the scope of his office.

The Nixon administration took a different course. Under Attorney General John Mitchell and his successors, the marshals were given significantly enhanced authorities over a much broader range of responsibilities. Between 1969 and 1974 the marshals inaugurated or consolidated programs in court security, personal security, witness security, air piracy, civil disturbances, internal inspections, and prisoner transportation. The Executive Office was radically transformed from a coordinating office to a full-fledged directorate of field activities. It was a revolutionary change that stripped the districts to the last remnant of their autonomy by centralizing the operations of the marshals. By the end, only the U.S. marshals' presidential commissions remained unchanged, though not unassaulted.

Between 1969 and 1989 the history of the marshals was the story of the headquarters' effort to establish control over the districts. Implicit in the struggle were emphases on centralization, professionalization, training, improved equipage, and a wide-ranging expansion of functional responsibilities. Unlike most organizations, which begin centralized and slowly expand outward, the marshals had a long tradition of diversification and decentralization. The centrifugal forces that naturally tug at any national organization were even stronger and more pronounced with the marshals.

A headquarters was mandatory if the marshals were to survive. It made possible the triple attributes essential to postwar America: specialization, professionalization, and bureaucratization. Chronic manpower shortages within the districts compelled the deputies to perform diverse duties. During the course of any single day, they moved from transporting a prisoner to protecting a judge to seizing property to serving a court order. In doing so, the deputies avoided developing specialties.

The headquarters solved that problem by housing the specialists. Unlike the districts, assignments at headquarters were concentrated on one aspect of the marshals' job. Experts in court security focused on the courts to the exclusion of everything else; those in witness security spent all their time tending witnesses. The experts could move from one division to another and even from headquarters to the field and back, but while they were in a division, they attended to that division exclusively. Thus, it was in headquarters that the experts first appeared and from headquarters that they began making their specialized demands on the districts. From their offices and divisions, the specialists called on the districts as they needed help and manpower.

The headquarters also developed professional standards for the marshals, then arranged training programs to instill those standards nationwide. Independence among the districts was shunned as the headquarters set about routinizing methods, procedures, and reports. Although unique methods within individual districts would never be entirely eradicated—the tradition of independence was too deeply rooted—the establishment and enforcement of professional standards and routines helped end the parochialism among the marshals. Deputies and headquarters staff could move freely among the districts with considerable assurance that individual operations were nationally recognizable.

In addition the headquarters bureaucratized the marshals. Separate divisions and offices were established. Forms were developed, promulgated, revised, withdrawn, and continually reissued. In 1988 a special committee recommended dropping more than a third of the three hundred forms spewing from headquarters to the districts. The reform, the districts naturally suspected, was just to make room for newer forms. Statistics were gathered, analyzed, reported, and filed away. Information was constantly disseminated through memos, newsletters, magazines, telephone calls, and Teletypes. By the late 1980s the headquarters communications center processed more than five hundred Teletypes a day. It was a cacophony of information from a bureaucratic chorus.

More important, the bureaucratization of the marshals helped promote organizational interests within the Department of Justice, the Office of Management and Budget, and the myriad other fiefdoms in Washington. It allowed one bureaucracy to talk to the other in a language that only bureaucracies comprehended. Turf battles were more easily won by bureaucrats hardened to the warfare. Increased budgets, resources, and equipment were more easily garnered; new responsibilities were more easily obtained. The bureaucracy identified the goals, developed the strategies, and joined the battles. Bureaucratization established the marshals behind a common front.

The struggle began with McShane's successor. Shortly after assuming office in early 1969, Attorney General Mitchell selected Carl C. Turner as the new chief marshal to supervise the ninety-three U.S. marshals and their six hundred deputies. With the appointment went a clear mandate to reorganize the marshals into a strong national organization capable of supporting and directing their diverse responsibilities.

Turner's credentials were impressive. A retired major general, he had devoted his army career to the military police. From 1964 to 1968 he had served as provost marshal general over the army's twenty-five thousand military police. When he retired in 1968, he set up his own security consulting business just outside Washington. After his appointment as chief marshal on March 24, 1969, he embarked on an aggressive campaign to centralize the marshals, absorbing most of the power within his grasp.[1]

Within six months, it became quite clear that Turner was a crook.

But during that time, he worked furiously to impose a stronger organizational structure on the marshals. He used as his model the military police, even to the point of suggesting that the marshals don uniforms. Whether Turner fully understood the marshals and their traditions, and whether he could have accomplished his goals, remains unclear. He did, however, move with amazing speed to rename the organization, strengthen its headquarters, and begin its expansion. Had he been an honest man, he might have accomplished even more.

Turner recognized two important flaws in the structure of the Executive Office for U.S. Marshals. The first was inherent in its original charter; the second dated to the organizational shuffle approved by Attorney General Ramsey Clark in November 1967. According to the charter, which had been codified by Department of Justice order 271-62, the head of the office was to "provide general executive assistance and supervision to the offices of the United States marshals, coordinate and direct the relationship of agencies of the Department with such offices, and approve the staffing requirements of the offices of the United States Marshals." That, Turner recognized, was not quite strong enough for his purposes.[2]

Second, on November 28, 1967, Attorney General Clark had approved a departmental reorganization transferring the Executive Office from the supervision of the deputy attorney general to the assistant attorney general for administration. Taking the office from the deputy attorney general reduced the bureaucratic position of the marshals within the department. Putting it under the administrative division rather than the criminal implied an even greater diminishment. In bureaucratic terms the change signaled that the marshals were not lawmen but administrators. The transfer was a clear reflection of McShane's reduced stature by 1967.[3]

Turner had no intention of accepting the arrangement. Within weeks of taking over, he moved to strengthen his own power and to reestablish the Executive Office within the department. His first step was to create the position of deputy chief U.S. marshal to bring aboard Donald H. Synnott, who had served with him for twenty-four years in the military police. Turner and Synnott embarked on a major reorganization of the marshals. Both men took office on March 24. On April 1, Turner asked Leo M. Pellerzi, the assistant attorney general for administration, for "clear-cut authority to 'direct' and 'supervise'" the marshals as a means "to achieve the desirable degree of U.S. Marshal responsiveness."[4]

Turner also wanted the Executive Office put back under the deputy attorney general with a new name, the United States Marshals Service. These proposals fit perfectly with the Nixon administration's general drive to strengthen law enforcement and streamline government operations. Attorney General Mitchell applauded Turner's suggestions; they were immediately implemented. On May 12, barely six weeks after taking office, Turner arranged the promulgation of Department of Justice order 415-69, which specified that "the Office of the Director, United States Marshals Service, shall be under the supervision of the Deputy Attorney General and shall direct and supervise the United States Marshals, coordinate and direct the relationship of other organizational units of the Department with the office of United States Marshals, and approve staffing requirements of such offices." The order gave Turner the authority he needed to launch his headquarters revolution.[5]

Turner also moved quickly on other fronts. On June 23 he asked for extensive powers over all personnel issues within the Marshals Service, including hiring, promoting, and resolving "all personnel problems for all Marshals offices." That was a significant departure from approving district staffing requirements. As Turner recognized, it was an essential step forward if the headquarters was to gain full control over the disparate districts. "I am not going to take a dogmatic approach on anything," he assured the department's director of personnel and training. "I don't want unnecessary prerogative—I want to help."[6]

In addition, Turner and Synnott planned the establishment of a headquarters field support unit to consolidate within the Marshals Service all the services currently provided by individual offices within the Department of Justice. "The unit," as Turner described it, "will be under the control and direction of this office and will coordinate and support field activities Service wide." Although Turner told his superiors that twenty-eight new positions would be required for the headquarters, privately he was planning on at least thirty-seven. And that was only the beginning.[7]

Department officials responded favorably. Leo M. Pellerzi, the department's administrative head, pointed out to Deputy Attorney General Richard Kleindienst that Turner's request for twenty-eight new positions "constitutes a 280 percent increase in staff," but it was "justified if the E O for U S Marshals is to function as a directorate for a field service." Pellerzi further observed, "If Carl Turner is to accomplish the improvements we have discussed, this staffing is necessary."[8]

Despite the rapidity with which Turner's reforms moved the Marshals Service forward, his past ensnared him. Throughout the summer of 1969, rumors and press reports implicated him in criminal activities, graft, and corruption in the army's enlisted men's clubs during his tenure as head of the military police. The pressure escalated when Reis Kash, whom Turner had brought into the Marshals Service from the army's criminal investigation division, testified against Turner before a congressional committee.

By September 1969 the pressure was unbearable. William E. Hall, whom Turner had hired the previous April as chief counsel, remembered sitting in his own office next door to Turner's late one Friday afternoon that September. Turner's office had its own outside exit. Hall heard the private telephone in Turner's office ring, then Turner answer it. A few minutes later, Turner's private door opened and closed. Hall never saw the director again. Later, Turner was convicted of graft and corruption, and deputy marshals escorted him to the federal penitentiary.[9]

After Turner's embarrassing resignation, Attorney General Mitchell looked within the Marshals Service to find the next director. He selected Wayne B. Colburn, a twenty-five-year veteran policeman who had put in an additional eight years as the U.S. marshal for the southern district of California in San Diego. Colburn was sworn in as director in January 1970. At that time the Marshals Service included ninety-three marshals and about six hundred deputies. The headquarters consisted of the director, his deputy, and the following offices: counsel, inspections, administration, field activities, and plans, training, and program. In all, it housed a staff of about forty professionals and support personnel.[10]

Colburn established his basic strategy for the Marshals Service within his first year. He recognized that the marshals' specialty was their diversity, that they were the government's experts at accepting new assignments. "During the last six months," he announced to the marshals in November 1970, "my staff and I have worked very hard pursuing the assignment of new missions to the Marshals Service (judicial security, air piracy, sensitive witness security). We realize that to thoroughly professionalize our Service we must have a variety of missions that will, in turn, enable us to establish career ladder opportunities."[11]

Colburn had three primary goals. First, he wanted to convert the office of U.S. marshal to civil service status with selection by the attorney general. Second, he wanted to establish a two-grade standard promotion route for the deputies. Finally, and most important to him, he wanted to obtain bureau status for the U.S. Marshals Service, putting it on a bureaucratic par with the other law enforcement agencies within the department. "The implementation of [these] proposals," he advised Deputy Attorney General Ralph Erickson on November 13, 1972, "is a prerequisite to true professionalization within the Service."[12]

Of the three goals, Colburn recognized that obtaining bureau status was the most crucial. "The primary intent of achieving bureau status," he advised Deputy Attorney General Kleindienst in June 1971, "is to upgrade the United States Marshals Service to a position of authority commensurate with its responsibilities." Bureau status would put the marshals on a level with the Immigration and Naturalization Service, the Bureau of Prisons, the Law Enforcement Assistance Administration, and various other law enforcement agencies.[13]

Bureau status also entailed considerable independence from the department. It would grant the Marshals Service power over its budget, personnel, procurements, and, to a significant extent, its various missions. "Due to the rapid expansion of the United States Marshals Service and its commensurate responsibilities, greater autonomy for dispositive action must be granted to the United States Marshals Service," Colburn consistently argued in his proposal. "Therefore to insure operational efficiency and reduce expenditures, this order creates and designates the United States Marshals Service as a Bureau within the Department of Justice."[14]

Colburn defined three main reasons for the designation. It would allow effective administration of the marshals by enhancing the authority of the headquarters. Second, it would release the Department of Justice from the "perfunctory burden" of supervising the Marshals Service. Finally, bureau status would increase operational efficiency and reduce expenditures by streamlining decision making within the service. The service could take dispositive actions itself, rather than constantly having to appeal to the department for permission to do things. In addition, bureau status would simplify access to all information pertinent to the Marshals Service. By centralizing authority, bureau status would permit more efficient utilization of resources and personnel.[15]

Every year between 1971 and 1973 Colburn battled to make the Marshals Service a bureau within the Department of Justice. Attorney

General Mitchell hesitated to approve the step. Although he had readily approved the earlier consolidation of authority within the service's headquarters, he believed that the service was yet too small to justify such a broad grant of independence. Colburn was forced to wait out Mitchell's tenure.

Mitchell resigned in 1972 to take charge of Nixon's reelection campaign. Shortly afterward, he was consumed by the uncontainable Watergate scandal involving high-level efforts to obstruct justice. As the courts and special prosecutors investigated the crimes committed by Nixon and his advisers, deputy marshals served the subpoenas, summonses, and other court process on the president and his lieutenants. It was a typically American phenomenon. Executive branch officials, acting under the orders of the judicial branch, served noxious orders on their superiors, including Mitchell.

During early 1973 the marshals contained the American Indian Movement's occupation of Wounded Knee, South Dakota, in the second-longest (as Abraham Lincoln would argue) civil uprising in American history. The response of the marshals during the seventy-one-day occupation helped convince the department that the service had reached a high level of professionalism that justified bureau status.

On May 10, 1973, barely two days after the occupation of Wounded Knee ended, Attorney General Kleindienst awarded Colburn with his long-sought bureau. The new charter delegated to the director full authority to "direct and supervise all activities of the United States Marshals Service." Those activities expressly included the execution of federal arrest warrants; the service of civil and criminal process; the "sustension" of custody of federal prisoners from arrest to delivery to prison or release; the protection of federal courts, jurists, court officers, and government witnesses; the prevention of air piracy; and the administration of a training school for marshals.

Furthermore, the director of the Marshals Service now worked under the general supervision and direction of the attorney general. To carry out its mission, the Marshals Service was given "relative autonomy in procurement and contracting matters, [and] the authority to take final action in matters pertaining to employment, direction, and general administration of personnel." The order satisfied all of Colburn's requests.[16]

But the charter did not last. Kleindienst was forced to resign because of Watergate, and Nixon replaced him with Elliot Richardson, a

Boston lawyer determined to hold back the growth of government. On October 17, 1973, five months after the charter was signed, Richardson revoked it. The revocation also stripped Colburn of his authority over procurement, contracting, and personnel, leaving him without clear control over the Marshals Service. For months afterward, he grappled with trying to restore even his original powers.[17]

Richardson resigned to protest Nixon's dismissal of the Watergate special prosecutor. His successor, William Saxbe, was more sympathetic to Colburn's goal. In May 1974, Colburn regained the bureau designation, with all its specified and implied powers. Yet the institutional memory of Richardson's revocation of the original order haunted the service and its successive directors. The new goal became to obtain bureau status by Congressional statute, thereby distancing it from fickle attorneys general.[18]

Colburn had a much easier time achieving a clear promotional route for his deputies. In January 1971 he obtained delegated authority from the department's personnel operations section "to take final action on matters pertaining to the employment, separation and general administration of personnel." Eighteen months later, Colburn established the class recruiting program, in which teams of headquarters specialists interviewed and selected candidates for deputy marshal.[19]

More important to Colburn was to revise the haphazard promotion of deputies by making promotion more rational and more routine. He proposed to establish "a two-grade progression series for the promotion of deputy United States marshal" as a way to enhance efficiency by attracting and keeping the most qualified individuals as deputies. "As a result," Colburn argued, "both the qualitative and quantitative job performance of United States Marshals Service personnel would be improved."[20]

In June 1973 the Civil Service Commission approved Colburn's plan. Deputies could now be hired at the GS-5 level, with automatic promotion to GS-7 after completion of a twelve-month probation period. Exemplary job performance would lead to promotion to GS-9. "Along with our Bureau status, the establishment of the deputy US marshal occupation as a two grade progression career plan surges us ahead in our pursuit of professionalism," Colburn proudly announced.[21]

There remained one major bastion prohibiting full professionalization: the political selection of U.S. marshals. The establishment of the headquarters had led to a steady chipping away of the marshals' autonomy. By 1973, headquarters fully controlled hiring, training, budgeting, and defining their missions. The only thing that headquarters did not control was their selection. That power still resided with the president and, by his traditional deferral, with the senator or congressional delegation.

Colburn launched his attack in November 1972. "With increased demands placed upon the Service as a result of widespread civil disobedience and organized crime," Colburn argued, "the United States Marshals Service can no longer effectively function as a loose confederation of ninety-four judicial districts." The political selection of marshals was "anachronistic since it provides no guarantee that the successful selectee possesses even minimum law enforcement experience," Colburn complained. "Moreover, the current method of appointment minimizes the effectiveness of the leadership of the Director of the United States Marshals Service, since many marshals consider that their authority is subject *only* to the supervision of the President and/or their congressional sponsor."[22]

His arguments were unpersuasive to Congress. The nomination of U.S. marshals was one of the few remaining political plums that senators could award. Colburn lost. He and subsequent directors were dependent on verbal agreements with the attorneys general that they would uphold disciplinary actions against wayward marshals. That support was always cautioned by the knowledge that U.S. marshals with powerful support were beyond reach. The U.S. marshals became the counterstructure in an otherwise structured organization.

Headquarters introduced a measure of stability in the professional life of deputies. Marshals came and went according to the fluctuations of American politics. Headquarters remained. The deputies came to look to it for procedural rules, training, guidance, support, and advancement. U.S. marshals were tolerated—sometimes just barely—depending on their attitude toward the service. To the extent that they wanted to participate in the activities of the service, the presidential appointees were welcome. But as the system evolved, headquarters avoided too much dependence on the marshals. It could not count on the quality of those political nominees as it could on the deputies it chose. As a practical result, the deputies were frequently torn between the demands of their district managers—the U.S. marshals—and headquarters. Headquarters offered the deputies a career. The marshals could not compete with that.

THE REVOLUTION TEMPERED, 1973

As part of Colburn's efforts to reform and restructure the Marshals Service, he described a new image for the marshals. "I have, in my testimony before various [Congressional] committees," he reported in November 1970, "committed you to be professional, semi-military oriented law enforcement officers." In 1971 Colburn created the Special Operations Group (SOG), an elite collection of a hundred or so specially trained, equipped, and uniformed deputies. Closely modeled on military response teams, SOG was designed to respond within hours to national emergencies and civil disturbances. By training, equipment, outlook, and mission, the members personified Colburn's image of "semi-military oriented law enforcement officers."[23]

SOG developed under the general direction of William E. Hall, whom Colburn made his assistant director for operations. Butler, Forsht, and Grider helped define the mission of the new unit, which they based largely on their experiences in desegregating the South and combatting antiwar demonstrators. As Grider pointed out, by 1971 they were too old for the rigorous training that SOG imposed upon its members. Grider had no desire to undergo the harsh basic training, running, physical exertion, and endurance tests in which the younger members of SOG reveled.[24]

A new group, led by William Whitworth, emerged to take control of SOG. They were more than just younger. They were also more disciplined, more willing to work together as a group, considerably more patient in following orders and directions than the old guard represented by Butler and Forsht. The hot-dog mentality that Butler and Forsht epitomized was shunned by SOG. Instead it favored a regimented, tightly controlled outfit.

Established because of the sixties history of civil disturbances, SOG soon stumbled upon its natural enemy. The activism of the civil rights and antiwar movement infected other special-interest groups, such as women, Hispanics, and Indians. The American Indian Movement

(AIM) began to demonstrate and attract attention around the time SOG was organized. The subsequent clashes with militant Indians determined the direction that SOG would take for the rest of the decade.

In early 1970, members of AIM took over Alcatraz Island in San Francisco Bay. Initially the federal government left them alone. Calling for better treatment of Indians and a reexamination of the century-old treaties, AIM used the occupation to publicize its demands.

In the early summer of 1971 other members of AIM occupied the Twin Cities Naval Air Station just outside Minneapolis. Unlike the occupation of the empty island, the new occupation disrupted naval operations at the facility. SOG members went to Minneapolis to evict the disgruntled Indians. The occupiers retreated to the base theater, which they barricaded. When the SOG members forced their way into the building, the Indians fought back with clubs, knives, and other weapons. Deputy Dan Dotson of Michigan suffered a broken arm and a severe cut on his head before the Indians were subdued.[25]

The Minnesota incident convinced officials in Washington that it was time to end the nineteen-month occupation of Alcatraz. Colburn, Hall, and a small contingent of SOG deputies arrived in San Francisco on June 10. The remainder of the SOG force was to arrive in a few days. Originally they planned to land in force on the island on June 16. On the morning of June 11, however, Whitworth watched as a boat carrying eleven Indians left the island with a cargo of copper tubing taken from the abandoned prison. The Indians sold the scrap copper on the mainland.

With the Indian population thus reduced, Colburn decided to act immediately. Gathering what force he could—about thirty men—he borrowed two Coast Guard cutters to take the deputies to the island. They arrived on Alcatraz early in the afternoon. No one opposed the landing. Moving quickly, Colburn and Hall established control of the island. The seventeen Indians left on Alcatraz were booted off. None were arrested.

Fearing that AIM might try to reoccupy Alcatraz, the marshals stayed on guard throughout the night. They uncovered large amounts of narcotics, weapons, ammunition, and other contraband left by the Indians. After a peaceful night, the marshals withdrew from the island the next day. Shortly thereafter, tour boats began again to take visitors to the historic prison.[26]

Afterward, AIM continued to agitate for Indian rights; Whitworth continued to train deputies as SOG members. Working with the FBI, Colburn and his lieutenants monitored the Indian movement. The Indians, however, remained relatively peaceful until the fall of 1972. At that time several hundred AIM members converged on Washington to demonstrate. They demanded that officials in the Bureau of Indian Affairs (BIA) find them a place to camp. Though BIA officials took them to several locations, the Indians peremptorily rejected them all. Finally, on November 3, the members of AIM took over the BIA building.

During the occupation, the marshals helped keep an eye on the building. Reis Kash, who took over as Colburn's associate director for operations when Hall became deputy director, gained entry to the BIA building by dressing up as a janitor for the General Services Administration. With an official-looking clipboard in hand, Kash marched through each floor barking orders on what to clean and what to fix to make the building habitable. He chided the Indians on their slovenly habits while carefully noting what toilet supplies they needed. Kash also took coded notes of the weaponry and preparations the Indians had made. He saw typewriters stacked in the stairwell, ready to bombard anyone who tried to rush the stairs. Sheets of glass and homemade weapons were strategically distributed. He reported to Colburn that the Indians clearly intended to resist.[27]

Kash's report, combined with other intelligence, persuaded officials in the Justice and Interior departments to negotiate. Although some plans were developed to storm the building, they were discounted as too risky. As finally resolved, the occupation ended on November 8 with the payment of $66,500 in "travel expenses" for the Indians to return home. Kash watched angrily as the money was distributed. It seemed to him and the other marshals a bad precedent.[28]

As the Indians made their paid trips home, both the marshals and the FBI stepped up surveillance of them. The intelligence information was reasonably sound, particularly because several members of AIM were faithful informants for the FBI. Their reports, combined with the movements of leading AIM members, soon revealed that AIM's next objective was the Pine Ridge, South Dakota, Sioux Indian Reservation. Some evidence indicated that they planned to seize the BIA building on the reservation.

According to the U.S. Court of Claims case *The Innocent Victims of the Occupation of Wounded Knee, South Dakota v. the United States,* which remains the best history of the occupation, between November 1972 and February 1973, the U.S. Marshals Service "was the agency receiving information about threats to the BIA building at the Pine Ridge Reservation because it had the only effective federal unit that was trained to combat civil disturbance." Concerned about the increased AIM activity in South Dakota, the Interior Department arranged with the Justice Department to use SOG deputies on a reimbursable basis.[29]

Over the winter of 1972–73, Dennis Banks, Russell Means, and other leaders of AIM stayed around Pine Ridge arguing with tribal leaders, demonstrating, and worrying Colburn and the marshals. Hall traveled several times to Pine Ridge for firsthand observations. Increased tensions convinced him and Colburn that he should activate SOG. Under the command of Kash and Grider (who was in charge of security for the Marshals Service), sixty-five SOG deputies arrived in mid-February to train the BIA police to secure the BIA building. Within a week the SOG force had grown to one hundred men. Between February 14 and February 27, SOG taught the BIA police the basic elements of riot control. "It was," according to the *Innocent Victims* decision, "a similar but less intensive type of special operations group training."[30]

In addition the SOG deputies established several roadblocks and observation points to try to prevent the introduction of weapons onto the reservation. The marshals were certain that AIM intended to seize the BIA building. "It seemed that the thrust of the frustration and anger of the AIM people at Pine Ridge was directed toward the Department of the Interior, the BIA, and the tribal leadership," the *Innocent Victims* decision pointed out, "all of which had offices at the Pine Ridge BIA headquarters."[31]

As part of their preparations, the SOG deputies fortified the BIA building. Windows were reinforced, tear gas was placed strategically throughout the building, and sandbag emplacements were built on the roof. By late February, Kash and Grider were satisfied that the building could not be stormed successfully. While they waited for AIM to move, they stepped up the training of the BIA police.[32]

Colburn toured the reservation on February 25. He was most concerned about the drain on the limited manpower of the Marshals Service and needed to return the deputies to their districts. He determined that the BIA building was well protected and that the police training was moving forward smoothly. On February 25 he ordered more than half of the SOG team home; the next day, only forty-seven deputies remained at the reservation.[33]

AIM members continued to demonstrate and cause sporadic small incidents. Occasionally, Indians were arrested carrying weapons or explosives, which served as constant reminders of the danger. But the arrests were infrequent enough, the quantities of armament insignificant enough, to cause some frustration among the marshals that nothing was going to happen. The intelligence reports, too, were mixed, largely because AIM leaders themselves had no idea what they wanted to do. They talked about taking the BIA building, about attacking the Sioux tribal leadership, about moving on to someplace else, but nothing much was ever done.

Kash returned home on February 28. As usual that evening, Grider and Hall went to dinner, then returned to their motel. A caravan of two hundred AIM members returned from one of their daily meetings. The cars drove past the Pine Ridge BIA building and turned onto the road leading to the small historic hamlet of Wounded Knee, which consisted of a handful of houses for the dozen residents, a trading post, and a white-steepled Catholic church on top of a hill. In December 1890, Wounded Knee had been the scene of the last Indian massacre by the U.S. Army. The church had housed the wounded, dying Indians.

With little forethought, AIM seized Wounded Knee, taking the residents hostage. Hall, Grider, and the remaining SOG deputies rushed back to the reservation. Later that night the FBI and the BIA police set up roadblocks along the four roads into Wounded Knee. Unconvinced that Wounded Knee was the true focus of the demonstration, the marshals maintained their vigil at the BIA building. "At this time no one knew whether the people in Wounded Knee were going to stay there," the *Innocent Victims* decision stated. "The law enforcement people did not think that they would; they thought that the AIM people might go into the BIA building after leaving Wounded Knee."[34]

As soon as Kash's plane landed in Washington, he turned right around and boarded a flight back west. Colburn reactivated SOG, dispatching more than a hundred deputies to South Dakota. When the occupiers made no move to leave Wounded Knee, the marshals deserted the BIA building to set up a siege around the hamlet. By March 1, Wounded Knee was surrounded by marshals and FBI agents. Although the ravines and crevasses of the terrain prohibited completely sealing the hamlet, the marshals and FBI maintained a fairly tight vigil. Both sides dug in to escape the Dakota cold. Within a few days, elaborate bunkers and trenches stretched along the hills surrounding Wounded Knee.[35]

Officials from the Justice Department opened negotiations with AIM leaders. Russell Means released a set of demands, mostly calling for Senate investigations of the treatment of Indians and the operation of the Bureau of Indian Affairs. The negotiations dragged on endlessly. Every morning, Justice Department officials drove past the FBI's roadblock number 1 to commence the day's discussions. Late in the afternoon they returned with little accomplished. Many of the deputies suspected that the officials were arriving with a full tank of gas but leaving with a nearly empty tank. The Indians had no trouble heating their bunkers and cooking their food.[36]

Frequently, firefights erupted between the marshals and the Indians. Almost every night, thousands of rounds were fired. For the Indians, it made good television news footage, and it gave the deputies something to do during their twelve-hour shifts. Because they were firing at each other at considerable distances, few people on either side were injured. Two Indians were killed; U.S. Marshal Lloyd H. Grimm was permanently paralyzed when a bullet severed his spine.

From the beginning, Attorney General Kleindienst insisted on a peaceful settlement. The marshals were expressly prohibited from storming the hamlet. The government's objectives, as described by the *Innocent Victims* decision, were "to contain the situation as closely as possible, be sure that nothing was done to unnecessarily jeopardize the lives of individuals at Wounded Knee, and be sure that the individuals involved in the occupation were prosecuted" and "that caution should be used so as not to unnecessarily provoke bloodshed." Trapped by the growing Watergate scandal, the Nixon administration wanted nothing controversial to happen.[37]

The marshals chafed. Most of the deputies thought that they could easily move in and retake Wounded Knee. After a week or so, Colburn even arranged to borrow some armored personnel carriers from the army. Thus equipped, the marshals felt confident that they could end the occupation in short order. But neither the White House nor the Justice Department would permit it.

The negotiations dragged on into the spring. Finally, on May 7, after several false starts, an agreement was reached. The next day, the marshals took back Wounded Knee. The occupiers were arrested and hauled away in buses. As part of the settlement, the marshals used bulldozers to cover over the bunkers and trenches. After seventy-one days, the Indian uprising was over.

Its principal effect was negative for both sides. The Indians achieved little but publicity for their demands. No reforms or significant changes in their treatment resulted. AIM itself faded away. Means, Banks, and the other leaders found themselves without a following, treated more as pests than saviors.

For the Marshals Service the occupation of Wounded Knee proved its ability to respond effectively as an organization. The marshals had professionally maintained their discipline, performed the tasks assigned them, and established reasonable procedures for relieving the men, rotating the stations, and controlling the situation. Two days after the occupation ended, Attorney General Kleindienst awarded Colburn with bureau status.

For many of the marshals who served there, Wounded Knee became the high point of their careers. For some, it was their first time in combat under fire. They had proved themselves. An unofficial "Wounded Knee club" mentality developed among the veterans. Those who were not at Wounded Knee could never quite belong; they would never understand. To a considerable extent, Wounded Knee divided the deputies into the veterans and the nonparticipants. An antipathy toward SOG and its elitism developed among those who would later call themselves the PODs, the plain old deputies. Within such a small, closely knit organization, the divisiveness was disruptive.

SOG spent the rest of the 1970s readying itself for more battles with Indians. Training focused on rural fights, on besieging isolated outposts that had been captured by hostiles. Wounded Knee confirmed Colburn's emphasis on the paramilitary. SOG became something just short of a small army, with members learning to parachute from airplanes, rappel from helicopters, and crawl silently through the tallgrass of the prairies. For many years, SOG remained confident that its nemesis would take the warpath again. No one seemed troubled that its skills were never used in action.

THE TOILS OF ANONYMITY, 1974–1983

After Wounded Knee, Colburn focused again on enhancing the professionalization of the marshals and increasing the authority of the headquarters over the districts. Training became more sophisticated. Deputies were sent to the Federal Law Enforcement Training Center for a twelve-week police school, followed by a one-week course on the duties of marshals. Although the police course was not strictly related to the responsibilities of the Marshals Service, it served as better preparation than the two-week sessions popular during the sixties.

In addition Colburn introduced government cars to the districts. Over a period of years each district acquired a fleet of cars and vans to use for official business. Oddly, many of the deputies resented the new acquisitions. Government cars robbed them of the 10 to 12 cents a mile they earned driving their own cars on duty.

Soon after the cars came radios, better weapons, and better office equipment. Teletypes were installed in each district office providing communications with other districts and with headquarters. Training of the accounting clerks and administrative personnel routinized procedures across district lines. An office of internal investigations tried to ensure that the routines were followed properly.

Yet, for all the standardization imposed by headquarters, the rapid growth in personnel and duties introduced a number of divisive issues within the Marshals Service. In the early 1970s Colburn brought in hundreds of new deputies. In the rush to recruit, the service paid scant regard to the suitability of the candidates. The careers of those deputies were noticeable for their personnel and discipline problems. The witness protection program had problems stemming from inexperience and rapid growth. It was not until the late 1970s, a decade after the program was assigned the Marshals Service, that the marshals felt comfortable with the logistic and security requirements of keeping former criminals alive.

A union of deputy marshals thrived during the 1970s, forcing management to negotiate delicate issues of overtime and duties and bringing to the fore some morale problems. During his last years in office, Colburn was plagued by a tenacious lawsuit charging the service with racial discrimination. Exonerating himself became Colburn's obsession, though the suit hung on long after his retirement in 1976.

The problems and divisions reflected a new aspect of the marshals. Their previous independence had largely insulated them from these types of problems that are typical of large organizations. The more cohesive and consolidated the service became, the more likely it was to squabble within itself. Deputies from different districts began talking to each other, sharing their gripes, emboldening themselves to do something about it. Unions, lawsuits, and personnel problems were the natural outgrowth.

In May 1976, Colburn retired to California. He had wrought a revolution from within the Marshals Service, but not without a cost. Colburn's style was to compel the issue, not build a consensus. A gruff, forceful man, he led by the strength of his personality, not by diplomacy. In a sad commentary, the Marshals Service's obituary for him, published after his death in June 1983, described him as "a fine man and a good man, and often a misunderstood man."[38]

William E. Hall succeeded Colburn as director in May 1976. Hall had entered the Marshals Service in 1969 as Turner's general counsel. Under Colburn, Hall had become assistant director for operations in 1971, then deputy director in 1973. No one understood the Marshals Service better than Hall; no one had enjoyed his vantage point in witnessing the dramatic changes in operations and organization during the seventies. When he became director, the Marshals Service stood poised and ready to continue the progress Colburn had induced.

Instead Hall chose, with a few notable exceptions, to consolidate Colburn's gains, not exploit them. A quiet, unassuming man, Hall shied from publicity, controversy, and attention. His management style was to build consensus, moving forward slowly and cautiously. When he discovered, to his chagrin, that his three assistant directors despised each other to the point that they could not sit in the same room together without fighting, Hall simply quit holding staff meetings. Hall frequently told his subordinates he wanted "to toil in anonymity."

In many ways Hall fit perfectly with the marshals in 1976. After the trauma of the sixties and the drama of the seventies, the marshals needed a breather. The organization that Hall inherited was racked by contention and dissent. Deputies were alienated from management; marshals were alienated from headquarters. The men needed time to adapt themselves to the modern Marshals Service.

Many marshals continued to have trouble with the adjustments. At a national conference held in Reston, Virginia, Hall spoke at length about the plans and directions he foresaw for the service. At the end of his remarks, a U.S. marshal stood up, held out his shiny gold badge, and boldly announced that the president of the United States had given him the badge and that he was not obliged to do what Hall said. Many of the other marshals silently agreed.

In confronting the dissension among the marshals, Hall chose to co-opt them by appointing one of their own as his deputy director. The choice was a masterstroke. In John J. Twomey, who had been the U.S. marshal in Chicago, Hall found someone who could pacify the other marshals even as he compelled them to accept headquarters' supervision. Throughout the country, the marshals rightfully believed that they had a friend highly placed in headquarters. With Twomey, the bitter pills of centralization and control would go down easier.

Hall had little time to promote new policies or reforms, even if he had been of a mind to. From the beginning, he frequently found himself on the defensive, trying to protect the Colburn advances. One of Colburn's last reforms, for example, was the establishment of a regional management structure. Five regional directors were placed throughout the country with direct control over the marshals in their region. The intent was to streamline the management of the service by providing easier, more focused attention on the districts within each region. Hall himself sought appointment as regional director in Atlanta, but Colburn's retirement interrupted his plans.

The Carter administration, which took office in January 1977, disliked the regionalization of the marshals. With the stroke of a pen, despite Hall's quiet objections, Attorney General Griffin Bell dismantled the regions.

Hall fared better when the Office of Personnel Management proposed downgrading the pay scale of deputies. In addition, when the Federal Law Enforcement Training Center moved to Glynn County, Georgia, Hall and his head of training, Gary Mead, took the opportunity to revamp the training system. Mead arranged an eight-week course in criminal investigation for the deputies, followed by an intensive three-week session devoted exclusively to the responsibilities of marshals. Subsequently, Hall and Mead added new courses on protective services, court security, and advanced deputy training.[39]

Hall's greatest accomplishment was an innovative exception to his normal style. In 1979 he allowed Deputy Director Twomey and the chief of witness security, Howard Safir, to swipe from the FBI the jurisdiction over federal fugitives. The FBI's limited resources and lack of attention had allowed the fugitive problem to multiply until, by 1979, an estimated 15,000 federal fugitives were loose on the streets.

Twomey first conceived the idea of the marshals' taking jurisdiction over federal fugitives. As the former warden of Joliet state penitentiary, he naturally focused on those who somehow escaped the judicial system.

When he became Hall's deputy, he promoted his idea, and Safir quickly developed the tactics to achieve it.

In a memorandum of understanding, approved by Deputy Attorney General Benjamin R. Civiletti on July 23, 1979, the separate jurisdictions between the marshals and the FBI were spelled out. The marshals took up the pursuit of escaped federal prisoners, bond defaulters, and federal probation, parole, and mandatory-release violators. The FBI retained jurisdiction over arrest warrants that its own investigations generated and over violators of the statutes concerning unlawful flight to avoid prosecution. The FBI kept the glamorous crimes and the high-profile criminals. From its point of view, it was merely giving the marshals jurisdiction over "lower priority matters in order to concentrate its resources on more complex investigations."[40]

The fugitive treaty with the FBI offered the marshals the avenue to escape their complete dependence on the courts and to prove their professionalism as law enforcement officers. Now they could mount investigations, pursue the fugitives, and make the arrests.

Under Safir's innovative leadership, the marshals cleared 9,500 of the 15,000 fugitive warrants during the first year of the program, a startling achievement. Typically, the marshals had more problems with the bureaucracy of fugitive investigations than with the actual pursuit. "The major obstacle," the service announced in October 1980, "was not the task of locating and arresting fugitives, as some outsiders perceived, but rather the new responsibility of preparing investigative reports and assisting the prosecutor during the pretrial investigations and the litigative process itself."[41]

The marshals did so much better at the fugitive program than the FBI because it was a much higher priority for them. Thus, they devoted more resources, more creative thinking, more effort, than the FBI had been able to afford. In late 1981 Hall and Safir launched the first Fugitive Investigation Strike Team (FIST) in Miami. Over a five-week period of investigations, the marshals nabbed 73 federal fugitives and 3 state fugitives. By the eighth FIST operation, completed in 1985, a total of 11,516 fugitives had been arrested.[42]

The theory of the FIST operations was cooperative, concentrated teamwork with state and local police officers devoted exclusively to the capture of the most important, dangerous, or deadly fugitives loose in a particular area. Most of the arrests resulted from old-fashioned, street-pounding police work, but the marshals spiced up the FIST operations by adding scams. In one, announcements were sent to the last known address of hundreds of fugitives informing them they had won tickets to a concert by Boy George, a transvestite singer generally despised by most police officers. Other scams involved free trips to the Bahamas, delivery of packages worth more than $100, and free tickets to a Washington Redskins football game. Each showed an underlying sense of humor for which cops are seldom suspected.[43]

The true test of the marshals' fugitive program came not with the large number of fugitives captured but with the arrest of one man who had escaped from the federal penitentiary in Lompoc, California. His name was Christopher Boyce, though some called him the Falcon, after his hobby. He had been convicted of selling top-secret defense information to the Russians. His escape caught the public's attention; his capture tested the marshals' ability to catch fugitives.

Howard Safir, the assistant director for operations, hounded his investigators to get Boyce. He recognized that only by capturing a high-profile fugitive like Boyce could the marshals guarantee their jurisdiction over all federal fugitives. A tough cop himself, Safir opened his daily staff meetings with the question, "Where is Christopher Boyce?" For a year his investigators cringed to answer him: No one knew.

They searched everywhere, following leads to South America, the Middle East, and Europe. Their greatest fear was that Boyce would make it to the Soviet Union and be protected there as a political prisoner. The deputies brought in psychologists and psychoanalysts to study Boyce's personality and predict where he might be. The districts were constantly reminded to keep alert for any evidence of Boyce's presence in their area. A task force devoted exclusively to Boyce's capture was established.

Still, Boyce eluded their efforts. For much of the time, he lived like a hermit in the mountains of Idaho. Every month or so he would come down to isolated towns to obtain supplies. Boyce's reclusion made him almost impossible to detect. He had disappeared, leaving no leads, no witnesses, no evidence. For as long as he lived that way, no police could catch him. But Boyce eventually returned to civilization, supporting himself by robbing banks.

After that, it was only a question of time. An informant alerted one of the deputies that he knew Boyce and knew where Boyce lived. The marshals managed to verify part of the informant's story, which gave them enough confidence in the man to follow his other leads. The trail led to a house in Beaver, Washington, and a boat dock down the road in La Push. Several days' surveillance of both places convinced Chief Deputy Robert Christman that Boyce was no longer at either one. Fortuitously, some of the deputies on the stakeout in Beaver chanced to overhear a conversation with two of the town's residents, who indicated that Boyce had gone to Port Angeles.

Buttressed by the headquarters' task force led by Thomas Kupferer and a team of FBI agents who wanted Boyce for bank robberies, the marshals raced to Port Angeles. They began checking Boyce's usual haunts, the sleazy motels and hamburger stands he liked. Early on the evening of August 21, 1981, the deputies spied Boyce sitting in his car at the Port Angeles Pit Stop. He had ordered a hamburger.

One car, driven by a deputy with a female FBI agent riding shotgun, pulled in next to Boyce's to verify his identity. At their signal, Kupferer, wearing his pistol in an ankle holster, walked past the front of Boyce's car. He paused just to the left, kneeling to tie his shoe. While Boyce watched him, the marshal car backed up, then pulled up to block Boyce into his parking space. Deputies Robert Dighera and Dave Neff, backed by deputies Dennis Behrend and Jack Cluff, came up behind Boyce.

With his gun in Boyce's ear, Neff barked out, "Drop the hamburger."

"Who are you guys?" Boyce asked.[44]

The next day, William Dempsey, the marshals' public information officer, called a press conference to announce Boyce's capture. Moments before the scheduled briefing, Dempsey saw Hall slip quietly out of the building. Safir and Deputy Director John Twomey were left to make the proud announcement.[45]

EPILOGUE

THE BICENTENNIAL IMPERATIVE

1983–1989

Late one October evening, 1988, we gathered in the director's office. Stephen Boyle and Ken Fulp of Congressional and Public Affairs brought wine. Jeff Miller, the special counsel to the director, chipped in with cheese and crackers. Deputy Director John Twomey crossed over from his office; Howard Safir and Gary Mead, now the associate directors for operations and administration, also came. Jack McCrory, the director's special assistant, and Claudia Peacock, the director's executive assistant, joined the celebration. Together we raised our glasses in a congratulatory toast to Director Stanley E. Morris.

Five years earlier, in October 1983, Morris had taken over from Hall. A fifteen-year veteran government manager, Morris had worked in the Office of Management and Budget and the Department of Health and Human Services before joining the Department of Justice as associate deputy attorney general. In the latter post, Morris had helped manage the department's sprawling bureaucracy. He had also been responsible for shepherding the Reagan administration's judicial appointments, including its nominees for U.S. marshal and attorney, through the White House and Congress. Morris understood how the government, especially the Department of Justice, worked. He used that knowledge to the advantage of the U.S. marshals.

That October evening, we toasted his accomplishments. In five years Morris established two major new programs, the National Asset Seizure and Forfeiture (NASAF) program and the Court Security Officers program. Through NASAF the marshals managed assets—cash, properties, and businesses—that had been seized from drug dealers and that the government could prove were obtained as a result of illegal drug activities. The marshals disposed of the assets, usually by selling them or inducting them into government service. Within four years, more than $1 billion in assets had been seized. They ranged from millions of dollars in cash to recording studios, bauxite mines, horse ranches, and factories.

The court security program represented an expansion of the centuries-old duty of the marshals to protect the courts. Under an agreement with the Administrative Office of the U.S. Courts, the marshals managed the hired guards and electronic security posted throughout each federal courthouse. Court security officers manned the magnetometers and X-ray machines guarding the entrances. Alarms and television cameras were set up throughout the court buildings. The electronics fed back to monitors in the marshals' offices. The program cost millions of dollars annually and required the marshals to supervise the work of hundreds of hired guards.

Under Morris, relations with the courts steadily improved. Despite a brief tiff with some judges over using deputies as bailiffs—a position from which Morris retreated—the federal judges came to accept the marshals and began turning to the Marshals Service for advice on security. At Morris's instigation, each district created court security committees to address local problems. The various judicial conferences also established security committees at the circuit and national level. After two hundred years the judges finally recognized the marshals as professionals.

Morris also modernized prisoner transportation by acquiring two Boeing 727 jets. A network of buses, vans, and smaller planes fed the jetliners with prisoners at scheduled stops in thirty-two cities every week. The prisoners were moved from local jails to serve their terms in federal penitentiaries or were taken to court for new trials. The planes moved more than eighty thousand prisoners a year.

During that five years the service managed three large-scale FIST operations and a number of smaller ones. Under a new memorandum of understanding negotiated in 1988 with the FBI, the marshals shifted their energy to clearing warrants against narcotics traffickers. In 1987

Morris and Safir launched a Warrant Apprehension Narcotics Team (WANT) operation that netted 210 fugitive drug felons. A second WANT operation, planned for late 1988, would apprehend 249 more.

To handle the growing workload, Morris obtained congressional approval to increase the number of deputy marshals by a third. When no one in the Department of Justice objected, he raised the average salaries of deputies by changing the service's pay structure. Hiring practices were improved to attract the best-quality candidates. For Morris, the Marshals Service was its people. Much of his energy was spent improving the work environment, the morale, and the training of his people.

Morris insisted on an improved quality of nominee for U.S. marshal. He negotiated with the senators to ensure that their nominees were qualified. At any one time, as many as eighty of the ninety-three marshals he supervised had law enforcement experience. Many were former deputies. Morris also moved quickly to dismiss errant marshals, getting the president to fire those who refused to follow his lead. After the first few dismissals, the problems with the U.S. marshals decreased remarkably.

As part of his emphasis on enhanced professionalism, Morris stressed physical fitness among the lawmen. He made participation in the service's Fitness in Total (FIT) exercise program a requisite for evaluations and promotions. One winter morning Morris, a faithful jogger, ran from downtown Manhattan to the district office in Brooklyn to prove to the deputies that if he had time to exercise, they could make the time too.

The equipment in each district—its radios, weapons, and office machinery—was improved and modernized. Local offices, many of which dated back fifty years, were renovated to improve the work environment and enhance office security. The service even hired a full-time architect to supervise its myriad construction projects.

During those five years, Morris streamlined the organizational lines between headquarters and the field. He established an advisory committee of U.S. marshals for himself and Twomey, and an advisory committee of chief deputies for Safir and Mead. He enhanced communications with the district offices through videotapes, memoranda, newsletters, and an award-winning magazine. Conferences, meetings, and ceremonies were moved from headquarters to the districts. Morris himself was constantly in the field. Within four years, he had visited each of the ninety-three districts.

In August 1988, Morris moved headquarters from its second-story offices in a Tysons Corner, Virginia, shopping mall to the top five floors of a new building across from the Pentagon. From his corner office, we could see Rosslyn, Virginia, and the new Russian embassy to the left all the way past the White House, the monuments, and the Capitol dome to National Airport on the right. The complex had a modern, secure communication center; space and equipment for various task forces; and plenty of room. Unlike the shopping mall, it felt like a professional place to do business.

Morris gave the marshals back their history. Working with the Smithsonian Institution, he sponsored a thirty-five-hundred-square-foot traveling museum exhibit commemorating the bicentennial of the marshals. The exhibit, which was booked in thirteen cities on its two-and-a-half-year tour, displayed more than three hundred artifacts, ranging from a seven-hundred-pound marble statue of an 1890s deputy marshal to Wyatt Earp's hand-drawn maps of his four gunfights. To help celebrate the bicentennial, Morris chartered the independent, nonprofit U.S. Marshals Foundation and invited two former attorneys general, two governors, two cowboy actors, one federal judge, and several millionaires to serve on its board of directors.

That October evening, we toasted the director for a more immediate success. The week before, Congress passed three major pieces of legislation to cap his achievements. The potent new drug bill allocated extra resources and manpower to the service. Congress also resolved that September 24, 1989, would be U.S. Marshals Day. The third bill, though, had occupied most of Morris's attention. It was the most important piece of legislation for the marshals since the Judiciary Act of 1789.

Buried deep within the drug bill was the Marshals Service Act of 1988, establishing the service as a bureau by statute rather than by attorney general fiat. The pursuit of fugitives and the protection of the courts and its participants were defined as duties for the marshals by law rather than by tradition or departmental assignment. Several efficiencies in the service of process and the employment of guards were also provided. The interim appointment of marshals was taken from district judges and assigned to the attorney general, which meant the director. Finally, the office of director was made a presidential appointment, putting it on a par with the U.S. marshals whom the director supervised.

Looking out over Washington that October evening, we seemed

poised on the edge. Safir spoke of new plans to go after fugitives, the opportunities posed by the enhanced authority to protect the courts, and ways to improve NASAF. Boyle talked optimistically of the chances for new legislation during the next session of Congress. Mead, too, seemed caught up in the moment, while Twomey's great good humor made all things seem possible that night. Each of us spoke earnestly, optimistically, as though the future stretched to infinity, beyond the upcoming November presidential election.

But Morris was the spark. The man exuded energy, an infectious vibrancy. He was a man in motion. Even when he sat, his hands were a study of movement. He continually shifted position or paced, chewed his nails or rubbed his head, as though by moving he could make things happen faster. Indeed, he did. His very presence quickened the pace.

That October evening, Morris spoke urgently of the changes wrought by the new legislation. With bureau status and a future presidential commission, he believed he was ready to tackle the marshals' presidential appointments. He wanted to look more closely at headquarters' organization because headquarters had not yet adjusted to the changes in the field. Morris intended to complete district automation, expand the pursuit of drug fugitives, and transfer the employment of court security guards from private contract corporations to the Marshals Service.

That October evening, frozen now in time and memory, seemed the pinnacle. Within a year the president would appoint Morris to another position. A new director would take over the Marshals Service.

Morris had transformed the agency. It was stronger now, more salient, better trained, and more professional than at any time in its history. Its duties were broader; it was better prepared, better equipped, and better managed to carry them out. Its relations with the judiciary, the department, and other lawmen were stronger than ever. Above all, the service approached its diverse duties with more confidence.

Morris had seen 1989 as an opportunity to define a bicentennial imperative for the marshals. The definition drove the organization forward, even as it used the marshals' history to carve out a distinct niche, enhance esprit de corps, and identify the inherent strengths of the service. Morris understood that the history of the marshals proved beyond doubt that innovation and flexibility were the essence of the U.S. marshals and their deputies. He used the bicentennial imperative to underscore those fundamental strengths.

Problems, Morris also understood, yet remained. The headquarters revolution had gone beyond imposing a centralized organization on the field. The marshals in the field groaned that headquarters–the Land of Oz, they called it–had no idea what was happening in the districts. Headquarters personnel put forth the opposite complaint, that the field was unsympathetic to the problems facing the service. In fact, they were both right. Until a way could be found to reconcile them, the service would become increasingly divided.

For five years Morris focused his attention and effort on programmatic changes and reforms in the field. With the exception of such new programs as NASAF, the headquarters organization and function was much the same as when William Hall left in 1983. At the same time, headquarters had become considerably more bureaucratized, and individual fiefdoms had developed. On occasion, but with disturbing frequency, the fiefdoms fell out of step with the broader objectives of the service.

The root of the problem lay in a basic indefiniteness about the function of headquarters. Was it operational or administrative? Did it control the field or support it? Directives issuing from headquarters were unclear on this issue. In the NASAF program, for example, the local U.S. marshal was legally responsible for seized property and assets, even though regional NASAF specialists, who reported directly to headquarters, managed those assets. Although much was still left to the discretion of the field, headquarters often demanded that the field do exactly–and sometimes only–what it was told.

The changes in the field, combined with the enhanced authorities of NASAF, court security, and the fugitive program, required a closer look at the way headquarters managed the service. The demands placed on the field sometimes seemed out of touch with its functions. An amazing array of collateral duties–tasks the deputies were to perform over and above their regular district assignments–was imposed, ranging from public affairs to threat analysis, from equal-employment-opportunity investigations to FIT coordinators. FIST and WANT operations, training exercises, assessment evaluations, and recruiting drives–headquarters operations all–competed with the normal operations of the districts.

Although much of this was an unavoidable result of the limited resources of the Marshals Service, much was not avoided. No central point at headquarters coordinated the directives issued to the field. As the marshals scrambled to respond to the incessant demands of the individual divisions, field operations inevitably suffered. Twomey, who had the impossible job of directly supervising the ninety-three U.S. marshals, frequently complained that within any single district, the U.S. marshal might be called out of town to attend a headquarters meeting on security standards, while the chief deputy was summoned to advise headquarters on merit promotions. Their deputies might be in training, on a FIST operation, or on a SOG mission. And headquarters was outraged when no one answered the phone.

Nor was the field free of problems. At the national conference in Philadelphia, convened by Morris in May 1987, Thomas Kupferer innocently announced the new headquarters policy that each district office should have a twenty-four-hour phone number published on the inside cover of public telephone books, right alongside the numbers for the local police and the FBI. Several marshals blindsided Kupferer with strenuous objections on a number of grounds, such as the added expense of answering services, local phone company rules, and so forth. It soon became clear, however, that their principal concern was that their weekends might be disturbed. Professionalism, those marshals were discovering, had its price.

There were other, higher prices. The Marshals Service was rapidly becoming more specialized. Given its traditional flexibility, specialization was not altogether beneficial. Increasingly, headquarters was reaching out across the districts to establish its own complex. The witness security, court security, enforcement, and NASAF headquarters divisions each created their own satellite organizations in the field that were responsive only to headquarters. The tendency, too, was to make promotions through the specialties, not the districts. The effect was not simply to encroach on the autonomy of the districts but to bypass the districts altogether.

The trend pointed toward the development of parallel organizations. Which would emerge supreme, the traditional districts or the new headquarters divisions? Some way was needed to integrate the two while retaining the benefits of each. Unless this merger could be effected, the parallel growth threatened to become destructively divergent.

The service remained too politicized. The presidential appointment of the U.S. marshals haunted the organization. It could never escape the taint of politics as long as its top district managers owed their appointments to political favors, not professional advancement. In the late 1980s a newly appointed U.S. marshal convened his staff to announce that he had paid $25,000 in political contributions to become the marshal. Therefore, he intended to enjoy the post and wanted no troubles from them.

However much the president and the Senate might unofficially emphasize professional criteria in proposing their nominations, until those standards were incorporated specifically into the selection, the marshals would suffer the burden of politics. The eighteenth-century need to appoint men who were prominent locally had been archaized by the twentieth-century need for professionalism.

Yet professionalism alone might not be enough. Appointment as U.S. marshal tended to cap a career, not continue one. It was a reward for previous services, not an opportunity to prove oneself in a new assignment. Marshal Romolo Imundi of southern New York (New York City) was an exemplary marshal, the first in a generation to earn reappointment to a second term. First appointed in 1982, Imundi nonetheless looked back to his forty years as a New York City policeman and homicide detective to confirm his self-worth. He defined himself as a New York City cop, not as a U.S. marshal. Although he managed one of the best-run districts, he accepted his marshal's commission as the capstone of a long, outstanding career. The deputies he managed saw their commissions as the opening of a career. The difference in viewpoint was profound.

The system strained the loyalties of the deputies. They were tugged between the demands of the local U.S. marshal and the demands of the service. The deputies dealt daily with their political supervisors, who controlled their work assignments and annual personnel evaluations, while they looked to headquarters for careers and promotions.

The deputies needed desperately to escape a debilitating inferiority complex that pervaded the service. During his six years in office, Morris was never able to overcome the service-wide impression that he was too good for the marshals and therefore would not remain long. Although a proud organization, deep within it lay the sense that the marshals had somehow peaked a century before when Wyatt Earp rode the range and Wild Bill Hickok held eights and aces. Too many people entered the service, took the deputy training, then left as soon as possible for better-paying jobs in other federal agencies or with state or local police.

Relations with the federal courts sometimes strained the service. In an early draft of the Marshals Service Act, Morris tried to take away the district judge's authority to demand a marshal in his courtroom at any time, for any reason. Instead, Morris proposed that the deputies go to court only if there was a legitimate security reason requiring a marshal. Pointing to numerous examples of deputies acting as simple bailiffs to the judges, Morris pleaded with Congress to allow the marshals the freedom to behave as professionals. The judges objected; Morris lost. The battle had put the local marshals squarely in the middle when both the district judges and headquarters turned to the local marshals to defend their point of view.

Times were changing, becoming more demanding on the already overstretched resources of the marshals. By 1989 the drug war consumed the Marshals Service. Well over 50 percent of its resources were expended on drug-related duties such as pursuing fugitives, securing the trials of dealers, protecting witnesses, seizing the ill-gotten gains of dealers, or transporting prisoners accused or convicted of drug crimes. The drug war clearly portended the greatest changes for American law enforcement. Not since the desegregation of the nation had the marshals been involved in such a profoundly crucial social phenomenon. Not since the moonshine wars and the settlement of the Indian Territory had they faced such danger.

A rash of high-security trials of drug lords, terrorists, and white supremacist groups required taking deputies from other hard-pressed districts to provide security at the trials. On several occasions, thirty or more deputies each were sent to such small district offices as Fort Smith, Arkansas; Reno, Nevada; and Hartford, Connecticut. The trials frequently lasted for months. Although the deputies were rotated, the overall drain on resources remained the same. The expense of housing and feeding the deputies was staggering, yet the threats to the courts could not be ignored.

Jail space was a chronic problem. Throughout the country, local jails filled up with local prisoners; federal inmates were turned away. Many marshals found themselves transporting prisoners over astounding distances because all the nearby jails were full. Deputies in San Francisco housed their prisoners in Los Angeles, a day's drive away. Washington, D.C., deputies drove four hours to take their prisoners to Petersburg, Virginia. Federal court orders prohibiting overcrowding in local jails frequently forced the issue. For the local jurisdictions the first step in obeying the court order was to boot out the federal prisoners.

Above all, the same schizophrenia that had plagued the marshals for two centuries remained. The deputies needed to be cops and accountants, as good with a gun as they were with a computer, a pencil, and a form. The job description for enforcement specialist demanded a trained investigator who could track down a fugitive felon. It also required someone who could investigate the local jails, filling out the proper forms to ensure that federal prisoners were maintained according to national standards. Deputies were trained to chase fugitives, protect witnesses, keep custody of prisoners, manage large businesses, and account for volumes of cash and assets. They spent more time in the classroom than on the shooting range and more time in the office than on the streets.

But the diverse talents combined into the great strengths of the Marshals Service: flexibility and innovation. That they did so much across such a wide range of duties prohibited the deputies from developing burdensome habits and rutted ways of doing things. Transporting prisoners and protecting witnesses made them better fugitive hunters, for it exposed them at close hand to the way criminals think and live. Managing assets and executing court orders involved them in a startling diversity that other police organizations usually shunned. No one would accuse the marshals, unlike the FBI, of developing a huge, monolithic organization.

For two hundred years the marshals had proved their ability to do their jobs regardless of the swirl of events around them. The strong tradition of innovation and creativity that developed could never be stifled by bureaucracy and professionalism.

As the marshals entered their bicentennial year, the imperative of that celebration, defined by Morris, was to continue moving forward, yet to glance back occasionally for reassurance. The long line of United States marshals and their deputies, stretching back to the presidency of George Washington and the birth of a nation, offered a heartening tradition of independence and flexibility. As the nation changed, so too had the marshals. As new problems evolved, so too would the marshals. In a nation of laws, they remained the lawmen.

NOTES

INTRODUCTION

1. *Augusta Chronicle and Gazette,* January 18, 1794; Robert Forsyth file, Office of the Historian, U.S. Marshals Service (hereinafter cited as Office of the Historian).

2. Gordon Kahl, press files, Office of Congressional and Public Affairs, U.S. Marshals Service.

3. U.S. Attorney A. J. Dallas to Secretary of State James Monroe, March 27, 1809, enclosing Marshal John Smith to Dallas, March 27, 1809; to secretary of state, April 17, April 18, May 1, and May 2, 1809, all in Miscellaneous Letters of the Secretary of State, Record Group 59, National Archives, Washington, D.C. (hereinafter cited as Misc. Letters). R. Smith to Dallas, March 31, 1809, Domestic Letters of the Secretary of State, RG 59 (hereinafter cited as Dom. Letters). Irving Brent, *James Madison: The President, 1809–1812* (Indianapolis: Bobbs-Merrill, 1956), 28–30. Henry J. Bourguignon, *The First Federal Court: The Federal Appellate Prize Court of the American Revolution, 1775–1787* (Philadelphia: American Philosophical Society, 1977), 101–34, 322–23.

4. Marshal Paul Strobach to Attorney General Benjamin Harris Brewster, May 3, 1884, Department of Justice, Source–Chronological Files (hereinafter cited as Source-Chron.): Ala., RG 60.

5. Marshal John M. McCalla to Attorney General Roger B. Taney, July 6,

1832, Attorney General Papers, Letters Received (hereinafter referred to as AG Letters Rec.): Ky., RG 60. The papers do not indicate the outcome of the controversy.

CHAPTER I

1. Frederick S. Calhoun, "The First Generation of U.S. Marshals: Part I," *Pentacle* (Summer 1985): 33–34.

2. Charles M. Andrews, *The Colonial Period of American History: England's Commercial and Colonial Policy* (New Haven, Conn.: Yale University Press, 1938), 226–27, 230–31; Bourguignon, *First Federal Court,* 29–35; Carl Ubbelohde, *The Vice-Admiralty Courts and the American Revolution* (Chapel Hill, N.C.: University of North Carolina Press, 1960), 203–9.

3. Bourguignon, *First Federal Court,* 41–77, 91–92, 116–21, 319–20, 328–43.

4. Dorothy S. Towle, ed., *American Legal Records,* vol. 3 (Washington, D.C.: American Historical Association, 1937), 17; Ubbelohde, *Vice-Admiralty Courts,* 10–11; John Franklin Jameson, ed., *Privateering and Piracy in the Colonial Period: Illustrative Documents*(New York: Macmillan, 1923), 279, 325, 345.

5. Charles Warren, "New Light on the History of the Federal Judiciary Act of 1789," *Harvard Law Review* 37 (November 1923): 53, 105, 109, 127–31; Edgar S. Maclay, ed., *Journal of William Maclay* (New York: D. Appleton and Co., 1890), 101.

6. Noble E. Cunningham, Jr., *The Process of Government under Jefferson* (Princeton, N.J.: Princeton University Press, 1978), 89, 97.

7. Secretary of State Timothy Pickering to Marshal David Randolph, February 11, 1797; to Attorney General Lee, March 7, 1797; to Marshal William Nichols, September 4, 1798, all in Pickering Papers, microfilm copy from Massachusetts Historical Society, Boston.

8. Secretary of State Edmund Randolph to Marshal David Lenox, July 21, 1794; E. Randolph to all marshals, January 3, 1795; Pickering to all marshals, March 25, 1797; Pickering to Jabez Fitch, March 16, 1799; Thomas Jefferson to all senators, January 9, 1809; Secretary of State John Quincy Adams to Marshal Tench Ringgold, November 25, 1820, all in Dom. Letters. Pickering to some marshals, March 1798; to all marshals, July 25, 1799; to Bradford, August 7, 1799, all in Pickering Papers. Marshal Samuel Bradford to Pickering, April 12, 1798; Marshal Aquilla Giles to Pickering, both in Misc. Letters.

9. Marshal James Prince to Commodore John Roberts, September 16, 1812, Misc. Letters; *In re Neagle,* 135 U.S. Reports 1.

10. "Act for the Enumeration of the Inhabitants of United States," *U.S. Congress,* 1790, 101–3; Carroll Wright, *History and Growth of the U.S. Census* (Washington, D.C.: GPO, 1900), 12–17.

11. Tobias Lear to some marshals, March 5, 1790, Papers of George Washington, Manuscript Division, Library of Congress, Washington, D.C. (hereinafter cited as Washington Papers). Lear to all marshals, March 5, 1790; Marshal Isaac Huger to George Washington, February 5, 1792, both in Misc. Letters. *Heads of Families at the First Census of the United States Taken in the Year 1790* (Baltimore: Genealogical Publishing, 1966).

12. Wright, *History and Growth of the U.S. Census,* 16–17.

13. Postmaster General Timothy Pickering to Secretary of State Thomas Jefferson, December 26, 1793, Misc. Letters.

14. Marshal Thomas Rutter to Acting Secretary of State Robert Smith, February 22, 1811; Smith to Marshal Andrew Moore, February 27, 1811; Monroe to Moore, June 1, 1811, all in Dom. Letters. Moore to secretary of state, May 22, 1811, Misc. Letters. Wright, *History and Growth of the U.S. Census,* 20–27.

15. Auditor's Office to Huger, warrant 5324, April 9, 1794, General Accounting Office, Miscellaneous Treasury Accounts of GAO, RG 217 (hereinafter cited as Misc. Treas. Accounts).

16. Secretary of the Treasury Alexander Hamilton to Marshal Phillip Bradley, May 31, 1793, Phillip Bradley Papers, Society of the Cininnatus, Washington, D.C. (hereinafter cited as Bradley Papers); secretary of the Treasury to collectors, January 23, 1797, General Records of Treasury Department, Circular Letters Sent (entry 47), set T, no. 0, RG 56 (hereinafter cited as Treas. Circ. Letters).

17. Secretary of the Treasury to collectors; to marshals, both January 23, 1797, Treas. Circ. Letters.

18. Marshal Robert Forsyth, warrant 1415, July 11, 1791; D. Randolph, warrant 2693, July 13, 1792, both in Misc. Treas. Accounts.

19. Marshal Thomas Lowry, warrant 1298, May 20, 1791; Marshal Nathaniel Ramsay, warrant 14317, July 30, 1791, both in Misc. Treas. Accounts.

20. Marshal John Skinner, warrant 1241, March 2, 1791; Lowry, warrant 1298, both in Misc. Treas. Accounts.

21. Hamilton to Bradley, July 2, 1793, Bradley Papers.

22. Washington to Benjamin Lincoln, August 14, 1791, in John C. Fitzpatrick, *Writings of George Washington* (Washington, D.C.: GPO, 1939), 336; Hamilton to Washington, January 14, 1795, in H. C. Syrrett, ed., *Papers of Alexander Hamilton,* vol. 18 (New York: Columbia University Press, 1972), 42.

23. Hugh Williamson to Washington, March 22, 1790, Washington Papers; Giles to President John Adams, April 17, 1797, Letters of Application and Recommendation during the Administration of John Adams, RG 59.

24. Deputy John C. Barrett to Marshal Joseph Scott, June 13, 1801, and November 17, 1802, both in Brock Collection–Joseph Scott Papers, Huntington Library, San Marino, Calif.

25. Judge Henry Innes to Secretary of State James Madison, January 18, 1802, Misc. Letters; Mary K. Bonsteel Tachau, *Federal Courts in the Early Republic: Kentucky, 1789–1816,* (Princeton, N.J.: Princeton University Press, 1978), 45.

26. Bill conveyed by Attorney General Edmund Randolph to Congress, 1790, in *American State Papers: Documents, Legislative and Executive, of the Congress of the United States,* vol. 1 (Washington, D.C.: Gales and Seaton, 1834), 35.

CHAPTER 2

1. District attorney of Massachusetts to Lear, August 24, 1793; deposition of Bradford and Samuel Brooks, August 1793, both in Misc. Letters.

2. Deposition of Bradford.

3. Hamilton to Washington, August 5, 1794, in Syrrett, *Papers of Hamilton,* vol. 16, 32–33; Leland D. Baldwin, *Whiskey Rebels: The Story of a Frontier Uprising* (Pittsburgh: University of Pittsburgh Press, 1939), 82–83. See also Thomas P. Slaughter, *The Whiskey Rebellion: Frontier Epilogue to the American Revolution* (New York: Oxford University Press, 1986).

4. Thomas Marshall to Tench Coxe, May 24, 1794; Coxe to John Neville, July 26, 1794, both in Records of the Internal Revenue Service, Whiskey Rebellion, 1792–96, RG 58. Lenox to Hamilton, September 8, 1794, in Syrrett, *Papers of Hamilton,* vol. 17, 203. Baldwin, *Whiskey Rebels,* 110–11.

5. Lenox to Hamilton, 206–7; Hugh H. Brackenridge, *Incidents of the Insurrection,* ed. Daniel Marder, vol. 1 (New Haven, Conn.: College and University Press, 1972), 23–24.

6. Lenox to Hamilton, 203–4; Baldwin, *Whiskey Rebels,* 113–14.

7. Lenox to Hamilton, 204–5; Baldwin, *Whiskey Rebels,* 116–17.

8. Lenox to Hamilton, 204–8; Baldwin, *Whiskey Rebels,* 117–20.

9. Lenox to Hamilton, 205.

10. Ibid.; Baldwin, *Whiskey Rebels,* 123.

11. Lenox to Hamilton, 205.

12. Ibid., 205–6.

13. Ibid., 207–9.

14. Ibid., 208; Attorney General William Bradford to Hamilton, August 23, 1794, Pennsylvania Whiskey Rebellion Collection, Manuscript Division, Library of Congress (hereinafter cited as Pa. Whiskey Rebellion Coll.).

15. E. Randolph to Washington, August 5, 1794, Washington Papers; August 2, 1794, in Syrrett, *Papers of Hamilton,* vol. 17, 10 n. 9.

16. Justice James Wilson to Washington, August 4, 1794, Pa. Whiskey Rebellion Coll.; August 5, 1794, in Syrrett, *Papers of Hamilton,* vol. 17, 24 n. 4.

17. Hamilton to Washington, September 19, 1794, Washington Papers, ser. 2; E. Randolph to U.S. Attorney William Rawle, October 3 and 8, 1794, both in Dom. Letters; Baldwin, *Whiskey Rebels,* 188–219, 241.

18. Hamilton to Washington, November 15 and 19, 1794, both in Papers of Alexander Hamilton, Manuscript Division, Library of Congress; Baldwin, *Whiskey Rebels,* 241–58, 263–64.

19. Petition for pardons, March 3, 1794; Lenox to Washington, June 3, 1796, both in Petitions for Pardon – George Washington's File, RG 59.

20. Tachau, *Federal Courts,* 64–65.

21. For information on the Fries Rebellion, see William W. H. Davis, *The Fries Rebellion, 1798–99* (New York: Arno Press and New York Times, 1969). Nichols to Pickering, March 11, 1799, Pennsylvania House Tax Collection, Manuscript Division, Library of Congress, is the marshal's report on the insurrection. Other documents in the Pennsylvania House Tax Collection flesh out the incident.

22. Rawle to Pickering, July 24 and September 19, 1799; District Attorney Richard Harrison to Pickering, August 17, 1799, all in Misc. Letters. James M. Smith, *Freedom's Fetters: The Alien and Sedition Laws and American Civil Liberties* (Ithaca, N.Y.: Cornell University Press, 1956), 398–417.

23. Smith, *Freedom's Fetters,* 270–71.

24. Ibid., 221, 223, 225.

25. Ibid., 223.

26. Ibid., 227–31.

27. Ibid., 231–35.

28. Warrant 5073, February 18, 1794, Misc. Treas. Accounts; Pickering to Fitch, June 29, 1798, Pickering Papers.

29. Smith, *Freedom's Fetters,* 238–41.

30. Ibid., 242–44.

31. Ibid., 244.

32. Carl R. Fish, *Removal of Officials by the Presidents of the United States: Annual Report of the American Historical Association for the Year 1899* (Washington, D.C.: GPO, 1900), 70–71.

33. Smith, *Freedom's Fetters*, 423; Elizabeth Lawson, *The Reign of Witches: The Struggle against the Alien and Sedition Laws* (New York: Civil Rights Congress, 1952), 49.

34. Cunningham, *Process of Government*, 166, 175, 182.

35. Max Farrand, "The Judiciary Act of 1801," *American Historical Review* 5 (1899–1900): 684–85.

36. Petition to Congress by Robert Robinson, in Clarence E. Carter, ed., *Territorial Papers of the United States: Northwest Territorial Papers, 1787–1803,* vol. 16 (Washington, D.C.: GPO, 1934–75), 93–94.

37. Circular to all marshals (two circulars); Madison to all marshals (except N.J., Ohio, Ky., and Tenn.), all May 29, 1805, Dom. Letters.

38. Marshal John Willard to secretary of state, August 14, 1807, Misc. Letters; secretary of state to Willard, April 19, 1808, Dom. Letters.

39. Monroe to Attorney General William Wirt, June 22, 1814; to J. Smith, June 30, 1814, both in Dom. Letters. Marshal John Eppinger to Monroe, January 23, 1815, Misc. Letters. Deputy Daniel Moore to Richard Rush, July 28, 1817; Moore to Wirt, January 5, 1818; C. I. Ingersoll to Wirt, January 13, 1818; Ames Ellmahler to Wirt, January 19, 1818; Wirt to Secretary of State Adams, January 27 and March 19, 1818, all in Papers of the Attorney General, Letterbook A1, RG 60 (hereinafter cited as AG Letterbook A1).

40. Prince to Monroe, January 29, 1813, Misc. Letters.

41. Prince to secretary of state, February 12, 1819, Misc. Letters.

42. Fifth Auditor Stephen Pleasanton to Acting Secretary of State Richard Rush, June 30, 1817; Assistant Secretary of State Rush to Pleasanton, July 2, 1817; Pleasanton to secretary of state, January 3 and 30, 1818, all in Misc. Letters.

43. Marshal Morton A. Waring to secretary of state, August 4, 1813, War of 1812 Papers, RG 59 (hereinafter cited as War of 1812 Papers); *Lockington v. Smith,* Federal Cases, no. 8448.

44. District Attorney Charles Ingersoll to secretary of state, January 23, 1817, Misc. Letters; *Lockington v. Smith.*

45. Marshal Thomas G. Thornton to attorney general, January 21, 1813, AG

Letterbook A1. Monroe to Marshal Peter Curtenius, April 5 and June 30, 1813; Monroe to marshals of Rhode Island, Connecticut, and Massachusetts, October 30, 1813, all in Dom. Letters. Waring to secretary of state, July 6, 1813; Prince to secretary of state, January 27, 1815, both in Misc. Letters.

46. Treaty on exchange of prisoners, November 12, 1812, War of 1812 Papers; Monroe to all marshals, March 1813, Dom. Letters.

47. Monroe to all marshals.

48. Ibid. Curtenius to secretary of state, July 2, 1813; Waring to secretary of state, July 6, 1813; Pleasanton to Adams, July 2, 1817; Pleasanton to secretary of state, July 2, 1817, all in Misc. Letters. Monroe to Colonel Lear, June 27, 1814, Dom. Letters.

CHAPTER 3

1. U.S. Attorney H. D. Gilpin to Secretary of the Treasury Levi Woodbury, October 29, 1835; to President Andrew Jackson, October 30, 1835, both in Records of the Department of the Treasury, Judiciary Letters Received, RG 56 (hereinafter cited as Treas. Judic. Letters Rec.).

2. Woodbury to Gilpin, November 2 and 11, 1835, both in Records of the Department of the Treasury, Judiciary Letters Sent, RG 56 (hereinafter cited as Treas. Judic. Letters Sent); Gilpin to Woodbury, December 11, 1835, Treas. Judic. Letters Rec.

3. Marshal John Patterson to Woodbury, January 29 and February 19, 1836, both in Treas. Judic. Letters Rec.

4. Gilpin to Woodbury, February 6, 1836, Treas. Judic. Letters Rec.

5. Woodbury to Marshal Patterson, February 23, 1836; Patterson to Woodbury, March 1, 1836; U.S. Attorney N. H. Swayne to Woodbury, March 2 and 3, 1836; Gilpin to Woodbury, March 11, 1836, all in Treas. Judic. Letters Rec.

6. Gilpin to Woodbury, March 22, 1836, Treas. Judic. Letters Rec.

7. Woodbury to U.S. Attorney R. G. Nichols, March 28, 1836; Gilpin to Woodbury, April 9, 1836; Patterson to Woodbury, July 2, 1836, all in Treas. Judic. Letters Rec.

8. Patterson to Woodbury, July 2, 1836, Treas. Judic. Letters Rec.; Woodbury to Patterson, July 8, 1836, Treas. Judic. Letters Sent.

9. Cunningham, *Process of Government*, 184, 187; Richard J. Richardson and Kenneth M. Vines, *The Politics of Federal Courts: Lower Courts in the United States* (Boston: Little, Brown, 1970), 59.

10. U.S. Attorney Joseph McIlwaine to Secretary of the Treasury Gabriel Duval, July 7 and October 17, 1805, both in Records of the Solicitor of the Treasury, Letters Received, RG 206 (hereinafter cited as Solicitor of the Treas. Letters Rec.).

11. Judge John Brayton to Monroe, May 13, 1813, Misc. Letters. U.S. Attorney George M. Bibb to Stephen Pleasanton, March 3, 1823, Solicitor of Treas. Letters Rec.

12. U.S. Attorney Jon Fiske to Monroe, May 7, 1818, Misc. Letters.

13. Secretary of the Treasury R. B. Taney to Marshal William M. Givin, January 27, 1834; fifth comptroller to U.S. attorneys, court clerks, and marshals, February 1, 1842; assistant secretary of the Treasury to Marshal Anderson Miller, June 17, 1843; Secretary of the Treasury R. J. Walker to Marshal D. A. Robertson, October 8, 1845; Walker to all marshals, July 1, 1846, all in Treas. Judic. Letters Sent.

14. Secretary of the Treasury to Marshal S. Meredith, September 18, 1851; Acting Secretary of the Treasury P. Clayton to late marshal Hiram H. Womack, August 15, 1859, both in Treas. Judic. Letters Sent.

15. Secretary of the Treasury to Marshal Benjamin Patteson, June 30, 1843; to Marshal Thomas M. Hope, November 18, 1844, both in Treas. Judic. Letters Sent.

16. Walker to William Field; to Marshal Elias Rector, both September 14, 1846, Treas. Judic. Letters Sent.

17. Walker to all marshals, July 1, 1846, Treas. Circ. Letters, vol. 3; Acting Secretary of the Treasury N. C. Young to Acting U.S. Attorney William G. Hale, August 3, 1847, Treas. Judic. Letters Sent.

18. Marshal Andrew Hull to Secretary of the Treasury Stephen Pleasanton, February 8, 1827, RG 206, Solicitor of Treas. Letters Rec.

19. Walker to Marshal John M. Allen, January 8, 1847; Walker to Marshal Austin Wing, February 9, 1847; Walker to Marshal James A. Cocke, August 3, 1847; Young to Marshal William Wagner, February 22, 1848, all in Treas. Judic. Letters Sent.

20. Waring to Adams, October 22, 1821, Misc. Letters; Marshal Abraham T. Hillyer to Secretary of the Interior Robert McClelland, May 13, 1853, AG Letters Rec.

21. Attorney General Caleb Cushing to President Franklin Pierce, April 15, 1853, Attorney General Papers, Letters Sent, RG 60.

22. Walker to all marshals, February 23, 1846, Treas. Circ. Letters. Marshal James Points to Walker, February 28, 1846; Marshal Thomas Fletcher to Walker,

March 9, 1846; Marshal Samuel Hays to Walker, April 6, 1846; Marshal Robert I. Chester to Walker, April 7, 1846, all in Treas. Judic. Letters Rec.

23. Marshal Burrington Anthony to Walker, February 28, 1846; Marshal Isaac Barnes to Walker, March 2, 1846; Marshal Jacob Gould to Walker, March 3, 1846; Marshal George M. Kern to Walker, March 3, 1846; Marshal Ely Moore to Walker, March 3, 1846; Marshal Thomas D. Condy to Walker, March 10, 1846; Marshal H. Willingham to Walker, March 10, 1846; Robertson to Walker, March 13, 1846; Marshal Moreau Forrest to Walker, March 18, 1846; Marshal John S. Rockwell to Walker, March 18, 1846; Marshal A. E. Wirig to Walker, March 26, 1846; Marshal S. H. Anderson to Walker, May 8, 1846, all in Treas. Judic. Letters Rec.

24. Secretary of State Martin Van Buren to Marshal Thomas Morris, April 14, 1831, Dom. Letters. G. G. and S. Howland to Morris, April 23, 1831; Morris to Van Buren, April 25, 1831, both in Misc. Letters. Marshal Chapman Coleman to Pleasanton, November 6, 1823, Solicitor of Treas. Letters Rec.

25. Marshal Mott L. Crawford to Secretary of the Treasury Levi Woodbury, May 1839; U.S. Attorney G. U. Gayle to Solicitor of the Treasury H. D. Gilpin, June 2, 1839, both in Treas. Judic. Letters Rec. Gilpin to Woodbury, June 19, 1839; Woodbury to Crawford, June 20, 1839, both in Treas. Judic. Letters Sent.

26. Secretary of the Treasury S. D. Ingham, circular to the district attorneys and marshals of the United States, March 25, 1829, enclosing "Extract of a Report from the Director of the Mint, March 16, 1829," Treas. Circ. Letters, vol. 2.

27. Robertson to Solicitor of the Treasury R. H. Gillett, November 4, 1848, Solicitor's Miscellaneous Closed Case File, RG 206 (hereinafter cited as Solicitor's Closed Case).

28. Deputy D. K. Goodin to Robertson, October 13, 1848, Solicitor's Closed Case.

29. Goodin to Robertson, October 19, 1848, Solicitor's Closed Case.

30. Robertson to Gillett, November 4 and 18, 1848, Solicitor's Closed Case.

31. District Attorney Asher Robbins (R.I.) to Adams, December 23, 1817; District Attorney Thomas Parker (S.C.) to Adams, December 26, 1817, both in Misc. Letters. The districts that reported no violations of the 1817 neutrality law included Maryland (District Attorney Elias Glenn to Adams, December 18, 1817, Misc. Letters), southern New York (District Attorney John A. Feake to Adams, December 20, 1817, Misc. Letters), Massachusetts (District Attorney George Blake to Adams, December 22, 1817, Misc. Letters), and Georgia (District Attorney William Davis to Adams, January 2, 1818, Misc. Letters).

32. Marshal Nathaniel Garrow to U.S. Attorney N. L. Benton, December 21, 1837 (two letters), both in Misc. Letters.

33. Collector of Customs P. A. Barker to Benton, December 23, 1837; Benton to Secretary of State John Forsyth, December 26, 1837, both in Misc. Letters. Forsyth to Garrow, January 5, 1838, mentioning Garrow's letter of December 28, 1837, Dom. Letters.

34. Forsyth to Garrow, January 5, 1838.

35. R. W. Ashley to Luke Baldwin, January 22, 1838; Brigadier General Donald MacLeod to Baldwin, ca. January 1838, both in R. W. Ashley Papers, Buffalo and Erie County Historical Society, Buffalo, N.Y. (hereinafter cited as Ashley Papers).

36. Ashley to Dr. Bond, March 1, 1838; MacLeod to Baldwin, March 4, 1838; MacLeod to James Thompson, March 7, 1838, all in Ashley Papers.

37. Donald MacLeod, *A Brief Review of the Settlement of Upper Canada by the VE Loyalists and Scotch Highlanders in 1783 and of the Grievances Which Compelled the Canadas to Have Recourse to Arms in Defense of Their Rights and Liberties in the Years 1837 and 1838; Together with a Brief Sketch of the Campaigns of 1812, '13, and '14: with an Account of the Military Executions, Burnings, and Sackings of Towns and Villages by the British in the Upper and Lower Provinces, during the Commotion of 1837 and '38* (Cleveland: FB Penniman, 1841), 216–17.

38. Ibid., 219.

39. Ibid., 231–32.

40. MacLeod to Dr. Duncombe, March 6, 1838; MacLeod to Silas Fletcher, March 26, 1838; MacLeod to Dr. E. Johnson, March 26, 1838; Ashley to MacLeod, April 15, 1838; Ashley to MacLeod, April 27, 1838, all in Ashley Papers. MacLeod, *Brief Review,* 237.

41. Marshal Demas Adams (Ohio) to Secretary of State Daniel Webster, March 8, 1842, Misc. Letters. For the continued problems with the Patriot army, see the following: A. Vail to Garrow, September 27, 1838; Forsyth to Garrow, December 11, 1838; Webster to D. Adams, September 25 and October 6, 1841, all in Dom. Letters. Marshal William Waddell (southern N.Y.) to J. Forsyth, November 20, 1838; Waddell to editor of *New York Gazette,* November 20, 1838; Garrow to Forsyth, November 29, December 19 and 25, and ca. December, 1838; Harvey Eldridge to Garrow, December 12, 1838; D. Adams to Webster, October 1 and 7, 1841; Marshal Joshua Howard (Mich.) to Webster, October 6, 1841, all in Misc. Letters.

42. U.S. Attorney J. Prescott Hall to Acting Secretary of the Interior William A. Graham, who forwarded the letter to the State Department, August 29, 1851, Misc. Letters.

43. Webster to marshals, district attorneys, and collectors, September 3, 1850, Dom. Letters.

44. Hall to secretary of state, April 22, 1851; statement by James Ridgeway, April 23, 1851, both in Misc. Letters.

45. Acting Secretary of State W. L. Derrick to Hall, April 23, 1851, Dom. Letters. Hall to Webster, April 24, 1851; to Graham, August 29, 1851, both in Misc. Letters.

46. Hall to Webster, April 24, 1851; Assistant U.S. Attorney William Evarts to Webster, April 26 and 28, 1851; Hall to Graham, August 29, 1851, all in Misc. Letters.

47. Evarts to Webster, April 29, 1851; Hall to Graham, forwarded to State Department, August 28 and 29, 1851; Marshal Henry F. Tallmadge to President Millard Fillmore, September 1, 1851; Hall to Secretary of the Interior A. H. H. Stuart, September 2, 1851, all in Misc. Letters. Webster to Tallmadge, May 30, 1851; Fillmore to Tallmadge, August 30, 1851; Derrick to respective attorneys and marshals on Atlantic Coast and Gulf of Mexico, September 2, 1851, all in Dom. Letters.

48. Charles H. Brown, *Agents of Manifest Destiny: The Lives and Times of the Filibusters* (Chapel Hill, N.C.: University of North Carolina Press, 1980), 75–77.

49. Ibid., 79–88; commander of the home squadron Foxhal A. Parker to secretary of state, September 6, 1851, Misc. Letters.

50. U.S. Attorney Henry Williams to secretary of state, September 3, 1851, Misc. Letters; Brown, *Agents of Manifest Destiny*, 89–91.

51. Williams to Marshal Isaac C. Mills, August 27, 1851, enclosed in Williams to secretary of state, September 4, 1851; Williams to secretary of state, September 3, 1851, both in Misc. Letters.

52. Williams to secretary of state, September 3 (letter) and September 4 (letter and telegram), 1851, all in Misc. Letters.

53. Deputy Collector John Portell to Derrick, September 6, 1851; Williams to secretary of state, September 10, 1851, both in Misc. Letters.

54. Marshal Charles Bingham to Derrick, September 10, 1851; Deputy Charles A. Labrizai to secretary of state, September 11, 1851, both in Misc. Letters.

55. Collector of customs I. M. Harrison to secretary of state, September 11, 1851; U.S. Attorney George Call, Jr., to secretary of state, September 12, 1851; collector of customs Isaah B. Hurt to secretary of the Treasury, forwarded to State Department, September 13, 1851, all in Misc. Letters.

56. Secretary of State William L. Marcy to U.S. attorneys in Louisiana, southern New York, Alabama, and Florida, June 5, 1854; to U.S. Attorney S. W. Inge, June 19, 1854, both in Dom. Letters. For information on the suspicions, rumors,

and investigations of the filibustering expeditions of the 1850s, see the following: Acting Secretary of State C. M. Conrad to U.S. marshals and attorneys in New York, Pennsylvania, Maryland, South Carolina, and Georgia, October 7, 1852; Marcy to Inge, November 2, 1853; Marcy to U.S. Attorney E. W. Moise (eastern La.), December 16, 1853, and February 15 and 17, 1855; Secretary of State Lewis Cass to U.S. Attorney John McKeon, September 17, 1857; Cass to U.S. Attorney Theodore Sedgewick (southern N.Y.), January 30 and February 10, 1858; Cass to U.S. attorneys in eastern Louisiana and southern New York, March 17, 1858, all in Dom. Letters. Inge to Marcy, December 23, 1853; Moise to Marcy, December 24, 1853, and February 8, 1855; Marshal Isaiah Rynders to McKeon, September 24, 1857; Sedgewick to Cass, February 11, 1858; U.S. Attorney Thomas J. Simmes (eastern La.) to Cass, March 25, 1858, all in Misc. Letters. Secretary of the Treasury James Guthrie to Hillyer, June 2, 1856, Treas. Judic. Letters Sent.

57. Brown, *Agents of Manifest Destiny,* 18.

CHAPTER 4

1. Marshal Lewis S. Partridge to Secretary of the Interior Jacob Thompson, November 28, 1859, AG Letters Rec.:Vt.

2. Brown, *Agents of Manifest Destiny,* 352–55.

3. Stanley W. Campbell, *The Slave Catchers* (Chapel Hill, N.C.: University of North Carolina Press, 1970), 117–20.

4. Marshal William Morel to Adams, July 27, 1820, Misc. Letters; Adams to U.S. Attorney Richard W. Habersham, August 10, 1820, Dom. Letters.

5. Wirt to Secretary of the Navy Domans, October 14 and 16, 1819, both in AG Letterbook A1, Misc.

6. Morel to Adams, September 4, 1820, Misc. Letters.

7. Marshal E. Levy to Adams, December 25, 1819, Misc. Letters.

8. Habersham to Adams, June 8, 1820; Prince to Adams, October 6, 1820; Marshal Waters Smith to Secretary of State Richard Rush, February 8, 1828, all in Misc. Letters. Adams to Prince, November 8, 1820, Dom. Letters.

9. Secretary of State Edward Livingston to Marshal John Nicholson; to Marshal Robert Crawford, both March 24, 1832, Dom. Letters. John Slidell to chief clerk Daniel Brent, April 9, 1832, Misc. Letters.

10. Marshal Albert Smith to Jackson, November 18, 1833; Waddell to Asbury Dickens, May 29, 1835; Marshal Samuel H. Duval to President Martin Van Buren, May 30, 1837; U.S. Attorney Charles S. Sibley to J. Forsyth, August 25, 1838; Gilpin to J. Forsyth, September 4, 1838, all in Misc. Letters.

11. On June 29, 1839, Deputy George I. Talmbauer of Florida reported to Secretary of the Interior Jacob Thompson rumors of a ship loaded with four hundred Africans due to dock in his district. Talmbauer suggested a general alert all along the coast to catch the vessel, but there is no documentation that such an alert was sounded. See Talmbauer to Thompson, June 29, 1839, Treas. Judic. Letters Rec.

12. Attorney General Jeremiah S. Black to U.S. Attorney James Conner, September 9, 1858, AG Letterbook A3, Misc.

13. Black to Conner, October 6, 1858, AG Letterbook A3, Misc.

14. Black to Conner, March 31, 1859, enclosing President James Buchanan to Conner, March 31, 1859, AG Letterbook A3, Misc.

15. Black to U.S. Attorney Joseph Ganahl, January 31, 1859, AG Letterbook A3, Misc.

16. Black to Ganahl, January 27 and 31, 1859; Black to Buchanan, February 1, 1859; Acting Attorney General Howell Cobb to Rynders, April 1, 1859; Cobb to special assistant attorney Henry R. Jackson, April 2, 1859; Cobb to U.S. Attorney A. J. Requier, April 2, 1859, all in AG Letterbook A3, Misc.

17. U.S. Attorney John H. O'Neile to Black, May 30, June 12, and July 7 and 15, 1857, all in AG Letters Rec.:Ohio; Black to O'Neile, June 7, 1857, AG Letterbook A3, Misc.; *Ex parte Sifford*, Federal Cases, no. 12848; Campbell, *Slave Catchers*, 161–64.

18. U.S. Attorney George Levitt to Attorney General John J. Crittenden, February 22, 1851, AG Letters Rec.:Mass.; Jane H. Pease and William H. Pease, *The Fugitive Slave Law and Anthony Burns: A Problem in Law Enforcement* (Philadelphia: J. B. Lippincott, 1975), 16; Campbell, *Slave Catchers*, 148–51.

19. U.S. Attorney John W. Ashmead to Webster, September 12, 1851; Commissioner Edward D. Ingraham to Ashmead, September 12, 1851, both in Misc. Letters. W. U. Hensel, *The Christiana Riot and the Treason Trials of 1851: An Historical Sketch* (New York: Negro Universities Press, 1911), 20–25. Jonathan Katz, *Resistance at Christiana: The Fugitive Slave Rebellion, Christiana, Pennsylvania, September 11, 1851, A Documentary Account* (New York: Thomas Y. Crowell, 1974), 65–75.

20. Hensel, *Christiana Riot;* Katz, *Resistance at Christiana.*

21. Derrick to Ashmead, September 13, 1851, Dom. Letters. Two days later, Derrick informed Ashmead that the commander of the troops at Fort Mifflin, Delaware, not Carlisle barracks, had been ordered to assist the marshal. See Derrick to Ashmead, September 15, 1851, Dom. Letters.

22. Hensel, *Christiana Riot*, 92–93.

23. Pease and Pease, *Fugitive Slave Law,* 21.

24. Ibid., 28–29; Campbell, *Slave Catchers,* 124–25.

25. U.S. Attorney B. F. Hallett to Pierce, May 27, 1854, AG Letters Rec.: Mass.; Campbell, *Slave Catchers,* 125–26; Pease and Pease, *Fugitive Slave Law,* 29–30.

26. Hallett to Pierce, May 27, 1854; Campbell, *Slave Catchers,*126–27; Pease and Pease, *Fugitive Slave Law,* 33.

27. Hallett to Pierce, May 27, 1854; Campbell, *Slave Catchers,*127; Pease and Pease, *Fugitive Slave Law,* 33.

28. Hallett to Pierce, May 27, 1854; Pease and Pease, *Fugitive Slave Law,* 41–42. Cushing's legal opinion remained the policy of succeeding administrations until 1878, when Congress passed the Posse Comitatus Law, prohibiting the use of federal troops by U.S. marshals. In the intervening years marshals relied heavily on soldiers, particularly in the South and the western territories after the Civil War.

29. Hallett to Pierce, May 31, 1854.

30. Campbell, *Slave Catchers,* 129–30; Pease and Pease, *Fugitive Slave Law,* 47–48.

31. Hallett to Cushing, June 22, July 8, September 12, and October 9, 1854, all in AG Letters Rec.:Mass.; Pease and Pease, *Fugitive Slave Law,* 49.

32. Hallett to Pierce, October 31, 1854, enclosing deposition by A. O. Butman, October 31, 1854, AG Letters Rec.:Mass.

33. Hallett to Cushing, November 25, 1854, AG Letters Rec.:Mass.

34. Hallett to Cushing, April 13, 1855 (two letters), AG Letters Rec.:Mass.

35. Hallett to Pierce, June 9, 1855, AG Letters Rec.:Mass.

36. For information on the Booth case, see AG Letters Rec.:Wis., 1854–61, and James I. Clark, *Wisconsin Defies the Fugitive Slave Law: The Case of Sherman M. Booth* (Madison, Wis.: State Historical Society of Wisconsin, 1955).

37. William C. Cochran, "The Western Reserve and the Fugitive Slave Law: A Prelude to the Civil War," *Western Reserve Historical Society Collections* 101 (January 1920): 122.

38. Ibid., 120–21.

39. Ibid., 125–31; Campbell, *Slave Catchers,* 164–65.

40. Campbell, *Slave Catchers,* 166–67.

41. Margaret Leech, *Reveille in Washington, 1860–1865* (New York: Harper and Brothers, 1941), 239–41.

CHAPTER 5

1. Marshal Ward Hill Lamon to "My Dear Mother," May 6, 1861, Ward Hill Lamon Papers, Huntington Library, San Marino, California (hereinafter cited as Lamon Papers). Allan Pinkerton and his detectives guarded the train Lincoln rode into Washington and were responsible for his protection on the trip.

2. Lamon to President Abraham Lincoln, n.d., Lamon Papers.

3. Governor Thomas Pickens's unaddressed letter authorizing Lamon to visit Fort Sumter, March 25, 1861; D. David to Lamon, March 30, 1861; Lamon to Pickens, April 1, 1861, all in Lamon Papers.

4. Secretary of the Interior Caleb B. Smith to Lamon, April 20, 1861; Lamon to Colonel J. D. Williams, August 19, 1861; Secretary of War Simon Cameron to Lamon, September 5, 1861; Lamon to Major General McClellan, September 16, 1861, all in Lamon Papers.

5. Lamon to Brigadier General James Cooper, March 14, 1862; Cooper to Lamon, March 16, 1861; Lamon to McClellan, September 16, 1861; Lamon to Representative William Kellogg, n.d., all in Lamon Papers.

6. Lamon to Secretary of War Edwin Stanton, April 27, 1865; Secretary of State William Seward to Lamon, June 10, 1865, both in Lamon Papers. Lamon's role in officiating at Lincoln's funeral was not exceptional. In 1841 Marshal Alexander Hunter of the District of Columbia handled the funeral arrangements for William Henry Harrison, the first president to die in office. See Marshal Alexander Hunter to President John Tyler, August 10, 1841, Misc. Letters.

7. Patteson to A. Lincoln, April 1, 1861, AG Letters Rec.:Ala.; William H. H. Tison to Buchanan, February 21, 1861, quoted in Homer Cummings and Carl McFarland, *Federal Justice: Chapters in the History of Justice and the Federal Executive* (New York: Da Capo Press, 1970), 187.

8. Marshal Henry D. Barrows to Attorney General Edward Bates, September 11 and April 7, 1862, both in AG Letters Rec.:Calif.

9. Cummings and McFarland, *Federal Justice*, 188–92.

10. U.S. Attorney John Hanna to Bates, April 14, 1863, enclosing Hanna to Marshal David G. Rose, April 7, 1863, AG Letters Rec.:Ind.

11. Cummings and McFarland, *Federal Justice*, 191.

12. "Habeas Corpus," n.d., unpublished draft manuscript, Lamon Papers.

13. Ibid.; Bates to U.S. Attorney George A. Caffrey, June 4, 1861, AG Letterbook B2, Misc.

14. "Habeas Corpus"; Cummings and McFarland, *Federal Justice,* 190.

15. "Habeas Corpus."

16. Bates to northern U.S. attorneys, May 6, 1861, AG Letterbook B2, Misc.; to Marshal Earl Bill, November 8, 1861, AG Letterbook B4, Misc.

17. Bates to Marshal D. L. Phillips, May 18, 1861, AG Letterbook B2, Misc.; to U.S. Attorney Asa S. Jones, July 1, 1861, AG Letterbook B4, Misc.

18. Bates to Jones, July 1, 1861, AG Letterbook B4, Misc.

19. U.S. Attorney A. Q. Keasbey to Bates, August 27, 1862, AG Letters Rec.:N.J.

20. Keasbey to Bates, April 24, 1863, AG Letters Rec.:N.J.; Bates to Keasbey, April 29, 1863, AG Letterbook C, Misc.

21. Barrows to Bates, November 20, 1862, and January 26, 1863, both in AG Letters Rec.:Calif.; Acting Attorney General T. J. Coffey to Marshal D. L. Phillips, July 22, 1863, AG Letterbook C, Misc.

22. Coffey to Marshal Benajah Deacon, August 29, 1861; Coffey to Marshal O. M. Norton, September 12, 1861; Coffey to Norton, October 4, 1861; Bates to Phillips, December 16, 1861, all in AG Letterbook B4, Misc.

23. Bates to U.S. Attorney Benjamin H. Smith, March 5, 1862; Bates to U.S. marshals in New York, Massachusetts, Pennsylvania, and Maryland, December 1, 1862; Bates, "General Instructions to District Attorneys and Marshals Relative to Proceedings under the Acts of Congress for Confiscation," January 8, 1863, all in AG Letterbook B5, Misc. Bates to U.S. Attorney F. Ball, August 28, 1863; to Stanton, April 7, 1864, both in AG Letterbook C, Misc.

24. Bates to Marshal John Underwood, October 9, November 12, and December 8, 1863, and April 26, 1864, all in AG Letterbook C, Misc.; Underwood to Bates, November 5, 1863, and n.d., both in AG Letters Rec.:Va.

25. Cummings and McFarland, *Federal Justice,* 209.

26. Marshal William Smythe to Attorney General Amos T. Akerman, August 7, 1871, Source-Chron.:Ga.

27. Attorney General Henry Stanbery to President Andrew Johnson, January 21, 1867, AG Letterbook F, Misc.

28. U.S. Attorney R. M. P. Smith to Akerman, January 4, 1871, Source-Chron.:Tenn.; Marshal J. H. Pierce to Akerman, July 12, 1871, Source-Chron.:Miss.

29. J. Pierce to Akerman, May 23 and June 24, 1871, both in Source-Chron.:Miss.; U.S. Attorney D. H. Starbuck to Attorney General George H.

Williams, February 24, 1872, Source-Chron.:N.C.; Marshal Robert W. Healy to G. Williams, October 6 and 16, 1874, both in Source-Chron.:Ala.

30. U.S. Attorney G. Wiley Welles to G. Williams, January 16, 1872, Source-Chron.:Miss.; G. Williams to Welles, January 23, 1872, Attorney General Instruction Book C, RG 60 (hereinafter cited as AG Instruction Book C); Healy to G. Williams, February 1, 1873, and October 16, 1874, both in Source-Chron.:Ala.

31. Smythe to G. Williams, January 23, 1873, Source-Chron.:Ga.; G. Williams to Marshal Y. E. Thomas (circular letter), September 30, 1874, AG Instruction Book E.

32. Marshal R. M. Wallace to G. Williams, September 18, 1872, Source-Chron.:S.C.

33. Welles to Akerman, November 3, 1871, Source-Chron.:Miss. G. Williams to Wallace, July 2, 1872, AG Instruction Book C. Marshal R. M. Douglas to G. Williams, April 13, 1874, Source-Chron.:N.C. Marshal W. Spence to G. Williams, June 10, 1874; Deputy Marshal Ed S. Wheat to chief clerk A. J. Falls, July 11, 1874, both in Source-Chron.:Tenn. G. Williams to Spence, June 16, 1874, AG Instruction Book D.

34. Welles to Akerman, September 18 and ca. September 18, 1871, both in Source-Chron.:Miss.

35. Akerman to all marshals, attorneys, commissioners, and deputies, July 28, 1870; to all U.S. attorneys and marshals, July 6, 1871, both in Circular Letters of the Attorney General to U.S. Marshals and Attorneys, RG 60 (hereinafter cited as AG Circ. Letters). Akerman to U.S. Attorney D. Y. Corbin, November 10, 1871; to U.S. Attorney John A. Minnis, November 11, 1871, both in AG Instruction Book C.

36. Akerman to David A. Newsom, January 8, 1872, AG Letterbook I, Misc.

37. Corbin to G. Williams, November 2, 1872, Source-Chron.:S.C. For reports of Klan outrages, see the following: Welles to G. Williams, April 2 and July 8, 1872; J. Pierce to G. Williams, June 20, 1872, all in Source-Chron.:Miss. Acting Attorney General B. H. Bristow to Welles, May 1, 1872, AG Instruction Book C.

38. G. Williams to Messrs. Porter, Kershaw, and Sims, July 31, 1873, AG Letterbook K, Misc.

39. G. Williams to U.S. Attorney J. R. Beckwith, June 16, 1873, AG Instruction Book D. Beckwith to G. Williams, June 17, 1873; Marshal S. B. Packard to G. Williams, September 6, September 10 (letter and telegram), and October 9, 1873, all in Source-Chron.:La.

40. Packard to G. Williams, April 2 and June 10, 1874; Beckwith to G. Williams, June 25, 1874, all in Source-Chron.:La. Cummings and McFarland,

Federal Justice, 242–44. Joe Gray Taylor, "Louisiana: An Impossible Task," in Otto H. Olsen, ed., *Reconstruction and Redemption in the South* (Baton Rouge, La.: Louisiana State University Press, 1980), 209–10.

41. Welles to G. Williams, April 5, 1873, Source-Chron.:Miss.

42. Welles to G. Williams, August 9, 1873, Source-Chron.:Miss.

43. G. Williams to Welles, November 13, 1873, AG Instruction Book D.

44. G. Williams to Minnis, October 27, 1873, AG Instruction Book D.

45. G. Williams to Corbin, March 17, 1874, AG Instruction Book D; Corbin to G. Williams, March 28, 1874, Source-Chron.:S.C.

46. G. Williams to U.S. Attorney Virgil S. Lusk, April 25, 1874, AG Instruction Book D, April 25, 1874.

47. U.S. Attorney Nick S. McAfee to G. Williams, August 31, 1874, Source-Chron.:Ala.

48. G. Williams to southern U.S. marshals and attorneys, September 3, 1874, AG Instruction Book E.

49. *U.S. v. Cruikshank,* 92 U.S. Reports 542.

50. Attorney General Charles Devens to J. Pierce, July 10, 1877; J. Pierce to Devens, July 13, 1877, both in Source-Chron.:Miss.

51. R. K. Baird to Devens, September 18, 1878; U.S. Attorney W. W. Murray to Devens, October 5, 1878, both in Source-Chron.:Tenn.

CHAPTER 6

1. David Neagle, testimony, RG 21, U.S. District Court, Northern District of California, Circuit Court Civil Case 10469, Transcripts "In the Matter of the Habeas Corpus of David Neagle," Regional Archives and Records Center, San Bruno, California.

2. Wallace to Devens, September 13, 1877, Source-Chron.:S.C.

3. Corbin to G. Williams, November 5 and December 16, 1874, and February 3 and 10, 1875; Deputy Alexander Mattison to G. Williams, December 28, 1874, and January 18, 1875, all in Source-Chron.:S.C.

4. Marshal R. P. Baker to Attorney General Alphonso Taft, November 21, 1876, Source-Chron.:Ala.

5. Marshal Edward S. Wheat to Taft, July 27, 1876, Source-Chron.:Tenn.

6. *Tennessee v. Davis,* 10 U.S. Reports 263. Three years later, having again

accepted appointment as a deputy marshal, Davis was killed by illicit distillers. See Marshal George N. Tillman to Attorney General Benjamin Harrison Brewster, June 27, 1883, Source-Chron.:Tenn.

7. G. Williams to U.S. Attorney R. C. Badger, December 4, 1874, AG Instruction Book E; Attorney General A. H. Garland to U.S. Attorney Andrew McLain, April 15, 1885, AG Instruction Book R.

8. *In re Neagle*.

9. Ibid.

10. Wallace to Devens, April 22, 1878; Deputy Collector H. H. Gillson to R. M. Wallace, April 23, 1878, both in Source-Chron.:S.C. Devens to R. M. Wallace, May 1, 1878; to U.S. Attorney S. C. Northrop, ca. May 1, 1878, both in AG Instruction Book H.

11. Lusk to G. Williams, December 23, 1873; Douglas to Devens, December 14, 1877, both in Source-Chron.:N.C.

12. Wallace to Devens, December 31, 1877, Source-Chron.:S.C.

13. Deputy Will W. Deavers to G. Williams, September 27, 1873, Source-Chron.:N.C. Marshal George Smith to G. Williams, August 22, 1874; U.S. Attorney James S. Botsford to G. Williams, August 31 and September 4, 1874, all in Source-Chron.:Mo. G. Williams to G. Smith, August 26, 1874, AG Instruction Book D. G. Williams to Secret Service chief H. C. Whitely, August 27, 1874; Acting Attorney General S. F. Phillips to Botsford, September 4, 1874; Falls to A. B. Newcomb, December 12, 1874; and February 4, 1875, all in AG Letterbook K.

14. Devens to Marshal M. J. Waldin, September 6, 1877, AG Instruction Book G; revenue agent George Clark to commissioner of the Internal Revenue Joseph S. Miller, December 10, 1887, Department of Justice Year Files (hereinafter cited as Year Files) 7616/87, RG 60.

15. Devens to Marshal George Turner, February 8, 1878, AG Instruction Book G; Attorney General William H. H. Miller to Marshal Richard R. Farr, September 5, 1890, AG Instruction Book 5.

16. G. Williams to G. Smith, March 18, 1875, AG Instruction Book E. Garland to Marshal E. M. Boykin, October 4, 1887; to Marshal W. W. Allen, October 6, 1887, both in AG Instruction Book X.

17. Devens to Waldin, September 6, 1877, AG Instruction Book G; Garland to Marshal J. R. Jordan, March 19, 1888, AG Instruction Book Z; Acting Attorney General G. A. Jenks to Marshal J. W. Nelms, July 19, 1888, AG Instruction Book 1.

18. Baker to Devens, September 25, 1877, Source-Chron.:Ala.; Garland to Marshal Thomas W. Scott, April 5, 1887, AG Instruction Book W.

19. Revenue agent William Somerville to commissioner of the Internal Revenue Green B. Raurn, May 14, 1879, Source-Chron.:Ga.; S. Phillips to U.S. Attorney George M. Thomas, November 10, 1884, AG Instruction Book Q; W. Miller to Marshal John C. Watts, September 13, 1891, AG Instruction Book 15.

20. "An Act Concerning the Attorney-General and the Attorneys and Marshals of the Several Districts," August 2, 1861, *U.S. Statutes at Large,* chap. 37; chief clerk John B. Kiss to U.S. Attorney George Y. Talbot, July 14, 1862, AG Letterbook B5, Misc.

21. "An Act to Give Greater Efficiency to the Judicial System of the United States," March 3, 1863, *U.S. Statutes at Large,* chap. 93.

22. Garland to Marshal W. A. Cabell, December 27, 1886, AG Instruction Book S.

23. G. Williams to Marshal W. G. Morris, March 15, 1872, AG Instruction Book C; to L. W. Day, December 3, 1873, AG Letterbook K, Misc.; to J. Pierce, October 14, 1874, AG Instruction Book E.

24. G. Williams to B. B. Smalley, September 27, 1873, AG Letterbook K, Misc.; G. Williams to Marshal Isaac T. Quimby, October 22, 1874, AG Instruction Book E; Garland to Marshal A. H. Keller, December 15, 1887, AG Instruction Book Y; Garland to Marshal H. C. Urner, March 8, 1888, AG Instruction Book Z.

25. *Illustrated Police News,* December 2, 1893.

26. W. Miller to Marshal B. W. Walker, November 22, 1889, AG Instruction Book 5.

27. S. Phillips to Turner, July 14, 1877, AG Instruction Book G; Brewster to Marshal D. B. Russell, February 13, 1885, AG Instruction Book R; Garland to former marshal Harrison Allen, November 9, 1885, AG Letterbook R, Misc.

28. Attorney General Edwards Pierrepont to judges, attorneys, and marshals, May 31, 1875, AG Circ. Letters.

29. Garland to deputies J. D. Goodman and E. W. Johnson, May 11, 1886, AG Letterbook R, Misc. Garland to former marshal J. J. Irvins, December 23, 1887, AG Letterbook T, Misc. W. Miller to A. E. Ratcliffe, June 26, 1889; to Deputy R. O. Grayson, May 28, 1889, both in AG Letterbook U, Misc.

30. Devens to U.S. attorneys, January 1878, AG Circ. Letters.

31. Pierrepont to Anthony Comstock, December 23, 1875, AG Letterbook L, Misc.

32. Devens to Lusk, June 6, 1877; to Marshal Algernon S. Gray, January 17, 1878, both in AG Instruction Book G. Devens to all marshals, January 1878, AG

Circ. Letters. Attorney General Richard Olney to Marshal W. B. Bunton, May 21, 1894, AG Instruction Book 39.

33. Statement of Belle Starr to Examiner David A. Fisher, September 25, 1886, Year Files 8435/86.

34. Examiner Joel W. Bowman to general agent Brewster Cameron, May 31, 1883; Cameron to Brewster, June 1, 1883; Bowman to Brewster, June 4, 1883, all in Source-Chron.:Ala.

35. *Annual Report of the Attorney General, 1883 and 1884,* 22–23 (1883), 17 (1884).

CHAPTER 7

1. Chief Justice Frank Dale to attorney general, May 21, 1894, Year Files 12014/92; Glenn Shirley, *West of Hell's Fringe: Crime, Criminals, and the Federal Peace Officer in Oklahoma Territory, 1889–1907* (Norman, Okla.: University of Oklahoma Press, 1978), 192.

2. Marshal E. D. Nix to attorney general, September 5, 1894, and July 30, 1895, both in Year Files 12014/92. Shirley, *West of Hell's Fringe,* 157–66.

3. Shirley, *West of Hell's Fringe,* 192–94.

4. Ibid., 194.

5. Marshal John Sherman to attorney general, February 25, 1879; U.S. Attorney Sidney M. Barry to attorney general, May 30, 1881, both in Source-Chron.:N.Mex. Larry D. Ball, *The United States Marshals of New Mexico and Arizona Territories, 1846–1912* (Albuquerque, N.Mex.: University of New Mexico Press, 1978), 84–95, 102.

6. Marshal J. H. Burdick to G. Williams, March 20 and August 3, 1874, both in Source-Chron.:Dak.Terr.

7. Marshal William S. Tough to attorney general, February 9, 1874; U.S. Attorney George R. Peck to Tough, February 1, 1875, both in Source-Chron.:Kan.

8. U.S. Attorney Joseph W. Huston to Taft, April 26, 1873, and August 23, 1876, both in Source-Chron.:Idaho. Marshal Thomas Purnell to attorney general (two letters), April 8, 1876; Superintendent C. T. Campbell to Devens, August 11, 1878; General Superintendent M. J. O'Brian to Devens, August 13, 1878, all in Source-Chron.:Tex. Marshal A. L. Morrison to Brewster, May 16, 1884, Source-Chron.:N.Mex.

9. U.S. Attorney E. P. Johnson to attorney general, June 28, 1877; Governor John W. Hoyt to Devens, December 16, 1878, both in Source-Chron.:Wyo.

10. Information on the Hole-in-the-Wall gang can be found in Year Files 16434/98 and in the Frank Hadsell Papers, Wyoming State Archives, Museums, and Historical Department, Cheyenne, Wyo.

11. Marshal Edward L. Hall to attorney general, January 21, 1897, Year Files 13065/96; Ball, *United States Marshals,* 203.

12. E. Hall to attorney general, August 24, 26 (three letters), 27, and 28 and October 3, 1896; October 5, 1896, enclosing Chief Deputy Horace W. Loomis to E. Hall, October 3, 1896, all in Year Files 13065/96.

13. E. Hall to attorney general, November 2 and 19, 1896, and January 21, 1897, Year Files 13065/96.

14. E. Hall to attorney general, March 25, May 1, June 9, and July 13, 1897, all in Year Files 13065/96.

15. Marshal W. M. Griffith to attorney general, July 17 and December 12 and 15, 1897; Marshal Creighton M. Foraker to attorney general, October 26, November 12, and December 12, 1897, all in Year Files 13065/96.

16. Foraker to attorney general, August 13, 1898; Griffith to attorney general, September 13, 1898, both in Year Files 13065/96.

17. Foraker to attorney general, July 19 and August 28, 1899, both in Year Files 13065/96.

18. Foraker to attorney general, August 28, 1899; U.S. Attorney W. B. Childers to attorney general, May 29, 1901, both in Year Files 13065/96.

19. Devens to Marshal Crowley P. Dake, July 15, 1879, AG Instruction Book I.

20. Garland to Cabell, June 25 and 27, 1887; to Marshal R. B. Reagan, July 7, 1887, all in AG Instruction Book X.

21. *Instructions to United States Marshals, Attorneys, Clerks, and Commissioners* (Washington, D.C.: GPO, 1899).

22. Assistant Attorney General John N. Hinckley to Deputy Marshal Jared Brown, February 18, 1868, AG Instruction Book A2; Garland to Deputy Samuel Howard, November 4, 1885, AG Letterbook R, Misc.

23. Marshal Smith O. Scofield to Attorney General James Speed, September 11, 1865, AG Letters Rec.:Mo.; Marshal Isaac Q. Dickason to attorney general, August 14, 1871, Source-Chron.:Ariz.; Marshal M. C. Hillyer to Brewster, received November 7, 1884, Year Files 1016/84.

24. Attorney General Ebenezer R. Hoar to Marshal Church Howe, June 15, 1869, AG Instruction Book A2.

25. Glenn Shirley, *Guardian of the Law: The Life and Times of William Matthew Tilghman* (Austin, Tex.: Eakin Press, 1988), 254–59.

26. Glenn Shirley, *Heck Thomas, Frontier Marshal* (Norman, Okla.: University of Oklahoma Press, 1962), 223–27, 235.

27. Ibid., 237–39.

28. Shirley, *West of Hell's Fringe*, 406–7.

29. Glenn Shirley, *Law West of Fort Smith: A History of Frontier Justice in the Indian Territory, 1834–1896* (Lincoln, Nebr.: University of Nebraska Press, 1968), 9–11.

30. W. Miller to Marshal Thomas B. Needles, April 18, 1889; G. Williams to J. W. Feebe, November 28, 1873, both in AG Instruction Book 3. W. Miller to Marshal R. L. Walker, July 23, 1889, AG Instruction Book 4.

31. Marshal James F. Fagan (circular letter), undated, Source-Chron.:Ark.

32. Shirley, *Law West of Fort Smith*, 215–16.

33. Ibid., 211–12.

34. Ibid., 223, 224, 226.

35. W. Miller to Needles, May 17 and June 5, 1889, both in AG Instruction Book 3.

36. U.S. Attorney H. Huckleberry to G. Williams, with enclosures, April 18, 1872; Marshal Logan H. Roots, by Deputy J. W. Donnelly, to G. Williams, April 26, 1872; Roots to G. Williams, May 7, 1872, all in Source-Chron.:Ark.; "The War in the Cherokee Nation," unsigned article in *New Era* (newspaper), n.d.

37. Roots to G. Williams, February 2, 1872, Source-Chron.:Ark.

38. G. Williams to Tough, March 21, 1874, AG Instruction Book D.

39. Marshal William F. Wheeler to attorney general, December 28, 1870, and January 22, 1871; Wheeler to G. Williams, July 22, 1873, and July 3 and 11, 1874; U.S. Attorney M. C. Page to G. Williams, July 25, 1873; U.S. Indian agent W. W. Alderson to G. Williams, July 9, 1874; Deputy Charles D. Hand to Wheeler, July 10, 1874; U.S. consul James W. Taylor, Winnipeg, Canada, to commissioner of Indian affairs, July 15, 1874, all in Source-Chron.:Mont.

40. Wheeler to Pierrepont, June 22, 1875, Source-Chron.:Mont.

41. Attorney General Wayne MacVeagh to Marshal Robert N. McLaren, June 13 and July 8, 1881; McLaren to MacVeagh, June 29, 1881; J. B. Blanchard to MacVeagh, July 19, 1881, all in Source-Chron.:Minn.

42. J. B. Blanchard to MacVeagh, July 19 and 24, 1881; Marshal H. R. Denny

to Brewster, April 7, 1882; Blanchard to U.S. Attorney D. B. Searle, August 5, September 5, October 5, and November 2, 1883; Charles J. Allen to Searle, August 15, 1883; Searle to Brewster, September 7, 1883; Blanchard to Brewster, December 3, 1883; Assistant U.S. Attorney C. A. Congdon to Brewster, December 1883, all in Source-Chron.:Minn.

43. Louis H. Roddis, "The Last Indian Uprising in the United States," *Minnesota History Bulletin* 3 (1919–20): 278.

44. Ibid., 276–77; Richard K. Kolb, "Last Stand at Leech Lake," *Army* (June 1987): 70–73.

45. *Minneapolis Tribune,* October 1 and 2, 1898; Roddis, "Last Indian Uprising," 278–79; Kolb, "Last Stand," 73–74.

46. Deputy Timothy J. Sheehan to President William McKinley, January 9, 1899, Papers of Timothy J. Sheehan, A.5541, Archives/Manuscripts Division of the Minnesota Historical Society, St. Paul, Minn. (hereinafter cited as Sheehan Papers).

47. Sheehan diary, September 29 and 30 and October 1, 1898, Sheehan Papers; Roddis, "Last Indian Uprising," 278–79.

48. Sheehan diary, October 3 and 4, 1898; *Minneapolis Tribune,* October 5, 1898; Roddis, "Last Indian Uprising," 279; Kolb, "Last Stand," 73.

49. Sheehan diary, October 5, 1898; Roddis, "Last Indian Uprising," 280–81; Kolb, "Last Stand," 73–74.

50. Roddis, "Last Indian Uprising," 281–82.

51. Sheehan diary, October 5 and 6, 1898; *Minneapolis Tribune,* October 6–16, 1898; Roddis, "Last Indian Uprising," 284–88; Kolb, "Last Stand," 74–79.

CHAPTER 8

1. U.S. consul George F. Seward to U.S. minister Anson Burlingame, September 30, 1863, enclosing untitled newspaper article, September 25, 1863, Legation Archives, Shanghai, China, RG 84 (hereinafter cited as Legation Archives), vol. 34, no. 225.

2. "An Act to Carry into Effect Provisions of the Treaties Between the United States, China, Japan, Siam, Persia, and Other Countries, Giving Certain Judicial Powers to Ministers and Consuls or Other Functionaries, of the United States in Those Countries, and for Other Purposes," June 22, 1860, *U.S. Statutes,* chap. 189.

3. G. Seward to chargé d'affaires D. S. Wells Williams, August 2, 1865, Legation Archives, vol. 35, no. 226.

4. R. D. McCarthy, "The Fenian Raid," *Niagara Frontier* 7 (Spring 1960): 25.

5. W. Seward to Speed, April 3, 1866, Dom. Letters. Speed to Marshal Edward Dodd; to U.S. Attorney William A. Dart, both April 3, 1866, AG Letterbook E, Misc.

6. Dart to Speed, June 3, 1866, AG Letters Rec.:N.Y.; deposition of Commander Andrew Bryson in habeas corpus hearing, June 5, 1866, Buffalo and Erie County Historical Society (hereinafter cited as BECHS); John O'Neill, *Official Report on the Attempt to Invade Canada* (New York: John J. Foster, 1870), 37–40; McCarthy, "Fenian Raid," 28.

7. "Writ of *Habeas Corpus*" for John Hay, Hugh Mooney, and John O'Neill, issued by the State of New York, June 4, 1866; "Warrant to Apprehend" John O'Neill, signed by U.S. Commissioner Perry G. Parker, June 5, 1866; trial record of writ of habeas corpus, June 5, 1866, all in BECHS; *Buffalo Morning Express,* June 5, 1866.

8. Speed to U.S. Attorney Dudley Dennison, June 13, 1866, AG Letterbook F, Misc.; Dart to Stanbery, August 9, 1866, AG Letters Rec.:N.Y.; Dennison to Stanbery, August 31, 1866, AG Letters Rec.:Vt.

9. Hoar to certain marshals, July 27, 1869; Hoar to U.S. Attorney William Dorsheimer, July 30, 1869; Acting Attorney General W. A. Field to Dorsheimer, August 27, 1869, all in AG Instruction Book A2. Dorsheimer to Hoar, August 4, 1869; Quimby to Hoar, August 6, 1869; Deputy William Hildreth to Quimby, August 12, 1869, all in AG Letters Rec.:N.Y. Field to Secretary of State Hamilton Fish, August 21, 1869; to Acting Secretary of State J. B. Davis, August 26, 1869, both in AG Letterbook H, Misc.

10. Field to certain district attorneys, September 10, 1869, AG Instruction Book A2.

11. Hoar to Fish, April 11 and 14, 1870, both in AG Letterbook H, Misc.

12. U.S. Attorney B. F. Fifield to Hoar, May 30, 1870, AG Letters Rec.:Vt.; O'Neill, *Official Report,* 24–27.

13. Hoar to Marshal George P. Foster, May 27 and 28, 1870, both in AG Instruction Book A2.

14. Fifield to Hoar, June 26, 1870, AG Letters Rec.:Vt.; Hoar to Fifield, July 4, 1870, AG Instruction Book A2; O'Neill, *Official Report,* 54–56.

15. G. Williams to U.S. Attorney Warren Cowles, February 21, 1872, AG Instruction Book C. Foster to Taft, November 17, 1876; Deputy Thomas Failey to Fifield, January 30, 1877; Fifield to Taft, January 31, 1877; Foster to Taft, February 5, 1877, all in Source-Chron.:Vt.

16. The best study of southern-style peonage is Pete Daniel, *The Shadow of*

Slavery: Peonage in the South, 1901–1969 (Urbana, Ill.: University of Illinois Press, 1972).

17. U.S. Attorney W. H. White to Garland, November 7 and 23 and December 5, 1885, and March 10 and April 2, 1886, all in Year Files 980/84.

18. "An Act to Execute Certain Treaty Stipulations Relating to Chinese," May 6, 1882, *U.S. Statutes,* chap. 126.

19. Jenks to Deputy W. H. Van Riper (Tex.), August 5, 1887, AG Letterbook S, Misc.

20. Van Riper to Garland, July 29, 1887, Year Files 980/84.

21. White to Garland, January 16, 1888; E. Hall to W. Miller, July 10, 1893, both in Year Files 980/84. Marshal P. A. Williams to Secretary of the Treasury John G. Carlisle, January 20, 1894, Treas. Judic. Letters Rec.

22. W. Miller to special assistant attorney George W. Schell, January 24, 1890, AG Instruction Book 5.

23. "Act of May 5, 1894."

24. Attorney General Joseph McKenna to Marshal Richard C. Ware, November 23, 1897, AG Instruction Book 85.

25. Marshal J. S. Williams to McKenna, November 27, 1897; Ware to McKenna, December 3, 1897, both in Year Files 980/84.

26. W. Miller to Schell, January 24, 1890, AG Instruction Book 5.

27. Chinese inspector J. Thomas Scharf to Carlisle, May 22 and June 24, 1896; acting secretary of the Treasury to Scharf, May 29, 1896; acting secretary of the Treasury to collector of customs, Burlington, Vt., San Francisco, and Portland, Oreg., May 29, 1896, all in Treas. Judic. Letters Rec.

28. Marshal Milton B. Duffield to Speed, November 10, 1865, AG Letters Rec.: Ariz.

29. U.S. Attorney D. J. Baldwin to G. Williams, March 30, 1872, Source-Chron.: Tex.

30. Baldwin to G. Williams, March 30, 1872 (two letters, one enclosing grand jury findings), both in Source-Chron.: Tex.

31. Baldwin to Devens, January 17, 1878; Deputy Kirkpatrick to Baldwin, February 18, 1878; Marshal William J. Phillips to Devens, May 3, 1878, all in Source-Chron.: Tex.

32. Baldwin to Taft, November 10, 1876, Source-Chron.: Tex.

33. MacVeagh to Dake, July 1, 1881, AG Instruction Book L.

34. Biographies of Arizona Marshals, Arizona Historical Society, Tucson, Ariz. (hereinafter cited as AHS); Ball, *United States Marshals,* 109.

35. Acting Governor John J. Gosper to Dake, November 28, 1881, Source-Chron.:Ariz.

36. MacVeagh to U.S. Attorney E. B. Pomroy, April 14, 1881, AG Instruction Book K; MacVeagh to Dake, August 10 and 27 and October 17, 1881, AG Instruction Book L.

37. Dake to S. Phillips, September 5, 1878, Source-Chron.:Ariz.; Ball, *United States Marshals,* 114–15.

38. Dake to Devens, August 19, 1878 (two letters), March 7, May 17, and July 14, 1879, and December 30, 1880; Arizona associate justice Charles Silent to Devens, September 6, 1878; Governor John P. Hoyt to Devens, September 9, 1878; Devens to Postmaster General D. M. Key, July 15, 1879, all in Source-Chron.:Ariz. Ball, *United States Marshals,* 114–15.

39. Pomroy to MacVeagh, June 23, 1881; Dake to MacVeagh, July 3, 1881, enclosing Deputy J. W. Evans to Dake, June 30, 1881; Evans to Dake, August 10, 1881, all in Source-Chron.:Ariz. Ball, *United States Marshals,* 114–15.

40. Pomroy to Devens, February 9, 1881, enclosing Evans to Dake, January 18, 1881; Dake to MacVeagh, May 30 and August 5, 1881; Evans to Dake, August 4, 1881, all in Source-Chron.:Ariz. Ball, *United States Marshals,* 118–19.

41. MacVeagh to Dake, June 15, 1881, Source-Chron.:Ariz.

42. Dake to S. Phillips, December 8, 1881 (letter and telegram), Source-Chron.:Ariz.

43. John Gilchrease, caption to *The Streetfight,* by Don Perceval, oil on canvas, 1966.

44. I am indebted to John Gilchrease for this description of the Earp street fight.

45. S. Phillips to Dake, November 17, 1881, AG Instruction Book L. Dake to S. Phillips, December 3 and 8, 1881, both in Source-Chron.:Ariz.

46. Wyatt Earp to Dake, December 19, 1881, quoted in Ball, *United States Marshals,* 123.

47. Ball, *United States Marshals,* 124–25.

48. Ibid., 124–26.

49. For information on Dake's financial difficulties with the Department of Justice, see Source-Chron.:Ariz. and Source-Chron (Accounts):Ariz.

50. General William Tecumseh Sherman to Brewster, April 12, 1882, Source-Chron.:Ariz.

51. Brewster to Dake, February 25, 1882, AG Instruction Book L; Dake to Brewster, May 3, 1882, Source-Chron.:Ariz.; Ball, *United States Marshals,* 125–26.

CHAPTER 9

1. Almont Lindsey, *The Pullman Strike* (Chicago: University of Chicago Press, 1967), 7–8.

2. Marshal Ben Spooner to Devens; Judge W. Q. Gresham to Devens, both July 24, 1877, Source-Chron.:Ind.

3. Ibid.

4. Spooner to Devens, July 25, 1877, Source-Chron.:Ind.

5. Ibid.

6. Spooner to Devens; Gresham to Devens, both July 26, 1877, Source-Chron.:Ind.

7. Devens to Spooner, July 26, 1877 (two letters); Gresham to Devens, July 27, 1877, all in Source-Chron.:Ind.

8. Devens to Spooner, July 27 and 28, 1877; Devens to G. W. Chase, July 28, 1877; Gresham to Devens, July 29, 1877, all in Source-Chron.:Ind.

9. Spooner to Devens, July 31, 1877, Source-Chron.:Ind.

10. Lindsey, *Pullman Strike,* 110–15.

11. Ibid., 12.

12. Primary documents on Coxey's march are in Year Files 4017/94. The best account of the march is Donald L. McMurry, *Coxey's Army: A Study of the Industrial Army Movement of 1894* (Seattle, Wash.: University of Washington Press, 1968).

13. Judge James H. Beatty to Olney, May 23, 1894; U.S. Attorney James H. Forney to Olney, May 28, 1894, both in Year Files 4017/94. McMurry, *Coxey's Army,* 224.

14. Lindsey, *Pullman Strike,* 123–31.

15. Ibid., 133.

16. Ibid., 135–50.

17. Ibid., 134, 260–61.

18. Olney to U.S. attorneys (circular letter), June 29, 1894; to U.S. Attorney

Burke (Ind.), June 30, 1894; to U.S. Attorney Leslie (Mont.), June 30, 1894; to U.S. Attorney Johnson (Colo.), June 30, 1894, all in AG Instruction Book 40.

19. Lindsey, *Pullman Strike,* 150.

20. Ibid., 245. Olney to Marshal John Arnold; to U.S. Attorney Thomas Milchrist, both June 30, 1894, AG Instruction Book 40.

21. Lindsey, *Pullman Strike,* 144.

22. Ibid., 154, 161; Special U.S. Attorney Edwin Walker to Olney, July 2 and 3, 1894, both in Subject Classification Files (hereinafter cited as Class. Files) 16-1-23, RG 60.

23. Lindsey, *Pullman Strike,* 161–62.

24. Ibid., 162–63.

25. Arnold to Olney, July 1, 1894, Class. Files 16-1-23.

26. Lindsey, *Pullman Strike,* 166.

27. Ibid., 165; E. Walker to Olney, July 2, 1894, Class. Files 16-1-23.

28. E. Walker to Olney; Arnold to Olney, both July 3, 1894, Class. Files 16-1-23. Lindsey, *Pullman Strike,* 164–65.

29. Arnold to Olney, July 2 and 3, 1894; E. Walker to Olney, July 3, 1894, all in Class. Files 16-1-23.

30. Olney to Milchrist, July 3, 1894, AG Instruction Book 41; Olney to Arnold, July 5, 1894, Class. Files 16-1-23; Lindsey, *Pullman Strike,* 171–74.

31. E. Walker to Olney, July 6, 1894, Class. Files 16-1-23; Lindsey, *Pullman Strike,* 205–8.

32. E. Walker to Olney, July 6, 1894, and n.d., both in Class. Files 16-1-23.

33. Olney to Arnold, July 10, 1894, AG Instruction Book 41; E. Walker to Olney, July 10, 1894, quoted in Lindsey, *Pullman Strike,* 167–68; Lindsey, *Pullman Strike,* 213, 217.

34. Lindsey, *Pullman Strike,* 208–12.

35. Olney to Marshal McDermott (Mont.), July 3, 1894; to Marshal Brinton (Ill.), July 4, 1894; to U.S. Attorney Brooks, July 13, 1894, all in AG Instruction Book 41.

36. Marshal George M. Humphrey to Olney, August 30, 1894, Class. Files 16-1-46; Lindsey, *Pullman Strike,* 168.

37. Arnold to Olney, July 11, 1894, Class. Files 16-1-23; Lindsey, *Pullman Strike,* 275–79.

38. E. Walker to Olney, July 14 and 20, 1894, both in Class. Files 16-1-23; Lindsey, *Pullman Strike,* 274–92.

39. Lindsey, *Pullman Strike,* 292–98.

40. Ibid., 298–305; U.S. Attorney H. S. Hoote to Olney, April 10, 1895, Class. Files 16-1-11.

41. Marshal Eugene Nolte to attorney general, August 27, 1909, Straight Numerical Files (hereinafter cited as Num. Files) 90755-139, RG 60.

42. Nolte to attorney general, August 11, 1909, Num. Files 90755-132; U.S. Attorney Charles A. Boynton to attorney general, September 24, 1909, Num. Files 90755-153.

43. Friedrich Katz, *The Secret War in Mexico: Europe, the United States, and the Mexican Revolution* (Chicago: University of Chicago Press, 1981), 29–35.

44. Nolte to attorney general, December 3, 1910, Num. Files 90755-332.

45. Nolte to attorney general, December 31, 1910, Num. Files 90755-39; Foraker to attorney general, December 31, 1910, Num. Files 90755-39; attorney general to Nolte, January 26, 1911, Num. Files 90755; collector of customs Cornelius O'Keefe to Marshal C. A. Overlock, February 6, 1911, AHS MS 820, S1 F247; attorney general to Secretary of State Philander C. Knox, February 13, 1911, Num. Files 90755-516.

46. U.S. Attorney A. I. McCormick to attorney general, February 23, 1911; Num. Files 90755-590; attorney general to Nolte, February 25, 1911, Num. Files 90755-571.

47. Brigadier General J. W. Duncan to adjutant general, February 21, 1911, Records of the Adjutant General's Office, AGO 1716354, add A246, RG 94; Nolte to attorney general, February 28, 1911, Num. Files 90755-592; attorney general to Nolte, March 7, 1911, Num. Files 90755-593.

48. Marshal Calvin G. Brewster to attorney general, February 16, 1911, Num. Files 90755-552; A. Brewster to attorney general, March 3, 1911, Num. Files 90755-611.

49. Nolte to attorney general, April 25, 1911, Num. Files 90755-788; Nolte to attorney general, May 9, 1911, Num. Files 90755-85——; C. Brewster to attorney general, n.d., Num. Files 90755-830.

50. Katz, *Secret War,* 40.

51. Acting Secretary of State Huntington Wilson to Attorney General George Wickersham, September 27, 1911, Num. Files 90755; Wickersham to U.S. Attorney McDaniel, November 19, 1911, Num. Files 90755-1096; J. C. Adkins to Wickersham, December 6, 1911, Num. Files 90755——.

52. Wickersham to Overlock, March 18 and 27, 1912, both in AHS MS 820, S1 F261.

53. Overlock to Wickersham, March 23, 1912, Num. Files 90755-1447. For reports on the increasing volume of smuggling, see Deputy Sheriff H. D. Hall to Overlock, April 1, 1912; U.S. Attorney [   ] to Overlock, April 4, 1912; Deputy A. A. Hopkins to Overlock, April 5, 8, 11, 25, and 29, June 1, and July 3, 1912; H. N. Gray to Overlock, April 7, 1912; J. H. Dyer to R. Lowrie, April 24, 1912; O'Keefe to Overlock, May 2, 1912; Deputy F. J. Taylor to Overlock, May 22 and September 4, 1912, all in AHS MS 820, S1 F262.

54. Frederick S. Calhoun, *Power and Principle: Armed Intervention in Wilsonian Foreign Policy* (Kent, Ohio: Kent State University Press, 1986), 39–42.

55. Ibid., 56.

56. Ibid., 49–51.

57. Ibid., 114–55.

58. H. C. Peterson and Gilbert C. Fite, *Opponents of War, 1917–1918* (Seattle, Wash.: University of Washington Press, 1957), 11; Arthur Link, "That Cobb Interview," *Journal of American History* 72 (June 1985): 7–17.

59. Assistant Attorney General Charles Warren to Attorney General Thomas W. Gregory, March 23, 1917, Class. Files 9-16-12-118.

60. Warren to Gregory, March 27, 1917, Class. Files 9-16-12-127; Warren to Gregory, March 28, 1917, Class. Files 9-16-12-120.

61. Gregory to chiefs of police, March 26, 1917; to U.S. marshals, March 27, 1917, both in AG Circ. Letters.

62. Gregory to Mr. Todd, March 29, 1917, Class. Files 9-16-12-119; Gregory to Secretary of War Newton D. Baker, April 1, 1917, Class. Files 9-16-½; Baker to Gregory, April 2, 1917, Class. Files 9-16-0½; "Outline and Illustrations of Procedure Followed in Interning of Alien Enemies During the World War," probably by Samuel Smith, n.d., Class. Files 9-16-12, sec. 1, exhibit 1.

63. Calhoun, *Power and Principle,* 152–54.

64. Gregory to U.S. attorneys and marshals, April 6, 1917, AG Circ. Letters; *Annual Report of the Attorney General of the United States for the Year 1917* (Washington, D.C.: GPO, 1918), 56.

65. David Kennedy, *Over Here: The First World War and American Society* (Oxford: Oxford University Press, 1980), 67–68, 87.

66. Warren to Marshal John D. Lynn (western N.Y.), May 26, 1917, Class. Files 9-16-4-122; Warren to Marshal Henry Behrendt, June 6, 1917, Class. Files

9-16-4-229; Marshal Samuel Randolph to Gregory, June 27, 1917, Class. Files 9-16-4-499; Gregory to Warren, September 14, 1917, Class. Files 9-16-4; Gregory to Marshal Frank J. Noonan (eastern Pa.), September 18, 1917, Class. Files 9-16-4; Warren to —— O'Brian, October 18, 1917, Class. Files 9-16-12-411; Gregory to U.S. marshals, November 28 and December 29, 1917, both in AG Circ. Letters; special assistant attorney general R. W. Sprague to —— O'Brian, October 1, 1918, Class. Files 9-16-4-2432; Sprague to —— O'Brian, November 2, 1918, Class. Files 9-16-11.

67. Warren to Mr. O'Brian, November 12, 1917, Class. Files 9-16-12; Gregory to U.S. marshals, January 5, 1918, AG Circ. Letters; "Outline and Illustrations."

68. Gregory to U.S. marshals, April 25 and May 6, 11, and 18, 1918; to U.S. attorneys and marshals, September 19, 1918, all in AG Circ. Letters. *Annual Report of the Attorney General of the United States for the Year 1918* (Washington, D.C.: GPO, 1919), 29, 30.

69. *Annual Report, 1917,* 56; *Annual Report, 1918,* 27; *Annual Report of the Attorney General of the United States for the Year 1919* (Washington, D.C.: GPO, 1920), 25.

70. U.S. Attorney J. Virgil Bourland to Gregory, May 9, 1917, Class. Files 9-16-1-4-1.

71. Warren to Bourland, May 22, 1917, Class. Files 9-16-1-4-1.

72. Adjutant general of the army to commanding general, northeastern department, Boston, May 24, 1917, Class. Files 9-16-12; Secretary of Labor William B. Wilson to secretary of war, June 29, 1917, Class. Files 9-16-12-122; assistant attorney general to Gregory, July 9, 1917, Class. Files 9-16-12-113; N. Baker to Gregory, July 17, 1917, Class. Files 9-16-12-156; Gregory to U.S. attorneys and marshals, July 18, 1917, Class. Files 9-16-12-166; Warren to Gregory, July 20, 1917, Class. Files 9-16-12-168 1/2; Gregory to N. Baker, August 21, 1917, Class. Files 9-16-12; Warren to Gregory, September 15, 1917, Class. Files 9-16-12-23; Gregory to U.S. attorneys and marshals, September 18, 1917, Class. Files 9-16-12-242; Gregory to U.S. marshals, n.d., Class. Files 9-16-12-52. Gregory to U.S. attorneys, marshals, and special agents, May 23, 1917, and April 27, 1918; Gregory to U.S. attorneys and marshals, July 18, 1917; E.D. to U.S. attorneys and marshals, January 5, 1918; Gregory to U.S. marshals, June 19, 1918, all in AG Circ. Letters.

73. Peterson and Fite, *Opponents of War,* 17; Kennedy, *Over Here,* 80.

74. Peterson and Fite, *Opponents of War,* 14; Kennedy, *Over Here,* 72, 83.

75. Peterson and Fite, *Opponents of War,* 117–18.

76. Gregory to U.S. attorneys and marshals, May 29, June 22, and October 8, 1917, and April 15, 1918; to U.S. attorneys, July 26, 1917; to U.S. attorneys, marshals, and special agents, December 1, 1917, all in AG Circ. Letters.

77. Memo to Gregory, December 18, 1918, Class. Files 9-16-12-1468; Gregory to U.S. marshals, December 23, 1918, Class. Files 9-16-12-1469. Attorney General A. Mitchell Palmer to U.S. attorneys, April 3, 1919; to U.S. attorneys and marshals, July 3, 1919, both in AG Circ. Letters. *Annual Report, 1919,* 26.

CHAPTER 10

1. Deathbed statement by Deputy J. Herbert Ray, February 2, 1935, attached to U.S. Attorney Mac Swinford to attorney general, February 13, 1935, Class. Files 125-30-1.

2. Swinford to attorney general, February 13, 1935.

3. Calhoun, *Power and Principle,* 35.

4. Homer Cummings and Carl McFarland, *Federal Justice: Chapters in the History of Justice and the Federal Executive* (New York: Macmillan, 1937), 496–97.

5. Gregory to U.S. attorneys and marshals, June 22, 1917, AG Circ. Letters.

6. Assistant Attorney General Rush L. Holland to Marshal James E. McClure, July 24, 1923, Department of Justice District Administration Files (hereinafter cited as Dist. Admin. Files) 14S331-479, RG 60.

7. Quoted in General Agent John W. Gardner, memorandum for Assistant Attorney General Sisson, January 29, 1930, Dist. Admin. Files 27X331-4.

8. Holland to U.S. marshals and deputy marshals, October 15, 1924; Attorney General John G. Sargent to all marshals, February 11, 1928, both in AG Circ. Letters.

9. Attorney General John W. Griggs to all marshals, February 27, 1900; Attorney General J. C. McReynolds to all marshals, August 21, 1914, both in AG Circ. Letters. *Instructions to United States Marshals, Attorneys, Clerks, and Commissioners* (Washington, D.C.: GPO, 1916), 31.

10. Special assistant to the attorney general John Lord O'Brian to Commander L. McCauley, December 21, 1917, Dist. Admin. Files 33S331.

11. Holland to U.S. Attorney William Hayward, May 18, 1923, Dist. Admin. Files 33S331-711; Holland to McClure, July 24, 1923, Dist. Admin. Files 14S331-479.

12. *Instructions* (1899), 25; *Instructions* (1916), 35.

13. *Instructions* (1899), 21–23.

14. Marshal William C. Hecht to Holland, November 29, 1922, Dist. Admin. Files 33S331-67.

15. Congressman Hamilton Fish, Jr., to Holland, December 13, 1922, Dist. Admin. Files 33S331-677.

16. Holland to Hecht, November 23, 1922, Dist. Admin. Files 33S331-67; to Fish, Jr., December 16, 1922, Dist. Admin. Files, 33S331——.

17. Fish, Jr., to Holland, December 26, 1922, Dist. Admin. Files 33S331-680.

18. Special assistant to the attorney general Warren F. Martin to Holland, January 17, 1923, Dist. Admin. Files 33S331-688.

19. Holland to Attorney General Harry M. Daugherty, January 18, 1923, Dist. Admin. Files 33S331-68; Holland to Fish, Jr., January 29, 1923, Dist. Admin. Files 33S331-688.

20. Fish, Jr., to Holland, February 1, 1923, Dist. Admin. Files 33S331-692; Senator James W. Wadsworth, Jr., to Holland, March 9, 1923, Dist. Admin. Files 33S331-697; Holland to Hecht, October 26, 1923, Dist. Admin. Files 33S331-727; Hecht to Holland, October 29, 1923, Dist. Admin. Files 33S331-73.

21. Assistant Attorney General Guy D. Goff to Marshal Henry F. Cooper, August 26, 1921, Dist. Admin. Files 37E331.

22. Holland to Marshal Victor Loisel (La.), November 20, 1923, Dist. Admin. Files 19E331.

23. Marshal John W. Van Heuvel to attorney general, December 18, 1923, Dist. Admin. Files 1S331-77.

24. Marshal Frederick L. Esola to attorney general, December 31, 1924, Dist. Admin. Files 5N331-415X.

25. Supervising Examiner John W. Gardner to attorney general, July 10, 1926, Dist. Admin. Files 14N331-88.

26. Assistant Attorney General G. A. Youngquist to Sisson, August 10, 1931, Dist. Admin. Files 14N331——.

27. Memorandum for Mr. Holland from R. A. Haynes, Prohibition Commissioner, October 19, 1922, Dist. Admin. Files 34E331-441; General Agent Gardner to Assistant Attorney General Marshall, July 26, 1927, Dist. Admin. Files 24X331.

28. John G. Harlan to Assistant Attorney General Willebrandt, September 22, 1924, Dist. Admin. Files 14N331-682; Assistant Attorney General [　] to Colonel Holland, July 31, 1924, Dist. Admin. Files 14N331-682.

29. Cummings and McFarland, *Federal Justice* (1937), 475.

30. Ibid., 476–77.

31. Ibid., 481–82.

32. Memorandum for the attorney general, "Subject: Railroad Strike and Steps Taken by the Department of Justice to Preserve the Peace of the United States," unsigned, July 12, 1922, Class. Files 16-150(1).

33. For documentation on the 1922 railroad strike, see Class. Files 16-150(1). After the strike, the department published an *Appendix to the Report of the Attorney General: 1922* entitled *Lawless Disorders and Their Suppression, 1922* (Washington, D.C.: GPO, 1922), which contained the bulk of the documents generated during the strike.

34. Memorandum for the attorney general, "Subject: Railroad Strike."

35. U.S. Attorney Dwight H. Green to attorney general, December 9, 1932, and departmental attachments, Dist. Admin. Files 14N331.

36. Alexander Holtzoff to attorney general, October 8, 1935, Class. Files 16-207.

37. Assistant Attorney General Samuel J. Graham to Marshal A. J. Wells, February 17, 1916, Dist. Admin. Files 4E331-71; Marshal Herman O'Connor to attorney general, October 18, 1916, Dist. Admin. Files 23W331-24.

38. Six district judges, southern district of New York, to attorney general, June 22, 1925, Dist. Admin. Files 33S331-850; J. D. Harris to Assistant Attorney General Marshall, June 25, 1925, Dist. Admin. Files 33S331——; Judge Augustus N. Hand to Colonel William Donovan, July 8, 1925, Dist. Admin. Files 33S331-85; Esola to attorney general, April 15, 1927, Dist. Admin. Files 5N331-480; Gardner to Marshall, March 3, 1928, Dist. Admin. Files 33E331-6; Attorney General Homer Cummings to Representative Emanuel Caller, March 25, 1933, Dist. Admin. Files 33E331-9.

39. "Appropriations Act of 1937," 1937, *U.S. Statutes,* 279; "An Act Further Defining the Number and Duties of Criers and Bailiffs in United States Courts and Regulating Their Compensation," 1944, *U.S. Statutes,* 796.

40. Administrative assistant to the attorney general to all marshals, October 13, 1937, AG Circ. Letters; Attorney General Frank Murphy to Marshal Ben. J. McKinney, February 23, 1939, AHS MS 978, S3 F115.

41. McKinney to Murphy, March 11 and May 22, 1939, AHS MS 978, S3 F115.

42. Marshal John Logan to all marshals, January 6 and 8, 1941; McKinney to Senator Carl Hayden, January 11, 1941; Logan to marshals, January 19 (two letters) and June 12, 1941; McKinney to Logan, June 14, 1941, all in AHS MS 978, S3 F138.

43. McKinney to Logan, January 11, 1941; Logan to McKinney, January 29, 1941, both in AHS MS 978, S3 F138.

44. T. D. Quinn, administrative assistant to the attorney general, December 19, 1941, AHS MS 978, S3 F160; January 23, 1942, AG Circ. Letters; January 15, 1945, AHS MS 978, S3 F117.

45. John Q. Cannon, administrative assistant to the attorney general, April 14, 1944, AG Circ. Letters.

46. *United States Marshals Bulletin* 1 (November 1946).

CHAPTER 11

1. Interview with Donald D. Forsht, July 9, 1985, Records of the Historian, U.S. Marshals Service, Washington, D.C. (hereinafter cited as Records of the Historian), 95–100.

2. "Tammany Man Named to Be U.S. Marshal," January 17, 1950; "Nominated by President to Be U.S. Marshal Here," February 28, 1950; "U.S. Marshal Here Defies Call to Quit," July 1, 1953; "Carroll Awaiting His Ouster Order," July 14, 1953, all in *New York Times*.

3. "U.S. Marshal Here Is Ousted Officially at a Cost to the Government of 75 Cents," *New York Times,* July 15, 1953.

4. Deputy Attorney General William P. Rogers to Attorney General Herbert Brownell, Jr., August 6, 1956, Bureau Status Files, Office of the Historian (hereinafter cited as Bureau Status Files).

5. Rogers to all U.S. marshals, November 30, 1956, Bureau Status Files.

6. Clive W. Palmer to Deputy Attorney General–Designee Byron White, January 5, 1961, Bureau Status Files.

7. Ibid.

8. Interview with Al Butler, August 12, 1985, Records of the Historian.

9. Interview with James J. P. McShane, Papers of James J. P. McShane, Kennedy Library, Boston.

10. Department of Justice press release, May 8, 1962, Bureau Status Files.

11. Telephone conversation with Frank Vandegrift, summer 1985.

12. Quoted in J. Anthony Lukas, "The Days of Hope and Glory" (review of Richard N. Goodwin, *Remembering America: A Voice from the Sixties* [New York: Little, Brown, 1988]), August 21, 1988, *Washington Post Book World*.

13. Juan Williams, *Eyes on the Prize: America's Civil Rights Years, 1954–1965* (New York: Viking, 1987), 252–87.

14. Ibid., 92–119.

15. Ibid., 195.

16. Interview with Jesse W. Grider, July 12, 1985, Records of the Historian.

17. Ibid.

18. Michael Dorman, *We Shall Overcome* (New York: Delacorte Press Book, n.d.), 20–21.

19. Interview with Butler.

20. Interviews with Butler and Forsht.

21. Interview with Hershel Garner, July 8, 1985, Records of the Historian.

22. Interview with Cecil Miller, July 9, 1985, Records of the Historian.

23. Conversation with Nicholas Katzenbach, March 1986.

24. Interviews with Butler, Forsht, and Garner.

25. Dorman, *We Shall Overcome,* 86–109.

26. Interview with Miller.

27. Ibid.

28. Dorman, *We Shall Overcome,* 104–9.

29. Ibid., 216–17.

30. Interview with Garner.

31. Interview with Frank Vandegrift, July 10, 1985.

32. Ibid.

33. Ibid. Interviews with James Redpath, July 5, 1985; William Shoemaker, July 9, 1985; William Stubblefield, July 11, 1985; Charles E. Burrows, January 22, 1986, all in Records of the Historian. Daily logs and shift reports, Bunker Files on Meredith at Ole Miss, Office of the Historian (hereinafter cited as Bunker Files).

34. Interview with Vandegrift; shift reports, Bunker files; Russell H. Barrett, *Integration at Ole Miss* (Chicago: Quadrangle Books, 1965).

35. Interview with Vandegrift; Barrett, *Integration.*

36. Interviews with Burrows, Redpath, Shoemaker, Stubblefield, and Vandegrift.

37. James Meredith, *Three Years in Mississippi* (Bloomington, Ind.: Indiana University Press, n.d.), 328.

38. White House tapes, September 30, 1962, Kennedy Library.

39. Department of Justice Statement of Organization, order 271-62, *Federal Register,* June 1, 1962, Bureau Status Files.

40. Remarks made by John Cameron at Attorney General John N. Mitchell's briefing on February 10, 1969, Bureau Status files.

41. "Difference Between the Missions of the Executive Office for United States Attorneys and the Executive Office for United States Marshals," unsigned memorandum, January 13, 1966; McShane to Assistant Attorney General L. M. Pellerzi, Administrative Division, September 25, 1968, both in Bureau Status Files.

42. Interview with Vandegrift.

43. Interview with Robert Christman.

44. Conversation with James O'Toole.

45. Interview with Butler.

46. Conversation with O'Toole.

CHAPTER 12

1. Department of Justice press release, March 24, 1969, Bureau Status Files.

2. Department of Justice Statement of Organization.

3. Department of Justice order 386-67, November 28, 1967, Bureau Status Files.

4. Chief Marshal Carl C. Turner to Deputy Attorney General Richard Kleindienst, March 28, 1969; to Assistant Attorney General Leo M. Pellerzi, April 1, 1969; to all U.S. marshals, April 3, 1969, all in Bureau Status Files.

5. Department of Justice order 415-69, May 12, 1969, Bureau Status Files; *Federal Register,* May 20, 1969, Bureau Status Files.

6. C. Turner to Kenneth J. Stallo, June 23, 1969, Bureau Status Files.

7. R. A. O'Connell, staff assistant, to William J. Neptune, chief of administration, July 3, 1969; Neptune to Donald Synnott, July 11, 1969; C. Turner to Pellerzi, July 25, 1969; Harold Jaeger, chief, budgets and accounts section, to Neptune, n.d., all in Bureau Status Files.

8. Pellerzi to Kleindienst, July 28, 1969, Bureau Status Files.

9. Interview with William E. Hall, July 30, 1986, draft manuscript, Office of the Historian.

10. Neptune to F. W. McGrail, building manager, Archives-Justice Field Office,

December 8, 1969; *Washington Star,* January 12, 1970, news clipping, both in Bureau Status Files.

11. *USMS Newsletter,* November 1970.

12. Wayne B. Colburn to Deputy Attorney General Ralph Erickson, November 13, 1972, Bureau Status Files.

13. Colburn to Kleindienst, June 9, 1971, Bureau Status Files.

14. Proposed bureau designation, ca. 1971, Bureau Status Files.

15. Colburn to Kleindienst, June 9, 1971, Bureau Status Files.

16. Department of Justice order 516-73, May 10, 1973; Colburn to Assistant Attorney General Robert G. Dixon, Jr., office of legal counsel, April 15, 1974, both in Bureau Status Files.

17. Colburn to Acting Attorney General Robert H. Bork, November 15, 1973; to Dixon, April 15, 1974, both in Bureau Status Files.

18. Department of Justice order 565-74, May 6, 1974, Bureau Status Files.

19. Charles M. Odell, chief, personnel operations section, to O. T. Berkman, personnel officer, U.S. Marshals Service, January 8, 1971, attachment C to Colburn to Kleindienst, June 9, 1971, Bureau Status Files; *USMS Newsletter,* June 1972.

20. Colburn to Erickson, November 13, 1972, Bureau Status Files.

21. *USMS Newsletter,* June 1973.

22. Colburn to Erickson, November 13, 1972.

23. *USMS Newsletter,* November 1970.

24. Interview with Grider.

25. *USMS Newsletter,* June 1971.

26. Ibid.

27. Interview with Reis Kash, February 7, 1985, draft transcript, Office of the Historian.

28. Ibid.; *The Innocent Victims of the Occupation of Wounded Knee, South Dakota v. the United States,* before the chief commissioner of the United States Court of Claims, n.d., Office of the Historian.

29. *Innocent Victims,* 58.

30. Ibid., 75.

31. Ibid., 70–71.

32. Ibid., 90.

33. Ibid., 89, 93.

34. Ibid., 104; interviews with Hall and Kash.

35. Interviews with Hall and Kash.

36. Interview with Kash; *Innocent Victims,* 106.

37. *Innocent Victims,* 112, 127.

38. *Pentacle* (July/August 1983): 13.

39. *U.S. Marshals Today* (July 1976): 8.

40. Deputy Attorney General Benjamin R. Civiletti to Director William H. Webster, FBI, July 23, 1979, approving W. Webster to Civiletti, June 29, 1979, Office of the Historian; *Pentacle* (November/December 1979).

41. *Pentacle* (September/October 1980), 2.

42. Ibid.; *Pentacle* (Summer 1985), 3–11.

43. *Pentacle* (Summer 1985), 3–11.

44. Interview with Robert Christman, October 3, 1986; conversations with Dennis Behrend, Thomas Kupferer, and Howard Safir; Robert Lindsey, *The Flight of the Falcon* (New York: Simon and Schuster, 1983), 307–11.

45. Conversation with William Dempsey.

INDEX